Collins

OCR GCSE

Combined Science

Combined Science

Foundation

OCR
Gateway
GCSE

Revision
Guide

**Fran Walsh, Eliot Attridge
and David Brodie**

Contents

Contents

Contents

Contents

Paper 3 Chemical Reactions

Paper 4 Predicting and Identifying Reactions and Products

Contents

Contents

Contents

Contents

Review Questions

Recap of KS3 Biology Key Concepts

1. Name **three** structures found in both plant and animal cells. [3]

2. Why do plants cells have a cell wall? [1]

3. Why do plants cells contain chloroplasts? [1]

4. What is an enzyme? [1]

5. What is the name of the enzyme that breaks down starch? [1]

6. The enzymes we use to break down food are proteins.

   How do high temperatures affect these proteins? [1]

7. What is the name of the sections of DNA, found on chromosomes, that are responsible for inherited characteristics? [1]

8. Which of the following characteristics in plants and animals are likely to be inherited?

   A flower colour in plants
   B fur colour in rabbits
   C weight in humans
   D blood group in humans
   E number of branches on a tree [3]

9. Where in the cell is DNA found? [1]

10. DNA exists as a coiled structure. What is the name we give to this structure? [1]

11. Respiration occurs in all living things. What is the purpose of respiration? [1]

12. Write down the equation for respiration. [2]

13. Plants carry out photosynthesis. Write the equation for photosynthesis. [2]

14. Plants can store the glucose produced in photosynthesis in their leaves. What is the glucose converted to for storage? [1]

15. Plants can also use the glucose produced by photosynthesis to build other molecules.

    Name **two** molecules made by the plant. [2]

16. What is diffusion? [1]

17. In the lungs, where does diffusion of oxygen happen? [2]

18 How are the structures in the lungs adapted for efficient diffusion? [3]

19 Put the following in order of size, starting with the smallest:

organ   cell   organ system   tissue [2]

20 Construct a food chain using the organisms below:

caterpillar   leaf   fox   bird [2]

21 What do the arrows in a food chain show? [1]

22 Which gas is taken in by plants during respiration? [1]

23 Which gas is taken in by plants during photosynthesis? [1]

24 Which gas is the main contributor to global warming? [1]

25 What does 'extinct' mean? [1]

26 What is a balanced diet? [3]

27 What are the **five** food groups? [5]

28 Give **three** examples of recreational drugs. [3]

29 Which organ is primarily affected by excessive alcohol consumption? [1]

30 What is the name of the substance found in red blood cells that carries oxygen? [1]

31 The diagram below shows the human respiratory system:

a) Which letter refers to the diaphragm? [1]

b) Which letter refers to the trachea? [1]

c) Which letter refers to the ribs? [1]

d) Oxygen and carbon dioxide are exchanged at structure **D**.

What is the name of this structure? [1]

e) By what process are oxygen and carbon dioxide exchanged? [1]

f) The respiratory system contains cells which produce mucus. What is the function of the mucus? [1]

Rib muscles — A

Bronchus

Bronchiole — B

D

C

Total Marks _____ / 56

Review Questions

Recap of KS3 Chemistry Key Concepts

1 Write down whether each substance in the table is an **element**, **mixture** or **compound**.

Name of Substance	Type of Substance
Distilled water	
Gold	
Glucose	
Salt water	

[4]

2 **a)** Look at the following chemical reactions and tick (✓) the **two** reactions that are written correctly.

    A magnesium + sulfuric acid → magnesium nitrate + hydrogen

    B copper oxide + hydrochloric acid → copper chloride + water

    C iron + phosphoric acid → iron phosphate + hydrogen

    D lithium oxide + nitric acid → lithium nitrate + hydrogen

[2]

b) When magnesium is burned in air, it produces a bright white light and a white, powdery residue.

    Write the **word equation** for the reaction.

[2]

3 Draw **three** diagrams to show the arrangement of particles in a **solid**, a **liquid** and a **gas**. [3]

4 For a metal to increase in temperature, its atoms must gain energy.

What type of energy must the metal atoms gain?

    A nuclear energy   **C** chemical energy

    B heat energy   **D** kinetic energy

[1]

5 Linda is stung by a bee.
The bee's sting is acidic.

a) What chemical is the opposite of an acid? [1]

b) Which of the following could neutralise an acid?

    A water   **C** vinegar

    B baking soda   **D** magnesium

[1]

6 Gold and platinum are among a few metals that can be found in their elemental form on Earth.

    a) Explain why these metals are found in their elemental form.   [2]

    b) Suggest why aluminium was discovered much later in human history than gold
       and platinum.   [4]

7 Ruth is using universal indicator to identify acids and bases.

    Suggest what colour universal indicator would turn for each of the examples below.

    a) Stomach acid   [1]

    b) Juice of a lime   [1]

    c) Tap water   [1]

    d) Hand soap   [1]

8 The diagram below shows the arrangement of atoms in four different substances.

A   **C**

B   **D**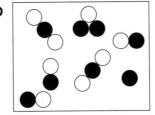

    a) Which box has a substance that is a mixture of compounds?   [1]

    b) Which box has a substance that could be pure carbon dioxide?   [1]

    c) Which box has a substance that could be a pure element?   [1]

9 In winter fish are able to survive in a fish pond, even when the fish pond freezes over.

    Explain what property of water enables the fish to survive.   [2]

Total Marks .... / 29

Review Questions

Recap of KS3 Physics Key Concepts

1 In what form do hydroelectric generating systems store energy?

A gravitational potential energy

C thermal energy

B elastic potential energy

D internal energy

[1]

2 Which of these is **not** a unit of energy?

A joule

C kilowatt

B kilojoule

D kilowatt-hour

[1]

3 Which of these **cannot** be detected by the human senses?

A infrared radiation

C sound waves

B radio waves

D visible light

[1]

4 Which of these is **not** part of the electromagnetic spectrum?

A infrared radiation

C sound waves

B radio waves

D visible light

[1]

5 Which of the following is a **contact** force?

A electric force

C gravitational force

B force of friction

D magnetic force

[1]

6 Which of these is a renewable energy resource?

A coal

C oil

B gas

D wind

[1]

7 What does an ammeter measure?

A electric charge

C electric potential difference

B electric current

D electrical resistance

[1]

8 Which of the following do atoms contain?

A only electrons

C only nuclei

B electrons and nuclei

D either electrons or nuclei [1]

9 What is the name of the device that is designed to transfer energy from one circuit to another?

A ammeter

C diode

B battery

D transformer [1]

10 The density of water is 1000kg/m³ and the density of aluminium is 2400kg/m³.

a) What is the mass of:

   i) 1m³ of water? [1]

   ii) 1m³ of aluminium? [1]

b) A bucket has a volume of 0.01m³. It is full to the brim with water.
   What is the mass of the water? [3]

c) If the same water is in the same bucket on the Moon, and none of it evaporates,
   what will be the mass of the water? [1]

d) The bucket of water will be easier to carry on the Moon. Explain why this is. [2]

e) What does evaporation of water from the bucket do to:

   i) the mass of water? [1]

   ii) the volume of water? [1]

   iii) the density of water? [1]

11 a) Two gases mix together easily.

   Explain this in terms of particles. [3]

b) Two solids do **not** mix together.

   Explain this in terms of particles. [2]

Total Marks _____ / 25

Cell Structures

You must be able to:

- Describe how light microscopes and staining can be used to view cells
- Explain how the main subcellular structures are related to their functions
- Explain how electron microscopy has increased understanding of subcellular structures.

The Light Microscope

- Light microscopes are useful for viewing whole cells or large subcellular structures.
- The specimen is placed on a glass slide, covered with a cover slip and placed on the stage of the microscope.
- The eyepiece and objective lenses magnify the object.
- A lamp provides illumination.
- **Magnification** is calculated by multiplying the magnification of the eyepiece lens by the magnification of the objective lens.
- Typical magnification is between 40 and 2000 times larger with a **resolution** of about 0.2 micrometres (μm).
- **Stains** can be used to colour whole cells and structures within cells, e.g. the nucleus, to make them easier to see.
- Sometimes a **mordant** is used, which fixes the stain to the structures.

Stained Bacteria Viewed using a Light Microscope

The Electron Microscope

- Electron microscopes are useful for viewing subcellular structures, such as ribosomes, mitochondrial membranes and nuclear membranes, in detail.
- They use a beam of electrons instead of a lamp.
- The specimen is placed inside a vacuum chamber.
- Electromagnets are used instead of lenses.
- The image is viewed on a TV screen.
- Typical magnification is 1 to 2 million times larger with a resolution of 2 nanometres (nm).

Bacteria Viewed using an Electron Microscope

SI Units and Interconverting Units

1 metre (m) = 1 000 000 micrometres (μm)
$1\mu m = 10^{-6}m$
1 metre (m) = 1 000 000 000 nanometres (nm)
$1 nm = 10^{-9}m$
To convert m to mm, multiply by 1000.
To convert mm to μm, multiply by 1000.
To convert μm to nm, multiply by 1000.

Typical Animal Cell

10–100μm

Bacteria

1–10μm

Chloroplast

0.5μm

Virus

80nm

Ribosome

25nm

Cell Membrane Thickness

20nm

Subcellular Structures

- The following structures are common to both animal and plant cells:
  - **nucleus** – controls the cell and contains genetic material in the form of chromosomes
  - **cytoplasm** – where most chemical reactions take place
  - **cell membrane** – a barrier that controls the passage of substances into and out of the cell and contains **receptor molecules**
  - **mitochondria** – contain the enzymes for cellular respiration and are the site of respiration.
- Additionally, plant cells contain:
  - **cell wall** – made from cellulose and provides structural support
  - **vacuole** – contains cell sap, which provides support
  - **chloroplasts** – contain **chlorophyll** and are the site of photosynthesis.

Types of Cells

- **Prokaryotes**, e.g. bacteria, have no nucleus – the nuclear material lies free within the cytoplasm.
- They may contain additional DNA in the form of a **plasmid**.
- **Eukaryotes**, e.g. human cheek cell, amoeba, plant cell, have a nucleus bound by a nuclear membrane.
- In eukaryotes, the cell wall is only present in plant cells.

A Prokaryote

Quick Test

1. The eyepiece lens of a light microscope is ×10 and the objective lens is ×4. What is the total magnification?
2. Which part of a cell is:
   a) the site of respiration?
   b) the site of photosynthesis?
   c) a barrier controlling what passes in and out of the cell?
   d) where most chemical reactions take place?
3. Name **two** structures found in plant cells, but not in animal cells.

Key Words

magnification
resolution
stain
mordant
receptor molecules
chlorophyll
prokaryote
plasmid
eukaryote

What Happens in Cells

You must be able to:

- Describe the structure of DNA
- Explain how enzymes work.

DNA

- Inside every cell is genetic material in the form of **DNA** (deoxyribonucleic acid).
- DNA is a **polymer** made of two strands of nucleic acid.
- The two strands are in the form of a **double helix**.
- DNA is found in the nucleus of the cell.

Double Helix

> **Key Point**
>
> There is genetic material, in the form of DNA, inside every cell. DNA provides a code to make proteins.

Enzymes

- Enzymes are biological catalysts and increase the rate of chemical reactions inside organisms.
- Enzymes are made of proteins and the amino acid chain is folded to make a shape into which **substrates** (substances) can fit.
- The place where the substrate fits is called the **active site**.
- Enzymes are specific and only substrate molecules with the correct shape can fit into the active site.
- This is called the 'lock and key' hypothesis.
- Enzymes are **denatured** when they lose their shape. The substrate no longer fits and the enzyme does not work.

> **Key Point**
>
> When enzymes are denatured, they change shape, so the substrate can no longer fit in the active site.

Substrate

Enzyme

Active site

Substrate fits into active site

Substrate is broken down and enzyme can be reused

Products

Factors Affecting Enzyme Action

- The rate of enzyme action is affected by temperature, pH, substrate concentration and enzyme concentration.
- High temperatures and deviation from the optimum (ideal) pH cause enzymes to lose their shape and become denatured.
- Low temperatures slow down the rate of reaction.
- Different enzymes have different optimum pH levels depending on where they act in the body.
- Many human enzymes have an optimum temperature of 37°C as this is normal human internal body temperature.
- As substrate concentration increases, the rate of enzyme activity increases to the point where all the enzymes present are being used.
- As enzyme concentration increases, the rate of enzyme activity increases to the point where all the substrate present is being used.

> **Key Point**
>
> When interpreting graphs about enzyme activity, remember – the steeper the line, the more rapid the increase or decrease in rate of enzyme activity.
>
> When explaining the shape of a graph, relate the explanation to scientific knowledge.

Presenting Data
How pH affects invertase activity

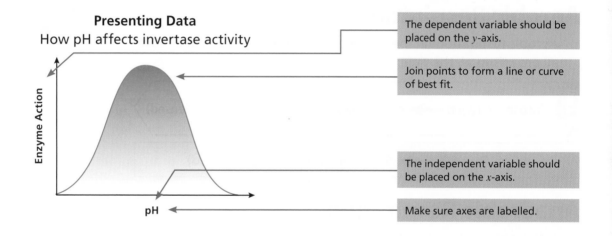

The dependent variable should be placed on the *y*-axis.

Join points to form a line or curve of best fit.

The independent variable should be placed on the *x*-axis.

Make sure axes are labelled.

Interpreting Data
How temperature affects invertase activity

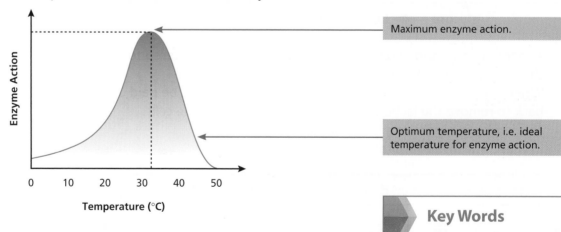

Maximum enzyme action.

Optimum temperature, i.e. ideal temperature for enzyme action.

> **Key Words**
>
> DNA
> polymer
> double helix
> substrate
> active site
> denature

Quick Test

1. How do enzymes affect chemical reactions?
2. State **three** factors that affect the action of enzymes.
3. Explain what is meant by the 'lock and key' hypothesis.

Respiration

You must be able to:

- Describe cellular respiration
- Compare aerobic and anaerobic respiration
- Describe the synthesis and breakdown of large molecules such as proteins, carbohydrates and lipids.

Cellular Respiration

- Cellular respiration happens inside the cells of all plants and animals. It occurs continuously and is controlled by enzymes.
- It is an exothermic reaction and releases energy in the form of a high energy molecule called ATP (adenosine triphosphate).

Aerobic Respiration

- Aerobic respiration (in the presence of oxygen) happens in almost all organisms all the time.

LEARN

> glucose + oxygen ⟶ carbon dioxide + water (+ energy released)

> $C_6H_{12}O_6 + 6O_2 \longrightarrow 6CO_2 + 6H_2O$ (+ energy released)

Key Point

Glucose is a member of the family of substances called sugars.

Anaerobic Respiration

- Cellular respiration can also happen anaerobically (without oxygen).
- In animal cells, anaerobic respiration produces lactic acid:

> glucose ⟶ lactic acid (+ energy released)

- Anaerobic respiration occurs when oxygen cannot be delivered to the cells fast enough, for example during vigorous activity.
- When exercise stops there is an oxygen debt, which must be paid back to remove the lactic acid that has accumulated in the cells.
- This is why the breathing rate is so fast.
- In yeast, anaerobic respiration produces ethanol:

> glucose ⟶ carbon dioxide + ethanol (+ energy released)

Key Point

Anaerobic respiration in yeast is called fermentation.

In everyday life, ethanol tends to be called alcohol.

	Where it Occurs	Oxygen	Breakdown of Glucose	ATP Yield per Mole of Glucose	Energy Released per Mole of Glucose
Aerobic	Mitochondria	Needed	Complete	38	2900kJ
Anaerobic	Cytoplasm	Not needed	Incomplete	2	120kJ

Breakdown of Biological Molecules

- We take in carbohydrates, proteins and lipids in our diet.
- These are all large molecules called **polymers**.
- During digestion, they are broken down by enzymes into smaller molecules, called **monomers**.
- Fats need to be broken down into small droplets to make them more digestible. This is called **emulsification**.
- In the small intestine, bile is responsible for emulsifying fats.

Name of Enzyme	Substrate it Acts Upon	Name of Monomers Produced
Carbohydrase	Carbohydrate	Glucose
Protease	Proteins	Amino acids
Lipase	Lipids (fats)	Fatty acids, glycerol

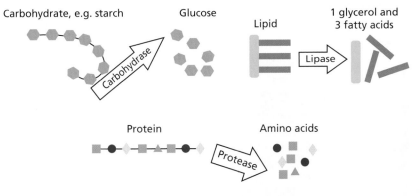

Synthesis of Biological Molecules

- Glucose, amino acids, glycerol and fatty acids are transported by the blood to the cells in the body.
- Inside the cells:
  - Glucose can be used in respiration.
  - Amino acids can be used to make useful proteins, e.g. enzymes and hormones.
  - Glycerol and fatty acids can be used to make useful lipids.
- Breakdown of proteins, carbohydrates and lipids produces the building blocks to synthesise the many different types of molecules that our bodies need to function.

Photosynthesis

You must be able to:

- Name organisms that photosynthesise and state why they are important
- Describe photosynthesis
- Describe experiments to investigate photosynthesis.

Photosynthesis

- Green plants and algae make their own food using **photosynthesis**.
- They trap light from the Sun to fix carbon dioxide with hydrogen (from water) to form glucose.
- The glucose is used by the plants and algae to build larger molecules, such as complex carbohydrates and proteins.
- These are then passed onto animals in the food chain.

Key Point

Photosynthetic organisms are the main producers of food and, therefore, biomass for life on Earth.

- The equation for photosynthesis is:

$$\text{carbon dioxide} + \text{water} \xrightarrow[\text{chlorophyll}]{\text{light energy}} \text{glucose} + \text{oxygen}$$

- Photosynthesis is an **endothermic** reaction.
- Photosynthesis occurs inside the chloroplasts, which contain **chlorophyll**.

Investigating Photosynthesis

- Watching gas bubble up from *Cabomba*, a type of pond weed, is a good visual demonstration of photosynthesis.
- The experiment can be used to investigate how the amount of light or the temperature of the water affects the rate of photosynthesis.

Palisade Cell

Packed with chloroplasts for photosynthesis.

A student carried out an investigation into the effect of light on photosynthesis.
They placed the apparatus shown below at different distances from a desk lamp and counted the number of bubbles produced in 5 minutes.
The results are shown in the table.

- Glass tube
- Water
- Beaker
- Funnel
- Pond weed

Distance of Lamp (cm)	0	5	10	15	20	25
Number of Bubbles	108	65	6	2	0	0

Evaluate the method and suggest possible improvements for further investigations.

Evaluation:
- It would have been better to use smaller distance intervals, e.g. 2.5cm, because there were not many bubbles after 5cm.
- It would have been difficult to count the bubbles at 0cm because they were quite fast. It would have been better to collect them and measure the volume of gas produced.
- Another improvement would be to count for a longer time as there were so few bubbles at 10 and 15cm.

When evaluating the method, consider:
- Was the equipment suitable?
- Were there enough results?
- Was it a fair test?
- Were the results reliable?

When suggesting improvements always state why they would make the experiment or results better.

Factors Affecting Photosynthesis

- The optimum temperature for photosynthesis is around 30°C.
- At 45°C, the enzymes involved start to become denatured.
- Increased carbon dioxide levels increase the rate of photosynthesis.
- Increasing the light intensity, increases the rate of photosynthesis.

1. What are a) the reactants and b) the products of photosynthesis?
2. Where in the cell does photosynthesis occur?
3. Why does photosynthesis stop at temperatures over 50°C?

Key Words

photosynthesis
endothermic
chlorophyll

Supplying the Cell

You must be able to:

- Explain how substances are transported by diffusion, osmosis and active transport
- Describe the stages of mitosis
- Give examples of specialised cells
- Explain the role of stem cells.

Transport of Substances In and Out of Cells

- Substances need to pass through cell membranes to get in and out of cells. This can happen in one of three ways:
  - **Diffusion** – the net movement of particles from an area of high concentration to an area of low concentration, i.e. along a concentration gradient.
  - **Active transport** – molecules move against the concentration gradient, from an area of low concentration to an area of high concentration. This requires energy.
  - **Osmosis** – the net movement of water from a dilute solution to a more concentrated solution through a **partially permeable** membrane.

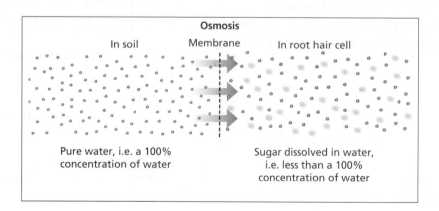

Key Point

Oxygen and glucose move into cells by diffusion. Carbon dioxide moves out of cells by diffusion.

Oxygen Glucose → Carbon dioxide → Waste products

Key Point

A concentration gradient is a measurement of how the concentration of something changes from one place to another.

Key Point

Glucose is moved from the intestine to the blood stream by active transport. Minerals from the soil move into root hair cells by active transport.

Key Point

A dilute solution has a high water potential. A concentrated solution has a low water potential. In osmosis, water diffuses from a region of high water potential to an area of low water potential.

Mitosis

- Mitosis is the division of cells to produce new cells.
- New cells are needed to replace those that die or are damaged.
- The growth and division of cells is called the **cell cycle**.
- The stages of mitosis are:
  1. Parent cell contains chromosomes.
  2. Chromosomes are copied.
  3. Chromatids (the two sets of chromosomes) pull apart.
  4. Two new cells created, each identical to parent.

Stages of Mitosis

Cell Differentiation

- Cell differentiation is when one cell changes into another type of cell.
- In animals this usually happens at an early stage of development and occurs to create specialised cells.
- In mature animal cells, differentiation is mostly restricted to replacement and repair.
- Many plant cells, however, maintain the ability to differentiate.
- Here are some examples of specialised cells:

Root Hair Cells	Ovum (Egg Cell)	Xylem	Sperm Cell	Nerve Cells
Tiny hair-like extensions increase the surface area of the cell for absorption.	Large cell that can carry food reserves for the developing embryo.	Long, thin, hollow cells used to transport water through the stem and root.	Has a tail, which allows it to move.	Long, slender axons that can carry nerve impulses.

Stem Cells

- Stem cells are undifferentiated cells that can differentiate to form specialised cells, such as muscle cells or nerve cells.
- Human stem cells can come from human **embryos**, in umbilical cord blood from new born babies or from adult **bone marrow**.
- Embryonic stem cells can differentiate into any type of cell.
- Adult stem cells can only differentiate into the cells of the type of tissue from which they came.
- Plant stem cells are found in **meristematic** tissue, which is usually in the tips of shoots and roots.
- Stem cells have the potential to provide replacement cells and tissues to treat Parkinson's disease, burns, heart disease and arthritis. The tissues made will not be rejected by the body.
- Stem cells can also be used for testing new drugs.

Key Point

There are ethical issues surrounding the use of stem cells, for example: Is destroying embryos taking a life? Is it right to dispose of human embryos? And who decides which people should benefit from such a treatment?

Key Words

diffusion
active transport
osmosis
partially permeable
cell cycle
embryos
bone marrow
meristematic

Quick Test

1. What are the differences between diffusion and active transport?
2. Name **two** molecules that diffuse into cells.
3. Why is mitosis important?
4. Where do **a)** embryonic and **b)** adult stem cells come from?

The Challenges of Size

You must be able to:

- Explain why organisms need exchange surfaces and transport systems
- Describe substances that need to be exchanged and transported
- Describe the human circulatory system.

Exchange Surfaces and Transport Systems

- Exchange surfaces allow efficient transport of materials across them by mechanisms such as diffusion and active transport.
- In simple **unicellular** organisms, the cell membrane provides an efficient exchange surface.
- **Multicellular** organisms, which have a smaller surface area to volume ratio, have developed specialised exchange surfaces.
- The following substances all need to be exchanged and transported:
  - oxygen and carbon dioxide
  - dissolved food molecules, e.g. glucose and minerals
  - **urea** (waste product from breakdown of proteins)
  - water.
- An efficient exchange system should have:
  - a large surface area to volume ratio
  - membranes that are very thin so diffusion distance is short
  - a good supply of transport medium (e.g. blood, air, etc.).

Two groups of students investigated how quickly coloured water diffused into agar cubes with a surface area of 24cm².

They repeated each test three times. Here are the results of one of their tests:

	Time Taken to Diffuse in Seconds			Average (Mean)
	1	2	3	
Group 1	122	124	126	124
Group 2	136	128	150	138

The data from Group 1 is **repeatable**. This is because all three times recorded are near to each other.

The data is not **reproducible**. This is because the data from Group 1 is different to Group 2.

The data from Group 1 is more **precise** as all the times are near the mean.

Key Point

The alveoli are the site of gas exchange in the lungs.

A Single Alveolus and a Capillary

Deoxygenated blood | CO_2 | Oxygenated blood | CO_2 | O_2 | O_2 | Alveolus

Key Point

The villi in the small intestine provide an exchange surface for the absorption of dissolved food molecules, such as glucose, amino acids, fatty acids and minerals.

A single villus
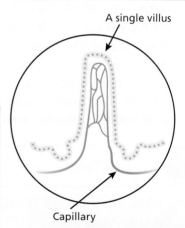
Capillary

You need to remember to evaluate data in terms of accuracy, precision, repeatability and reproducibility.

Measuring in second intervals is more accurate than measuring in minutes.

The Human Circulatory System

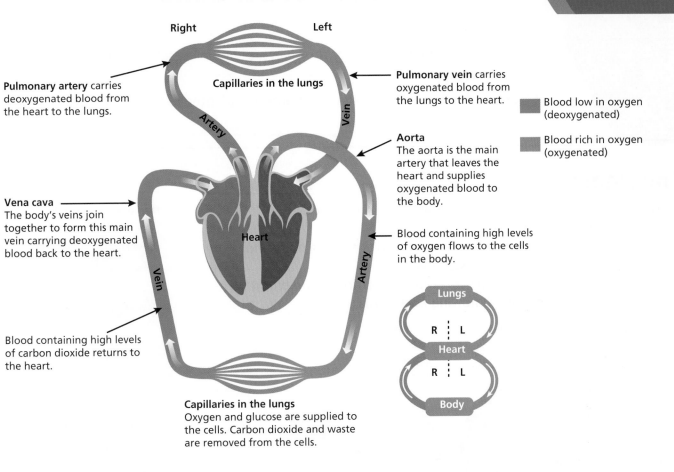

Right **Left**

Pulmonary artery carries deoxygenated blood from the heart to the lungs.

Capillaries in the lungs

Pulmonary vein carries oxygenated blood from the lungs to the heart.

Artery

Vein

Aorta
The aorta is the main artery that leaves the heart and supplies oxygenated blood to the body.

Vena cava
The body's veins join together to form this main vein carrying deoxygenated blood back to the heart.

Heart

Blood containing high levels of oxygen flows to the cells in the body.

Vein

Artery

Blood containing high levels of carbon dioxide returns to the heart.

Blood low in oxygen (deoxygenated)

Blood rich in oxygen (oxygenated)

Lungs

R | L

Heart

R | L

Body

Capillaries in the lungs
Oxygen and glucose are supplied to the cells. Carbon dioxide and waste are removed from the cells.

- Humans have a double circulatory system with two loops:
  - one from the heart to the lungs
  - one from the heart to the body.
- The advantage of a double circulatory system is that it can achieve a higher blood pressure and, therefore, a greater flow of blood (and oxygen) to tissues.
- Substances transported by the circulatory system include oxygen, carbon dioxide, dissolved food molecules, hormones, antibodies, urea and other waste products.
- The right side of the circulatory system carries deoxygenated blood. The left side carries oxygenated blood.

Quick Test

1. What are **three** features of an efficient exchange system?
2. Why do multicellular organisms need specialised exchange systems?
3. What are the advantages of a double circulatory system?

The Heart and Blood Cells

You must be able to:

- Explain how the structures of the heart and blood vessels are adapted to their functions
- Explain how red blood cells and plasma are adapted to their functions.

The Heart

- The heart pumps blood to the lungs and around the body.
- It is made mostly of muscle.
- The left ventricle needs to pump blood round the whole body and, therefore, has thicker, more muscular walls.
- The valves between atria and ventricles and ventricles and blood vessels, are to prevent blood flowing backwards.

Flow of Blood Through the Heart

From body to right atrium

↓

To right ventricle

↓

To lungs via pulmonary artery

↓

From lungs to left atrium via pulmonary vein

↓

To left ventricle

↓

To body via aorta

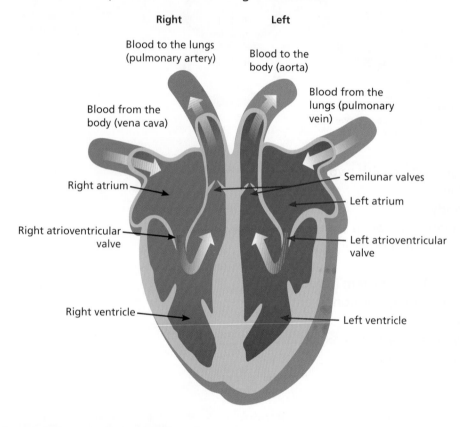

Right

Left

Blood to the lungs (pulmonary artery)

Blood to the body (aorta)

Blood from the body (vena cava)

Blood from the lungs (pulmonary vein)

Right atrium

Semilunar valves

Left atrium

Right atrioventricular valve

Left atrioventricular valve

Right ventricle

Left ventricle

Red Blood Cells

- Red blood cells carry oxygen.
- They have a biconcave disc shape that maximises the surface area for absorbing oxygen.
- They contain haemoglobin, which binds to oxygen in the lungs and releases it at the tissues.
- Red blood cells do not have a nucleus, which means there is more space to carry oxygen.

Blood Vessels

- There are three types of blood vessel: arteries, veins and capillaries.

- Arteries carry blood away from the heart.
- Veins carry blood to the heart.
- Capillaries deliver nutrients to cells and remove waste products from them.
- Arteries have thick outer walls with thick layers of elastic and muscle fibres because they have to carry blood under high pressure.
- Veins have a large lumen (cavity or opening) and thin walls, since blood is under low pressure.
- Veins also have valves to stop blood flowing backwards.
- Capillaries have very thin, permeable walls to allow substances to easily pass into and out of tissues.

Plasma

- Plasma is the pale coloured liquid part of blood. It transports:
  - hormones
  - antibodies
  - nutrients, such as glucose, amino acids, minerals and vitamins
  - waste substances, such as carbon dioxide and urea.

Quick Test

1. How are arteries adapted to carry blood under high pressure?
2. What happens at the capillaries?
3. How is a red blood cell adapted to its function of carrying oxygen?

Key Words

atria
ventricles
haemoglobin
lumen

Plants, Water and Minerals

You must be able to:

- Explain how plants take in water and mineral ions
- Describe the processes of translocation and transpiration
- Explain how xylem and phloem are adapted to their functions
- Explain how water uptake in plants is measured and the factors that affect it.

Mineral and Water Uptake in Plants

- Plants need to take in water for photosynthesis and minerals for general health. These are taken in through the roots.
- Root hair cells have a large surface area to maximise absorption of water and minerals.
- Their cell membrane is thin, which also helps absorption.
- Water enters root hair cells by osmosis.
- Minerals enter root hair cells by active transport.
- There are three essential minerals that plants need to be healthy:
  - nitrates
  - phosphates
  - potassium.

A Root Hair Cell

Transport Systems in Plants

- Plants have two types of transport tissue: xylem and phloem.
- The xylem and phloem are found in the stem of the plant.
- Movement of glucose from the leaf to other parts of the plant by phloem tissue is called translocation.

Cross-Section of a Stem

Phloem vessels carry food substances up and down the plant

Xylem

Phloem

Xylem vessels carry water up from the roots

Tissue Properties	Xylem Vessels	Phloem Vessels
What does it transport?	Xylem transports water and minerals from the soil to other parts of the plant.	Phloem transports the glucose made in the leaf by photosynthesis to other parts of the plant.
How is it adapted to its function?	Xylem vessels are made of dead cells. They have a thick cell wall and hollow lumen. There are no cell contents and no end cell walls, therefore, there is a continuous column for water to move up.	Phloem vessels are made of living cells. They have lots of mitochondria to release energy to move substances by active transport.

Transpiration

- Transpiration is the upward flow of water from roots to leaves, from where it evaporates into the atmosphere.
- The more water a plant loses via the leaves, the more water it will need to take in through the roots.

$$\text{rate of transpiration} = \frac{\text{volume of water lost}}{\text{time}}$$

A Potometer

- A **potometer** can be used to measure water uptake.
- As water is lost from the leaves, the air bubble moves to the left.
- Water is lost through **stomata** in the leaves.
- Plants can close stomata to reduce water loss. However, this closure also reduces the intake of carbon dioxide, which will limit photosynthesis.

Water Uptake and Transpiration

- The factors that affect water uptake and transpiration are:
  - wind velocity
  - temperature
  - humidity.
- You need to analyse distributions of data and predict the shape of graphs.

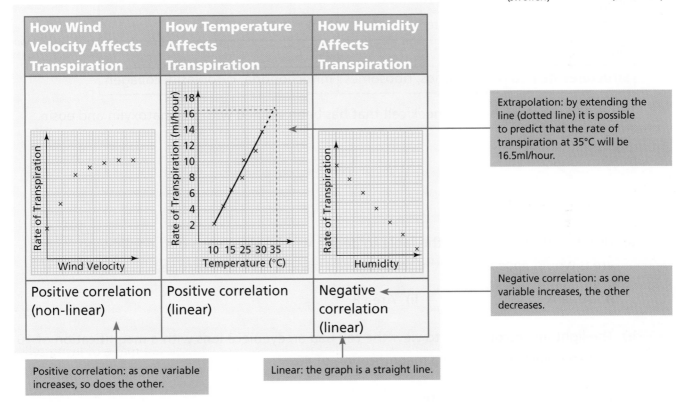

How Wind Velocity Affects Transpiration	How Temperature Affects Transpiration	How Humidity Affects Transpiration
Positive correlation (non-linear)	Positive correlation (linear)	Negative correlation (linear)

Extrapolation: by extending the line (dotted line) it is possible to predict that the rate of transpiration at 35°C will be 16.5ml/hour.

Negative correlation: as one variable increases, the other decreases.

Positive correlation: as one variable increases, so does the other.

Linear: the graph is a straight line.

Quick Test

1. Name the **three** essential minerals plants need for good health.
2. What is transported by:
   a) xylem?
   b) phloem?
3. Give **three** factors that affect the rate of transpiration.

Key Words

translocation
potometer
stomata

Practice Questions

Cell Structures

1. Complete the table below using a tick or cross to indicate if the structures are present or absent in each of the cells.

Structure / Cell	Cell Wall	Cytoplasm	Nuclear Membrane	Cell Membrane	Chloroplasts
Plant					
Animal					
Bacterium					

[3]

2. Haematoxylin and eosin is a common stain made of two components.
The table below gives some information about each of the components.

Component	Haematoxylin	Eosin
Colour	black / blue	pink
Type of stain	basic	acidic
Structures stained	nucleic acids, ribosomes	mitochondria, cytoplasm, collagen

The diagram below shows a cheek cell that has been stained with haematoxylin and eosin.

a) Use the information from the table to decide which colour each of the following areas would appear when the cell is viewed using a light microscope:

   i) Area A   ii) Area B   [2]

b) The light microscope used to view the cell had an eyepiece lens with a magnification of 10 and an objective lens with a magnification of 40.

   What is the total magnification?   [1]

3. The table below gives the diameter of two different cells.

Cell	Diameter
A	3000nm
B	4.5μm

Which cell is larger?   [1]

Total Marks _____ / 7

What Happens in Cells

1. The figure on the right shows a DNA molecule.

    a) The two chains of the DNA molecule form a coiled structure.

    What is the name of this structure? [1]

    b) Where in the cell is DNA found? [1]

2. The diagram below is about enzyme action.

    a) Label the enzyme, substrate and active site. [3]

    b) Describe what will happen to the enzyme at temperatures above 50°C. [2]

    c) Name **one** factor, other than temperature, that affects enzyme activity. [1]

    Total Marks _____ / 8

Respiration

1. The table below compares aerobic and anaerobic respiration.

    Complete the table using words from the list.

    complete   incomplete   cytoplasm   low   high   mitochondria

	Aerobic	Anaerobic
Where it occurs		
Energy release		
Breakdown of glucose		

[6]

2 Complete the equation for aerobic respiration:

_____ + _____ → _____ + _____ + energy   [4]

Total Marks _____ / 10

Photosynthesis

1 Complete the word equation for photosynthesis:

$$\text{_____ + _____} \xrightarrow{\textbf{light energy}} \text{_____ + _____}$$ [4]

2 The cell on the right is packed with subcellular structures that contain the enzymes for photosynthesis.

a) What is the name of this cell?   [1]

b) What is the name of the structures that are the site of photosynthesis?   [1]

c) What is the name of the green pigment inside these structures?   [1]

Total Marks _____ / 7

Supplying the Cell

1 The drawing below shows a single celled organism called an amoeba.

a) Name **two** substances that pass through the cell membrane into the amoeba.   [2]

b) By what process will the carbon dioxide produced by respiration move out of the amoeba?   [1]

c) Choose the correct word to complete the sentence below.

Amoeba is a **unicellular / multicellular** organism.   [1]

2 Complete the sentences by choosing the best words from the selection below.

You do **not** have to use all the words.

| low | between | chloroplasts | energy | uneven | against | net | high | slow |

Diffusion is the _____ movement of particles from an area of _____

concentration to an area of _____ concentration. Active transport moves particles

_____ a concentration gradient and requires _____ .   [5]

3 Which of the following statements best describes osmosis?

A Osmosis is the movement of particles from an area of high water potential to an area of low water potential.

B Osmosis is the movement of particles from an area of low water potential to an area of high water potential.

C Osmosis is the movement of water from an area of high water potential to an area of low water potential.

D Osmosis is the movement of water from an area of low water potential to an area of high water potential.   [1]

4 Mitosis is a form of cell division that produces new cells.

Give **two** reasons why the body needs to produce new cells.   [2]

5 Human stem cells can be made to differentiate into different types of cells.

From where are adult stem cells obtained?   [1]

6 Many people are against using embryonic stem cells to treat human diseases.

Give **one** ethical reason why people may be against this.   [1]

Total Marks _____ / 14

Practice Questions

The Challenges of Size

1 The diagram below shows an exchange system in humans.

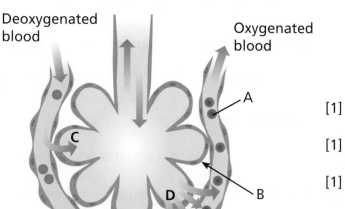

a) In what organ of the body would you find this exchange system? [1]

b) What structure is letter **A**? [1]

c) What structure is letter **B**? [1]

d) Movement of what substance is represented by arrow **C**? [1]

e) Movement of what substance is represented by letter **D**? [1]

Total Marks .... / 5

The Heart and Blood Cells

1 The diagram below shows the human heart.

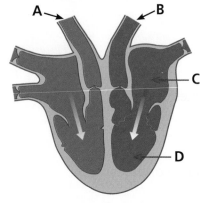

a) What are the names of the parts labelled **A–D**? [4]

b) What is the name of the valve found between parts **C** and **D**? [1]

c) What is the function of the valve found between parts **C** and **D**? [1]

d) When blood flows through part **A**, where is it going? [1]

2 Match each blood vessel on the left to **two** statements on the right with straight lines.

Blood Vessel

| Capillary |

| Artery |

| Vein |

Statements

| Has valves |

| Smallest blood vessels |

| Thick muscular walls |

| Small lumen |

| Thin permeable walls |

| Large lumen |

[6]

3 Name **three** substances carried by plasma.   [3]

Total Marks _____ / 16

Plants, Water and Minerals

1 Complete each statement below by naming the correct process.

   a) Minerals move into root hair cells by…   [1]

   b) Water moves into root hair cells by…   [1]

   c) Oxygen moves into the alveoli by…   [1]

   d) Glucose moves from the intestine to the blood by…   [1]

2 The guard cells to the right are found on the underside of a leaf.

   What is their function?   [2]

3 Transpiration is movement of water in a plant from roots to leaves.

   For each of the following changes, state whether it will **increase** or **decrease** the rate
   of transpiration.

   a) Increase in wind velocity   [1]

   b) Increase in temperature   [1]

   c) Increase in humidity   [1]

Total Marks _____ / 9

Coordination and Control

You must be able to:

- Describe the structure of the nervous system
- Explain how the body produces a coordinated response
- Explain a reflex arc and its function.

The Nervous System

- The nervous system is composed of two parts:
  - the **central nervous system** – the brain and spinal cord
  - the **peripheral nervous system** – all the other nerve cells that connect to the central nervous system.
- The nervous system receives **stimuli** from the environment, via **receptors** in sense organs, and coordinates a response.

Neurones

- Messages are carried to different parts of the body as electrical impulses via **neurones**.

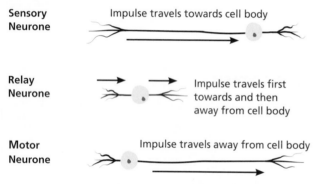

Sensory Neurone — Impulse travels towards cell body

Relay Neurone — Impulse travels first towards and then away from cell body

Motor Neurone — Impulse travels away from cell body

- Sensory neurones carry impulses from receptors to the central nervous system.
- Relay neurones pass the impulse to a motor neurone.
- Motor neurones send the impulse to an **effector**, which is a muscle or gland that produces a response.
- The connection between two neurones is a gap called a **synapse**.
- When the impulse reaches the synapse, it stimulates the release of neurotransmitter chemicals from the neurone.
- The chemicals diffuse across the gap and bind to receptors on the next neurone.
- This triggers a new electrical impulse.
- At the synapse the message goes from electrical to chemical and back to electrical.

Coordinated Responses

- In a voluntary (coordinated) response, there may be a number of possible responses.
- The impulse is sent to the brain, which makes a decision as to the best responses.

Sense Organs

Sense Organ	Receptors Detect
Eye	Light
Ear	Sound
Nose	Smell
Tongue	Taste
Skin	Touch, pressure, pain, temperature change

Chemical transmitter released here

A Synapse

Impulse

Neurone A

Receptor area

Cell body of neurone B

Electrical impulse generated in neurone B

The Reflex Arc

- Reflexes are automatic responses to certain stimuli. You do not think about them.
- The function of a reflex is to protect the body.
- The response doesn't involve the brain – the pathway goes via the spinal cord, so it is quicker.
- A reflex response happens faster than a coordinated response. Example reflexes include touching a hot object, the pupil of the eye getting smaller in bright light and the 'knee jerk' reaction.

Touching a Hot Object

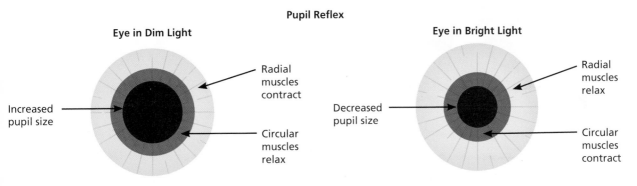

Spinal cord

2 Sensory neurone

3 Relay neurone

4 Motor neurone

Spinal nerve

5 Effector cells, in this case a muscle

1 Receptor

Hot plate (stimulus)

1 Receptors in hand detect pain.

2 Impulse sent via sensory neurone to central nervous system.

3 Impulse crosses synapse to relay neurone.

4 Impulse crosses synapse and is passed along motor neurone.

5 Response by effector muscle is to move hand away.

Pupil Reflex

Eye in Dim Light

Radial muscles contract

Increased pupil size

Circular muscles relax

Eye in Bright Light

Radial muscles relax

Decreased pupil size

Circular muscles contract

Quick Test

1. What are the **two** parts of the nervous system?
2. What is the function of a:
   a) sensory neurone?
   b) motor neurone?
   c) relay neurone?
3. What do the receptors detect in the:
   a) eye?
   b) ear?
4. Describe what happens at a synapse.

Key Words

central nervous system
peripheral nervous
 system
stimuli
receptor
neurone
effector
synapse

The Endocrine System

You must be able to:

- Describe how hormones can coordinate a response
- Describe the role of hormones in the menstrual cycle.

The Endocrine System

- Hormones are chemical messengers produced by endocrine **glands**.
- They are released directly into the blood, which carries them to the target organ.
- The cells of the target organ contain receptors to which the hormone can bind.

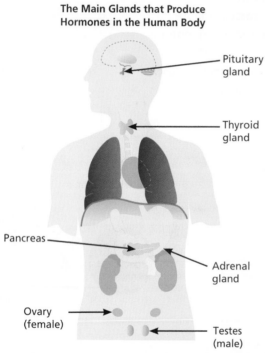

The Main Glands that Produce Hormones in the Human Body

Pituitary gland

Thyroid gland

Pancreas

Adrenal gland

Ovary (female)

Testes (male)

> **Key Point**
>
> In animals, hormones are transported around the body in the blood and affect target tissues and organs.

Gland	Hormone(s) Produced	Function
Pituitary	LH, FSH	Involved in reproduction
Pituitary	ADH	Controls water content of blood
Pituitary	Growth hormone	Stimulates growth
Thyroid	Thyroxine	Controls metabolism
Pancreas	Insulin	Controls blood glucose levels
Adrenal	Adrenaline	Fight or flight
Ovaries	Oestrogen and progesterone	Reproduction and secondary sexual characteristics
Testes	Testosterone	Secondary sexual characteristics

Hormones in the Menstrual Cycle

- Three hormones each play a different role in the menstrual cycle.
- **Oestrogen** – causes build-up of the uterus wall.
- **Progesterone** – maintains the lining of the womb.
- **Follicle-stimulating hormone (FSH)** – stimulates release of an egg because it stimulates the ovaries to produce oestrogen.

The Menstrual Cycle

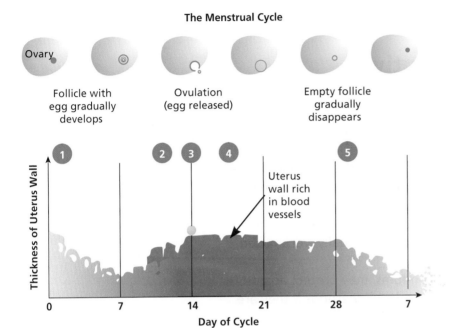

Ovary

Follicle with egg gradually develops

Ovulation (egg released)

Empty follicle gradually disappears

Uterus wall rich in blood vessels

Thickness of Uterus Wall

Day of Cycle

1 Uterus lining breaks down (i.e. a period).

2 Repair of the uterus wall. Oestrogen causes the uterus lining to gradually thicken.

3 Egg released by the ovary.

4 Progesterone and oestrogen make the lining stay thick, waiting for a fertilised egg.

5 No fertilised egg so cycle restarts.

Key Point

Ovulation (the release of an egg) takes place when the lining of the uterus is at its thickest, so that the egg can implant into the lining if it is fertilised.

Quick Test

1. What hormone is secreted by:
   a) the testes?
   b) the thyroid gland?
2. Give **three** ways in which messages transmitted by hormones are different from messages transmitted by neurones.
3. How does FSH help to stimulate the release of an egg?

Key Words

gland
oestrogen
progesterone
follicle-stimulating
   hormone (FSH)

Hormones and Their Uses

You must be able to:

- Explain the use of hormones as contraceptives and their advantages and disadvantages
- Evaluate the personal, social, economic and environmental implications of applications of science.

Hormones as Contraceptives

- Oestrogen can be used as a method of contraception.
- When taken daily, the high levels produced inhibit production of follicle-stimulating hormone (FSH) so egg development and production eventually stop.
- Progesterone also reduces fertility by causing a thick sticky mucus to be produced at the cervix, which prevents sperm from reaching the egg.
- There are over 15 methods of contraception.
- Hormonal contraceptives like the pill are very effective but can cause side effects and do not protect against sexually transmitted diseases (STDs).
- Barrier forms of contraception like condoms, may protect against STDs. They can be less reliable than hormonal methods if they are not used correctly.

Key Point

Most contraceptive pills combine progesterone and oestrogen.

The progesterone-only pill is less effective.

	The Contraceptive Pill	Condoms
Advantage (High priority)	• More than 99% effective	• 98% effective • Protect against sexually transmitted diseases
Advantage (Low priority)	• Can reduce the risk of getting some types of cancer	
Disadvantage (High priority)	• Does not protect against sexually transmitted diseases	
Disadvantage (Low priority)	• Can have side effects	• Can only be used once

Key Point

You need to be able to evaluate risks and make decisions based on the evaluation of evidence. Decisions should always be justified.

When making a decision, divide the information into advantages and disadvantages and prioritise them.

Oral Contraceptive

Evaluating Evidence

- You need to be able to:
  - evaluate the **social**, **economic** and **ethical** implications of scientific developments
  - understand the power and limitations of science.
- Scientific developments have the potential to improve the quality of life for many people but they can also create issues.

Scientific developments create issues	

Social issues – the effect on people

Ethical issues – who has the right to decide which embryos 'live' or are destroyed?

Economic issues – is the cost of developments worth the rewards?

Advances in IVF

New techniques offer the possibilities of improving a patient's odds of having a baby through in vitro fertilisation.

A single IVF cycle has about a 32% chance of resulting in a live birth and, to improve the odds, doctors often implant several embryos in the uterus during a single IVF cycle. This leads to high rates of twins and triplets, which can impact on the health of both mother and baby.

Chromosome abnormality is the main cause of miscarriage. Screening chromosomes involves taking cells from the embryo at day five to see if the normal number of chromosomes is present. Embryos with extra or missing chromosomes are not used. More research is needed on screening chromosomes, with a larger number of patients, to definitively determine the degree of benefit, especially since the cost of screening is around £2000 per patient.

Monitoring cell divisions is a technique that takes thousands of pictures of the embryos dividing at an early stage. If the division is atypical, the embryos are not used. Monitoring cell division has the advantage that it costs less and is less invasive.

Science has limititations

Science does not have an answer for everything – we still do not know enough about why the incidence of failure in IVF is so high.

There are also questions that science cannot answer, such as when does an embryo become a person? Is destroying an embryo the same as taking a life? Different people will have different opinons.

> **Quick Test**
>
> 1. What **two** hormones are commonly used in the contraceptive pill?
> 2. Suggest **two** advantages of using hormonal methods of contraception.
> 3. Suggest **two** disadvantages of using hormonal methods of contraception.
> 4. What do you understand by the terms **social**, **economic** and **ethical**?

> **Key Words**
>
> contraception
> social
> economic
> ethical

Maintaining Internal Environments

You must be able to:

- Explain why it is important to maintain a constant internal environment
- Explain how blood sugar levels in the body are controlled
- Compare Type 1 and Type 2 diabetes.

Homeostasis

- **Homeostasis** means keeping the internal body environment constant.
- The body needs to control levels of water, glucose and salts to ensure chemicals can be transported effectively into and out of cells by osmosis and active transport.
- It also needs to maintain a constant temperature, since chemical reactions in the body are catalysed by enzymes that function best at their optimum temperature.

Control of Blood Sugar Levels

- Sugar in the blood comes from the food we eat.
- The blood sugar (glucose) levels are controlled by the **pancreas**.
- The pancreas produces **insulin**:
  - insulin causes cells to become more permeable to glucose
  - glucose moves from the blood into cells.
- Insulin also causes the liver to turn excess glucose into glycogen.

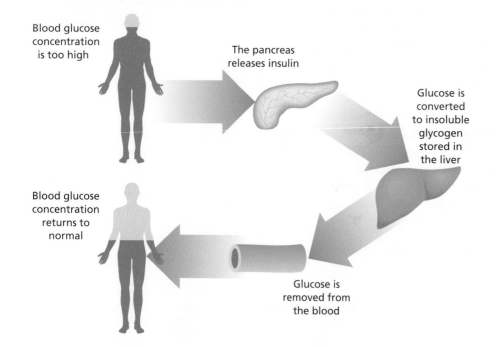

Blood glucose concentration is too high

The pancreas releases insulin

Glucose is converted to insoluble glycogen stored in the liver

Blood glucose concentration returns to normal

Glucose is removed from the blood

Diabetes

- Diabetes is a condition that causes a person's blood sugar level to become too high.
- There are two types of diabetes:

	Type 1	Type 2
Incidence	Less common	Most common
Onset	Develops suddenly, often at a young age	Develops gradually, often in people over 40 who may be overweight
Cause	Pancreas does not produce insulin	Not enough insulin is produced or cells are not affected by insulin
Treatment	Insulin injections for life, plus eating sensibly	Healthy eating, exercise, possible medication

Key Point

Type 2 diabetes cannot be treated with insulin injections.

- The graph below compares the blood glucose (sugar) concentrations of a diabetic and non-diabetic person after drinking glucose.

- The diabetic's starting blood glucose level is higher than the non-diabetic's.
- The rise in the diabetic's blood glucose level is higher than the non-diabetic's.
- It takes longer for the diabetic's blood glucose level to return to its original level.

Quick Test

1. Why is it important to maintain a constant body temperature?
2. Which type of diabetes can develop as a result of being overweight?
3. a) What is the name of the organ that produces insulin?
   b) What effect does insulin have on the body?

Key Words

homeostasis
pancreas
insulin

Recycling

You must be able to:

- Give examples of cycled materials and explain why cycling of materials is important
- Recall the key points in the carbon and nitrogen cycles
- Explain the role of microorganisms in cycling of materials.

The Importance of Recycling

- Living things are made of substances they take from the world around them.
- Plants take in elements such as carbon, oxygen, nitrogen and hydrogen from the air or from the soil.
- The plants turn the elements into complex carbohydrates, which are eaten by animals.
- These elements must be returned to the environment so they can be used by other plants and animals.
- Elements are recycled through biotic (living) components of an ecosystem (animals, plants, decomposers) and also abiotic (non-living) components (oceans, rivers, atmosphere).

> **Key Point**
>
> Carbon, nitrogen and water are vital substances for all living things and must be recycled.

The Water Cycle

- All living organisms need water to grow and survive.
- Water cycles through the atmosphere, soil, rivers, lakes and oceans.
- The water cycle is important to living organisms because it influences climate and maintains habitats.
- It also ensures there is flow of fresh water into lakes, rivers and the sea, and carries important nutrients.

The Nitrogen Cycle

- Nitrogen in the air must be turned into a form that plants can use by nitrogen fixation.
- Lightning 'fixes' nitrogen in the air and turns it into nitrates in the soil.
- Nitrogen-fixing bacteria in plant roots turn nitrogen into nitrates.
- Nitrogen is used to make fertilisers.
- Decomposition is the process by which dead animals and plants are turned into ammonium compounds by putrefying bacteria.
- Ammonium compounds are turned into nitrates by nitrifying bacteria.
- Denitrifying bacteria turn nitrates in the soil into nitrogen gas.

The Carbon Cycle

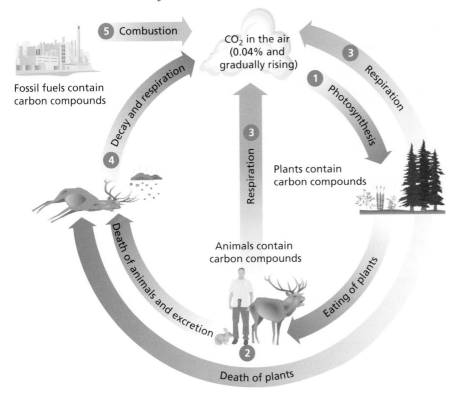

1. Carbon dioxide is taken out of the atmosphere by plants when they photosynthesise.
2. The carbon in plants passes to animals when they are eaten.
3. Animals and plants respire releasing carbon dioxide back into the air.
4. Microorganisms **decompose** dead organisms and waste, and release carbon dioxide when they respire.
5. Combustion releases carbon dioxide into the atmosphere.

Decay

- Microorganisms such as bacteria and fungi are called **decomposers**.
- They cause decay by releasing enzymes that break down compounds.
- They need water and a suitable temperature to survive.
- **Detritivores**, such as earthworms and woodlice, break down decaying material into small pieces, increasing its surface area and speeding up decay.

> **Key Point**
>
> Carbon dioxide is put back into the atmosphere by three types of respiration – animal, plant and microbial – along with combustion, and is removed by photosynthesis.

> **Key Words**
>
> biotic
> abiotic
> nitrogen fixation
> decompose
> decomposers
> detritivores

> **Quick Test**
>
> 1. Why is the water cycle important to living organisms?
> 2. Name the **four** types of bacteria that are involved in the nitrogen cycle.
> 3. How is carbon removed from the atmosphere?

Interdependence

You must be able to:

- Describe the different levels of organisation in an ecosystem
- Explain how factors can affect communities
- Describe the importance of interdependence and competition in the community.

Levels of Organisation within an Ecosystem

- An ecosystem is a place or habitat together with all the plants and animals that live there.
- The plants and animals within an ecosystem form the **community**.
- A **population** is all the animals or plants of the same species within a community.

Word	Definition
Producer	All plants – they use the Sun's energy to produce food
Herbivore	An animal that eats only plants
Consumer	All animals – they consume food
Carnivore	An animal that eats only animals
Omnivore	An animal that eats both animals and plants

Remember to use scientific vocabulary, terminology and definitions.

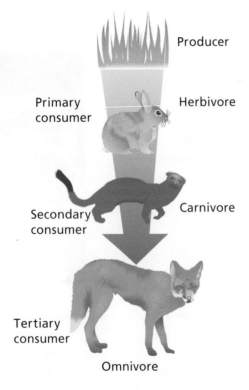

Producer

Primary consumer   Herbivore

Secondary consumer   Carnivore

Tertiary consumer

Omnivore

Key Point

Producers use energy from the Sun to make food.

Factors Affecting Communities

- Biotic factors are living organisms or things that influence or affect ecosystems, for example:
  - number of predators
  - food availability
  - number of insects to pollinate plants
  - disease
  - human activity, such as mining, which may destroy habitats.
- Abiotic factors are non-living conditions or things that affect ecosystems and the organisms in them, for example:
  - temperature
  - light intensity
  - moisture levels
  - pH of soil
  - salinity (salt levels) of water.

Interdependence and Competition

- The organisms within a community may depend on other organisms for food (predation) or shelter.
- Sometimes an organism lives on another organism, e.g. mistletoe lives on trees and absorbs nutrients from the tree.
- This type of dependence is known as parasitism.
- Mutualism is a state in which two organisms depend on each other and both benefit, e.g. a bee feeds from a flower and the flower is pollinated.
- Organisms within a community will compete with each other:
  - animals compete for food, space, water, mates
  - plants compete for space, water, light, minerals.

> **Key Point**
>
> Mutualism benefits both organisms. Parasitism only benefits one organism and harms the other organism.

Oxpecker birds remove and eat ticks and larvae from the skin of buffalo. This is an example of mutualism – both species benefit.

> **Quick Test**
>
> 1. Explain the difference between a community and a population.
> 2. Suggest **two** biotic factors and **two** abiotic factors that affect a community.
> 3. Name **three** things for which animals may compete.
> 4. What is the difference between parasitism and mutualism?

> **Key Words**
>
> community
> population
> predation
> parasitism
> mutualism

Review Questions

Cell Structures

1 Draw a line from each cell part to the correct description.

Cell Part

| Cell membrane |
| Mitochondria |
| Chloroplast |
| Cell wall |

Description

| Contains chlorophyll |
| Gives support |
| Controls movement of substances in and out of the cell |
| Contains the enzymes for respiration |

[3]

Total Marks .... / 3

What Happens in Cells

1 Explain what happens to an enzyme if the temperature is too high. [2]

2 Choose the correct word from each pair in bold to complete the passage about enzymes.

Enzymes are **protein / carbohydrate** molecules.

They are made up of **glucose / amino acid** chains.

They **slow down / speed up** the rate of reactions in the body and are **rejuvenated / denatured** by high temperatures.

The temperature that an enzyme works best at is called the **optimum / normal** temperature. [5]

Total Marks .... / 7

Respiration

1 Tom is running up a hill.
Every few minutes he stops because he has to catch his breath by breathing deeply and his legs muscles feel painful.

a) What is the name of the substance that has built up in Tom's muscles and is causing pain? [1]

b) Why does Tom get out of breath? [4]

c) When Tom reaches the top of the hill he rests for 10 minutes and then begins to walk slowly back down.

   i) What kind of respiration is occurring in Tom's cells as he starts his descent? [1]

   ii) Write the equation for this type of respiration. [2]

   iii) Where in the cell does this type of respiration occur? [1]

Total Marks _____ / 9

Photosynthesis

1   Carol and Letisha are neighbours.
They both have greenhouses in which they are growing lettuces.
Carol keeps her greenhouse warm using an electric heater.
Letisha uses a heater that burns paraffin, which is a fossil fuel.

a) Why do both Carol and Letisha heat their greenhouses? [2]

b) Letisha says she will get bigger lettuces because a paraffin heater is better for the plants than an electric heater.

   Suggest why she says this. [2]

c) Apart from heating the greenhouses, what else could they do to increase the yield? [1]

d) Write the word equation for photosynthesis. [2]

2   Complete the sentences about photosynthesis by choosing the correct word from the list.

chloroplast light water absorbs oxygen carbon dioxide releases chlorophyll

The green colour in plants is caused by a pigment called _____, which

_____ light energy from the Sun to use in photosynthesis. In addition to

light, photosynthesis requires _____, which is absorbed by the roots, and

_____, which enters the plants through the leaf. [4]

Total Marks _____ / 11

Review Questions

Supplying the Cell

1 Root hair cells absorb water from the soil. How are they adapted for absorbing water? [1]

2 The diagram shows a working muscle cell.

a) Suggest what substance molecule **A** is most likely to be. [1]

b) What is the name of cell **B**? [1]

c) **C** is a blood vessel.

   Which of the following is **C** most likely to be?

   A an artery

   B a vein

   C a capillary [1]

Total Marks _____ / 4

The Challenges of Size

1 The pictures show a unicellular organism called a *Paramecium* and a monkey, which is a multicellular organism.

Oxygen is able to pass into the *Paramecium* through the cell membrane.

a) By what process will this happen? [1]

b) Explain why the monkey has a specialised transport system that delivers oxygen to the lungs, but the *Paramecium* does not. [3]

Total Marks _____ / 4

The Heart and Blood Cells

1 The diagram below shows two blood vessels.

A   **B**

a) Which blood vessel will carry blood at high pressure? [1]

b) Which blood vessel has thick muscular walls? [1]

c) Which blood vessel has valves? [1]

d) Which blood vessel has the largest lumen? [1]

e) Draw an arrow on vessel **A** to show the lumen. Label it L. [1]

Total Marks _____ / 5

Plants, Water and Minerals

1 Through which process do plants lose water?
Put a tick (✓) in the box next to the correct answer.

Translocation	
Transpiration	
Transfusion	

[1]

2 The diagram shows a cross-section through the stem of a plant.

a) What is the name of the tubes labelled **A**? [1]

b) Name **one** substance transported in the tubes labelled **A**. [1]

c) Which statement below best describes the tubes labelled **A**?
Put a tick (✓) in the box next to the best answer.

Made of living cells with large channels in end walls	
Made of dead cells with end walls removed	
Made of living cells packed with mitochondria	

[1]

3 What is the name of the process by which minerals move into plant roots against a concentration gradient? [1]

Total Marks _____ / 5

Practice Questions

Coordination and Control

1 Complete the table below about sense organs and the stimuli that they detect.

Sense Organ	Stimulus Detected
eye	a)
b)	sound
nose	c)
d)	taste
skin	e) _____ and f)

[6]

2 The passage below is about nerve impulses.

Choose the correct word from each pair.

Messages are carried by neurones as **electrical / chemical** impulses.

The junction between two neurones is called a **synapse / intersection**.

When the impulse reaches this junction, **hormones / neurotransmitters** are released.

These cross the gap and bind to **antigens / receptors** on the next neurone.

[4]

3 Which **two** structures make up the central nervous system?

A brain

B eye

C spinal cord

D peripheral nerves

E heart

[2]

4 Name the type of neurone being described in each sentence.

  a) Carries impulses from the central nervous system to effectors. [1]

  b) Carries impulses from receptors to the central nervous system. [1]

  c) Only found within the central nervous system. [1]

Total Marks .... / 15

The Endocrine System

1 Hormones are produced by glands.

  How do they travel to their site of action? [1]

2 Hormones play an important role in control of the menstrual cycle.

  Draw a line from each hormone to its function.

  Hormone   **Function**

  oestrogen   stimulates the release of an egg

  progesterone   causes the lining of the uterus to thicken

  FSH   maintains the lining of the uterus   [2]

Total Marks .... / 3

Hormones and Their Uses

1 Oral contraceptives may contain oestrogen and progesterone, or progesterone on its own.

  a) Give **one** disadvantage of the progesterone-only pill. [1]

  b) How does progesterone help to prevent pregnancy? [1]

  c) Where in the body are oestrogen and progesterone produced? [1]

  d) Give **one** disadvantage of using oral contraceptives. [1]

Total Marks .... / 4

Maintaining Internal Environments

1 Insulin increases the permeability of cells to glucose, so glucose can move from the blood into the cells.

   a) By what process does the glucose move from the blood into the cells?   [1]

   b) For what process is the glucose required?   [1]

2 Gordy has type 2 diabetes.
   He goes out for a meal with his brother who does not have diabetes.
   The graphs below show the blood glucose levels of Gordy and his brother before and after the meal.

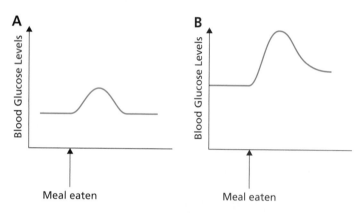

Which graph is most likely to be Gordy's? Give **two** reasons for your answer.   [2]

Total Marks _____ / 4

Recycling

1 Draw a line from each process in the nitrogen cycle to the type of bacteria involved.

Process	Type of Bacteria
nitrogen gas turned into nitrates by bacteria in plant roots	denitrifying
animal and plant material and waste products turned into ammonium compounds	putrefying
ammonium compounds turned into nitrates	nitrogen-fixing
nitrates turned into nitrogen gas	nitrifying

[3]

2 The diagram shows the carbon cycle.

a) What letter represents each of the following processes?

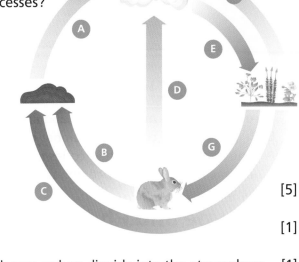

CO₂ in air (0.04%)

i) Photosynthesis

ii) Animal respiration

iii) Consumption

iv) Microbial respiration

v) Plant respiration [5]

b) What process is shown by the letter **B**? [1]

c) Name a process, **not** shown on the diagram, that releases carbon dioxide into the atmosphere. [1]

Total Marks _____ / 10

Interdependence

1 Divide the words below into **biotic** and **abiotic** components of an ecosystem.

animals   bacteria   rivers   trees   soil   sea   detritivores   [7]

2 Some students noticed that the grass growing in one part of the school field was longer and greener than grass growing in another area.

Suggest **three** factors that may be affecting the growth of the grass. [3]

3 a) Cleaner fish feed off dead skin and parasites on larger fish.

Explain why this is an example of mutualism. [3]

b) A dog tapeworm lives inside the intestines of a dog and absorbs its food.
The dog may lose weight and become sick.

What type of relationship is this? Underline the correct word.

mutualism   parasitism   symbiosis [1]

Total Marks _____ / 14

Genes

You must be able to:

- Explain the relationship between genes, chromosomes and the genome
- Describe how genes and the environment influence phenotype.

Genes and Chromosomes

- **Chromosomes** are made of **DNA** and are found inside the nucleus.
- Each chromosome contains a number of **genes**.
- A gene is section of DNA that codes for a protein.
- A **genome** is an organism's complete set of DNA, including all of its genes.

Genotype and Phenotype

- Genes are responsible for our characteristics.
- We have two copies of every chromosome in our cells, therefore, we have two copies of each gene.
- The different forms of each gene are called **alleles**.
- We use capital and lower case letters to show if alleles are **dominant** or **recessive**.
- If two dominant alleles are present, e.g. BB, the dominant characteristic is seen, e.g. brown eyes.
- If two recessive alleles are present, e.g. bb, the recessive characteristic is seen, e.g. blue eyes.
- If one of each allele is present, e.g. Bb, the dominant character is seen, e.g. brown eyes.
- In the case of eye colour for example, brown eyes are dominant and would be shown as BB or Bb.
- Blue eyes on the other hand, are recessive and would be shown as bb.
- The **phenotype** is the characteristic that is seen, e.g. blue eyes.
- The **genotype** is the genes that are present, e.g. bb.

A Cell

Chromosomes

A Section of Chromosome

← A gene

A Section of DNA

A Section of Uncoiled DNA

	A person who is **heterozygous** has two different alleles.	A person who is **homozygous** has both alleles the same.
Genes on Chromosomes		
Alleles	One allele for blue eyes, one for brown eyes	Both alleles are for blue eyes
Heterozygous or Homozygous	Heterozygous	Homozygous
Genotype	Bb	bb
Phenotype	Brown eyes	Blue eyes

> **Key Point**
>
> Capital letters represent dominant alleles.
>
> Lower case letters represent recessive alleles.

> **Key Point**
>
> A human body cell has 46 chromosomes, arranged in 23 pairs.

Environment and Phenotype

- Inherited variation is caused by the genes inherited from parents.
- Environmental variation is caused by environmental factors, e.g. diet.
- The phenotype of an organism is often the result of both genetic and environmental variation.
- For example:
    - a person who inherits light skin may, through prolonged exposure to the sun, develop darker skin
    - a person who inherits 'tall' genes may not grow tall if poorly nourished.
- Some characteristics show continuous variation, for example height. A person can be tall or short or anywhere in between the two.
- Characteristics that show discontinuous variation have a limited number of possible values. For example, blood groups are either A, B, AB or O.

> **Key Point**
>
> Height and weight are both examples of continuous variation.

Characteristics Controlled Solely by Inheritance
Eye colour
Hair colour
Blood group
Inherited diseases

Factors that are Influenced by Environment and Inheritance
Height and weight
Intelligence
Artistic or sporting ability
Skin colour

Quick Test

1. What is a genome?
2. How do we show whether an allele is dominant or recessive?
3. Suggest **two** characteristics that may be affected by the environment.
4. Give an example of:
    a) continuous variation
    b) discontinuous variation.

> **Key Words**
>
> chromosome
> DNA
> gene
> genome
> allele
> dominant
> recessive
> phenotype
> genotype
> heterozygous
> homozygous
> continuous
> discontinuous

Genetics and Reproduction

You must be able to:

- Describe meiosis and explain its role in genetic variation
- Use genetic crosses to determine the outcomes for sex and other characteristics
- Describe the work of Mendel in developing our understanding of genetics.

Meiosis

- Meiosis is a type of cell division that produces **gametes**.
- The cell divides twice to produce four gametes with genetically different sets of chromosomes.
- Gametes have half the number of chromosomes as body cells. This is called a **haploid** number.

| Cell with two pairs of chromosomes (diploid cell). | Each chromosome replicates itself. | Chromosomes part company and move to opposite poles. | Cell divides for the first time. | Copies now separate and the second cell division takes place. | Four haploid cells (gametes), each with half the number of chromosomes of the parent cell. |

- When the gametes fuse in fertilisation, the normal **diploid** number of chromosomes is restored.
- Fusion of gametes is a source of genetic variation.

Determination of Sex

- Sex inheritance is controlled by a whole chromosome rather than a gene.
- In humans, the 23rd pair of chromosomes in males contains an X and a Y chromosome; females have two X chromosomes.

> ### Key Point
>
> The chance of having a male child is always 50%, as is the chance of having a female child.

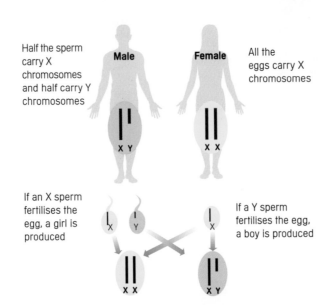

Half the sperm carry X chromosomes and half carry Y chromosomes

Male

X Y

Female

X X

All the eggs carry X chromosomes

If an X sperm fertilises the egg, a girl is produced

X

Y

X

If a Y sperm fertilises the egg, a boy is produced

X X

X Y

Genetic Crosses

- A genetic cross looks at the possible outcomes for offspring with parents of the same or different genotypes.
- All the offspring of a cross between a homozygous dominant and a homozygous recessive will appear to have the dominant characteristic.
- A cross between two heterozygous parents will give a ratio of three offspring with the dominant characteristic to one with the recessive.

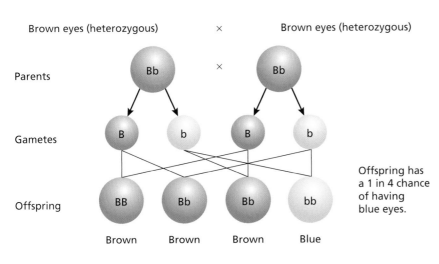

Key Point

Most of the characteristics we exhibit are not controlled by a single gene, but are the result of multiple gene inheritance.

Quick Test

1. What is the difference between a haploid cell and a diploid cell? Give an example of each.
2. Explain the role of meiosis in genetic variation.
3. An individual has sex chromosomes XX. Are they male or female?
4. Explain why there is a 50/50 chance of having a male or female baby.

Key Words

gamete
haploid
diploid

Natural Selection and Evolution

You must be able to:

- Understand there is extensive genetic variation within a population and relate this to evolution
- Explain how the development of ideas on evolution have impacted on modern biology, including the impact on classification systems.

Evolution and Natural Selection

- Evolution is the gradual change in the inherited characteristics of a population over a large number of generations, which may result in the formation of a new species.
- Charles Darwin's theory of evolution suggested:
  - There is much variation within a species.
  - There is a struggle for survival and organisms have more offspring than can survive.
  - Those that are best adapted to their environment are likely to survive, breed and pass on their genes to the next generation (survival of the fittest).
  - Those that are least well adapted are likely to die.

Mutations

- Mutations in genes results in multiple variants of any one gene.
- Usually the mutations have no effect on the phenotype of the organism.
- Occasionally, the mutation may influence the phenotype.
- If the mutation results in a characteristic that gives the organism an advantage over organisms without the characteristic, the organism is more likely to survive, breed and pass on the mutated gene to its offspring.

Using Darwin's idea of survival of the fittest, you might hypothesise:

'Animals that are better camouflaged are less likely to be seen by predators.'

A model can be used to test this hypothesis using blue, green, red and brown strands of wool:

- Thirty 5cm strands of each colour of wool are scattered randomly in a field.
- A group of students are given 1 minute to find as many strands as they can.

Using the model, you might predict that:

- More red and blue strands of wool will be found because they are not camouflaged.
- Fewer green and brown strands will be found because they are better camouflaged.

Key Point

Evolution by natural selection relies on random mutations.

Key Point

Scientific models are used to explain and predict the behaviour of real objects or systems that are difficult to observe directly.

Evidence for Evolution

- The fossil record gives us evidence of change over a long period of time, however there are gaps in this record.
- **Antibiotic resistance** provides evidence for evolution – bacteria divide very rapidly, so evolution by natural selection can be seen in a very short period of time:
  - A mutation may cause a bacterium to be resistant to an antibiotic.
  - Most of the bacteria in the population are killed by the antibiotic.
  - The antibiotic-resistant bacteria multiply rapidly to form a colony of resistant bacteria.

Developments in Classification Systems

- Developments in biology have had a significant impact on classification systems.
- The binomial classification system places organisms into groups based on a large number of characteristics such as anatomy, physiology, biochemistry and reproduction.
- This helps us to understand how organisms are related to each other.
- Darwin's theory of evolution provided a new explanation for how to group organisms:
  - nearness of descent
  - phylogeny (the sequence of events involved in the evolution of a species).
- **Phylogenetic** systems of classification help us understand the evolutionary history of organisms:
  - DNA sequencing can be used to show if organisms share common ancestors.
  - DNA sequencing has led to some organisms being reclassified.

Natural Classification of Sumatran Orang-utan

Level	Example
Kingdom	Animalia
Phylum	Chordata
Class	Mammalia
Order	Primates
Family	Hominidae
Genus	*Pongo*
Species	*Pongo abelii*

The Bornean orang-utan, *Pongo pygmaeus*, shares the same genus, which shows they are closely related. They developed as two separate species following the separation of Borneo and Sumatra.

Phylogenetic Tree

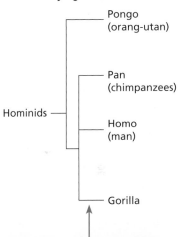

This shows that man, chimps, gorillas and orang-utans all share a common ancestor. It is thought that man is more closely related to gorillas than orang-utans.

Quick Test

1. Explain the process of natural selection.
2. Explain how antibiotic resistance develops.
3. How does DNA sequencing help to classify organisms?

Key Words

mutation
antibiotic resistance
phylogenetic

Monitoring and Maintaining the Environment

You must be able to:

- Explain how to carry out field investigations into the distribution and abundance of organisms in a habitat.

Distribution and Abundance

- Scientists studying the environment often want to investigate:
  - the distribution of an organism (where it is found)
  - the numbers of organisms in a given area or habitat.
- The following apparatus can be used for sampling:

Apparatus	What it is Used For
Pooter	Catching small insects on the ground
Pitfall traps	Catching small crawling insects
Pond net	Catching water invertebrates, small fish
Sweep net	Catching flying insects
Quadrat	Sampling the number of plant species
Line transects	Sampling the distribution of plant species

- A key can be used to identify the organisms found.

> **Key Point**
>
> It is important to gain a better understanding of the environment by collecting and interpreting data. This information is essential if we want to maintain the environment and variety of life.

A Quadrat

A Pooter

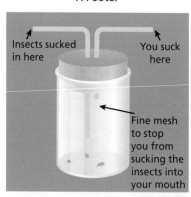

Insects sucked in here

You suck here

Fine mesh to stop you from sucking the insects into your mouth

A Pitfall Trap

A Sweep Net

The Capture–Mark–Recapture Method

- Capture–mark–recapture is a method commonly used to estimate the population size of a particular animal.
- Over a set number of hours or days, animals are caught, marked and then released.
- After a period of time, to allow the animals to redistribute themselves, a second sample is caught, some of which will already be marked.

$$\text{population size} = \frac{\text{number in 1st sample} \times \text{number in 2nd sample}}{\text{number in 2nd sample that are marked}}$$

In a garden, 12 snails were caught in a trap overnight.
Their shells were marked with a spot of blue paint and they were released.
The following night 8 snails were caught in the trap, of which 4 were marked.

$$\text{population size} = \frac{(12 \times 8)}{4} = \frac{96}{4} = 24$$

Using Quadrats

- Follow the steps below to estimate the number of plants in a field:
  1. Measure the area of the field.
  2. Randomly place a number of quadrats (1 square metre) in the field.
  3. Count the number of plants in each quadrat.
  4. Work out the mean number of plants per quadrat.
  5. Multiply by the number of square metres in the field.

Area of field = 50m²

Quadrat	1	2	3	4	5
No. of Plants	8	4	7	3	6

Average number of plants per m² = 5.6
Estimated number of plants in whole field = 5.6 × 50 = 280

Quick Test

1. What piece of apparatus would you use for catching dragonflies in an area of marsh land?
2. Using the capture–mark–recapture method, researchers trapped, marked and released 20 red squirrels. A week later, they caught 10 red squirrels, 4 of which were marked. What is the estimated population size of squirrels?

Key Words

habitat

Investigations

You must be able to:

- Explain how to determine the number of organisms in a given area
- Plan and explain investigations
- Select appropriate apparatus and recognise when to apply sampling techniques
- Translate data and carry out statistical analysis, identifying potential sources of error
- Recognise the importance of peer review of results.

Planning and Carrying Out Investigations

- When planning an investigation many factors must be considered and certain steps should always be followed.

At the edge of the school field are some large trees that shade part of the field for much of the day.
A group of students wanted to find out if the shade from the trees affected the number of dandelions growing in the field.

Investigation:
How is the distribution of dandelions affected by light and shade?

> The rationale for the investigation can be incorporated into the title.

Hypothesis:
There will be more dandelions growing the further you get from the trees because there will be more light.

> The hypothesis should always be based on scientific knowledge.

Method:

1. Measure a transect from the trees to the edge of the field.
2. At 5-metre intervals along the transect, place a quadrat on the ground.
3. Count the number of dandelions in each quadrat.
4. Carry out two more transects, parallel to the first one, and count the dandelions in each quadrat. This will improve the reliability of the results.
5. Work out the average number of dandelions at each distance from the trees.

> Apparatus should always be appropriate, e.g. you would not use a ruler to measure 5-metre intervals.

> Scientists use sampling and look at several small areas to get a good representation of the whole area.

> Any data recorded should be reliable, which means readings should be repeated.

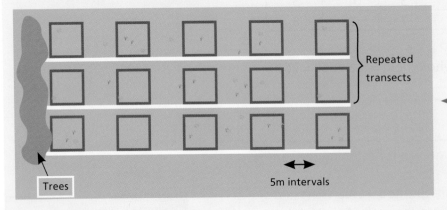

Repeated transects

Trees

5m intervals

> A diagram often helps to clarify the method.

Results:

Distance from Trees (m)	0	5	10	15	20
Number of Dandelions in Each Transect	8	9	7	6	5
	8	8	7	2	6
	9	6	5	6	4
Mean Number	8.3	7.7	6.3	4.7	5.0

Data needs to be presented in an organised way, e.g. tables are useful for presenting data clearly.

Data sometimes needs to be analysed statistically by calculating the mean, mode or median.

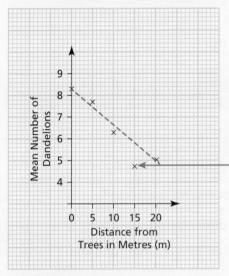

Line graphs are often useful for spotting anomalous results, which are often due to human errors, e.g. misreading the tape measure, or may occur randomly by chance.

Conclusion:
- The results show that the further you go from the trees, the fewer dandelions are growing, i.e. the opposite of what was predicted.

Evaluation:
- It was difficult to control variables such as the moisture content of the soil and the ground temperature, which could have affected the number of dandelions.
- To improve the experiment, a digital light meter could have been used to give some light readings for each quadrat.
- The experiment could be repeated at a different time of the year.

The evaluation should consider the method and results and what improvements could be made.

If the conclusion is different to what was predicted, the question 'why' must be asked and this may generate a new hypothesis, which can then be tested.

Key Point

Systemic / systematic errors occur when the same error is made every time. Systematic errors are only likely to be discovered if someone else tries to repeat the experiment and does not achieve the same results.

Key Point

A **peer review** is when one scientist evaluates another's experiment. This is valuable for scrutinising the design of the experiment and the validity of the data, and providing credibility.

Key Words

rationale
hypothesis
sampling
reliable
anomalous
systemic / systematic error
peer review

Quick Test

1. How do you ensure results from an investigation are reliable?
2. What is an anomalous result?
3. What are systemic / systematic errors?
4. Why is peer review important?

Resources and the Environment

You must be able to:

- Describe how human interactions affect ecosystems
- Explain the benefits and challenges of maintaining biodiversity
- Explain the impact of the selective breeding of food plants and animals
- Describe the process of genetic engineering and the benefits and risks of using gene technology in food production.

Human Interaction

- Humans need to obtain and produce resources to survive.
- Their interactions have a huge impact on ecosystems.

Interaction	Impact
Deforestation	• Loss of habitat and biodiversity.
Pesticide use	• Gets into food chains and reduces biodiversity. • Kills insects that may be an important part of the food chain.
Over fishing	• Fish stocks drop to a level where breeding is affected.
Hunting	• Many animals are now becoming endangered.
Farming single crops (monocultures)	• Reduces biodiversity since pollen is only available for a short period of time.
Captive breeding programmes	• Increases the numbers of animals that are endangered.
Creating nature reserves	• Protects native species and increases their numbers.
Passing laws to protect animals	• Protects endangered species.
Reforestation by planting native trees	• Increases biodiversity.
Sustainable fishing	• Allows healthy fish stock levels to be maintained so reproduction occurs.

Biodiversity

- The greater the biodiversity, the greater the stability of an ecosystem and the greater the opportunity for medical discoveries.
- Biodiversity boosts the economy, e.g. a greater variety of plants means a greater variety of crops.
- The challenges of maintaining diversity arise due to:
  - **Political issues** – conservation strategies are often politically sensitive and there may be difficulty in gaining agreements between local, national and global partners.
  - **Economic issues** – conservation is often expensive, for example, trying to monitor conservation schemes.

Key Point

Not all human interactions with the environment have a negative impact.

Ecotourism

- **Ecotourism** aims to reduce the impact of tourism on environments by:
  - not interfering with wild life
  - leaving a low carbon footprint
  - supporting the local community, e.g. buying local produce.
- It is an example of **sustainable** development.

Revise

Selective Breeding

- **Selective breeding** is the process of finding plants or animals with the best characteristics and breeding them.
- The process is repeated many times until the desired characteristic is present in all offspring.
- Selective breeding has been used to produce:
  - disease-resistant wheat
  - dairy cattle that give high milk yields
  - wheat that grows in areas of high salt levels.

Genetic Engineering

- Genetic engineering involves altering the genome of an organism by adding a gene, or genes, from a different organism.
- It uses enzymes to 'cut and paste' genes.

Benefits of GM Foods	Risks of GM Foods
Higher crop yields	Once out in the wild it is impossible to recall genetically modified organisms
More nutritious crops	Genetically modified organisms may breed with other non-GM organisms passing on these new foreign genes into the wild population, for example, spread of herbicide-resistant genes might lead to 'super weeds'
Crops can grow in harsh environments	We do not know the long-term effects of eating GM food; GM foods may harm the consumer, for example, causing allergic reactions
Crops resistant to pests and disease	
Better flavour food	
Food with longer shelf life	

Monitoring and Maintaining Health

You must be able to:

- Describe different types of diseases
- Describe how diseases spread and how this spread may be reduced
- Describe defence responses in animals to disease
- Explain how white blood cells and platelets are adapted to their function.

Diseases

- **Communicable** diseases are easily transmitted.
- They are caused by bacteria, viruses, fungi, protoctista or parasites.
- Sometimes diseases interact with each other, for example:
  - People with HIV (human immunodeficiency virus) are more likely to catch tuberculosis (TB) than those without HIV because of a weakened immune system.
  - Infection with some types of human papillomavirus can lead to the development of cervical cancer.

Spread of Disease

- Communicable diseases can be spread in humans in a number of ways, as shown in the table below:

Method of Spread	Examples
In the air through droplets, when people sneeze or cough	Chicken pox, tuberculosis, colds
By eating contaminated food	*Salmonella* food poisoning
By drinking contaminated water	Cholera
Contact – person to person or person to object	Athlete's foot
Animals – through bites or scratches	Malaria

- Spread of disease in humans can be reduced by good hygiene:
  - handle and prepare food safely
  - wash hands frequently
  - sneeze into a tissue then bin it
  - do not share personal items, e.g. a toothbrush
  - get vaccinated
  - do not touch wild animals.
- Communicable diseases can spread rapidly and infect millions of people globally.
- Statistics on the incidence and spread of communicable diseases are collected by Communicable Disease Centres.

Key Point

Health is more than just the absence of disease. It is defined as a state of complete physical, mental and social wellbeing.

Key Point

HIV is the virus that causes AIDS. It is possible to have the virus but not have AIDS. The virus is usually sexually transmitted and attacks the immune system making sufferers vulnerable to infection. There is no cure, but there are treatments to help manage the disease.

Key Point

Scientific quantities (i.e. statistics) allow us to predict likely trends in the number of cases of diseases and how the disease will spread nationally and globally. This is very important when planning for a country's future health needs.

Human Defences Against Disease

- Human's first line of defence is to stop microorganisms entering the body:
  - the skin acts as a physical barrier
  - **platelets** help the blood to clot and seal wounds to prevent pathogens entering
  - mucous membranes in the lungs produce mucus, which traps microorganisms
  - acid in the stomach kills microorganisms in food.

White Blood Cells

- White blood cells engulf and destroy microbes by a process called **phagocytosis**.

Phagocytosis

White blood cell (phagocyte)

Microorganisms invade the body.

The white blood cell surrounds and ingests the microorganisms.

The white blood cell starts to digest the microorganisms.

The microorganisms have been digested by the white blood cell.

- Some white blood cells, called B lymphocytes, also produce **antibodies**.
- The lymphocyte recognises **antigens** on the surface of the invading pathogen.
- It produces antibodies that lock onto the antigen.
- The antibodies are specific for that antigen.

Antibody Production by White Blood Cells

Microorganisms (antigens) invade the body.

The white blood cell forms antibodies.

The antibodies cause the microorganisms to clump.

The white blood cell destroys the microorganisms.

> ### Key Point
>
> There are two types of white blood cell involved in defence:
>
> - Phagocytes destroy microorganisms by ingestion.
> - Lymphocytes produce antibodies and form memory cells.

Quick Test

1. Name **four** groups of organism which cause disease.
2. Suggest **three** ways diseases can be spread in humans.
3. Give **three** human defences against disease.
4. What is the difference between HIV and AIDS?

> ### Key Words
>
> communicable
> platelets
> phagocytosis
> antibody
> antigen

Prevention and Treatment of Disease

You must be able to:

- Explain the role of vaccination and medicines in the prevention and treatment of disease
- Describe the process of developing new medicines.

Vaccination

- Vaccination (or immunisation) prevents people from getting a disease.
- The vaccine contains a dead or weakened version of the disease-causing organism.
- White blood cells (B lymphocytes) recognise the antigens present in the vaccine and produce antibodies.
- Memory cells are also produced that will recognise the disease-causing organism should the body come into contact with it again.
- If this happens, they will make lots of antibodies very quickly to prevent the person catching the disease.

Key Point

Vaccinations provide protection against communicable diseases.

Memory Cells and Antibody Production

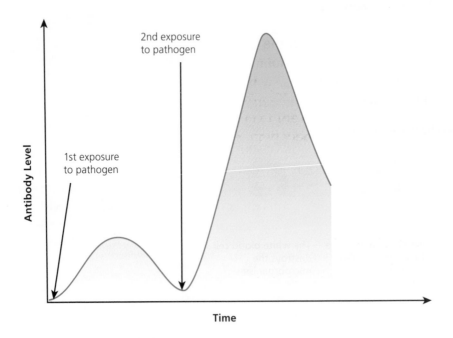

- If a large percentage of the population have been vaccinated, only a small percentage of the population will be at risk from catching the disease and passing it on to others.
- Vaccination is important in controlling the spread of disease.
- It is often possible to have one injection that vaccinates against several different diseases.

Common Vaccinations Available in the UK	
Vaccination	**Age Offered**
5-in-1 (diphtheria, tetanus, whooping cough, polio and Hib (Haemophilus Influenzae Type B)	8 weeks
Pneumococcal	8 weeks
Meningitis B	8 weeks
Rotavirus	8 weeks
Measles, mumps and rubella (MMR) vaccine	1 year
HPV (girls only)	13 years
Flu vaccine	65 years

Key Point

It is important to finish a course of antibiotics. Even when a person is feeling better, there are still infectious organisms in the body.

Antibiotics, Antivirals and Antiseptics

- Antibiotics, e.g. penicillin, are used to treat bacterial infections.
- They cannot be used for viral infections because viruses are found inside cells and the antibiotic would damage the cell.
- Antivirals are drugs that treat viral infections.
- Antiseptics are chemicals that kill microorganisms outside
  the body. They can be used on skin, on surfaces and on wounds.

Developing New Medicines

- New medicines must be tested for toxicity, efficacy (effectiveness) and dosage before they are released to the public.
- There are a number of stages in developing a new drug:
  1. Tested on computer models or cells grown in the laboratory.
  2. Tested on animals, e.g. mice.
  3. Tested on small numbers of healthy volunteers in clinical trials (low doses often used).
  4. Further clinical trials on people with the disease, using control groups who are given a placebo.

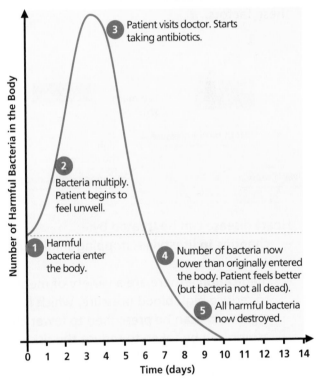

The Effect of Antibiotics on Infection

Number of Harmful Bacteria in the Body (y-axis) vs *Time (days)* (x-axis)

1. Harmful bacteria enter the body.
2. Bacteria multiply. Patient begins to feel unwell.
3. Patient visits doctor. Starts taking antibiotics.
4. Number of bacteria now lower than originally entered the body. Patient feels better (but bacteria not all dead).
5. All harmful bacteria now destroyed.

Quick Test

1. How does vaccination work?
2. Distinguish between antibiotics, antivirals and antiseptics.
3. What are the **three** diseases that the MMR vaccination offers protection against?
4. Give **three** reasons why scientists must test new medicines before they are made available for public use.

Key Words

memory cells
antibiotic
antiviral
antiseptic
placebo

Non-Communicable Diseases

You must be able to:

- Recall some non-communicable diseases, suggest factors that contribute to them and evaluate data on them
- Evaluate some of the treatments for cardiovascular disease
- Discuss benefits and risks associated with using stem cells and gene technology in medicine
- Suggest why understanding the human genome is important in medicine.

Non-Communicable Diseases

- Many non-communicable diseases have contributory factors linked to lifestyle factors.
- Many of these factors interact with each other.
- For example, poor diet and lack of exercise can lead to obesity, which in turn is a risk factor for many diseases such as type 2 diabetes and cardiovascular disease.
- The arrows on the diagram below show the complex interaction of these factors.

> **Key Point**
>
> Cancer occurs when a cell mutates and begins to grow and divide uncontrollably.

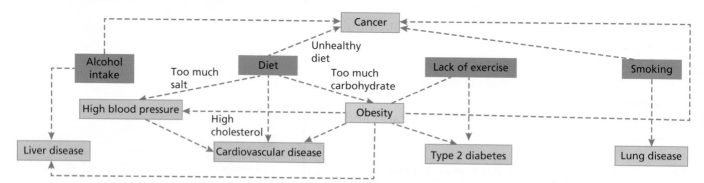

- Heart disease can be treated by:
  - **changes to lifestyle** – stopping smoking, eating healthily, exercising more
  - **medication** – there are a variety of medicines that can be taken to reduce high blood pressure, which is linked to heart disease, e.g. statins can be prescribed to lower cholesterol levels and aspirin can be taken to reduce the risk of further heart attacks
  - **surgery** – stents can be placed in narrowed arteries and heart transplants can replace damaged or diseased hearts.

> **Key Point**
>
> Cardiovascular disease is disease of the heart and / or blood vessels.

Evaluating Data

- Smoking and lung cancer in the UK:

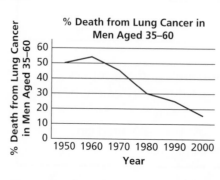

> **Key Point**
>
> You will often be asked to evaluate data to suggest the link between two variables.

- While the two graphs on smoking (on page 74) cannot prove that lung cancer is caused by smoking, they do suggest that as the percentage of men smoking decreased, so too did deaths from lung cancer.
- It is, therefore, likely that the two variables are linked.

Use of Stem Cells in Medicine

- Stem cells are cells which can differentiate to become any cell type found in the body (see page 25).
- They can be used to make new tissue and to replace tissues damaged by disease, e.g. to grow new nerve tissue to treat paralysis, or new heart valves to replace faulty ones.
- There are benefits and risks associated with using stem cells, as shown in the table below.

Potential Uses for Stem Cells

Benefits	Risks
Personal benefits to the person undergoing treatment	The stem cells may form tumours in the patient so may worsen the disease
Benefits to society since the process will provide knowledge that could lead to better future treatments	Stem cells may be rejected by the patient, which could lead to organ failure
Stem cells can be used to test new drugs	

- There are many ethical issues associated with using stem cells, e.g. some say that the use of stem cells sourced from human embryos is unethical and violates human rights as the embryos have 'no choice'.

Use of Gene Technology in Medicine

- Gene technology could be used in medicine to replace faulty genes, offering a cure for inherited conditions such as cystic fibrosis or diabetes.
- Replacing a faulty gene in the body has proved difficult to do.
- A virus is used to deliver the new gene and there are risks that the virus could harm the patient or deliver the gene to the wrong cell.

The Human Genome

- Genes can affect our chances of getting certain diseases.
- By studying the human genome, scientists hope to be able to predict the likelihood of a person getting a particular disease.
- Preventative action can then be taken.
- This is an example of personalised medicine.

> **Key Point**
>
> Some people are worried about the speed of developments in gene therapy, and are concerned that society does not fully understand the implications of these developments.

> **Quick Test**
>
> 1. How does diet impact on cardiovascular disease?
> 2. What is cancer?
> 3. What are the **three** options for treatment of cardiovascular disease?
> 4. Give **one** risk of using stem cell technology in medicine.

> **Key Words**
>
> cardiovascular
> statin
> stent

Coordination and Control

1 Bryn runs into the road without looking. There is a car coming towards him.
The driver of the car has to brake suddenly.

    a) What sense organ does the driver use to see Bryn?   [1]

    b) Was braking a reflex action or a voluntary response for the driver?   [1]

    c) The response was to push down on the brake pedal – what was the effector that
    carried out the response?   [1]

2 The diagram shows a neurone.

    a) What type of neurone is shown?   [1]

    b) Put an arrow on the diagram to show the direction of an impulse through the neurone.   [1]

> **Total Marks** .... / 5

The Endocrine System

1 The diagram below shows how the thickness of the lining of the womb changes during the
menstrual cycle.

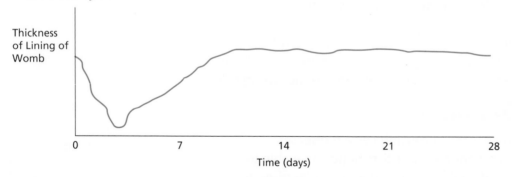

Oestrogen causes the lining of the womb to thicken.

Which of the following statements best describes how oestrogen levels change?
Put a tick (✓) in the box next to the best answer.

Oestrogen levels will increase from day 14 to day 21.	
Oestrogen levels will increase from day 0 to day 2.	
Oestrogen levels will increase from day 2 to day 14.	

[1]

> **Total Marks** .... / 1

Hormones and Their Uses

1 Complete the passage below about oral contraceptives by choosing the correct words from the list. You do **not** have to use all the words.

side effects   sexually transmitted diseases   FSH   more

less   oestrogen   progesterone

Oral contraceptives are taken to prevent pregnancy. The combined pill contains the hormones

_____ and _____. It is _____ reliable than the progesterone-

only pill. One of the disadvantages of using the contraceptive pill is it can cause _____. [4]

Total Marks _____ / 4

Maintaining Internal Environments

1 The flow chart shows the control of blood glucose levels by the hormone insulin.

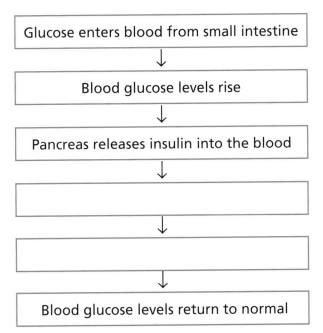

Glucose enters blood from small intestine

↓

Blood glucose levels rise

↓

Pancreas releases insulin into the blood

↓

[ ]

↓

[ ]

↓

Blood glucose levels return to normal

a) By what process is glucose absorbed into the blood? [1]

b) Complete the fourth and fifth level in the flow chart. [2]

Total Marks _____ / 3

Recycling

1   The diagram below shows a bean plant.

Root nodules

a) What type of bacteria will be present in the root nodules?   [1]

b) Why are these bacteria important to the nitrogen cycle?   [2]

2   Carbon is an element that is continually recycled in nature.

What process in the carbon cycle is represented by each of the arrows in the diagram below?

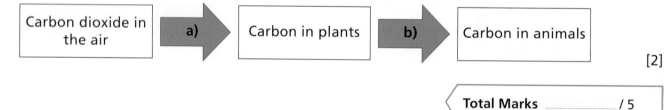

| Carbon dioxide in the air | a) | Carbon in plants | b) | Carbon in animals |

[2]

Total Marks _____ / 5

Interdependence

1   In a community, the numbers of animals stay fairly constant.
This is because of limiting factors, which stop any one population from becoming too large.

Suggest **two** limiting factors.   [2]

2   The red and grey squirrel live in the same habitat.

a) Suggest **three** things they will compete for.   [3]

b) The table below gives some information about red and grey squirrels.

	Grey Squirrel	Red Squirrel
Origins	Introduced in last 150 years	Native to Britain
Diet	Omnivores – like acorns and other nuts and berries, eggs and young chicks	Mostly vegetarian but cannot digest acorns
Size	50cm; 400–550 grams in weight	40cm; 280–340 grams in weight
Litter Size	1–8 young	1–8 young
Litters per Year	2	1

Using the table above, suggest why the number of grey squirrels have increased over the past 100 years. [2]

3 Finish the sentences about a rock pool using words from the box.

You do not have to use all the words.

habitat	artificial	community	natural	population	niche

A rock pool is an example of a _____ ecosystem.

The plants, fish and water invertebrates make up the _____.

The _____ of mussels in the rock pool is likely to be larger than that of the crabs. [3]

4 Below is a list of factors that affect the distribution of seaweed.

Divide the factors into **biotic** and **abiotic** factors.

A the aspect of the beach (which direction it faces)

B the temperature

C accessibility of the beach to humans

D the amount of fishing in the area

E the slope of the beach [5]

Total Marks _____ / 15

Genes

1. Put the following structures in order of size, starting with largest.

   nucleus   **gene**   **cell**   **chromosome**   [1]

2. The diagram below shows the pairs of alleles for genes that code for tongue rolling, eye colour and attached earlobes.

   Use the diagram to answer the following questions.

   a) Is tongue rolling dominant or recessive?   [1]

   b) Is the individual homozygous or heterozygous for eye colour?   [1]

   c) What is the genotype for attached earlobes?   [1]

   Total Marks _____ / 4

Genetics and Reproduction

1. Fill in the spaces on the diagram below to show how many chromosomes are present in each of these human cells.

   Sperm   Egg   Fertilised egg cell

       +   =

   _____   _____   _____   [3]

2. In meiosis, how many gametes are produced from one parent cell?   [1]

3 Cystic fibrosis in an inherited disease caused by a recessive gene.

People who have one dominant and one recessive allele are known as carriers.

People who have two recessive alleles will have cystic fibrosis.

The diagram shows a cross between two carriers of cystic fibrosis.

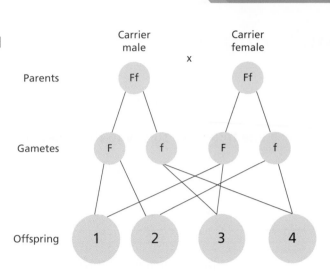

a) For each of the offspring, 1–4, write their genotype. [4]

b) What are the numbers of the offspring who will be carriers? [2]

c) Which number offspring will have the disease? [1]

Total Marks _____ / 11

Natural Selection and Evolution

1 Evolution is a slow process but can be seen quickly when bacteria develop antibiotic resistance.

Explain how antibiotic resistance develops. [3]

2 The diagram below shows a phylogenetic tree.

Use the diagram to decide which pair of organisms is most closely related in each question below.

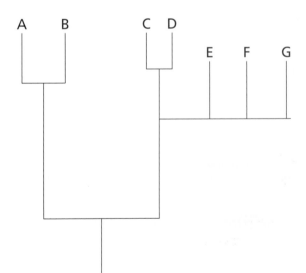

a) Organisms **C** and **D** or Organisms **B** and **C**? [1]

b) Organisms **E** and **F** or Organisms **D** and **E**? [1]

c) Organisms **C** and **G** or Organisms **A** and **G**? [1]

Total Marks _____ / 6

Practice Questions

Monitoring and Maintaining the Environment

1 Some students wanted to survey the variety of organisms in an area by a canal.

Draw a line from each survey to the best piece of apparatus for the students to use.

Survey	Apparatus

Survey

The variety of water invertebrates in the canal

The variety of plants growing by the side of the canal

The variety of flying insects in the long grass by the side of the canal

The variety of invertebrates found under the hedges along the side of the canal

Apparatus

quadrat

pitfall trap

sweep net

pond net

[3]

2 Some students used the capture–mark–recapture method to estimate the number of slugs in a garden.
In their first sample they caught 12 slugs, which they marked.
In their second sample, which was collected a few days later, there were 10 slugs of which four were marked.

What is the estimated population size of slugs in the garden? Show your working. [2]

Total Marks _____ / 5

Investigations

1 Look at the diagram of a pea, before and after germination.

If provided with water and a suitable temperature, germination should take about three days.

A group of students want to find out the optimum temperature for germination of the pea.

Before   After

Describe an investigation the students could do. Your description should include how to ensure the investigation is a fair test. [5]

Total Marks _____ / 5

Resources and the Environment

1 The following statements are about selectively breeding cows that produce good quantities of meat. They are not in the correct order.

A Offspring that produce a lot of meat are chosen.
B A cow and a bull that provide good quantities of meat are chosen as the parents.
C The offspring are bred together.
D The process is repeated over many generations.
E The parents are bred with each other.

Put the statements in the correct order. [1]

Total Marks _____ / 1

Monitoring and Maintaining Health

1 Draw a line from each disease to the method by which it is spread.

Disease	Method of Spread
malaria	contact
cholera	by air
tuberculosis	by water
athlete's foot	animal vector

[3]

2 The following paragraph is about tuberculosis.

Choose the correct word from each pair in bold to complete the sentences.

Tuberculosis (TB) is a disease that affects the **lungs / liver**.

People who have **HIV / cancer** are more likely to catch TB because their **circulatory / immune** system is already weakened. [3]

3 Which of the following statements about HIV and AIDS are **true**?

A AIDS is caused by HIV.
B AIDS can be cured if diagnosed early.
C The HIV virus can be treated with antivirals to prolong life expectancy.
D The virus can be spread by droplets in the air. [2]

4 White blood cells recognise antigens on the surface of microorganisms and produce antibodies to attack them.

a) Look at the diagram. Which letter corresponds to the microorganism, the antigen and the antibody? [2]

b) What is the name of the white blood cell that produces antibodies?
   Circle the correct answer.

   phagocyte   **lymphocyte**   **blastocyte**   [1]

Total Marks _____ / 11

Prevention and Treatment of Disease

1 Paul goes to the doctor with earache.
The doctor prescribes antibiotics and tells Paul that he must be sure to finish the course even if he feels better.

a) What type of organism may be responsible for Paul's earache? [1]

b) Why did the doctor tell Paul to finish the course even if he is feeling better? [2]

c) Dakota goes to the doctors because she has a sore throat.
   The doctor does not give her antibiotics.

   Suggest why. [2]

2 Put the stages below, about developing new medicines, in order.

   A   Tests on animals
   B   Tests on healthy volunteers
   C   Clinical trials
   D   Tests on computer models or cells grown in the laboratory   [3]

3 Explain why it is important to test new drugs before they are released to the public. [3]

4 In the early 1800s, a doctor called Semmelweiss suggested that 'something' on the hands of doctors and surgeons caused infections and could be spread from patient to patient. By insisting that doctors washed their hands, he reduced patient deaths on hospital wards from 12% to 1%.

a) What was the 'something' on the hands of doctors and surgeons? [1]

b) In modern hospitals, staff, patients and visitors are encouraged to wash their hands regularly.

   i) What type of substance is used in hand wash in hospitals? [1]

   ii) Suggest **one** precaution, other than hand washing, that surgeons take to reduce the spread of infection. [1]

Total Marks _____ / 14

Non-Communicable Diseases

1 Beatrice has been told that her arteries are coated with fatty deposits and that her cholesterol levels are above normal.
The doctor wants to treat her with a drug to reduce her cholesterol levels.
The doctor tells her she may need an operation to make her arteries wider.

a) Suggest what drug the doctor may want to prescribe. [1]

b) What could be placed inside Beatrice's arteries to make them wider? [1]

2 Many lifestyle factors influence how likely it is that someone will suffer from certain diseases.

Explain the link between diet and heart disease. [3]

3 Ben goes to the doctor for an annual check up.
He drinks about 30 units of alcohol a week and is considerably overweight.
The doctor takes Ben's blood pressure and finds it is high.

What advice should the doctor give Ben? [4]

4 What are **two** conditions for which obesity is a risk factor? [2]

5 Which of the following statements best describes cancer?

A Cells begin to grow in the wrong place.
B Cells become infected with cancer chemicals.
C Cells begin to grow and divide uncontrollably. [1]

Total Marks _____ / 12

Particle Model and Atomic Structure

You must be able to:

- Use the particle model to explain states of matter and changes in state
- Describe the structure of the atom
- Explain how the atomic model has changed over time
- Calculate the number of electrons, protons and neutrons in atoms, ions and isotopes.

Particle Theory of Matter

- The particle theory of matter is based on the idea that all matter is made up of small particles.
- It is used to explain the structure and properties of solids, liquids and gases.

States of Matter

- When particles are heated (given energy), the energy causes them to move more.
- Even in a solid, the particles vibrate.
- At 0°C, water changes state from solid to liquid. This is called the melting point.
- The water molecules move faster as the water is heated.
- At 100°C, the water molecules change from liquid to gas. This is called the boiling point.
- When a substance is changing state, the temperature remains constant.
- If gaseous water is cooled, the molecules slow down as they lose kinetic energy and liquid water forms.
- Changes in state are physical changes – it is relatively easy to go back to a previous state.
- Chemical changes are permanent changes where an atom or molecule chemically joins to another atom or molecule.
- The particle model uses circles or spheres to represent particles.

The Atom

- The atom is the smallest part of an element that retains the properties of that element.
- Atoms are very small, with a radius of about 1^{-10}m and a mass of about 10^{-23}g.
- An atom has a central, positively charged nucleus, surrounded by shells of negatively charged electrons.
- The radius (width) of the nucleus is far smaller than that of the whole atom.
- The nucleus is made up of protons and neutrons.
- An atom has no overall charge because the charges of the (positive) protons and (negative) electrons cancel each other out.

> ### Key Point
>
> The particles within a substance only have no movement at absolute zero (–273.15°C). At all other temperatures the particles will vibrate.

Atomic Particle	Relative Charge	Relative Mass
Proton	+1	1
Neutron	0	1
Electron	–1	0.0005 (zero)

> ### Key Point
>
> No matter how many electrons or neutrons there are in an atom, it is the number of protons that defines an element and its properties.

The History of the Atom

- The model of atomic structure has changed over time.
- In the early 1800s, John Dalton proposed that all atoms of the same element were identical.
- In 1897, J. J. Thomson discovered the electron and put forward the 'plum pudding model' with charges spread evenly throughout the atom.
- In 1911, Ernest Rutherford with his assistants, Geiger and Marsden, discovered that the atom had a dense centre – the nucleus – by firing alpha particles at gold foil.
- In 1913, Niels Bohr predicted that electrons occupy energy levels or orbitals.

Mass Number and Atomic Number

- The mass number is the total number of protons and neutrons in an atom.
- The atomic number is the number of protons in an atom.
- An ion is formed when an element gains or loses electrons.

Element	Symbol	Mass Number	Atomic Number	Protons	Neutrons	Electrons
Hydrogen	$^{1}_{1}H$	1	1	1	1	0
Helium	$^{4}_{2}He$	4	2	2	2	2
Sodium	$^{23}_{11}Na$	23	11	11	11	12

number of protons = atomic number

number of electrons = number of protons (in an atom)

number of neutrons = mass number – atomic number

- Isotopes are atoms of the same element that have:
  - the same atomic number
  - a different mass number, due to a different number of neutrons.
- For example, carbon has three main isotopes:

Isotope	Symbol	Mass Number	Atomic Number	Protons	Neutrons	Electrons
Carbon-12	$^{12}_{6}C$	12	6	6	6	6
Carbon-13	$^{13}_{6}C$	13	6	6	7	6
Carbon-14	$^{14}_{6}C$	14	6	6	8	6

Taking away the atomic number from the mass number gives the number of neutrons. So, there are two extra neutrons in chlorine-37 compared to chlorine-35.

Chlorine has two isotopes:

$^{35}_{17}Cl$	Mass number = 35
	Atomic number = 17

$^{37}_{17}Cl$	Mass number = 37
	Atomic number = 17

35 – 17 = 18 neutrons   37 – 17 = 20 neutrons

Quick Test

1. What are isotopes?
2. How many neutrons does an element have with a mass number of 14 and an atomic number of 6?
3. Why have different models of the atom been proposed over time?

Purity and Separating Mixtures

You must be able to:

- Suggest appropriate methods to separate substances
- Work out empirical formulae using relative molecular masses and relative formula masses
- Calculate the R$_f$ values of different substances that have been separated using chromatography.

Purity

- In chemistry something is pure if all of the particles that make up that substance are the same, e.g. pure gold only contains gold atoms and pure water only contains water molecules.
- All substances have a specific boiling point at room temperature and pressure.
- Comparing the actual boiling point to this known value is a way of checking the purity of a substance.
- Any impurities cause the substance to boil at a different temperature.

> ### Key Point
>
> In the world outside the lab, 'pure' is often used to describe mixtures, e.g. milk. This means that nothing has been added; it does not indicate how *chemically* pure it is.

Relative Atomic, Formula and Molecular Mass

- Every element has its own relative atomic mass (A_r).
- This is the ratio of the average mass of one atom of the element to one-twelfth of the mass of an atom of carbon-12.
- For example, the relative atomic mass of magnesium is 24 and of oxygen is 16.
- The relative molecular mass (M_r) is the sum of the relative atomic masses of each atom making up a molecule.
- For example, the M_r of O_2 is $2 \times 16 = 32$.
- The relative formula mass (M_r) is the sum of the relative atomic masses of all the atoms that make up a compound.

magnesium   oxygen

Calculate the relative formula mass of H_2O.
H: $2 \times 1 = 2$
O: $1 \times 16 = 16$
H_2O: $2 + 16 = 18$

> Multiply the number of atoms of each element in the molecule by the relative atomic mass.

> Add them all up to calculate the M_r.

Empirical Formula

- The empirical formula is the simplest whole number ratio of each type of atom in a compound.
- It can be calculated from the numbers of atoms present or by converting the mass of the element or compound.

> ### Key Point
>
> Always show your working-out when calculating empirical formulae. You will be less likely to make mistakes if you do.

What is the empirical formula of a compound with the formula $C_6H_{12}O_6$?

$C = \dfrac{6}{6} = 1 \qquad H = \dfrac{12}{6} = 2 \qquad O = \dfrac{6}{6} = 1$

The empirical formula is written as CH_2O.

> Work out the smallest ratio of whole numbers by dividing each by the smallest number. This would be $C_1H_2O_1$.

> Remember, the 1 is not written.

- For example, all alkenes have the empirical formula C_1H_2 although the 1 is not written, so it would be appear as CH_2.

What is the empirical formula of a compound containing 24g of carbon, 8g of hydrogen and 32g of oxygen?

Elements	Carbon	:	Hydrogen	:	Oxygen
Mass of element	24	:	8	:	32
A_r of element	12	:	1	:	16
$\dfrac{\text{Mass of element}}{A_r}$	2	:	8	:	2
Divide by smallest number	÷ 2		÷ 2		÷ 2
Ratio of atoms in empirical formula	1	:	4	:	1

List all the elements in the compound.

To find the number of moles, divide the mass of each element by its relative atomic mass.

Divide each answer by the smallest number in step 2 to obtain a ratio.

The ratio may have to be scaled up to give whole numbers.

The empirical formula is therefore CH_4O.

Remember, it is incorrect to write the 1 for an element.

Separation Techniques

- Techniques that can be used to separate mixtures include:
- **Filtration** – a solid is separated from a liquid (e.g. copper oxide solid in copper sulfate solution).
- **Crystallisation** – a solvent is evaporated off to leave behind a solute in crystal form (e.g. salt in water).
- **Distillation** – two liquids with significantly different boiling points are separated, i.e. when heated, the liquid with the lowest boiling point evaporates first and the vapour is condensed and collected.
- **Fractional distillation** – a mixture of liquids with different boiling points are separated (e.g. petrol from crude oil).
- Chromatography – substances in a mixture are separated using a **stationary phase** and a **mobile phase**.
  - **Paper chromatography** – this is useful for separating mixtures of dyes in solution (e.g. dyes in ink).
  - **Thin layer chromatography (TLC)** – this is more accurate than paper chromatography and uses a thin layer of an inert solid for the stationary phase.
  - **Gas chromatography** – this separates gas mixtures by passing them through a solid stationary phase.
- Substances separated by chromatography can be identified by calculating their R_f values.

 $$R_f = \frac{\text{distance moved by the compound}}{\text{distance moved by the solvent}}$$

- Separated substances can be identified by comparing the results to known R_f values.

> **Key Point**
>
> Substances move up the stationary phase at different rates depending upon their properties. The rate will remain the same as long as the conditions are the same.

Stationary phase (paper)
Level reached by solvent
Three substances have been separated from the original mixture
Original spot
Pencil line
Mobile phase (solvent)

> **Key Words**
>
> relative atomic mass (A_r)
> relative molecular mass (M_r)
> relative formula mass (M_r)
> chromatography
> stationary phase
> mobile phase
> R_f value

Quick Test

1. What is the relative formula mass of $Mg(OH)_2$?
2. What is paper chromatography used to separate?
3. What is the empirical formula of a compound with the formula C_2H_6?

Bonding

You must be able to:

- Explain how metals and non-metals are positioned in the periodic table
- Describe the electronic structure of an atom
- Draw dot and cross diagrams for ions and simple covalent molecules.

The Periodic Table

- An element contains one type of atom.
- Elements cannot be chemically broken down into simpler substances.
- There are about 100 naturally occurring elements.
- The design of the modern periodic table was first developed by Mendeleev.
- Elements in Mendeleev's table were placed into groups based on their atomic mass.
- Mendeleev's method was testable and predicted elements not yet discovered.
- However, some elements were put in the wrong place because the values used for their atomic masses were incorrect.
- The modern periodic table is a modified version of Mendeleev's table.
- It takes into account the arrangement of electrons, the number of electrons in the outermost shell, and atomic number.

Groups

- A vertical column of elements in the periodic table is a group.
- Lithium (Li), sodium (Na) and potassium (K) are in Group 1.
- Elements in the same group have similar chemical properties because they have the same number of electrons in their outer shell (or energy level).
- The number of outer electrons is the same as the group number:
  - Group 1 elements have one electron in their outer shell.
  - Group 7 elements have seven electrons in their outer shell.
  - Group 0 elements have a full outer shell.

Periods

- A horizontal row of elements in the periodic table is a period.
- Lithium (Li), carbon (C) and neon (Ne) are in Period 2.
- The period for an element is related to the number of occupied electron shells it has.
- For example, sodium (Na), aluminium (Al) and chlorine (Cl) have three shells of electrons so they are in the Period 3.

> **Key Point**
>
> The number of protons in a nucleus of an element never changes. That's why the periodic table shows the atomic number.

Metals and Non-Metals

- The majority of the elements in the periodic table are metals.
- Metals are very useful materials because of their properties:
  - They are lustrous, e.g. gold is used in jewellery.
  - They are hard and have a high density, e.g. titanium is used to make steel for drill parts.
  - They have high tensile strength (are able to bear loads), e.g. steel is used to make bridge girders.
  - They have high melting and boiling points, e.g. tungsten is used to make light-bulb filaments.
  - They are good conductors of heat and electricity, e.g. copper is used to make pans and wiring.
- Metals can react with non-metals to form ionic compounds.
- For example, metals react with oxygen to form metal oxides.

Electronic Structure

- An element's position in the periodic table can be worked out from its **electronic structure**.
- For example, sodium's electronic structure is 2.8.1 (atomic number = 11):
  - It has three orbital shells, so it can be found in Period 3.
  - It has one electron in its outer shell, so it can be found in Group 1.
- The electronic structure can also be shown using a dot and cross diagram, in which each cross represents an electron.

Sodium atom, Na
2.8.1

Sodium ion, Na^+
$[2.8]^+$

$+\ 1e^-$

Chemical Bonds

- Chemical bonds are *not* physical structures.
- They are the transfer or sharing of electrons, which leads to the atoms involved becoming more stable.
- An **ionic bond** is formed when one or more electrons are donated by one atom or molecule and received by another atom or molecule.
- When an ionic compound is in solution, or in a molten state, the ions move freely.
- When an ionic compound is solid, ions are arranged in a way to cancel out the charges.
- A **covalent bond** is formed when atoms share electrons to complete their outermost shell.

 Positively charged ion   Negatively charged ion

Models of Bonding

You must be able to:

- Describe and compare the type of bonds in different substances and their arrangement
- Use a variety of models to represent molecules
- Identify the limitations of different models.

Models of Bonding

- **Models** can be used to show how atoms are bonded together.
- Dot and cross diagrams can show:
  - each shell of electrons or just the outer shell
  - how electrons are donated or shared.
- Methane is a **covalent** compound. Each molecule is made up of a carbon atom joined to four hydrogens (CH_4).

Methane, CH₄

Methane, CH₄

Each line or shared pair of electrons shows a covalent bond.

Methane, CH₄

- ◯ H
- ⬤ C

- Ball and stick models give an idea of the 3D shape of a molecule or compound.
- Each model has limitations:
  - The scale of the nucleus to the electrons is wrong in most models.
  - Models show bonds as physical structures.
  - Most models do not give an accurate idea of the 3D shape of a molecule.
  - The bond lengths are not in proportion to the size of the atoms.
  - Models aid our understanding about molecules, but they are not the real thing.

Ion Formation

- Metals give away electrons to become positive ions:

Sodium atom, Na
2.8.1

Sodium ion, Na⁺
[2.8]⁺

+ 1e⁻

- Non-metals gain electrons to become negative ions:

Chlorine atom, Cl
2.8.7

Chloride ion, Cl⁻
[2.8.8]⁻

+ 1e⁻

> **Key Point**
>
> Scientists use models to help solve problems. As atoms are too small to be seen with the naked eye, models are a helpful way of visualising them.

Sodium gives away a single electron to become a Na⁺ ion.

Chlorine gains an electron to become a Cl⁻ ion.

- **Ionic bonds** are the electrostatic forces of attraction that hold the ions together.

Simple Molecules

- When non-metals or non-ionic molecules join together, the atoms share electrons and form a covalent bond. These are called **simple molecules**.
- Hydrogen gas, H_2, is a covalent molecule.

 Hydrogen Atoms   **A Hydrogen Molecule**

Covalent bond

Outermost shells overlap

Giant Covalent Structures

- **Giant covalent structures** are formed when the atoms of a substance form repeated covalent bonds.
- Silicon dioxide is a compound made up of repeating silicon and oxygen atoms joined by single covalent bonds.

Polymers

- A **polymer** is formed when repeated units are covalently bonded together.
- For example, when lots of ethene molecules are joined together they form poly(ethene).

Ethene Monomers   **Poly(ethene) Polymer**

Metals

- Metal atoms are held together by strong metallic bonds.
- The metal atoms lose their outermost electrons and become positively charged.
- The electrons can move freely from one metal ion to another.
- This causes a sea of **delocalised** (free) electrons to be formed.

Silicon atom
Oxygen atom
Covalent bond

Atoms are shown by their element symbol. Bonds are shown with lines. Two lines together indicate a double bond (two covalent bonds between atoms).

Free electron
Positive metal ion

Key Words

model
covalent
ionic bond
simple molecule
giant covalent structure
polymer
delocalised

Quick Test

1. What is meant by the term 'sea of delocalised electrons'?
2. Give **two** limitations of a dot and cross model of a covalent compound.
3. What is meant by the term 'giant covalent structure'?

Properties of Materials

You must be able to:

- Describe how carbon can form a wide variety of different molecules
- Explain the properties of diamond, graphite, fullerenes and graphene
- Explain how the bulk properties of materials are related to the bonds they contain
- Understand that many useful materials are formulations of mixtures, e.g. alloys.

Carbon

- Carbon is the sixth element in the periodic table and has an atomic mass of 12.
- Carbon is in Group 4 because it has four electrons in its outer shell.
- This means that it can make up to four covalent bonds with other atoms.
- It can also form long chains of atoms and rings.
- There is a vast variety of naturally occurring and synthetic (man-made) carbon-based compounds, called organic compounds.

Allotropes of Carbon

- Each carbon atom can bond with up to four other carbon atoms.
- Different structures are formed depending on how many carbon atoms bond together.
- These different forms are called allotropes of carbon. They do not contain any other elements.
- Graphite is formed when each carbon atom bonds with three other carbon atoms:
  - Graphite has free electrons so it can conduct electricity, e.g. in electrolysis.
  - The layers are held together by weak bonds, so they can break off easily, e.g. in drawing pencils and as a dry lubricant.
- Graphene is a single layer of graphite:
  - In this form, the carbon is 207 times stronger than steel.
  - Graphene has free electrons so it can conduct electricity.
  - It is used in electronics and solar panels.
- Diamond is formed when each carbon atom bonds with four other carbon atoms:
  - Diamond cannot conduct electricity, as all its outermost electrons are involved in bonding.
  - Diamonds are very hard. They are used in drill bits and polished diamonds are used in jewellery.
  - Diamond is extremely strong because each atom forms the full number of covalent bonds.
- Fullerenes are tubes and spherical structures formed using only carbon atoms:
  - They are used as superconductors, for reinforcing carbon-fibre structures, and as containers for drugs being introduced into the body.

Graphite

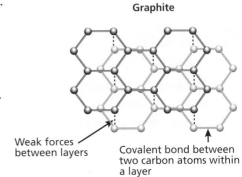

Weak forces between layers

Covalent bond between two carbon atoms within a layer

Graphene

Diamond

Covalent bond between two carbon atoms

Buckminsterfullerene

Carbon atom

Strong covalent bond

Bonding and Changing State

- Bonding is an attraction between atoms in elements and compounds.
- If the attraction is weak, then it is easy to separate the atoms compared to those with a stronger attraction.
- The ions in ionic substances are more easily separated when they are in solution or molten, as they can move about freely.
- When an ionic substance is in its crystal (solid) form, i.e. when the distance between ions is at its smallest, it is very difficult to separate the ions due to the strong electrostatic forces.
- They form a giant lattice structure.
- The melting point of ionic substances is, therefore, very high.
- For example, the melting point of NaCl is 801°C.
- Covalent bonds are very strong.
- If there are a lot of bonds, e.g. in a giant covalent compound, the melting point will be very high (higher than for ionic compounds).
- For example, graphite melts at 3600°C.
- Simple covalent molecules have very low boiling points.
- The simplest gas, hydrogen, melts at −259°C and has a boiling point of −252.87°C.
- This is because the intermolecular forces that hold all the molecules together are weak and, therefore, easily broken.

Bulk Properties

- The properties of materials are related to:
  - the different types of bonds the molecules contain
  - the ways in which the bonds are arranged
  - the strength of the bonds in relation to the intermolecular forces.
- Ionic and covalent bonds are always stronger than intermolecular forces.
- The individual atoms do not have the same properties as the bulk material.

Alloys

- Alloys are a mixture of elements, containing at least one metal.
- An alloy has different properties to the individual elements.
- The elements in some alloys stop the metal atoms from slipping past one another when a force is applied (making it stronger).
- Steel is an alloy – it is a mixture of iron, carbon and other metals (depending on the type of steel).
- Brass is a mixture of copper and zinc and bronze is an alloy of copper and tin.
- Mixing these elements in different proportions produces alloys with different properties.

> **Key Words**
>
> organic
> allotropes
> graphene
> fullerenes
> intermolecular force
> alloy

> **Quick Test**
>
> 1. What is meant by the term 'organic compound'?
> 2. Why is diamond so strong?
> 3. Explain, giving an example, what allotropes are.

Review Questions

Genes

1 Corey describes himself to his friend, listing the features below.

For each feature, state whether it is caused by **genetics**, the **environment** or a **combination** of both.

a) 1.6 metres tall

d) Weight 90kg [2]

b) Blue eyes

e) Scar on left cheek [2]

c) Pierced eyebrow [1]

2 Sickle cell anaemia is a serious inherited blood disorder. The red blood cells, which carry oxygen around the body, develop abnormally.
It is caused by a recessive gene and a person with sickle cell anaemia must have two recessive alleles.

Use the letters **A** = no sickle cell anaemia and **a** = sickle cell anaemia.

a) What would be the phenotype of someone with the following alleles?

   i) AA   ii) Aa   iii) aa [3]

b) What would be the genotype of someone who was a carrier of sickle cell anaemia? [1]

3 Lesley was studying variation within her class.
She collected information on her friends' height, weight, eye colour, shoe size and whether they had freckles.

a) Divide the list above into continuous and discontinuous variations. [5]

b) Lesley plotted a bar chart of her results for shoe size.

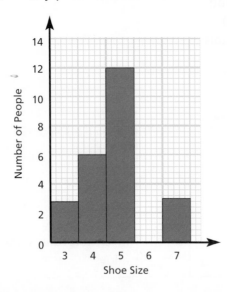

i) Seven people in Lesley's class wear a size 6 shoe. Plot this information on the chart. [1]

ii) Suggest how many people in Lesley's class might wear size 8 shoes. [1]

Total Marks _____ / 16

Genetics and Reproduction

1 What is the name of the type of cell division that leads to the formation of gametes? [1]

2 In humans, brown eyes is the dominant trait and blue eyes is the recessive trait.

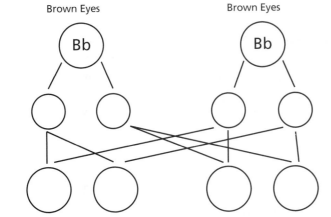

Brown Eyes   Brown Eyes

Parental

Bb   Bb

Gametes

Offspring

a) Complete the genetic cross above. [2]

b) Are the parents homozygous or heterozygous for eye colour? [1]

c) What is the ratio of brown eyes to blue eyes in the offspring? [1]

d) Circle the correct option in the sentence below.

If both parents had blue eyes, there would be a **0% / 25% / 50% / 75% / 100%** chance that their offspring will have blue eyes. [1]

Total Marks .... / 6

Natural Selection and Evolution

1 In 1753, Carl Linnaeus classified the grey wolf as *Canis lupus,* the domestic dog as *Canis canis* and the coyote as *Canis latrans.*
In 1993, analysis of mitochondrial DNA from all three animals showed:
- the grey wolf and domestic dog share 99.8% of their DNA
- the grey wolf and coyote share 96% of their DNA.
Following this discovery, the domestic dog was reclassified as *Canis lupus familiaris.*

a) Which of the words in the table describes the word '*Canis*'?
Put a tick (✓) in the box next to the correct option.

Family	
Genus	
Species	

[1]

b) Suggest why the domestic dog was reclassified. [1]

c) Apart from results of DNA sequencing, suggest **one** other reason why organisms may need to be reclassified. [1]

d) There are many species of dogs. What is meant by the word 'species'? [1]

Total Marks .... / 4

Monitoring and Maintaining the Environment

1 A group of students are asked to estimate the number of dandelions on the school field.
The field is a rectangle 100 metres long and 50 metres wide.
The students decide to use 1m² quadrats.

a) What is the best way for the students to use the quadrats?

    A Place the quadrats randomly across the field.

    B Place the quadrats where there are dandelion plants growing.

    C Place quadrats in all four corners of the field.   [1]

b) Calculate the area of the school field.   [1]

c) The students estimate that the mean number of dandelions per quadrat is 1.7

   What is the estimated number of dandelions on the school field?   [1]

Total Marks .... / 3

Investigations

1 Some students wanted to investigate the distribution of the meadow buttercup plant in the
area around a local river. They had read that the meadow buttercup prefers damp areas to dry areas.

The equipment they used is shown below.

Tape measure   Quadrat   Moisture meter

The students' hypothesis was: 'Meadow buttercups prefer damp areas to dry areas'.

a) Describe how the students could use the equipment to test their hypothesis.
In your answer you should make reference to how each piece of equipment would be used. [5]

b) Another group of students were investigating the distribution of water snails in the river. They used a pond net to sweep through the water and counted the number of snails in the net. They did this 10 times in total before repeating the investigation further upstream. Their results are shown below.

	Number of Snails in the Net at Each Sweep									
Downstream	3	6	5	4	6	2	2	3	4	4
Upstream	6	1	8	7	10	8	7	6	9	9

i)   Calculate the mean, mode and median number of snails in one sweep of the downstream sample. [3]

ii) Which is the anomalous result in the upstream data? [1]

iii) Suggest **two** reasons for this anomalous result. [2]

Total Marks _____ / 11

Resources and the Environment

1 Which of the following is an example of genetic engineering?

A Placing a gene in barley plants to make them drought resistant.

B Treating wheat with hormones to make a dwarf variety.

C Taking the pollen from one type of lily and using it to pollinate a different type of lily with the hope of creating a new variety. [1]

2 Scientists use selective breeding with a range of organisms.

Draw **one** line from each organism to the quality that scientists would want to selectively breed for.

Organism	Quality
wheat	sweet tasting
potato plant	large grain size
tomato plant	large tubers

[2]

Total Marks _____ / 3

Monitoring and Maintaining Health

1 Use the diseases listed below to answer the questions.

malaria   **flu**   **athlete's foot**   **tuberculosis**

a) Which disease is caused by a fungus? [1]

b) Which disease is caused by a virus? [1]

c) Which disease would be treated with antibiotics? [1]

2 The diagram below shows one way in which the body deals with invading microorganisms.

a) What is the name of this process? [1]

b) What type of cell is involved in this process? [1]

3 The human body has a number of mechanisms to prevent microorganisms from gaining entry.

Describe how each of the following helps to defend the body.

a) Platelets [2]

b) Mucous membranes in the respiratory system [1]

4 Our white blood cells produce antibodies when foreign microorganisms invade our bodies.

Use the diagram below to explain why antibodies produced in response to the TB bacterium will **not** protect us against cholera.

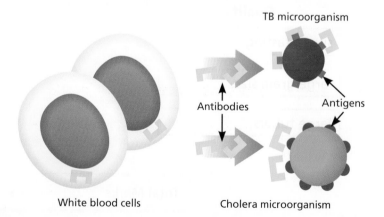

TB microorganism

Antibodies

Antigens

White blood cells   Cholera microorganism [3]

Total Marks .... / 11

Prevention and Treatment of Disease

1 Tanya and Charlie are best friends.
Tanya has been immunised against measles, but Charlie has not.
They come into contact with someone who has measles.
Charlie catches measles, but Tanya does not.

a) What was in the measles vaccine that Tanya was given? [1]

b) Explain why Tanya does **not** catch measles, but Charlie does. [3]

c) How is measles spread from one person to another? [1]

d) Charlie goes to the doctor. The doctor advises plenty of rest and painkillers if necessary.

Why does the doctor **not** prescribe antibiotics for Charlie? [2]

2 When new drugs are developed in the laboratory they are eventually tested in clinical trials.

State **two** ways that drugs are tested before clinical trials. [2]

3 In clinical trials, a control group of patients are often given a placebo.

What is the purpose of the control group? [1]

Total Marks .... / 10

Non-Communicable Diseases

1 The table below shows how the percentage of adults with obesity in the United States changed over a 50-year period.

Year	1962	1974	1980	1994	2002	2008	2012
% Adults with Obesity	13	13	15	23	31	35	36

a) Plot a line graph of these results. [3]

b) Use the graph to predict what the percentage of people with obesity will be in 2015. [1]

c) Name **two** diseases that people with obesity are more likely to suffer from than people of normal weight. [2]

Total Marks .... / 6

Particle Model and Atomic Structure

1 Look at the heating curve for water.

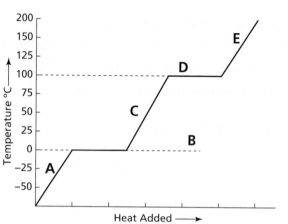

  a) Which point, **A**, **B**, **C**, **D** or **E**, indicates the boiling point?   [1]

  b) Describe what will happen to the particles in water as the temperature changes from −50°C to −25°C.   [2]

2 Which of the following scientists discovered the electron in 1897?

  A John Dalton

  B J.J. Thomson

  C Ernest Rutherford

  D Niels Bohr   [1]

3 Look at the following elements on your periodic table and answer the questions below: **lithium**, **oxygen**, **neon**, **silicon** and **calcium**.

  a) Which element has a mass number of 20?   [1]

  b) Which element has an atomic number of 20?   [1]

  c) What would the mass number of an isotope of Si be if it had two extra neutrons?   [1]

4 Water vapour at 140°C was cooled to −40°C.

  a) Draw a labelled diagram showing the changes that take place during the cooling process. [4]

  b) Describe what happens to the particles in the water as it cools.   [2]

5 What are the charges and relative masses of:

  a) an electron?   **b)** a proton?   **c)** a neutron?   [6]

Total Marks _____ / 19

Purity and Separating Mixtures

1 a) What does the term **pure** mean in chemistry? [1]

b) Describe how boiling points can be used to help identify a pure substance. [2]

2 Athina is separating food colourings using chromatography.

a) Calculate the R_f value for the two colours in **X**. Show your working. [3]

b) Which of the food colourings, **A, B, C, D** or **E**, matches **X**? [1]

3 A compound has the formula $C_8H_8S_2$.

What is its empirical formula? [1]

4 What is the empirical formula of a compound containing 84g of carbon, 16g of hydrogen and 64g of oxygen? Show your working. [3]

5 What is the best method for separating water from an ink solution?

A distillation **C** evaporation

B filtration **D** chromatography [1]

Total Marks _____ / 12

Bonding

1 Look at the following chemical symbols from the periodic table.

a) Write down the atomic number for each element. [2]

b) Potassium oxide has the formula: K_2O.
Work out the **relative formula mass** for K_2O. [1]

c) Calculate the **relative molecular mass** for oxygen. [1]

1	11	12	6
H	**Na**	**Mg**	**C**
hydrogen	sodium	magnesium	carbon
1.0	23.0	24.3	12.0
8	19	20	13
O	**K**	**Ca**	**Al**
oxygen	potassium	calcium	aluminium
16.0	39.1	40.1	27.0

2 a) Why do elements in the same group of the periodic table have the same properties? [1]

  b) Lithium, carbon and neon are in the same period.

  What feature do these elements share? [1]

3 The electronic structure of potassium, K, is written as 2.8.8.1.

  a) Which of the following dot and cross diagrams represents K?

A	B	C	D	E	F

  [1]

  b) Write down the electronic structures for **B** and **E**. [2]

  c) What do the **X** symbols represent in the diagrams? [1]

Total Marks _____ / 10

Models of Bonding

1 a) Describe what is meant by the term **ion**. [1]

  b) Draw the dot and cross diagram for a sodium ion, Na^+, and a chloride ion, Cl^-. [2]

2 a) Describe what is meant by the term **covalent bond**. [2]

  b) Chlorine gas, Cl_2, is a covalent molecule.

  Use a dot and cross diagram to show the covalent bond between the chlorine atoms. [2]

3 Silicon dioxide is a compound that forms a giant covalent structure.

  a) What is meant by the term **giant covalent structure**? [2]

  b) Water freezes into ice.
  Although it can form giant structures, ice is not a **giant covalent structure**.

  Suggest why this is the case. [2]

Total Marks _____ / 11

Properties of Materials

1 a) Explain how carbon can form a variety of different molecules.   [3]

   b) Describe what is meant by the term **allotrope**.   [1]

   c) Give the names of **three** allotropes of carbon.   [3]

2 Graphene is used in electronics and solar panels.

   Graphene

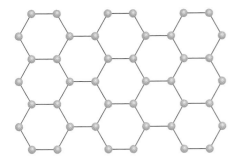

   a) Explain why graphene is used for these purposes.   [2]

   b) Other than cost, explain why diamond is **not** used for these purposes.   [1]

   c) Draw the structure of diamond.   [2]

3 Ionic compounds can conduct electricity.

   a) Describe the conditions required for an ionic compound to conduct electricity.   [2]

   b) Why do ionic compounds in their crystalline form typically have very high melting points?   [2]

4 Simple covalent compounds typically have very low melting points.

   Which of the following would have the lowest melting point?

   A CH_4

   B H_2O

   C H_2

   D O_2 [1]

   Total Marks _____ / 17

Introducing Chemical Reactions

You must be able to:

- Use names and symbols to write formulae and balanced chemical equations
- Describe the states of reactants and products in a chemical reaction.

Law of Conservation of Mass

- The law of conservation of mass means that no atoms are created or destroyed.
- This means that, in a chemical reaction, the mass of the products will always equal the mass of the reactants.
- The atoms in a reaction can recombine with other atoms, but there will be no change in the overall number of atoms.
- This allows chemists to make predictions about chemical reactions. For example:
  - What might be formed when chemicals react together?
  - How much of the chemical or chemicals will be made?

Key Point

Chemicals are not 'used up' in a reaction. The atoms are rearranged into different chemicals.

Formulae and State Symbols

- Compounds can be represented using formulae, which use symbols and numbers to show:
  - the different elements in the compound
  - the number of atoms of each element in a molecule of the compound.
- A small subscript number following a symbol is a multiplier – it tells you how many of those atoms are present in a molecule.
- If there are brackets around part of the formula, everything inside the brackets is multiplied by the number on the outside.

> Sulfuric acid has the formula H_2SO_4.
> This means that there are two hydrogen atoms, one sulfur atom and four oxygen atoms.

The ratio of the number of atoms of each element in sulfuric acid is $2H : 1S : 4O$.

> $Ca(NO_3)_2$
> This means that there is one calcium atom and two nitrate (NO_3) groups.
> In total there are one calcium, two nitrogen and six oxygen atoms present in this compound.

- There are four state symbols, which are written in brackets after the formula symbols and numbers:
  - (s) = solid
  - (l) = liquid
  - (g) = gas
  - (aq) = aqueous (dissolved in water).

$$H_2O(l) \qquad CO_2(g) \qquad H_2SO_4(aq) \qquad S_8(s)$$

Balancing Equations

- Equations show what happens during a chemical reaction.
- The reactants are on the left-hand side of the equation and the products are on the right.
- Remember, no atoms are lost or gained during a chemical reaction so the equation must be balanced.
- There must always be the same number of each type of atom on both sides of the equation.
- A large number written before a molecule is a **coefficient** – it is a multiplier that tells you how many copies of that whole molecule there are.

  $2H_2SO_4(aq)$ means there are two molecules of $H_2SO_4(aq)$ present.

- To balance an equation:

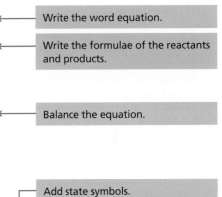

Reactants			→	Products
magnesium	+	oxygen	→	magnesium oxide
Mg	+	O_2	→	MgO
$2Mg(s)$	+	$O_2(g)$	→	$2MgO(s)$

Write the word equation.

Write the formulae of the reactants and products.

Balance the equation.

Add state symbols.

- You should be able to balance equations by looking at the formulae, without drawing the atoms. For example:

calcium carbonate	+	nitric acid	→	calcium nitrate	+	carbon dioxide	+	water
$CaCO_3$	+	HNO_3	→	$Ca(NO_3)_2$	+	CO_2	+	H_2O
$CaCO_3$	+	$2HNO_3$	→	$Ca(NO_3)_2$	+	CO_2	+	H_2O
$CaCO_3(s)$	+	$2HNO_3(aq)$	→	$Ca(NO_3)_2(aq)$	+	$CO_2(g)$	+	$H_2O(l)$

- Equations can also be written using displayed formulae. These must be balanced too.

Key Point

If you find the numbers keep on increasing on both sides of an equation you are trying to balance, it is likely you have made a mistake. Restart by checking the formulae and then rebalancing the equation.

Key Words

products
reactants
formulae
solid
liquid
gas
aqueous
coefficient

Quick Test

1. What is the formula of calcium hydroxide?
2. Write the balanced symbol equation for the reaction:
   sodium + chlorine → sodium chloride.
3. How many of each atom are present in this formula: $2MgSO_4$?

Chemical Equations and Energetics

You must be able to:

- Recall the formulae of common ions and use them to deduce the formula of a compound
- Explain the difference between endothermic and exothermic reactions
- Draw and label reaction profiles for an endothermic and an exothermic reaction.

Formulae of Common Ions

- Positive ions are called **cations**.
- Negative ions are called **anions**.
- There are a number of common ions that have a set **charge**.
- It is useful to learn these, although the charges can be worked out if necessary.

Positive Ions (Cations)		Negative Ions (Anions)	
Name	**Formula**	**Name**	**Formula**
Hydrogen	H^+	Chloride	Cl^-
Sodium	Na^+	Bromide	Br^-
Silver	Ag^+	Fluoride	F^-
Potassium	K^+	Iodide	I^-
Lithium	Li^+	Hydroxide	OH^-
Ammonium	NH_4^+	Nitrate	NO_3^-
Barium	Ba^{2+}	Oxide	O^{2-}
Calcium	Ca^{2+}	Sulfide	S^{2-}
Copper(II)	Cu^{2+}	Sulfate	SO_4^{2-}
Magnesium	Mg^{2+}	Carbonate	CO_3^{2-}
Zinc	Zn^{2+}	Hydrogen carbonate	HCO_3^-
Lead	Pb^{2+}		
Iron(II)	Fe^{2+}		
Iron(III)	Fe^{3+}		
Aluminium	Al^{3+}		

> ### Key Point
>
> Although ionic compounds are written as a formula (e.g. $CuCl_2$), they are actually dissociated when in solution, i.e. the ions separate from each other.

- The roman numerals after a transition metal's name tell you its charge, e.g. iron(II) will have the charge Fe^{2+} and iron(III) will have the charge Fe^{3+}.
- When combining ions to make an ionic compound, it is important that the charges cancel each other out so the overall charge is neutral.

$Cu^{2+} + Cl^-$

The formula is: $CuCl_2$

> Two negative charges are needed to cancel the charge on the copper cation. These will come from having two chloride ions.

Reactions and Temperature

- In a chemical reaction, energy is taken in or given out to the surroundings.
- **Exothermic** reactions release energy to the surroundings causing a temperature rise, e.g. when wood burns through combustion.
- The energy given out by exothermic chemical reactions can be used for heating or to produce electricity, sound or light.
- **Endothermic** reactions absorb energy from the surroundings and cause a temperature drop.
- For example, when ethanoic acid (vinegar) and calcium carbonate react, the temperature of the surroundings decreases.
- Endothermic reactions can be used to make cold packs, which are used for sports injuries.

Activation Energy

- Most of the time chemicals do not spontaneously react.
- A minimum amount of energy is needed to start the reaction. This is called the **activation energy**.
- For example, paper does not normally burn at room temperature.
- To start the combustion reaction, energy has to be added in the form of heat from a match. This provides enough energy to start the reaction.
- As the reaction is exothermic, it will produce enough energy to continue the reaction until all the paper has reacted (burned).

Reaction Profiles

- A graph called a **reaction profile** can be drawn to show the energy changes that take place in exothermic and endothermic reactions.

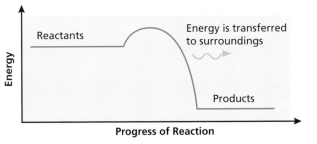

Reaction Profile for an Exothermic Reaction

Reaction Profile for an Endothermic Reaction

Quick Test

1. What are the formulae of barium oxide, copper fluoride and aluminium chloride?
2. Aluminium ions have a charge of 3^+ and oxide ions have a charge of 2^-. What is the formula of aluminium oxide?
3. What is 'activation energy'?
4. Draw a reaction profile for an endothermic reaction.

Key Words

cations
anions
charge
exothermic
endothermic
activation energy
reaction profile

Types of Chemical Reactions

You must be able to:

- Explain whether a substance is oxidised or reduced in a reaction
- Predict the products of reactions between metals or metal compounds and acids
- Describe techniques to measure pH.

Oxidation and Reduction

- When oxygen is added to a substance, it is oxidised.
- When oxygen is removed from a substance, it is reduced.
- The substance that gives away the oxygen is called the oxidising agent.
- The substance that receives the oxygen is the reducing agent.

copper oxide + hydrogen ⟶ copper + water

Copper oxide is the oxidising agent (it loses the oxygen). Hydrogen is the reducing agent (it gains the oxygen to form water).

Acids and Alkalis

- When an acid or alkali is dissolved in water, the ions that make up the substance move freely.
    - An acid produces hydrogen ions, $H^+(aq)$.
    - An alkali produces hydroxide / hydroxyl ions, $OH^-(aq)$.
- For example, a solution of hydrochloric acid, HCl, will dissociate into $H^+(aq)$ and $Cl^-(aq)$ ions.
- A solution of sodium hydroxide, NaOH, will dissociate into $Na^+(aq)$ and $OH^-(aq)$ ions.

low pH = lots of H^+ lots of OH^- = high pH

Neutralisation

- Neutralisation occurs when an acid reacts with an alkali or a base, to form a salt and water.

acid + base ⟶ salt + water

- For example, hydrochloric acid reacts with sodium hydroxide to produce sodium chloride and water:

$HCl(aq) + NaOH(aq) \longrightarrow NaCl(aq) + H_2O(l)$

- The reaction can be rewritten to only show the species that change:

$H^+(aq) + OH^-(aq) \longrightarrow H_2O(l)$

Reacting Metals with Acid

- Many metals will react in the presence of an acid to form a salt and hydrogen gas.

metal + acid ⟶ salt + hydrogen

Key Point

Remember, ionic substances separate from each other when dissolved or molten. The ions move freely and are not joined together.

Key Point

Water is not an ionic compound. It is a polar molecule (it has positively charged hydrogen and negatively charged oxygen), which means that ionic substances can dissolve easily into it.

- The reactivity of a metal determines whether it will react with an acid and how vigorously it reacts.
- Metals can be arranged in order of reactivity in a **reactivity series**.
- If there is a reaction, then the name of the salt produced is based on the acid used:
  - Hydrochloric acid forms chlorides.
  - Nitric acid forms nitrates.
  - Sulfuric acid forms sulfates.

magnesium + hydrochloric acid ⟶ magnesium chloride + hydrogen

$$Mg(s) + 2HCl(aq) \longrightarrow MgCl_2(aq) + H_2(g)$$

Reacting Metal Carbonates with Acid

- Metal carbonates also react with acids to form a metal salt, plus water and carbon dioxide gas.

LEARN

metal carbonate + acid ⟶ salt + water + carbon dioxide

- The salts produced are named in the same way as for metals reacting with acids.

magnesium carbonate + sulfuric acid ⟶ magnesium sulfate + water + carbon dioxide

$$MgCO_3(s) + H_2SO_4(aq) \longrightarrow MgSO_4(aq) + H_2O(l) + CO_2(aq)$$

Measuring pH

- Indicators change colour depending on whether they are in acidic or alkaline solutions.
- Single indicators, such as litmus, produce a sudden colour change when there is a change from acid to alkali or vice versa.
- **pH** is a scale from 0 to 14 that provides a measure of how acidic or alkaline a solution is.
- Universal indicator is a mixture of different indicators, which gives a continuous range of colours.
- The pH of a solution can be estimated by comparing the colour of the indicator in solution to a pH colour chart.
- pH can also be measured electronically using an electronic data logger with a pH probe, which gives the numerical value of the pH.

Reactivity Series

The higher the metal is positioned the more readily it reacts with oxygen. This is useful for protecting metals lower down against corrosion. →

These metals slowly react with oxygen and corrode away. →

This metal will very slightly discolour to show oxygen has had very little effect. It very rarely corrodes. →

These metals remain → unaffected by oxygen.

Most Reactive — Sodium, Calcium, Magnesium, Aluminium, Zinc, Iron, Lead, Copper, Gold, Platinum — Least Reactive

Key Point

Judging something using the eye is a qualitative measurement and has more variation than a quantitative measurement, such as a pH reading from a pH probe.

Key Words

oxidised
reduced
oxidising agent
reducing agent
acid
alkali
neutralisation
base
salt
reactivity series
pH

Quick Test

1. What gas is made when metal carbonates react with acid?
2. What salt is made when zinc oxide is reacted with nitric acid?
3. Write the word equation for the reaction between copper oxide and sulfuric acid.

Electrolysis

You must be able to:

- Predict the products of electrolysis of simple ionic compounds
- Describe electrolysis in terms of the ions present.

Simple Electrolysis

- Ionic compounds can be broken down into simpler substances using an electric current.
- In **electrolysis**, the solution containing the ionic compound (e.g. copper(II) sulfate solution) is called an **electrolyte**.
- When the electrolyte melts or dissolves, the ions in the compound dissociate.
- Metals and hydrogen form positive ions, called **cations**.
- Non-metals form negative ions, called **anions**.
- The negative electrode is called a **cathode** and the positive electrode is called the **anode**.
- When electricity is passed through the electrolyte, the ions move.
- The cations will move to the cathode and the anions will move to the anode.
- At the cathode, the metal ions gain electrons to become metal atoms.
- At the anode, the non-metal ions lose electrons to become non-metal atoms.

> ### Key Point
>
> Unless the ions can move (i.e. the substance is in solution or molten) electrolysis will not occur.

Electrolysis of molten sodium chloride takes place when the compound is heated beyond its melting point (801°C).

Na(s) forming on surface of cathode.

Types of Electrodes

- **Inert electrodes** do not react during electrolysis.
- Typically they are made from carbon.

Electrolysis of Copper Sulfate Solution with Carbon Electrodes

Oxygen gas collected and tested with glowing splint

Cathode
Anode
Carbon electrodes
Copper metal deposited at cathode
Copper sulfate solution

- Electrodes can be made out of inert metals instead, such as platinum, which will not react with the products of electrolysis. However, platinum electrodes are very expensive.
- Non-inert or **active electrodes** can be used for processes such as electroplating.
- For example, using copper electrodes with copper sulfate solution:

Electrolysis of Copper Sulfate Solution with Active Electrodes

- In the electrolysis above, if the cathode were replaced with a metal object it would become covered in copper metal, i.e. it will be copper-plated.

Electrolysis of Dilute Sulfuric Acid

- Dilute sulfuric acid (acidified water) can undergo electrolysis.
- This produces oxygen at the anode and hydrogen gas at the cathode.
- The reaction is carried out in suitable apparatus to allow the gases to be collected.

Quick Test

1. In what state must an ionic substance be for electrolysis to occur?
2. At which electrode will oxygen form during electrolysis?
3. Describe how you could silver-plate a key using electrolysis.

Key Words

electrolysis
electrolyte
cations
anions
cathode
anode
inert electrode
active electrode

Predicting Chemical Reactions

You must be able to:

- Describe the properties of elements in Group 1, Group 7 and Group 0
- Predict possible reactions of elements from their position in the periodic table
- Work out the order of reactivity of different metals
- Describe the tests to identify gases produced in a chemical reaction.

Group 1

- Group 1 metals all have one **electron** in their outer shell.
- The outer shell can take a maximum of eight electrons (for elements 3–20) or two for H and He.
- Elements are **reactive** because atoms will gain or lose electrons until they have a full outer shell.
- The first three elements in the group are lithium (Li), sodium (Na) and potassium (K).
- It is easier for a Group 1 metal to donate its outermost electron than gain seven more electrons to achieve a full outer shell.
- The elements in Group 1 have similar physical and chemical properties.
- Density increases going down the group.
- The first three metals float on water.
- The Group 1 metals become more reactive going down the group.
- This is because the outermost electron gets further away from the nucleus, so the force of attraction between the electron and nucleus is weaker.

Reactivity increases, and melting and boiling points decrease as you go down the group.

Group 7

- The non-metals in Group 7 are known as the **halogens**.
- They all have seven electrons in their outer shell, so they have similar chemical properties.
- It is easier for a Group 7 halogen to gain a single electron than donate seven electrons to achieve a full outer shell.
- Fluorine (F), chlorine (Cl), bromine (Br) and iodine (I) are halogens.
- The elements in Group 7 have similar physical and chemical properties.
- Their melting and boiling points are very low and they are not very dense.
- Unlike the alkali metals, halogens become less reactive going down the group.
- This is because the closer the outer shell is to the nucleus, the stronger the force of attraction, and the easier it is to gain an electron.

Reactivity decreases, and melting and boiling points increase as you go down the group.

Group 0

- The non-metals in Group 0 are known as the **noble gases**.
- These elements all have a full outer shell and do not react with other elements.

Predicting Reactivity

- In general, for metals:
  - the lower down the group, the more reactive the element
  - the fewer the electrons in the outer shell, the more reactive it will be.
- For example, potassium (K) and calcium (Ca) are in the same period on the periodic table.
- K is more reactive than Ca because Ca has two electrons in its outer shell and K only has one.
- A metal higher in the reactivity series can displace another metal from a compound, e.g. copper is lower than magnesium in the reactivity series, so it will be displaced by magnesium.

$$CuSO_4(aq) + Mg(s) \longrightarrow MgSO_4(aq) + Cu(s)$$

- In general, for non-metals:
  - the higher up the group, the more reactive the element
  - the greater the number of electrons in the outer shell, the more reactive it will be.

> **Key Point**
>
> The reactivity series also includes hydrogen and carbon. Although non-metals, these elements also displace metals.

Metal Reactions with Acids and Water

- Very reactive metals will react with acid to form metal salts + hydrogen:

> **metal + acid ⟶ metal salt + hydrogen**

- Reactive metals react with water to form metal hydroxides + hydrogen.
- The more reactive the metal, the quicker it will donate its outer electron(s). Positive metal ions are formed.

> **magnesium + water ⟶ magnesium hydroxide + hydrogen**
> $$Mg(s) + 2H_2O(l) \longrightarrow Mg(OH)_2(aq) + H_2(g)$$

$Mg(OH)_2$ is an ionic compound so it will dissociate into $Mg^{2+}(aq)$ and $OH^-(aq)$ ions.

Identifying Gases

Gas	Properties	Test for Gas
Oxygen, O_2	A colourless gas that helps fuels burn more readily in air.	Relights a glowing splint.
Carbon dioxide, CO_2	A colourless gas produced when fuels are burned in a sufficient supply of oxygen.	Turns limewater milky.
Hydrogen, H_2	A colourless gas. It combines violently with oxygen when ignited.	When mixed with air, burns with a squeaky pop.
Chlorine, Cl_2	A green poisonous gas that bleaches dyes.	Turns damp indicator paper white.

> **Quick Test**
>
> 1. Which of these halogens would be the least reactive: bromine, chlorine, fluorine or iodine?
> 2. Explain why caesium is more reactive than lithium.
> 3. Which of the following metals will displace copper from $CuSO_4$: silver, platinum, lithium?

> **Key Words**
>
> electron
> reactive
> halogen
> noble gas
> reactivity series

Particle Model and Atomic Structure

1 Tad places a cup of water on a windowsill.
When he returns four days later, he notices that all of the water has disappeared.

a) What has happened to the water? [1]

b) Tad decides place another cup on the windowsill.

What would Tad need to do to increase the rate of water loss? [1]

c) Draw two boxes:

i) In one box show the arrangement of the water particles in the cup. [1]

ii) In the other box, draw the arrangement of water particles in the air. [1]

2 Which of the following is the approximate **mass** of an atom?

A 1×10^{-1}g   B 1×10^{-10}g   C 1×10^{-15}g   D 1×10^{-23}g   [1]

3 Complete the table showing the structure of an atom.

Subatomic Particle	Relative Mass	Relative Charge
	1	
Neutron		0 (neutral)
Electron		

[5]

4 In 1911, Geiger and Marsden fired alpha particles at gold foil.
They expected all of the alpha particles to pass straight through the atoms.
Instead, a substantial number bounced straight back.

a) What subatomic particle must have been present in the middle of the atom for this to happen? [1]

b) Suggest why only some of the alpha particles bounced back. [2]

5 For each of the following elements, work out how many **neutrons** are present:

2
He
helium
4.0

11
Na
sodium
23.0

23
V
vanadium
50.9

[3]

Total Marks _____ / 16

Purity and Separating Mixtures

1 Sanjit is testing a mystery pure substance.
He heats the substance until it boils.

  a) How could he confirm the identity of the substance? [2]

  b) Sanjit now takes a sample of water and boils it.
  He finds that the water boils at 101°C.

  Assuming that the thermometer is working correctly, why does the water boil at
  this temperature? [2]

2 What is the empirical formula of each of the following substances?

  a) $C_6H_{12}O_6$ [1]

  b) CH_3COOH [1]

  c) $CH_3CH_2CH_2COOH$ [1]

3 Calculate the relative formula masses of the following compounds:

  a) $C_6H_{12}O_6$ b) CH_3COOH [2]

  c) CO_2 d) H_2SO_4 [2]

4 What is the scientific term for a substance created by mixing two or more elements, at least
one of which is a metal? [1]

5 Three substances are separated using thin layer chromatography.

Substance	R_f Value
A	0.6
B	0.3
C	0.7

Which substance travelled the furthest in the solid stationary phase? [1]

Total Marks _____ / 13

Review Questions

Bonding

1   Which of the following scientists first devised the structure of the modern periodic table? Circle the correct answer.

Bohr   Mendel   Mendeleev   Marsden   Rutherford   Thomson   [1]

2   Here are the electronic structures of five elements:

Element	Electronic Structure
A	2.1
B	2.8.1
C	2.8.3
D	2.8.8
E	2.2

a)   Which elements are in Period 2 of the periodic table?   [2]

b)   Which elements are in the same group?   [2]

c)   Which is the most reactive metal?   [1]

d)   What is the atomic number of each element?   [5]

3   The majority of elements in the periodic table are metals.

a)   Give **three** properties of metals.   [3]

b)   What is the general name given to the product formed when a metal reacts with oxygen?   [1]

c)   What type of compound is formed when metals react with non-metals?   [1]

> Total Marks .... / 16

Models of Bonding

1   Which of the following diagrams correctly shows the bonding for fluorine gas (F_2)?

A   B

C   D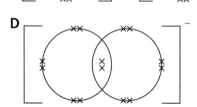

[1]

2 Draw a dot and cross diagram to show the covalent bonds in **methane** (CH₄). [2]

3 What advantage do ball and stick models have over dot and cross diagrams? [2]

4 Show, using dot and cross diagrams, how magnesium becomes a magnesium ion. [2]

Total Marks _____ / 7

Properties of Materials

1 Carbon has a number of different **allotropes**.

a) What is meant by the term **allotrope**? [1]

b) Graphite is used as a dry lubricant in air compressors.

Referring to the structure of graphite, explain why it is a good dry lubricant. [4]

c) Diamonds are often used in drill bits.

Referring to the structure of diamond, explain why diamonds are used in drill bits. [3]

d) Give **one** use of graphene. [1]

2 One type of fullerene is a tube made entirely of carbon atoms.

Which of the following is **not** a property of this material?

A conducts electricity

B conducts heat

C lubricant

D high melting point [1]

Total Marks _____ / 10

Practice Questions

Introducing Chemical Reactions

1. What is the **law of conservation of mass**? [1]

2. a) What do the **subscript** numbers that appear after an element symbol mean, e.g. Cl_2? [1]

   b) Write the number of atoms of each element shown in each formula below:

   i) $C_6H_{12}O_6$ [2]

   ii) CH_3CH_2COOH

   iii) H_2O_2 [2]

   iv) $Ca(NO_3)_2$ [2]

3. Write down the **four** state symbols. [1]

4. Write the **balanced symbol equations** for the following reactions, including state symbols:

   a) magnesium + oxygen → magnesium oxide [2]

   b) lithium + oxygen → lithium oxide [2]

   c) calcium carbonate + hydrochloric acid → calcium chloride + carbon dioxide + water [2]

   d) aluminium + oxygen → aluminium oxide [2]

Total Marks _____ / 15

Chemical Equations and Energetics

1. What are the charges on these common ions?

   a) copper(II)   b) oxide   c) iron(III)   d) sulfide [4]

2. a) A reaction gives out energy to the environment.

   What type of reaction is it? [1]

   b) A reaction takes in energy from the environment.

   What type of reaction is it? [1]

3. Give **two** ways in which the energy released from a reaction can be used. [2]

4. Explain what is meant by the term **activation energy**. [1]

5 Draw a reaction profile for an exothermic reaction. [1]

6 Draw a reaction profile for an endothermic reaction. [1]

Total Marks _____ / 11

Types of Chemical Reactions

1 Which of the following reactions involve a reactant being oxidised?

   A magnesium + oxygen → magnesium oxide

   B water (solid) → water (liquid)

   C copper + oxygen → copper oxide

   D barium carbonate + sodium sulfate → barium sulfate + sodium carbonate [2]

2 For each of the following reactions, write a balanced equation, including state symbols. Then state which species has been oxidised and which has been reduced.

   a) sodium + chlorine → sodium chloride [3]

   b) magnesium + oxygen → magnesium oxide [3]

   c) lithium + bromine → lithium bromide [3]

   d) copper(II) oxide + hydrogen → copper + water [3]

3 What ions are produced by:

   a) an acid? [1]

   b) an alkali? [1]

4 What is the general equation for the neutralisation of a base by an acid? [1]

5 Dilute sulfuric acid and sodium hydroxide solution are reacted together.

   a) Write the balanced symbol equation for the reaction. [2]

   b) Which ions are not involved in the reaction? [2]

6 Claude adds an acid to an alkali to make a neutral solution.

a) Describe how Claude can measure the pH of the solution as the experiment progresses using universal indicator paper. [2]

b) Claude wants to measure the pH more accurately.

Which of the following would he use?

A litmus paper

B data logger

C laptop

D phenolpthalein [1]

7 Nitric acid and sodium hydroxide are reacted together.

a) Write the balanced symbol equation for the reaction. [2]

b) Which ions are cations? [2]

c) Which ions are anions? [2]

> Total Marks .... / 30

Electrolysis

1 What are the ions of a) metals and b) non-metals called? [2]

2 What is 'electrolysis'? [1]

3 Why is it not possible to carry out electrolysis on crystals of table salt (sodium chloride) at room temperature and pressure? [1]

4 a) Why are inert electrodes often used in electrolysis? [1]

b) Platinum can be used as an inert electrode.
However, platinum electrodes are rarely used.
Explain why. [1]

5 Electrolysis is used to copper-plate objects.

The diagram shows the apparatus for electroplating using copper and a metal object in copper(II) sulfate solution.

What are ions **X** and **Y**? [2]

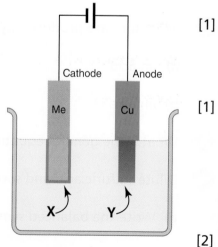

> Total Marks .... / 8

Predicting Chemical Reactions

1 Which of the following statements is **correct** about a Group 7 element?

    A It conducts electricity.   **C** It dissolves in water to make bleach.

    B It is malleable.   **D** It reacts with water to form hydrogen.   [1]

2 How many electrons are in the outermost shell of a Group 1 element?   [1]

3 Sort the following elements into order of reactivity, with the most reactive first:

    bromine   chlorine   fluorine   iodine   [1]

4 **a)** Draw the electronic structure of sodium (atomic number 11) and potassium (atomic number 19).   [2]

    b) Sodium is placed into a container of water.
    It moves around rapidly on top of the water and burns with a yellow flame.

    Describe what happens when potassium is placed into a container of water.   [2]

    c) Which of the following best describes why potassium reacts differently to sodium?

        A Sodium is denser than potassium.

        B Potassium is denser than sodium.

        C Potassium's outermost electron is closer to the nucleus.

        D Potassium's outermost electron is further away from the nucleus.   [1]

5 Look at the periodic table on page 265.

    Which is the **least** reactive Group 2 metal?   [1]

6 Zinc is reacted with sulfuric acid:

    $Zn(s) + H_2SO_4(aq) \rightarrow ZnSO_4(aq) + H_2(g)$

    What **ions** will be formed in this reaction?   [1]

7 Describe the test for hydrogen gas.   [2]

Total Marks .... / 12

Controlling Chemical Reactions

You must be able to:

- Suggest methods for working out the rate of reaction
- Describe factors that affect the rate of reaction
- Explain how surface area to volume ratios change in solids
- Analyse the rate of reaction using a graph.

Rates of Reaction

- The **rate of reaction** is a measure of how much product is made in a specific time.
- It can be measured in:
  - g/s or g/min for mass changes
  - cm^3/s or cm^3/min for volume changes.
- Chemical reactions stop when one of the reactants is used up.
- The amount of product produced depends on the amount of reactant(s) used.
- Often there is an excess of one of the reactants.
- The one that is used up first is the limiting reactant.

Changing the Temperature

- Chemical reactions happen when particles collide with enough energy for the reactants to bond together or split apart.
- The more successful **collisions** there are between particles, the faster the reaction.
- At low temperatures, the particles move slowly as they have less **kinetic energy**.
- This means that the particles collide less often, and with lower energy, so fewer collisions will be successful – the rate of reaction will be slow.
- At high temperatures, the particles move faster as they have more kinetic energy.
- This means that particles successfully collide more often, and with higher energy, giving a faster rate of reaction.

Changing the Concentration of Liquids

- In a reaction where one or both reactants are in low concentrations, the particles will be spread out in solution.
- The particles will collide with each other less often, so there will be fewer successful collisions.
- If there is a high concentration of one or both reactants, the particles will be crowded close together.
- The particles will collide with each other more often, so there will be many more successful collisions.
- To measure the effect of concentration on rate of reaction, create a series of different concentrations of a reactant by diluting a stock solution of known concentration.
- Once a range of at least five different concentrations has been created, the reactants can be reacted together.

Low Temperature

High Temperature

Low Concentration

High Concentration

Changing the Pressure of Gases

- When a gas is under a low **pressure**, the particles are spread out.
- The particles will collide with each other less often, so there will be fewer successful collisions.
- When the pressure is high, the particles are crowded more closely together.
- The particles therefore collide more often, resulting in many more successful collisions.
- It difficult to carry out an experiment where gas pressure is changed in a school laboratory.
- Specialised equipment is needed to ensure that the pressure can be maintained and measured.

Low Pressure

High Pressure

Changing the Surface Area of Solids

- The larger the **surface area** of a solid reactant, the faster the reaction.
- Powdered solids have a large surface area compared to their volume – they have a high surface area to volume ratio.
- This means there are more particles exposed on the surface for the other reactants to collide with.
- The greater the number of particles exposed, the greater the chance of them colliding successfully, which increases the rate of the reaction.
- As a result, powders react much faster than a lump of the same reactant.
- To measure the effect of surface area on rate of reaction, take the reactant and create a set of different surface areas, e.g. by cutting the solid into progressively smaller sections.
- Once a suitable range of surface areas has been created, they can then be reacted with the other reactant.

Lump of Solid (Large Particles)   Powdered Solid (Small Particles)

Analysing the Rate of Reaction

- From a graph you can find out the following:
  ① How long it takes to make the maximum amount of products:
     Draw a vertical line from the beginning of the flat line (which indicates the reaction has finished) down to the x-axis (time).
  ② How much product was made:
     Draw a horizontal line from the highest point on the graph across to the y-axis.
  ③ Which reaction is the quicker:
     Compare the gradient (steepness) of graphs for the same reaction under different conditions.
- $\frac{1}{time}$ is **proportional** to the rate of reaction.

Volume of CO_2 Produced (cm^3)

45°C

30°C

Time (minutes)

The line is steeper for the 45°C line, so the rate is faster.

relative rate of reaction for
$45°C = \frac{1}{5min} = 0.2$

relative rate of reaction for
$30°C = \frac{1}{10min} = 0.1$

Quick Test

1. What is the effect of increasing the temperature of a reaction mixture?
2. How could the rate of reaction be increased in a reaction involving gaseous reactants?
3. Describe the surface area to volume ratio of a large block of calcium carbonate compared to calcium carbonate powder.

Key Words

rate of reaction
collisions
kinetic energy
pressure
surface area
proportional

Catalysts, Activation Energy and Equilibria

You must be able to:

- Describe the characteristics of catalysts and their effect on the rate of reaction
- Explain the action of catalysts in terms of activation energy
- Recall that some reactions may be reversed by altering the reaction conditions
- Describe a dynamic equilibrium.

Effect of Catalysts

- A **catalyst** is a substance that speeds up the rate of a chemical reaction without being used up or changed in the reaction.
- Catalysts are very useful materials, as only a small amount is needed to speed up a reaction involving large amounts of reactant.
- You can see how a catalyst affects the rate of reaction by comparing graphs of reactions with and without the catalyst.
- The graph on the right shows two reactions that eventually produce the same amount of product.
- One reaction takes place much faster than the other because a catalyst is used.
- As catalysts are not used up in a reaction, they are not a reactant.
- When a catalyst is used in a reaction, the name of the catalyst is written above the arrow in the equation.
- For example, hydrogen peroxide is relatively stable at room temperature and pressure. It breaks down into water and oxygen very slowly.
- In the presence of the **inorganic** catalyst, manganese(IV) oxide, the breakdown is very rapid.

> ### Key Point
>
> When looking at a graph, it may be obvious which line is steeper but it pays to calculate the gradient as well.

Without a catalyst: hydrogen peroxide $\longrightarrow$ water + oxygen (very slow)

With a catalyst: hydrogen peroxide *manganese(IV) oxide* water + oxygen (very fast)

Catalysts and Activation Energy

- Catalysts work by lowering the **activation energy** for a reaction.
- This means that the reaction is more likely to happen, because less energy is needed to get it started.
- This may be achieved by providing a surface for the reactants to temporarily **adhere** to (stick to).
- Adhering to the catalyst's surface uses electrons, weakening the bonds in the reactants, lowering the activation energy.

Biological Catalysts

- **Enzymes** and certain pigments are biological catalysts.
- They are proteins and, as with inorganic catalysts, they lower the activation energy for a reaction.
- Examples include:
  - **amylase** – an enzyme that breaks down the starch (a polymer) into glucose
  - **chlorophyll** – a pigment that catalyses photosynthesis
  - **catalase** – an enzyme that, like manganese(IV) oxide, can break down hydrogen peroxide into water and oxygen.

Reversible Reactions and Equilibrium

- Most chemical reactions are of the type: reactants → products
- The reaction is complete, i.e. it is an **irreversible** reaction.
- There are, however, some reactions that are **reversible**.
- A reversible reaction can go forwards or backwards if the reaction conditions are changed.
- A reversible reaction can reach **equilibrium** (a balance).
- This means that the rate of the forward reaction is equal to the rate of the reverse reaction.
- A closed system is one where the conditions of the reaction (such as pressure and temperature) are not changed and no substances are added or removed.
- At equilibrium in a closed system:
  - there is no change in the amounts and concentrations of reactants and products
  - reactants are reacting to form products and products are reacting to re-form reactants at the same rate.
- This is called a **dynamic equilibrium**.
- For example, heating a mixture of hydrogen and iodine gas:

$$H_2(g) \quad + \quad I_2(g) \quad \rightleftharpoons \quad 2HI(g)$$

  - Unlike an irreversible reaction, the reactants will *not* completely form hydrogen iodide.
  - When the reaction starts, the forward reaction producing HI will dominate.
  - This is because the concentration of HI will be very low.
  - As the concentration of HI increases, the rate of the reverse reaction (making H_2 and I_2) will also increase.
  - Eventually the rate of the forward reaction will equal the rate of the reverse reaction.
  - The reaction is in dynamic equilibrium.

Surface of catalyst

> ## Key Point
> Don't forget, catalysts are not used up in a reaction.

> ## Key Point
> The ⇌ symbol indicates a reversible reaction.

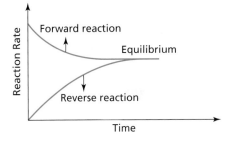

Key Words
catalyst
inorganic
activation energy
adhere
enzymes
irreversible
reversible
equilibrium
dynamic equilibrium

Quick Test

1. What does the gradient (steepness) of a reaction graph tell you?
2. How do catalysts affect activation energy?
3. Which biological molecules can catalyse a reaction?

Improving Processes and Products

You must be able to:

- Describe how to extract metals from their ores using carbon
- Explain the use of electrolysis to extract metals higher than carbon in the reactivity series.

Industrial Metal Extraction Using the Reactivity Series

- It is only the least reactive metals that are found in their pure, elemental form (e.g. gold, platinum).
- All other metals react with other elements to form **minerals**, which are substances made up of metal compounds (typically oxides, sulfides or carbonates).
- An **ore** is a rock that contains minerals from which a metal can be extracted profitably.
- Carbon, when heated with a metal oxide, will **displace** a metal that is below it in the reactivity series.
- The products formed will be molten metal and carbon dioxide.
- An example is the extraction of copper from its ore.
- There are a number of different ores of copper. Each is a different copper compound.
- For example, cuprite is copper(I) oxide (Cu_2O) and chalcocite is copper(I) sulfide (Cu_2S).
- In the school laboratory, the displacement reaction can easily be demonstrated with pure copper(II) oxide.

---

copper(II) oxide + carbon $\longrightarrow$ copper + carbon dioxide

---

Extracting Copper from Copper(II) Oxide

Loose plug of mineral wool to stop mixture shooting out

Mixture of copper oxide and carbon

Heat

> ### Key Point
>
> Carbon is a non-metal. However, in displacement reactions, it can displace less reactive metals as if it were one.

- The copper(II) oxide used in laboratories is free of impurities, which means displacement can take place more effectively.
- In industry, the reactions are scaled up to maximise the amount of metal that can be extracted.

Industrial Metal Extraction Using Electrolysis

- Metals that are higher than carbon in the reactivity series cannot be displaced from their compounds by carbon.
- Industrial chemists use electrolysis to extract metals instead.
- The ore is heated to high temperatures to make it molten so that the ions move freely.
- The mixture is poured into an electrolytic cell with electrodes made of carbon.
- A typical example is the extraction of aluminium from its ore:
  - The aluminium ore is bauxite, which consists mainly of aluminium oxide (Al_2O_3).
  - The reaction is: aluminium oxide $\rightarrow$ aluminium + oxygen
  - The oxygen reacts with the carbon anode to form carbon dioxide.
  - This wears the anode out, so it has to be replaced regularly.

Aluminium Electrolysis

Steel case

Carbon anode

Molten bauxite (Al_2O_3)

Graphite cathode

Molten aluminium

Quick Test

1. Galena is an ore containing lead. Suggest an appropriate method for extracting the lead.
2. Why do the anodes have to be replaced regularly in the electrolysis of molten aluminium?

Key Words

minerals
ore
displace
electrolysis

Life Cycle Assessments and Recycling

You must be able to:

- Describe the differences between industrial and laboratory scale production
- Describe a life cycle assessment for a material or a product
- Explain recycling and evaluate when it is worth undertaking.

Scales of Production

- Manufacturing chemicals on an industrial scale is very different to producing chemicals in a laboratory.

Laboratory Production	Industrial Production
Small quantities of chemicals used	Large quantities of chemicals used
Chemicals are expensive to buy	Bulk buying means chemical are cheaper
Energy usage is not an issue	There is a need to reduce costs and, therefore, energy usage
Equipment is usually glassware	Large-scale expensive factory equipment is needed
Chemists work on each reaction	Automation is common

Life Cycle Assessments

- A **life cycle assessment** is used to determine the environmental impact of a product throughout its life cycle.
- A product can be viewed as having four stages in its life cycle:
  1. Obtaining raw materials
  2. Manufacture
  3. Use
  4. Disposal.
- For each stage, the assessment looks at how much energy is needed, how **sustainable** the processes are, and what the environmental impact is.

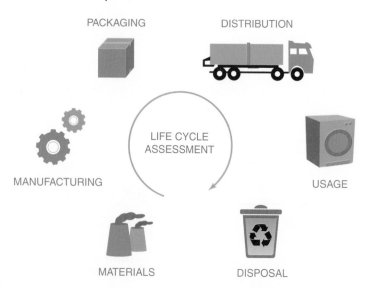

PACKAGING   DISTRIBUTION

LIFE CYCLE ASSESSMENT

MANUFACTURING   USAGE

MATERIALS   DISPOSAL

> **Key Point**
>
> Manufacture includes the processes and materials used to make the product and packaging, and distribution.

Plastic Bags	Paper Bags
Plastic bags are made out of plastic.	Paper bags are made from wood pulp.
The plastic is made from crude oil, which is not renewable.	The wood pulp is made from trees, which are renewable.
Making the plastic requires a lot of energy (for fractional distillation and cracking) and is not sustainable.	This means that paper bags are sustainable (low environmental impact).
The environmental impact of making the bags is high, as oil is running out.	Paper bags are often only used once. Therefore, they are disposed of in large numbers.
Plastic bags are often only used once, are non-biodegradable and disposed of in landfill sites.	Paper bags can be recycled and repulped to make new bags.

Recycling

- Recycling is the process of taking materials and using them to make new products, e.g. making a vase from a glass bottle.
- Recycling materials means:
    - less quarrying for raw materials is required
    - less energy is used to extract metals from ores
    - the limited ore and crude oil reserves will last longer (saves natural resources)
    - disposal problems are reduced.
- It is important to evaluate whether an object should be recycled or not.
- Sometimes recycling could be more environmentally damaging than just disposal.
- For example, plastic objects that are placed in recycling bins may have contaminants – they would have to be deep cleaned, which the recycling companies can't do due to high costs.

> **Key Point**
>
> Being environmentally friendly is seen as an advantage when marketing and selling a product.

> Computer circuit boards could end up in landfill, but once reusable components are removed, they can be used in a number of products, e.g. the covers for notebooks.

> **Quick Test**
>
> 1. Why is returning glass bottles to a store for refilling *not* an example of recycling?
> 2. Suggest why some plastics are not suitable for recycling.
> 3. What is the purpose of a life cycle assessment?

> **Key Words**
>
> life cycle assessment
> sustainable
> renewable

Crude Oil

You must be able to:

- Explain the processes of fractional distillation and cracking
- Describe alternatives to crude oil as a fuel source.

Crude Oil

- Crude oil is a fossil fuel that formed over millions of years in the Earth's crust.
- It has become crucially important to our modern way of life.
- It is the main source of chemicals for the petrochemical industry, for making plastics and fuels such as petrol and diesel.
- The hydrocarbons present in crude oil are used extensively throughout the chemical industry.
- Crude oil is a finite resource, which means it is being used up much faster than it is being replaced.

> ### Key Point
>
> It is important to recognise that the components of crude oil can be changed into many other chemicals, including fuel, medicines and plastics.

Fractional Distillation

- Crude oil is a mixture of many hydrocarbons that have different boiling points.
- The hydrocarbon chains generally all belong to the alkane homologous series (general formula C_nH_{2n+2}).

Alkane	Methane, CH_4	Ethane, C_2H_6	Propane, C_3H_8	Butane, C_4H_{10}
Displayed Formula	$\begin{array}{c} H \\ | \\ H-C-H \\ | \\ H \end{array}$	$\begin{array}{c} H \quad H \\ | \quad | \\ H-C-C-H \\ | \quad | \\ H \quad H \end{array}$	$\begin{array}{c} H \quad H \quad H \\ | \quad | \quad | \\ H-C-C-C-H \\ | \quad | \quad | \\ H \quad H \quad H \end{array}$	$\begin{array}{c} H \quad H \quad H \quad H \\ | \quad | \quad | \quad | \\ H-C-C-C-C-H \\ | \quad | \quad | \quad | \\ H \quad H \quad H \quad H \end{array}$

- The longer the chain, the greater the intermolecular forces, so the higher the boiling point.
- This means that crude oil can be separated into useful fractions (parts) that contain mixtures of hydrocarbons with similar boiling points.
- The process used is fractional distillation.
- The crude oil is heated in a fractionating column.
- The column has a temperature gradient – it is hotter at the bottom of the column than at the top:
  - Fractions with low boiling points leave towards the top of the fractionating column.
  - Fractions with high boiling points leave towards the bottom of the fractionating column.

Fractional Distillation Tower

Cool
(approximately 25°C)

Refinery gases / LPG
(bottled gas)

Petrol
(fuel for cars)

Naphtha (making
other chemicals)

Kerosene/Paraffin
(aircraft fuel)

Diesel (fuel for
cars/lorries/buses)

Heated
crude oil

Fuel oil (fuel for
power stations/ships)

Hot
(approximately 350°C)

Bitumen (tar for
roofs and roads)

Small molecules

Low boiling point

Evaporate easily

Burn easily

Large molecules

High boiling point

Don't evaporate
easily
Don't burn easily

Cracking

- There is not enough petrol in crude oil to meet demand.
- A process called **cracking** is used to change the parts of crude oil that cannot be used into smaller, more useful molecules.
- Cracking requires a catalyst, high temperature and high pressure.
- Petrol can be produced in this way, as can other short-chain hydrocarbons used to make polymers for plastics and fuels.
- For example, C_6H_{14} can be cracked to form C_2H_4 (ethene) and C_4H_{10} (butane).

Key Point

Intermolecular forces between chains of hydrocarbons are not bonds. However, the energy required to pull them apart can be thought of like bond energies.

Quick Test

1. What is meant by the term 'cracking'?
2. Why do longer-chain hydrocarbons have higher boiling points?
3. Give **three** fractions of crude oil and **one** use for each.

Key Words

fractional distillation
cracking

Interpreting and Interacting with Earth's Systems

You must be able to:

- Describe how the Earth's atmosphere has developed over time
- Explain the greenhouse effect
- Describe the effects of greenhouse gases.

The Earth's Atmosphere

- The current composition of the Earth's atmosphere is 78% nitrogen, 21% oxygen and 1% other gases, including 0.040% (400ppm) carbon dioxide.
- The Earth's atmosphere has not always been the same as it is today – it has gradually changed over billions of years.
- A current theory for how the Earth's atmosphere evolved is:
  1. A hot, volcanic Earth released gases from the crust.
  2. The initial atmosphere contained ammonia, carbon dioxide and water vapour.
  3. As the Earth cooled, its surface temperature gradually fell below 100°C and the water vapour condensed into liquid water.
  4. Some carbon dioxide dissolved in the newly formed oceans, removing it from the atmosphere.
  5. The levels of nitrogen in the atmosphere increased as nitrifying bacteria released nitrogen.
  6. The development of primitive plants that could photosynthesise removed carbon dioxide from the atmosphere and added oxygen.

The Greenhouse Effect

- The Earth's atmosphere does a very good job at keeping the Earth warm due to the greenhouse effect.
- Greenhouse gases prevent infrared radiation from escaping into space.
- Carbon dioxide, methane and water vapour are powerful greenhouse gases.

Infrared radiation

> **Key Point**
>
> The atmosphere is very thin. If the Earth were the size of a basketball, the atmosphere would only be as thick as a layer of clingfilm wrapped around it.

> **Key Point**
>
> Scientists take a variety of samples from all over the planet and analyse them to build models of the gases that were present in the atmosphere at different times in Earth's history.

> **Key Point**
>
> Scientific consensus (over 97% of scientists globally) is that it is extremely likely humans are the main cause of climate change.

Climate Change and the Enhanced Greenhouse Effect

- Evidence strongly indicates that humans have contributed to increasing levels of carbon dioxide, creating an enhanced greenhouse effect.
- Three key factors have affected the balance of carbon dioxide in the atmosphere:
  1. Burning fossil fuels, which releases CO_2 into the atmosphere.
  2. Deforestation over large areas of the Earth's surface, which reduces photosynthesis, so less CO_2 is removed from the atmosphere.
  3. A growing global population, which directly and indirectly contributes to the above factors.
- Carbon dioxide levels have increased from approximately 0.028%, at the time when humans first started using industrial technology, to the 0.040% seen today.
- As a result, the average global temperatures are changing, bringing about changes in weather patterns (climate change) over the entire planet.
- The evidence points to humans being the main cause of global climate change. However, these are still controversial issues.
- There are natural sources of greenhouse gases, e.g. volcanic eruptions, carbon dioxide emissions from the oceans and respiration.

- Detailed global temperature and CO_2 measurements were not made in the past, so scientists have to take samples and model what the atmosphere was like at different times.
- There is still a lot of research being carried out to gather more evidence and improve the climate models.
- To slow or stop climate change, we need to:
  - Reduce our reliance on fossil fuels, and find and use alternative energy sources.
  - Be more aware of our energy use and not waste energy.
  - Implement carbon capture schemes, such as planting forests – the forests store carbon whilst they are growing.
  - Reduce waste sent to landfill – waste often produces methane gas, which has a greater greenhouse effect than carbon dioxide.

Quick Test

1. What was the main source of carbon dioxide, methane and ammonia in the Earth's early atmosphere?
2. What process led to the large amount of oxygen in the atmosphere?
3. Which greenhouse gas is produced by landfill sites?

Key Words

atmosphere
greenhouse effect
infrared
enhanced greenhouse effect
fossil fuels
carbon capture

Air Pollution and Potable Water

You must be able to:

- Describe the effects of CO, SO_2, NO_x and particulates in the atmosphere
- Describe methods for increasing potable water.

Carbon Monoxide, Sulfur Dioxide and Oxides of Nitrogen (NO_x)

- When hydrocarbons are combusted with oxygen, they will produce carbon dioxide (CO_2) and water.
- If there is not enough oxygen, carbon monoxide (CO) is produced.
- Carbon monoxide is toxic.
- It bonds more tightly to haemoglobin than oxygen does, starving the blood of oxygen so that the body suffocates slowly.
- Gas appliances need to be checked regularly for this reason.
- Burning fossil fuels produces large amounts of carbon monoxide.
- Sulfur dioxide (SO_2), in small quantities, is used as a preservative in wine to prevent it from going off.
- Sulfur dioxide is produced when fossil fuels are burned.
- It is also produced in large quantities during volcanic eruptions.
- Sulfur dioxide dissolves in water vapour in the atmosphere causing acid rain, which kills plants and aquatic life, erodes stonework and corrodes ironwork.
- SO_2 also reacts with other chemicals in the air forming fine **particulates**.
- Nitrogen and oxygen from the air react in a hot car engine to form nitrogen monoxide (NO) and nitrogen dioxide (NO_2).
- NO_x is used to refer to the various nitrogen oxides formed.
- They can cause photochemical smog and acid rain.

Key Point

CO attaches to the haemoglobin because the shape of the CO molecule is so similar to the O_2 molecule.

Particulates

- Particulates are very small, solid particles that can cause lung problems and **respiratory** diseases.
- If a fuel is burned very inefficiently, carbon (soot) is produced.
- As well as causing respiratory problems, soot can coat buildings and trees in a black layer.
- Realising the dangers of **air pollutants**, governments have passed laws dictating the maximum levels that are allowed to be emitted, with the aim of improving air quality.

Potable Water

- Although the surface of the planet is covered in water, much of it is not safe to drink.
- Approximately 26% of the world's population only has access to unsafe water (e.g. contaminated by faeces).
- Providing potable water (water that is safe to drink) is an important goal for many countries.

Treating Waste Water

- When rain water goes down a drain, the toilet is flushed or a bath is emptied, the water enters the sewage system.
- This water is treated at a sewage treatment works before being piped to the tap:
  1. The water is filtered to remove large objects.
  2. The water is held in a **sedimentation tank** to remove small particulates.
  3. Bacteria are added to break down the particulates.
  4. Fine particles are removed by filtration.
  5. Chlorine is added to kill bacteria.
  6. The water is **ultra-filtered** through special membranes and stored in reservoirs.
  7. It is then treated before being piped back to the tap.

Desalination

- The majority of the world's water is in the seas and oceans.
- The water contains dissolved salt, which means it is undrinkable.
- **Desalination** (removing the salt to make the water drinkable) is an expensive process.
- There are two ways this can be achieved:
- **Evaporation / condensation:**
  1. Heat the salt water to boiling point to evaporate the water off.
  2. Cool the water vapour to recondense it into liquid form.
- **Reverse osmosis:**
  1. The salt water is filtered and passed into an osmosis tank.
  2. The salt water is forced against a partially permeable membrane.
  3. The membrane only lets water pass through, separating out the salt molecules.
  4. The water has chemicals added (e.g. chlorine) to kill bacteria.
- Both processes are very expensive due to their high energy needs.

> **Key Point**
>
> All water molecules are identical, even if they have passed through other organisms.

> **Key Words**
>
> particulates
> respiratory
> air pollutants
> sedimentation tank
> ultra-filtered
> desalination
> reverse osmosis

Quick Test

1. What is the biggest source of CO in the atmosphere?
2. Why is chlorine often added to drinking water?
3. What is meant by the term 'potable water'?

Review Questions

Introducing Chemical Reactions

1   Write down the number of atoms of each element in each of the following compounds.

     a) H_2SO_4 [1]

     b) $Cu(NO_3)_2$ [1]

     c) CH_3CH_2COOH [1]

     d) C_2H_6 [1]

2   Balance the following equations:

     a) $CuO(s) + H_2SO_4(aq) \rightarrow CuSO_4(aq) + H_2O(l)$ [2]

     b) $Mg(s) + O_2(g) \rightarrow MgO(s)$ [2]

     c) $Mg(OH)_2(aq) + HCl(aq) \rightarrow MgCl_2(aq) + H_2O(l)$ [2]

     d) $CH_4(g) + O_2(g) \rightarrow CO_2(g) + H_2O(l)$ [2]

3   What information does a chemical formula provide?

     A   the ratio of different atoms in a substance

     B   what mass of reactant will be used up

     C   what mass of product will be formed

     D   how much the reaction will cost   [1]

> **Total Marks** .... / 13

Chemical Equations and Energetics

1   Atu pulls a muscle whilst playing rugby.
     A cold pack is applied to his leg to help cool the muscle and prevent further injury.
     The pack contains ammonium nitrate and water.
     When the pack is crushed, the two chemicals mix and ammonium nitrate dissolves endothermically.

     a)   What is meant by the term **endothermic**?   [1]

     b)   Where does the energy come from that enables the pack to work?   [1]

2 The table below shows the names and formulae of some common ions.

Fill in the missing information to complete the table.

Name of Ion	Formula
carbonate	
lithium	
	Fe^{3+}
	O^{2-}
sulfate	

[5]

Total Marks .... / 7

Types of Chemical Reactions

1 Which **two** of the following reactions are oxidation reactions?

A aluminium + oxygen → aluminium oxide

B sodium chloride + silver nitrate → silver chloride + sodium nitrate

C copper sulfate + sodium hydroxide → copper hydroxide + sodium sulfate

D copper + oxygen → copper oxide [2]

2 Look at the following reaction:

iron(III) oxide + carbon monoxide → iron + carbon dioxide

a) Which species is being **reduced**? [1]

b) Which species is being **oxidised**? [1]

c) Write the balanced symbol equation for the reaction. [2]

3 Underline the **acid** in each reaction.

a) $Mg(OH)_2(aq) + 2HCl(aq) \rightarrow MgCl_2(aq) + 2H_2O(l)$ [1]

b) $H_2SO_4(aq) + 2NaOH(aq) \rightarrow Na_2SO_4(aq) + 2H_2O(l)$ [1]

c) $2CH_3COOH(aq) + 2Na(s) \rightarrow H_2(g) + 2CH_3COONa(aq)$ [1]

d) $2HF(aq) + Mg(s) \rightarrow MgF_2(aq) + H_2(g)$ [1]

Review Questions

4. Part of the reactivity series is shown in the diagram on the right.

   When a metal is reacted with an acid it forms a metal salt, plus hydrogen gas. For example:

   lead + sulfuric acid → lead sulfate + hydrogen

   calcium + sulfuric acid → calcium sulfate + hydrogen

   a) Which of the two reactions has the fastest initial reaction? [1]

   b) A metal **X** is reacted with sulfuric acid.
      It reacts violently compared with the other two reactions.

      Where would **X** be placed on the reactivity series? [1]

Reactivity Series

Most Reactive
Sodium
Calcium
Magnesium
Aluminium
Carbon
Zinc
Iron
Lead
Hydrogen
Copper
Gold
Platinum
Least Reactive

Total Marks _____ / 12

Electrolysis

1. In what state(s) will ionic compounds conduct electricity? [1]

2. Masum is carrying out the electrolysis of water and sulfuric acid.

   a) Which of the following would be the most appropriate material for the electrodes?

      A wood

      B copper

      C carbon

      D plastic [1]

   b) Write the names of the anions and cations involved in this electrolysis. [2]

   c) Metals such as aluminium only started to be extracted after the invention of electric circuits.

      Suggest why. [2]

Total Marks _____ / 6

Predicting Chemical Reactions

1 Which of the following properties does **not** apply to a Group 1 element?

   A conducts electricity

   B is malleable

   C dissolves in water to make bleach

   D reacts with water to form hydrogen [1]

2 Which of the following dot and cross diagrams could show a Group 0 element?

   A   **B**   **C**   **D** [1]

3 Sort the following elements into order of reactivity, with the most reactive first:

   caesium   lithium   potassium   rubidium   sodium [1]

4 **a)** Write the electronic configuration of each of the following elements:

   i) Li   **ii)** Mg   **iii)** Al   **iv)** O [4]

   b) Pieces of lithium, magnesium and aluminium are placed into test tubes containing water. The results for Al and Mg are shown in the diagram below:

   Draw what would be seen in the tube containing the lithium. [1]

   c) What gas is produced in the reaction? [1]

5 The decomposition of hydrogen peroxide in the presence of a catalyst produces oxygen.

   Describe the test for oxygen gas. [2]

Total Marks .... / 11

Practice Questions

Controlling Chemical Reactions

1. Niamh is investigating the effect of temperature on the breakdown of hydrogen peroxide in the presence of the catalyst manganese(IV) oxide.

   In each experiment Niamh uses a different temperature. All other factors are kept the same.

   Niamh's results are shown in the graph below.

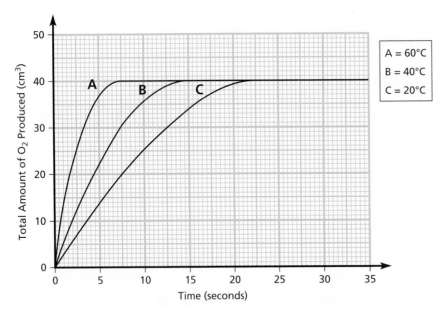

A = 60°C
B = 40°C
C = 20°C

   a) In which experiment is the reaction the **slowest**?   [1]

   b) Write a suitable conclusion for the investigation.   [1]

2. Which of the following could affect the rate of reaction?

   A time

   B surface area

   C concentration

   D volume   [2]

   Total Marks .... / 4

Catalysts, Activation Energy and Equilibria

1 Explain, in terms of activation energy, how a catalyst affects the rate of reaction. [2]

2 Body cells sometimes produce hydrogen peroxide, H_2O_2.
Hydrogen peroxide is dangerous in the human body.
The enzyme, catalase, speeds up the breakdown of hydrogen peroxide.

hydrogen peroxide $\xrightarrow{\text{catalase}}$ water + oxygen

a) Why is catalase written above the reaction arrow? [1]

b) In what way is catalase different to manganese(IV) oxide, which can also
   break down hydrogen peroxide? [2]

3 Temperature affects particle movement.

a) Draw two diagrams to show reacting particles at:

   i) a low temperature. [1]

   ii) a high temperature. [1]

b) Explain why reactions are faster at a higher temperature. [3]

4 A dynamic equilibrium can be reached when there is a closed system.

Explain what is meant by the term **closed system**. [2]

5 Alex is carrying out an experiment.
He ensures that he sets up a closed system and heats a mixture of hydrogen and iodine.

Which of the following is **not** true for a closed system at equilibrium?

A The amount of reactant remains the same.

B The amount of reactant decreases.

C The amount of product remains constant.

D Reactants react to form products and products react to form reactants at the same rate. [1]

Total Marks _____ / 13

Practice Questions

Improving Processes and Products

1 Which of the following metals **cannot** be displaced by carbon?

    A iron   **C** copper

    B magnesium   **D** lead   [1]

2 Zac is extracting copper using carbon displacement.
He sets up the equipment as shown below:

Loose plug of mineral wool

Mixture of copper(II) oxide and carbon

Heat

    a) Write the word equation for the displacement of copper from copper(II) oxide by carbon.   [1]

    b) Suggest why there is a loose plug of mineral wool in the top of the tube.   [1]

3 Which of the following is used to extract metals that are more reactive than carbon from their ores?

    A magnetism   **C** explosives

    B chromatography   **D** electrolysis   [1]

4 For an ionic compound, such as sodium chloride, to be electrolysed, which of the following statements is **true**?

    A The amount of metal in the compound has to be greater than 90%.

    B The ionic compound needs to be molten or in solution.

    C A catalyst needs to be added to the ionic compound.

    D The ionic compound needs to be in a gaseous state.   [1]

Total Marks .... / 5

Life Cycle Assessments and Recycling

1. Which of the following factors are analysed as part of a life cycle assessment?

   A colour   D manufacture   G recycling

   B disposal   E popularity   H transport

   C history   F price   I use   [1]

2. Each year thousands of mobile phones are disposed of in landfill sites.
   Many of the materials used in the manufacture of mobile phones could be recycled.

   a) What is meant by the term 'recycled'? [1]

   b) Explain why it is important to recycle materials. [4]

   c) Suggest why some of the parts of a mobile phone will not be recycled, even though
   technically it may be possible to do so. [1]

3. The following factors are considered when making a disposable plastic bag.

   Which factors would **not** be suitable for inclusion in a life cycle assessment?

   A which bags customers prefer to use

   B the environmental impact of disposing of the bags

   C the energy required to dispose of the bags

   D the energy required to make the bags from plant fibres

   E how much should be charged for the bag [2]

Total Marks _____ / 9

Practice Questions

Crude Oil

1 Fractional distillation is used to separate the fractions in crude oil.

Fraction

→ LPG

→ Petrol

→ **W**

→ **X**

→ Heating oil

→ Heavy fuel oil

Y→

→ **Z**

a) Choose words from the list below to label **W**, **X**, **Y** and **Z** on the diagram:

   Bitumen   **Crude oil**   **Diesel**   **Paraffin**   [3]

b) Where is the **lowest temperature** in the column?   [1]

2 Which of the following is **not** a member of the alkane homologous series?

A C_2H_6

B C_4H_{10}

C C_6H_{14}

D C_8H_{10} [1]

3 Crude oil can be cracked.

a) What is meant by the term 'cracked'?   [1]

b) Why is crude oil cracked?   [2]

c) Give **two** conditions needed for cracking crude oil.   [2]

Total Marks .... / 10

Interpreting and Interacting with Earth's Systems

1 Look at the graph showing the relationship between temperature and carbon dioxide levels.

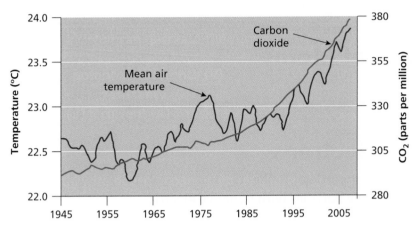

a) Describe the general trend in air temperature in relation to carbon dioxide levels. [1]

b) Explain why carbon dioxide concentrations are linked to temperature increases. [2]

Total Marks .... / 3

Air Pollution and Potable Water

1 Which of the following is the correct explanation for the term **potable water**?

A Ultra-pure water made from the process of reverse osmosis.

B Water that is stored in pots and taken from village to village.

C Water that is safe to drink.

D Water that needs to be sterilised. [1]

2 The World Health Organisation has guidelines about the maximum amount of particulates that should be in the air.

a) What are particulates? [1]

b) What part of the body is most likely to be affected by particulates? [1]

Total Marks .... / 3

Matter, Models and Density

You must be able to:

- Explain that matter is made of atoms and describe the structure of an atom
- Understand that nuclei and electrons exert an electric force on each other
- Associate the different behaviours of solids, liquids and gases with differences in forces and distances between atoms and molecules
- Describe and calculate density.

A Simple Model of Atoms

- Matter is made of atoms.
- Sometimes an atom can be pictured as a very small ball – the ball is a model of an atom.

Inside Atoms – Electrons

- Every atom has even smaller particles inside it.
- J. J. Thomson discovered tiny particles with negative electric charge, called electrons.
- He suggested that electrons are like currants in a plum pudding.
- He also knew that a whole atom is electrically neutral – with no overall electric charge.
- So the electrons must be balanced by a positive charge within each atom.
- Thomson suggested that the part of the atom with positive electric charge was like the soft 'sponge' of a plum pudding.
- The plum pudding is Thomson's model of an atom.

Inside Atoms – Nuclei

- Other scientists discovered small positively charged particles that come out from some kinds of radioactive material at very high speed. They called them alpha particles.
- Ernest Rutherford asked two of his assistants – Hans Geiger and Ernest Marsden – to fire some of these particles at very thin sheets of gold.
- They expected the alpha particles to shoot straight through the gold atoms, like bullets through cake.
- However, some bounced back. This is called alpha scattering.

> ### Key Point
>
> Atoms and small molecules are very small – about 1×10^{-10}m in diameter. That's 0.1nm.

Models of Atoms

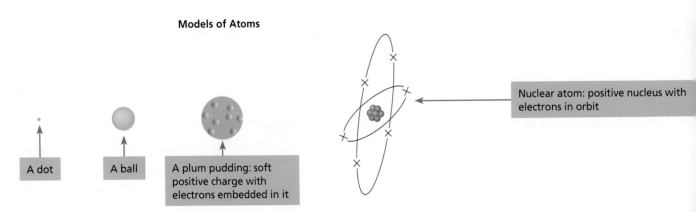

A dot

A ball

A plum pudding: soft positive charge with electrons embedded in it

Nuclear atom: positive nucleus with electrons in orbit

- Atoms must contain something very dense and positively charged to cause the scattering.
- Rutherford concluded that the positive electric charge must be concentrated into a very tiny space deep inside each atom.
- He called this the **nucleus** of the atom.
- Niels Bohr, from Denmark, improved this nuclear model by describing the pathways of electrons in **orbit** around the nucleus.

Mass and Charge in Atoms

- The electric charge inside an atom is shared equally between the electrons (negative) and the nucleus (positive). But the nucleus has nearly all of the **mass**.
- Electric charge can cause **forces** between atoms.
- The forces hold atoms together to make solids and liquids.
- Some atoms can form groups held together by electric force. These groups are **molecules**.
- Water is made of molecules – each one has two hydrogen (H) atoms and one oxygen (O) atom, so water is H_2O.
- In gases, the forces between particles are very weak. So gases spread out into the space around them.
- Gases have much lower **density** than solids and liquids, e.g.
  - The density of air is approximately $1.2kg/m^3$.
  - The density of solid iron is about $7800kg/m^3$.
- Density is a **ratio** of mass to **volume**: mass is divided by volume to work out density.
- The unit of density is the kilogram per cubic metre (kg/m^3).

LEARN

$$density\ (kg/m^3) = \frac{mass\ (kg)}{volume\ (m^3)}$$

Particles in a Solid, Liquid and Gas

Gas

Liquid

Solid

Quick Test

1. State **three** facts about electrons.
2. Outline the evidence that led Rutherford to conclude that atoms have nuclei.
3. State the type of electric charge that nuclei have.
4. What holds the atoms of your body together?
5. Suggest why it is easy to walk through air but difficult to walk through walls.

Temperature and State

You must be able to:

- Understand that many materials can change between three states
- Explain that supplying energy to a material can change its internal energy by increasing its temperature or changing its state
- Define and make calculations using specific heat capacity and specific latent heat
- Explain gas pressure and the effects of changing the volume and temperature.

Changes of State

- Some changes of state, e.g. melting (solid to liquid), **sublimating** (solid to gas) and boiling (liquid to gas), need the material to gain energy.
- For other changes of state, e.g. condensing (gas to liquid) and freezing (liquid to solid), the material loses energy.
- There is no change in the structures of atoms during a change of state.
- However, their energy and speed and the distance apart and force between them can change.
- Changes of state are not **chemical changes**. They are **physical changes**. They are **reversible**.
- The mass of material does not change during a change of state. Mass is **conserved**.
- Volume and density usually change during a change of state.
- The **internal energy** of a solid or liquid is linked to the forces between its atoms or molecules, as well as to the motion of the atoms or molecules.
- The internal energy of a gas is simpler. The forces between the atoms or molecules are insignificant, so internal energy is just the total kinetic energy of all of the atoms or molecules in the gas.

Specific Latent Heat

- The amount of energy needed to melt a substance is different for all substances, e.g.
  - It takes about 23000 joules of energy to melt 1kg of lead.
  - It takes about 335000 joules of energy to melt 1kg of ice.
- These values are called the **specific latent heat** of melting for lead and water: 23000 joules per kilogram (J/kg) for lead and 335000J/kg for ice.
- A substance has a different value of specific latent heat for the change of state from liquid to gas. This is called the specific latent heat of vaporisation.

> **thermal energy for a change in state =**
> **mass × specific latent heat**

Key Point

Supplying energy to a material can increase its temperature or change its state.

Energy gained can raise the temperature, e.g. from −5°C to 0°C. Extra energy can change the state from solid to liquid or even from solid to gas. If ice loses energy, its temperature goes down.

Energy gained can raise the temperature, e.g. from 10°C to 80°C. Further energy gained can change the state, from liquid to gas. Loss of energy can lower the temperature or cause liquid to become solid.

Giving more energy to hot gas raises its temperature. If it loses energy, its temperature can fall or it can change state from gas to liquid.

Specific Heat Capacity

- Energy isn't just needed for a change of state. It is also needed to raise the temperature of a material.
- It takes about 450J to raise the temperature of 1kg of iron by 1°C (or by 1K).
- It takes about 4200J to raise the temperature of 1kg of water by 1°C (or 1K).
- These values are the **specific heat capacities** of iron and water: 450J/kg°C for iron and 4200J/kg°C for water.
- The specific heat capacity of a material is the energy needed to raise the temperature of 1kg by 1°C (or 1K).

> **change in thermal energy =**
> **mass × specific heat capacity × change in temperature**

Gas Pressure

- A gas in a box exerts **pressure** on all of the walls of the box because its molecules **bombard** the walls.
- Most gases have atoms in small groups or molecules. This includes oxygen and hydrogen, where each molecule is a pair of atoms.
- The faster the particles in a gas move, the bigger the pressure. So pressure is related to temperature.
- If the box is made smaller:
  - the particles become closer together and the walls are hit more often by the gas molecules
  - there is more pressure on the walls, so pressure also depends on the volume of the box.

Key Point

Temperature can be measured in degrees Celsius (°C), or in kelvin (K). Zero kelvin is the lowest possible temperature. Ice melts at 0°C or 273K. Water boils at 100°C or 373K. A temperature difference of 1°C is the same as a difference of 1K.

Key Point

The energy needed for temperature change can be predicted if the specific heat capacity of the material and its mass is known.

Molecular Bombardment and Gas Pressure

Key Words

sublimate
chemical change
physical change
reversible
conserved
internal energy
specific latent heat
specific heat capacity
pressure
bombard

Quick Test

1. Name **one** quantity that changes when a substance changes state and **one** quantity that does not change.
2. Explain whether or not temperature always changes when a substance gains energy.
3. If the specific latent heat of melting of iron is 267 000J/kg, calculate how much energy will be needed to melt 1 tonne (1000kg).
4. If the specific heat capacity of air is 1006J/kg°C, calculate how much energy will be needed to raise the temperature of a room containing 100kg of air by 10°C (if none of the air escapes).
5. Use ideas about molecules to explain why increasing the temperature of a gas (but keeping its volume the same) causes an increase in pressure.
6. Use ideas about molecules to explain why increasing the volume of a gas (but keeping its temperature the same) causes a decrease in pressure.

Journeys

You must be able to:

* Make measurements and calculations of speed, time and distance
* Calculate the kinetic energy of a moving body
* Understand the importance of vector quantities (displacement, velocity and acceleration) when considering motion
* Interpret displacement–time and velocity–time graphs
* Calculate acceleration.

Measurements of Distance and Time

* Rulers and tape measures can be used to measure everyday distances or lengths.
* Technologies like radar can also be used to measure distances, including very long ones.
* A car's mileometer measures the number of rotations of a wheel and multiplies this by the circumference of the wheel to give total distance travelled.
* Clocks and stopwatches measure everyday times.
* Computer systems have clocks with very small divisions of time. They can measure very short times.

Speed and Velocity

* Miles per hour (mph) can be used to measure the speed of vehicles.
* However, in the standard international **SI system**, metres per second (m/s) is used.
* 1 m/s is equal to 3.6 kilometres per hour (km/h or kph) and 2.24 mph.
* Distance and speed are **scalar quantities** (without direction).
* They are used when direction is not important.
* When thinking about energy, direction is not important.
* The energy of a moving body is called **kinetic energy**, which is measured in joules (J).

> **LEARN**
> **kinetic energy (J) = 0.5 × mass (kg) × (speed (m/s))²**

* This equation can be used for predicting journeys:

> **LEARN**
> **distance travelled (m) = speed (m/s) × time (s)**

* When direction is important, **displacement** and **velocity** are used.
* Quantities with direction are **vector quantities**.
* Arrows of different lengths and directions can be used to compare different displacements and different velocities.
* A negative vector quantity means it is in the reverse direction.

$$\text{velocity} = \frac{\text{displacement}}{\text{time}}$$

> ### Key Point
>
> You must be able to rearrange the distance equation to work out speed and time, i.e.
>
> $$\text{speed} = \frac{\text{distance}}{\text{time}}$$
>
> $$\text{time} = \frac{\text{distance}}{\text{speed}}$$
>
> If the speed on a journey varies, the average speed is given by the total distance divided by the total time.

Graphs of Journeys

- Displacement–time graphs can be used to describe journeys.
- The **slope** or **gradient** of a displacement–time graph is equal to velocity.

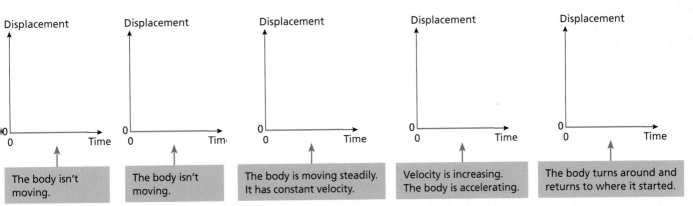

The body isn't moving.

The body isn't moving.

The body is moving steadily. It has constant velocity.

Velocity is increasing. The body is accelerating.

The body turns around and returns to where it started.

- Velocity–time graphs can be used to describe the same journeys.

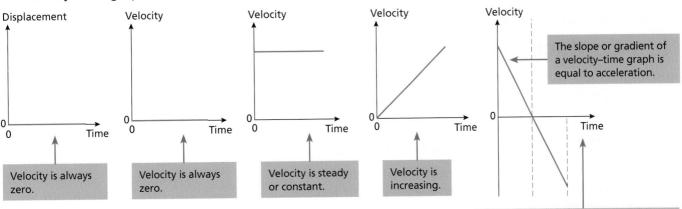

Velocity is always zero.

Velocity is always zero.

Velocity is steady or constant.

Velocity is increasing.

The slope or gradient of a velocity–time graph is equal to acceleration.

The velocity is high to start with and becomes zero. Then it becomes negative, i.e. in the opposite direction. That is how the body gets back to where it started.

Acceleration

- **Acceleration** is rate of change of velocity. It is a vector quantity.

LEARN

$$\text{acceleration (m/s}^2) = \frac{\text{change in velocity (m/s)}}{\text{time (s)}}$$

$$\text{(final velocity (m/s))}^2 - \text{(initial velocity (m/s))}^2 = 2 \times \text{acceleration (m/s}^2) \times \text{distance (m)}$$

- When an object is released close to the Earth's surface, it accelerates downwards at approximately 10m/s².
- This is called **acceleration in free fall** (g).

Quick Test

1. Calculate the kinetic energy, in joules (J), of a ball of mass 0.5kg moving at 16m/s.
2. Calculate how long a 100km journey would take at an average speed of 40kph.
3. Calculate the acceleration, in m/s², of a car that goes from standstill (0m/s) to 24m/s in 10s.

Key Words

SI system
scalar quantity
kinetic energy
displacement
velocity
vector quantity
slope
gradient
acceleration
acceleration in free fall (g)

Forces

You must be able to:

- Calculate combinations of forces that act along the same line
- Understand that forces act in pairs of the same size but opposite direction
- Recall that acceleration is not possible without net force, and a net force always produces acceleration.

Contact Force

- You can push and pull objects by making contact with them.
- The force you apply can be partly or completely a force of **friction**.
- Friction acts parallel to the surface of the object.
- You can also push at right-angles to the object. This is called a **normal force**.
- Force is measured in newtons, N.

Non-Contact Force

- Two magnets can attract or **repel** each other without touching.
- Electric force also acts without contact (without touching).
- Gravity provides another force that can act at a distance.

Gravitational and Electric Force

- All objects that have mass experience gravitational force.
- All objects with electric charge experience electric force.
- Gravitational force is always attractive, so there must be only one kind of mass.
- The Earth attracts you. The force, measured in N, is your weight.
- Electric force can be attractive or repulsive, so there must be two kinds of electric charge – positive and negative.

Net Force

- The overall force for a combination of forces is called their **resultant force** or **net force**.
- When there is a net force on an object it *always* accelerates.
- When there is no force at all on an object or the forces are balanced, it *never* accelerates. (It can move, but the motion never changes.)
- A body stays still or keeps moving at constant velocity unless an **external force** acts on it. That idea is called **Newton's first law**.

Direction of Force

- The direction of a force makes a big difference to the effect it has.
  - Two forces of the same size acting in opposite directions do *not* cause acceleration, so the net force is zero.
  - Two forces acting in the same direction add together to produce a bigger net force.

Key Point

Force is a vector quantity – direction matters. Arrows can be drawn to show forces.

Key Point

Forces act between pairs of objects. The objects experience force of the same size, but opposite direction.

Key Point

If net force is not zero, the forces are unbalanced and there is acceleration. If motion is steady and in a straight line, velocity is constant and there is no acceleration.

The forces add together.

Normal reaction force

Your weight

- When you push an object, you experience a force of the same size and in the opposite direction.
- **Newton's third law** states that for every force there is an equal and opposite force.

Force and Acceleration

- Net force is related to acceleration in a fairly simple way:
  - acceleration is bigger when force is bigger
  - but smaller when mass is bigger.

$$\text{force (N)} = \text{mass (kg)} \times \text{acceleration (m/s}^2\text{)}$$

- This equation is a form of **Newton's second law**.

> A car of mass 1500kg and a truck of mass 7500kg are waiting at a red traffic light.
> When the light changes to green, both vehicles accelerate away at 4m/s².
>
> What is the net force acting on **a)** the car and **b)** the truck?
>
> **a)** force on car = mass × acceleration
>
> $\qquad\qquad$ = 1500 × 4
>
> $\qquad\qquad$ = 6000N
>
> **b)** force on truck = 7500 × 4
>
> $\qquad\qquad\quad$ = 30 000N

Key Point
Acceleration involves change of motion – change of velocity (which can be a change in size or direction, or both). When there is net force there is always acceleration.

Because the truck has greater mass, the net force is much greater than that of the car.

Quick Test
1. Name the kind of force that keeps you in your seat.
2. Name the kind of force that holds your body together.
3. State what is necessary, in terms of forces, for acceleration to happen.

Key Words
friction
normal force
repel
resultant force
net force
external force
Newton's first law
Newton's third law
Newton's second law

Force, Energy and Power

You must be able to:

- Select from a range of equations so that you can analyse and predict motion
- Understand 'doing work' as mechanical energy transfer.

Force, Work and Energy

- When a force acts and a body accelerates as a result of this force, energy is supplied to the body.
- We say that the force does **work** on the body.
- The amount of work done and the energy supplied to the body are the same:

> **LEARN**
>
> **work done (J) = energy supplied =**
> **force × distance (m) (along the line of action of the force)**

- The unit of energy is the joule (J).

$$1J = 1N \times 1m$$

- Work must be done to overcome **friction** as well as to cause acceleration.
- When there is friction, some or all of the energy causes heating.
- In some situations, some of the work done increases an object's **potential energy**.

> **LEARN**
>
> **(in a gravity field) potential energy (J) =**
> **mass (kg) × height (m) × gravitational field strength, g (N/kg)**

How much energy has to be transferred to a mass of 2.5kg to lift it 4m above the ground?

potential energy = mass × height × g ← Write out the equation.

= 2.5 × 4 × 10 ← Write out the matching values.

= 100J ← Always write the answer with the correct unit.

Energy Stores and Transfers

- Energy can be stored in different ways, e.g.
  - in the **kinetic energy** of a moving body
  - as **gravitational potential energy**
  - as **elastic potential energy**
  - as **thermal energy**.

Key Point

The work done is equal to the energy supplied.

- Energy can be taken from these stores and transferred to other systems.
- Sometimes the energy becomes thinly spread out and only heats the surroundings of a process. Then it cannot be usefully transferred.

$$\text{energy transferred (J)} = \text{charge (C)} \times \text{potential difference (V)}$$

- Wasted energy **dissipates** in the surroundings.

Power

- Energy can be transferred quickly or slowly.
- The rate of transfer of energy is **power**.

$$\text{power (W)} = \text{rate of transfer of energy (J/s)}$$
$$= \frac{\text{energy (J)}}{\text{time (s)}}$$

- Doing work is one way of transferring energy. It is energy transfer involving force and distance.
- So, when work is done:

LEARN

$$\text{power (W)} = \frac{\text{work done (J)}}{\text{time (s)}}$$

If you transfer heat energy to your surroundings at a rate of 90W, how much energy will you lose in one hour?
(1 hour is 3600 seconds.)

$$\text{power} = \frac{\text{energy}}{\text{time}}$$ ← Write out the equation.

Rearrange to equation to make energy the subject.

$$\text{energy} = \text{power} \times \text{time}$$ ← Write out the matching values.

$$= 90 \times 3600$$

$$= 324\,000\text{J}$$ ← Don't forget the units.

Write out the equation.

Rearrange to equation to make energy the subject.

Write out the matching values.

Don't forget the units.

Key Point

No matter what happens inside a system, its energy cannot change unless it exchanges energy with other systems.

Key Point

A bow and arrow, with the bowstring pulled back, is an example of an energy storage system. It's an elastic potential energy store.

Key Words

work
friction
potential energy
kinetic energy
gravitational potential energy
elastic potential energy
thermal energy
dissipate
power

Quick Test

1. An ice skater can move in a straight line at almost constant speed without needing to supply more energy. Explain, in terms of force and distance, how that is possible.
2. When you lean against a wall you are not doing work. Explain why in terms of force and distance.
3. Describe the relationship between power and energy.

Changes of Shape

You must be able to:

- Distinguish between plastic and elastic materials
- Distinguish between linear and non-linear relationships
- Understand that for a linear relationship, the slope or gradient is constant
- Recall that a planet's gravitational field strength depends on its mass.

Extension and Compression

- A pair of forces acting outwards on an object can stretch it, or **extend** it, even if the forces are balanced and there is no acceleration.
- A pair of forces acting inwards on an object can **compress** it.
- Combinations of forces can also bend objects.
- Change of shape can be called **deformation**.

Elastic and Plastic Deformation

- When forces make an object change shape, but it returns to its original shape when the forces are removed, the deformation is said to be **elastic**.
- If the object keeps its new shape when the deforming forces are removed, the deformation is **plastic**.

Extension of Springs

- A spring experiences elastic deformation unless the force applied is large enough to exceed the elastic limit of the spring. Then the spring may be permanently stretched.
- For a spring, unless the force is very large, the amount of extension is **proportional** to the size of the deforming force.
- When the force changes, the amount of the extension changes by the same proportion.
- A graph of extension and applied force is a straight line – the relationship between force and extension is **linear.**

> **Key Point**
>
> A spring will behave elastically, unless its elastic limit is exceeded.

Weaker spring

Stronger spring

 Steep slope; large gradient

Shallow slope; small gradient

- The gradient of the graph is different for individual springs. It is called the **spring constant**.

> force exerted on a spring (N) =
> extension (m) × spring constant (N/m)

- The graph produced by a rubber band is not a straight line. The relationship is **non-linear**.

Energy Stored by a Stretched Spring

- Stretching a spring involves force and distance (the extension) in the same direction. So work must be done to stretch a spring.

> work done = average force × distance = $\left(\dfrac{\text{final force}}{2}\right)$ × distance
>
> work done = energy transferred in stretching (J) =
> 0.5 × spring constant (N/m) × (extension (m))^2

Mass and Weight

- In physics, we treat **weight** as a type of force, so we measure it in newtons (N). It is the force on an object due to gravity.
- Different **planets** and **moons** have different **gravitational field strengths** (g) at their surface. This means that objects have different weights on different planets and moons.
- Weight is related to mass:

> weight = gravity force (N) =
> mass (kg) × gravitational field strength, g (N/kg)

- On Earth, g = 10N/kg; on the Moon, g = 1.6N/kg; near the surface of Jupiter, g = 26N/kg.

Quick Test

1. A pair of forces that act on an object along the same line are balanced (equal size, opposite direction) and cannot accelerate the object. What effect can they have?
2. State which of the following show **elastic** behaviour and which show **plastic** behaviour:
   a) a guitar string
   b) a piece of modelling clay
   c) a saw blade when it is flicked
   d) a saw blade when a large force bends it permanently.
3. Physics distinguishes between mass and weight and uses different units (kg for mass and N for weight). Explain why we usually do not pay attention to about this difference in everyday life on Earth.

Electric Charge

You must be able to:

- Recall that in everyday objects there are many atoms, each with electrons
- Recall that friction can transfer some electrons from one object to another, so that both objects become charged
- Understand that electric current in metal conductors, including wires, is a result of the flow of large numbers of electrons
- Understand that resistance to current produces heat, which transfers energy from the circuit to the surroundings.

Electric Force and Electric Charge

- Electric force can be attractive or repulsive and can act at a distance.
- Electric force acts between bodies that have net charge.
- There are two types of charge – positive and negative.
- When many charged particles, such as electrons, move together they form an **electric current**.
- In a **neutral** atom, the negative charge of the electrons is balanced by the positive charge of the nucleus.
- The unit of charge is the coulomb (C).

Key Point

Electric force holds atoms together. It is the dominant force between individual atoms and between the nuclei of atoms and electrons.

Electrostatic Phenomena

- Forces between objects much larger than atoms can be observed when there is an imbalance of positive and negative charge.
- The observations, or **phenomena**, are called static electricity, or **electrostatics**, because the charged particles are not flowing.
- Friction can **transfer** electrons from one object to another:
  - one object will have an excess of electrons and a negative charge
  - the other object will have a shortage of electrons and a positive charge.
- When objects become charged in this way, then they exert electrical force – attraction or repulsion – on other charged objects.

Key Point

All electrons are the same. They are extremely small and they all have the same negative charge.

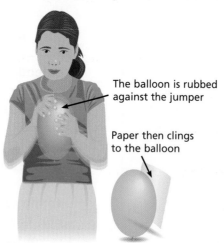

The balloon is rubbed against the jumper

Paper then clings to the balloon

- In the space between objects with different levels of charge, there can be strong forces on the charged particles inside atoms.
- Electrons can then escape from atoms of air, for example.
- Then the air conducts electricity and a spark occurs.

Electric Current

Metals are conductors of electricity.

When many electrons move in the same direction in a wire, there is an electric current.

Electric current inside a closed loop of wire can be continuous if the electrons experience continuous force from a source of energy. Batteries and cells, for example, can create continuous force.

Ammeters are used to measure current.

They are connected into circuits so that the circuit current flows through them.

Current is measured in amperes, sometimes referred to as 'amps', (A).

Current is equal to rate of flow of charge:

LEARN

$$current\ (A) = \frac{charge\ flow\ (C)}{time\ (s)}$$

$$charge\ flow\ (C) = current\ (A) \times time\ (s)$$

Unless it is isolated (cut off) from other objects, a conductor cannot keep excess electric charge, because electrons flow in or out of it too easily.

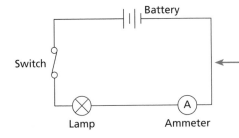

Battery

Switch

Lamp

Ammeter

> For a current to flow in this circuit there must be an energy supply and a complete loop (or closed circuit).

Resistance

- Current can flow through an electrical conductor, such as a metal wire, but there is always some resistance to the flow.
- This resistance means that a wire can be heated by an electrical current. Energy passes from the wire to the surroundings.
- Resistance is measured in ohms (Ω).

> **Key Point**
>
> In any electrical conductor, there is always some resistance to the flow of current.

> **Key Words**
>
> electric current
> neutral
> phenomenon
> electrostatics
> transfer
> conductor
> battery
> cell
> ammeter
> resistance

> **Quick Test**
>
> 1. What are the two types of electric force?
> 2. a) Outline how an object, such as an inflated balloon, becomes electrically charged.
>   b) Explain why it is **not** possible to charge a metal spoon in the same way as the balloon.
> 3. What is the difference between charge and current?
> 4. Describe how resistance causes transfer of energy from a circuit.

Circuits

You must be able to:

- Understand that resistance to current produces heat, which transfers energy from the circuit to the surroundings
- Understand that a potential difference, or voltage, is needed to keep a current going around a circuit
- Investigate the relationship between current and voltage for different components.

Circuits and Symbols

- A system of symbols is used to represent the different **components** in circuits.
- The components in electrical circuits can be connected in **series** or in **parallel** (see pages 164–165)

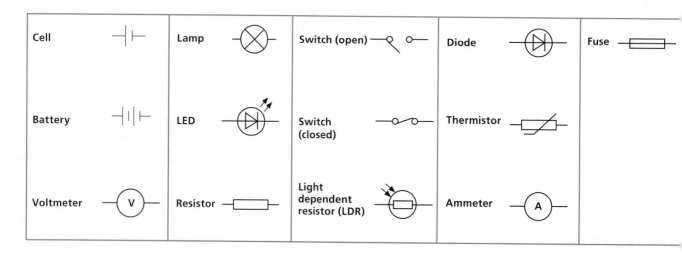

Potential Difference or Voltage

- Batteries and other power supplies can replace the energy that is transferred out of the wires and components in a circuit.
- Batteries and other power supplies only work when they are part of a circuit.
- A battery has a **positive terminal** (which attracts negative charge, so it attracts electrons) and a **negative terminal** (which repels negative charge).
- The abilities of batteries or other power supplies to provide energy to moving charge in a circuit can be compared using **potential difference** or **voltage**.
- Potential difference or voltage is measured in volts (V).

> **LEARN**
>
> energy transferred (J) = charge (C) × potential difference (V)

- **Voltmeters** are used to measure potential difference or voltage.
- A voltmeter is connected to two points. The circuit current does not flow through a voltmeter.

> **Key Point**
>
> For continuous current, a continuous potential difference and a continuous loop of conductor (such as wire and other components) are necessary.

> **Key Point**
>
> The potential difference between two points in a circuit is 1V if 1J of energy is transferred when 1C of charge passes between the points.

A voltmeter measures a difference between two points in a circuit.

Current, Potential Difference and Resistance

- An increase in potential difference can increase the current in a circuit.
- An increase in resistance in a circuit can decrease the current.

LEARN

$$\text{current (A)} = \frac{\text{potential difference (V)}}{\text{resistance } (\Omega)}$$

$$\text{potential difference (V)} = \text{current (A)} \times \text{resistance } (\Omega)$$

Wire with Little Heating

Current

Constant resistance

0   Voltage

Current–Voltage Relationships

- If the temperature of a metal wire doesn't change, its resistance doesn't change.
    - Current is proportional to voltage.
    - A current–voltage (I–V) graph is a straight line that passes through the **origin** of the graph.
    - The relationship between current and voltage is linear.
- For a wire that gets hotter as voltage and current get bigger, the resistance increases and the relationship between current and voltage is non-linear.
- This happens in a filament lamp, in which the wire is white hot.
- A **thermistor** behaves in the opposite way to a wire.
- As it becomes hotter, more electrons become free to move, so its resistance goes down.
- For a thermistor the current–voltage relationship is also non-linear.
- Thermistors are sensitive to changes in temperature.
- This means thermistors can be used as electrical temperature **sensors**.
- **Diodes** and **light dependent resistors (LDRs)** also have non-linear current–voltage relationships.
- Diodes only allow current in one direction. When a voltage is in the 'reverse' direction, no current flows.
- For LDRs, when the light intensity increases the resistance goes down.

A Wire That Gets Hot at a Higher Voltage (e.g. A Filament Lamp)

Current

Resistance changes when the wire gets hot.

0   Voltage

Diode (Reverse Voltage Produces Zero Current)

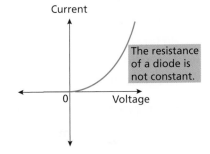

Current

The resistance of a diode is not constant.

0   Voltage

Key Words

component
series
parallel
positive terminal
negative terminal
potential difference
voltage
voltmeter
origin
thermistor
sensor
diode
light dependent resistor (LDR)

Quick Test

1. Outline what can cause the current in a simple circuit to **a)** increase and **b)** decrease.
2. Explain why a current–voltage graph for a wire becomes curved when the wire becomes hot.
3. What happens to the resistance of a thermistor when its temperature increases?

Resistors and Energy Transfers

You must be able to:

- Calculate the resistance of two or more resistors in series or in parallel
- Understand that resistors transfer energy out of circuits by heating and motors are used to transfer energy out of circuits by doing work
- Recall that rate of transfer of energy is power
- Perform calculations on power, energy, voltage, current and time for use of electricity by appliances at home.

Resistors in Series

- Resistors can be connected in series – one after the other.
- Since both resistors resist current, their net (total) resistance is greater than their individual resistance.
- The current in each of the resistors must be the same.
- Current is the flow of charge and, if there is only one route for it to flow along, it must be the same at all points.

The current flowing through R_1, R_2 and R_3 is the same

Key Point

When two resistors are in series, current must pass through both of them.

- If the current is the same in two resistors but the resistances are different, the voltages must be different.
- The relative size of the voltages is the same as the relative size of the resistances.

Resistors in Parallel

- Resistors can be connected in parallel – one alongside the other.
- This gives current two routes to follow, so the net (total) resistance is smaller than either of the resistors on their own.
- Resistors in parallel have the same voltage.
- If the resistances of two resistors in parallel are different:
  - they do not carry the same current
  - the current will be larger in the smaller resistor.

Key Point

When two resistors are in parallel, some of the current will go through one resistor and the rest through the other.

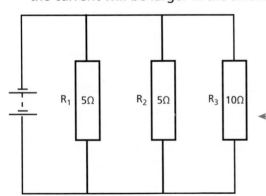

The voltage in R_1, R_2 and R_3 is the same.

Transfer of Energy

- Current in resistors heats them. Thermal energy is transferred.
- Motors also transfer energy. They do that by exerting force that can make objects move – they do work.
- Motors are not designed to provide heat, but they do transfer some energy by heating their surroundings.

Electrical Power

- The rate at which a component in a circuit transfers energy is its power, measured in watts (W) or kilowatts (kW).
- Since power is rate of transfer of energy:

LEARN

$$\text{power} = \frac{\text{energy transferred}}{\text{time}}$$

- Energy can be measured in joules (J), kilojoules (kJ) and kilowatt-hours (kWh).
- In circuits, power is related to current and voltage:

LEARN

power (W) = potential difference (V) × current (A)
= (current (A))² × resistance (Ω)

What is the power of a device that has a current of 4A when the potential difference (voltage) is 230V?

power = potential difference (voltage) × current ← Write out the equation.

= 230 × 4 ← Write out the matching values.

= 920W ← Remember, the unit of power is watts (W).

> ### Key Point
>
> One watt (W) and one joule (J) are small. So kW (1000 W) are often used for power of domestic appliances. The kilowatt-hour (kWh) is then used for measuring energy. A kilowatt-hour is the energy transferred in 1 hour by an appliance with a power of 1kW.

Quick Test

1. Describe how motors transfer energy out of a circuit.
2. A resistor has a current of 1.5A and a potential difference of 12V.
   a) Calculate how much heat energy it transfers to its surroundings in 60 seconds.
   b) What is the power of the resistor?

> ### Key Words
>
> series
> parallel

Review Questions

Controlling Chemical Reactions

1 Jude is carrying out an investigation into how temperature affects the rate of reaction.
He uses the reaction between sodium thiosulfate and hydrochloric acid:

$$Na_2S_2O_3(aq) + 2HCl(aq) \rightarrow 2NaCl(aq) + S(s) + SO_2(g) + H_2O(l)$$

The reactants in this reaction are colourless.
Sulfur produced in the reaction makes the solution turn an
opaque yellow colour.
Jude uses a cross drawn under a beaker to help measure the
reaction rate.

Jude carries out the reaction at three different temperatures using
water baths.

a) Which of the following safety precautions should be taken during this experiment?

   A no naked flames

   B keep the lab well ventilated

   C wear eye protection

   D keep a fire extinguisher nearby   [2]

b) The graph shows the reaction at two different temperatures.
Jude also carried out the reaction at 35°C.

Draw the line to show the results you would expect for 35°C.

[1]

Total Marks .... / 3

Catalysts, Activation Energy and Equilibria

1 Catalysts are often used in chemical reactions.
Modern car engines use a catalyst in the exhaust system.

Oxidising-Reducing Catalyst

Engine-out gases: HC, CO, NO_x

a) What is a catalyst? [1]

b) Suggest why a car engine needs to have a catalytic converter. [2]

c) Draw a graph to show how the **activation energy** for a reaction is affected by the presence of a catalyst. [2]

3-way catalytic converter

H_2O
N_2
CO_2
other gases

2 Photosynthesis is represented by the equation:

$$6CO_2(g) + 6H_2O(l) \xrightarrow{\text{chlorophyll}} C_6H_{12}O_6(s) + 6O_2(g)$$

Why is chlorophyll included in this reaction?

A It is the pigment that makes leaves green.

B It is the site of photosynthesis.

C It interacts with catalysts (enzymes) in photosynthesis.

D It makes oxygen. [1]

3 Heating a mixture of hydrogen and iodine gas is a reversible reaction:

$$H_2(g) + I_2(g) \rightleftharpoons 2HI(g)$$

When the reaction is carried out in a closed system a dynamic equilibrium will eventually be reached.

Use the following words to complete the sentences below.
Each word may be used once, more than once or not at all.

forward   reverse H_2 I_2 HI

At the beginning of the reaction, when the reactants are first mixed, the _____

reaction is dominant. Over time, the concentration of _____ increases and so

the _____ reaction will increase. Eventually, the rate of the forward reaction

will equal the rate of the _____ reaction. [4]

Total Marks _____ / 10

Review Questions

Improving Processes and Products

1 Which of the following metals cannot be extracted from its ore using carbon?

    A lithium

    B iron

    C copper

    D lead   [1]

2 The industrial electrolysis of aluminium ore takes place in large electrolyte cells like the one shown below.

Steel case   Graphite anode

Molten bauxite (Al_2O_3)

Graphite cathode   Molten aluminium

Which part of the cell will have to be replaced regularly?   [1]

Total Marks _____ / 2

Life Cycle Assessments and Recycling

1 A life cycle assessment can be divided into four stages.
The four stages are listed below, but they are in the wrong order:

    A Disposal of the product.
    B Obtaining raw materials / producing the materials needed for the product.
    C Use of the product.
    D Making the product.

a) List the stages in the correct order. [1]

The table below shows the results of life cycle assessments for three different types of bottle stops: corks, synthetic (plastic) corks and metal screw caps.

	Totals for 1000 Units		
	Cork	Synthetic Cork	Metal Cap
Energy Use (MJ)	1250	4500	5600
Fossil Fuel Use (kg)	27	54	149
Waste	46	1	90
Greenhouse Gas Emissions (kg CO_2)	40	81	231
Fresh Water Use (litres)	8400	4010	4200

b) Give **two** ways in which the manufacture of synthetic corks is **more** environmentally friendly than the manufacture of corks and metal caps. [2]

c) The metal used to make the caps is aluminium.

Suggest why using aluminium results in the highest CO_2 emissions. [2]

d) Which type of cap uses the least energy? [1]

e) What major advantage do aluminium caps have over the other two types? [1]

Total Marks .... / 7

Crude Oil

1 The following are fractions of crude oil:

bitumen   petrol   diesel   paraffin

Which fraction has the **lowest** boiling point? [1]

Total Marks .... / 1

Interpreting and Interacting with Earth's Systems

1. Carbon dioxide levels are increasing globally.

   The Kyoto agreement was an international agreement, made in 2012, to reduce CO_2 levels to a certain level.

   One way to capture carbon dioxide is to inject it into wells, which are between 800 and 3300m deep, to store the greenhouse gas.

   The table below shows:
   - the estimated number of wells that are now needed to keep CO_2 at the 2015 levels
   - the number of wells predicted by the Kyoto agreement in 2012.

Year	Wells Now Needed to Meet Kyoto Target Levels	Wells Predicted in 2012
2015	100 176	40 332
2020	120 342	60 498
2025	140 508	80 664
2030	160 674	100 830

   a) Explain why it is important to reduce the CO_2 levels in the atmosphere. [3]

   b) Suggest why the number of wells needed to meet the Kyoto target now is greater than was predicted. [2]

   c) Calculate the percentage increase in the wells now needed to meet Kyoto target levels from 2015 to 2030. [1]

   d) Scientists believe that human activity has caused climate change.

      Give **two** ways in which humans are believed to have increased the amount of CO_2 in the atmosphere. [2]

2. These statements explain how scientists think that our modern-day atmosphere evolved.

   1. Nitrogen gas was released from ammonia by bacteria in the soil.
   2. The modern atmosphere consists of nitrogen, oxygen and a very small amount of carbon dioxide.
   3. Plants evolved and used carbon dioxide for photosynthesis, producing oxygen as a by-product.
   4. Volcanoes gave out ammonia, carbon dioxide, methane and water vapour.
   5. As the Earth cooled, water fell as rain, which led to the formation of oceans.

Which is the correct order of this happening?

A 4, 5, 1, 3, 2

B 2, 5, 3, 1, 4

C 1, 4, 3, 5, 2

D 4, 3, 1, 5, 2   [1]

Total Marks _____ / 9

Air Pollution and Potable Water

1 Explain why carbon monoxide is poisonous to mammals.   [3]

2 Which of the following is **not** a consequence of air pollution from SO_2?

A acid rain   B phytochemical smog

C fine particulates   D lung disease   [1]

3 Give **two** chemical methods for making drinking water from sea water.   [2]

4 The diagram shows a form of reverse osmosis.

a) Name the part of the diagram labelled **X**.   [1]

b) Suggest where this method of producing water is most likely to be needed.   [2]

Total Marks _____ / 9

Practice Questions

Matter, Models and Density

1 Complete the sentence.

An atom must be electrically neutral if:

A it is an ion.   **C** it has equal numbers of protons and neutrons.

B it is a molecule.   **D** it has equal numbers of protons and electrons.   [1]

2 Which of these is a unit of volume?

A m   **C** m^3

B m^2 **D** m^4 [1]

3 Why are gases less dense than solids and liquids?

A their particles are further apart   **C** their particles are smaller

B their particles are closer together   **D** their particles are bigger   [1]

4 An object has a mass of 0.24kg and a volume of $0.0001m^3$.

What is the density of the object?   [3]

Total Marks _____ / 6

Temperature and State

1 Which of these is **not** a change of state?

A evaporation   **C** boiling

B expansion   **D** sublimation   [1]

2 Which of the following best describes how the internal energy of a sample of material can be changed?

A only by change of state

B only by change of temperature

C by change of state or change of temperature   [1]

3   Describe what happens to the particles in a gas when it is heated.   [3]

4   When a liquid is heated, what can happen to its particles?   [2]

Total Marks _____ / 7

Journeys

1   Which of these is **not** a unit of speed?

   A   mph   C   m/s

   B   km/h   D   kg/s   [1]

2   How far can you walk in 3 hours at an average speed of 4km/h?

   A   0.75km   C   7km

   B   1.33km   D   12km   [1]

3   Which of these is a unit of energy?

   A   joule   C   pascal

   B   newton   D   watt   [1]

4   What happens to the speed of the Earth as it orbits the Sun?

   A   it decreases   C   it increases

   B   it stays the same   D   it changes direction   [1]

5   How far can you travel in 1 hour at an average speed of:

   a)   24km/h?   [3]

   b)   40mph?   [2]

   c)   4m/s?   [3]

6   Volume is a scalar quantity but force is a vector quantity.

   a)   What is the difference between a vector and a scalar quantity?   [1]

   b)   Give another example of a vector quantity.   [1]

   c)   Give another example of a scalar quantity.   [1]

7 A plane takes off in Hong Kong and lands in London 12 hours later. The distance of the journey is 6000km.

    a) What is its average speed in km/h? [3]

    b) What is its average speed in m/s? [2]

Total Marks _____ / 20

Forces

1 Which of these forces requires contact?

    A electric or electrostatic force   **C** gravitational force

    B frictional force   **D** magnetic force [1]

2 Which graph shows acceleration?

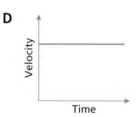

    [1]

3 If a ball is kicked along the ground it eventually slows down and stops, i.e. it decelerates.

    What force causes this deceleration? [1]

4 What does Newton's first law say about force? [1]

5 What does Newton's third law say about force? [1]

Total Marks _____ / 5

Force, Energy and Power

1 Which of these is necessary for doing work?

A energy

B mass

C pressure

D velocity [1]

Total Marks _____ / 1

Changes of Shape

1 What word describes the behaviour of a material that keeps its new shape after a deforming force is removed?

A elastic

B plastic

C compressed

D extended [1]

2 In physics, what is weight?

A a quantity measured in kilograms (kg)

B a quantity measured in joules (J)

C the force of gravity

D the gravitational field strength [1]

Total Marks _____ / 2

Electric Charge

1 Why can an object, such as a balloon, become charged when rubbed?

A friction creates electrons

B friction destroys electrons

C friction transfers electrons

D friction gives electrons extra charge [1]

2 What is produced by the movement of many electrons in the same direction?

    A an electric charge   **B** an electric current   **C** an electric resistance   [1]

3 What is the unit of resistance?

    A amp   **B** coulomb   **C** ohm   **D** volt   [1]

4 Complete the sentence.

To experience electric force, a body must have:

    A positive charge.   **C** either positive or negative charge.

    B negative charge.   **D** positive and negative charge.   [1]

> **Total Marks** _____ / 4

Circuits

1 What voltage is needed to drive a 2.5A current through a 20Ω resistor?

    A 8V   **B** 20V   **C** 22.5V   **D** 50V   [1]

2 Which of these diagrams shows the correct connection of an ammeter and a voltmeter?

A

C

B

D

    [1]

3 How does a resistor transfer energy to its surroundings?

    A heating   **B** doing work   **C** storing energy   **D** creating energy   [1]

4 At what rate does a resistor transfer energy if it carries a current of 0.5A and is connected to a voltage of 1.5V?

A 0.75W   B 1.0W   C 2.0W   D 3W   [1]

5 Which of these equations is **not** correct?

A charge moved = current × time

B potential difference = current × resistance

C energy transferred = power × time

D resistance = current × potential difference   [1]

6 Explain what each of the following components are used for.

a) battery or cell   e) diode   [2]

b) ammeter   f) thermistor   [3]

c) voltmeter   g) LDR   [3]

d) resistor   [1]

Total Marks _____ / 14

Resistors and Energy Transfers

1 Which of these circuits has the least resistance? (All of the resistors are identical.)

A

C

B

D   [1]

Total Marks _____ / 1

Magnetic Fields

You must be able to:

- Relate diagrams of magnetic field lines to possible forces
- Recall that strong electromagnets can be made from coils of wire
- Understand that an electric current in a wire creates a magnetic field.

Magnetic Fields

- Magnets can exert force without contact.
- Magnetic force can be attractive or repulsive.
- Every magnet has two poles – a north pole and a south pole.
- The **magnetic field** is the space around a magnet in which its force can act.
- **Magnetic field lines** are used in diagrams to represent direction of force that would act on a small north pole at different places in a magnetic field.
- The distances between magnetic field lines show the strength of the magnetic field at different places.

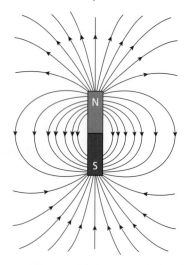

Permanent and Induced Magnets

- Some iron and steel objects are **permanent magnets**.
- Others become magnetic when they are in a magnetic field – that kind of magnetism is called **induced magnetism**.

The Earth's Magnetic Field

- The Earth has a magnetic field, as if there is a huge magnet inside.
- Compass needles line up along magnetic field lines if they are free to do so.
- A compass needle that is free to move up and down as well as round and round, dips towards or away from the ground.
- These compasses show that in most places the Earth's magnetic field is not parallel to the ground.

 Key Point

The Earth's geographic and magnetic poles are not located in the same places.

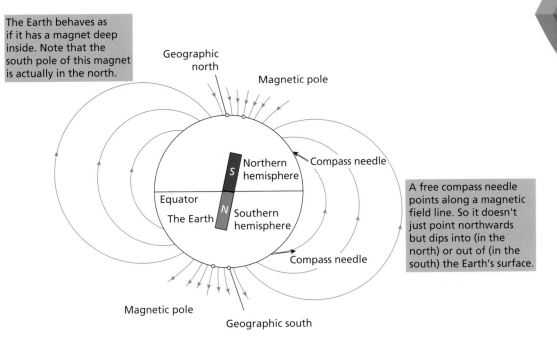

The Earth behaves as if it has a magnet deep inside. Note that the south pole of this magnet is actually in the north.

A free compass needle points along a magnetic field line. So it doesn't just point northwards but dips into (in the north) or out of (in the south) the Earth's surface.

Magnetic Field Due to an Electric Current

- Wires with electric current have a magnetic field.
- The strength of the magnetic field at a point around a wire with current depends on the size of the current and also on the distance from the wire.
- A coil of wire with an iron core can be a strong electromagnet.
- This can also be called a solenoid.

A Solenoid

Key Point

The magnetic force on a wire carrying an electric current provides the principle of electric motors.

Quick Test

1. Sketch the magnetic field pattern around a bar magnet.
2. Describe the similarities and differences between the magnetic field around a solenoid and the magnetic field around a permanent bar magnet.

Key Words

magnetic field
magnetic field lines
permanent magnetism
induced magnetism
electromagnet
solenoid

Wave Behaviour

You must be able to:

- Describe wave motion in terms of amplitude, wavelength, frequency and period
- Recall and apply the wave speed formula
- Describe the differences between transverse and longitudinal waves.

Properties of Waves

- All waves have a:
  - **frequency** – the number of waves passing a fixed point per second, measured in hertz (Hz)
  - **amplitude** – the maximum displacement that any particle achieves from its undisturbed position in metres (m)
  - **wavelength** – the distance from one point on a wave to the equivalent point on the next wave in metres (m)
  - **period** – the time taken for one complete oscillation in seconds (s).

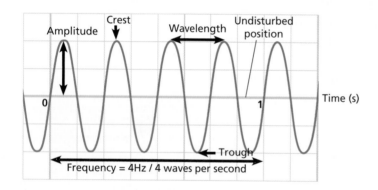

Transverse and Longitudinal Waves

- There are two types of wave: **transverse** and **longitudinal**.
- All waves transfer energy from one place to another.
- For example, if a stone is dropped into a pond, ripples travel outwards carrying the energy. The water does not travel outwards (otherwise it would leave a hole in the middle).
- The particles that make up a wave **oscillate** (vibrate) about a fixed point. In doing so, they pass the energy on to the next particles, which also oscillate, and so on.
- The energy moves along, but the matter remains.
- In a transverse wave, e.g. water wave, the oscillations are perpendicular (at right-angles) to the direction of energy transfer.
- This can be demonstrated by moving a rope or slinky spring up and down vertically – the wave then moves horizontally.
- In a longitudinal wave, e.g. sound wave, the oscillations are parallel to the direction of energy transfer.
- This can be demonstrated by moving a slinky spring moving back and forward horizontally – the wave also moves horizontally.

Transverse Waves

Hand movement up and down

Direction of wave movement

Longitudinal Waves

Hand movement in and out

Compression Rarefaction

Direction of wave movement

Sound Waves

- Vibrations from a source pass into a nearby material or medium and travel through as sound waves.
- Sound waves travel more easily through solids and liquids than through gases.
- However, sound waves can reach our ears by travelling through air.
- Sound waves are longitudinal waves.
- The speed of sound in air is about 330–340m/s.

Wave Speed

- The speed of a wave is the speed at which the energy is transferred (or the wave moves).
- It is a measure of how far the wave moves in one second and can be found with 'the wave equation':

> **LEARN**
>
> **wave speed (m/s) = frequency (Hz) × wavelength (m)**

- Ripples on the surface of water are slow enough that their speed can be measured by direct observation and timing with a stopwatch.
- As waves are transmitted from one medium to another, their speed and, therefore, their wavelength changes, e.g. water waves travelling from deep to shallow water or sound travelling from air into water.
- As the wave's speed changes, it experiences refraction.
- Refraction involves a change in direction of travel of the waves.
- The frequency does not change because the same number of waves is still being produced by the source per second.
- Because all waves obey the wave equation, the speed and wavelength are directly proportional:
  - doubling the speed, doubles the wavelength
  - halving the speed, halves the wavelength.
- A ripple tank can be used to model this behaviour in transverse waves.

Refraction

Shallow water

Boundary →

Deep water

Refracted wave

Incident wave

Change in direction and wavelength due to change in wave speed

> **Quick Test**
>
> 1. What are the units of **wavelength**, **frequency** and **wave speed**?
> 2. Calculate the frequency of a sound wave with wavelength 2m that travels at 320m/s.
> 3. Summarise the difference between transverse and longitudinal waves.

Electromagnetic Radiation

You must be able to:

- Understand that vision is based on absorption of light in the eyes
- Use a ripple model of light to illustrate reflection and refraction
- Describe the electromagnetic spectrum, including sources, uses and hazards of different kinds of electromagnetic radiation
- Understand that high frequency radiation can ionise, and that ionisation can cause chemical changes in our bodies that can be harmful.

Light Waves

- Light travels as vibrations of electrical and magnetic fields – it is an **electromagnetic wave**.
- The vibrations are at right-angles to the direction of travel – light waves are **transverse waves**.
- Different frequencies or wavelengths of visible light have different effects on the cells in the **retinas** in our eyes.
- As a result, different electrical changes happen in our brains and we see different colours.
- When light travels from a source (an emitter of light):
  - no material travels
  - it transmits energy from the source to anything that absorbs it.
- When light is completely absorbed, it loses all of its energy and ceases to exist.

Key Point

Electromagnetic radiation transfers energy from the source to anything that absorbs it.

The Electromagnetic Spectrum

- The **electromagnetic spectrum** includes radio waves and **microwaves**, **infrared**, visible light, **ultraviolet (UV)**, **X-rays** and **gamma rays**.
- These radiations all have the same speed in a vacuum.
- It is called the speed of light and is 300 000 000 m/s or 3×10^8 m/s.
- Radio waves have the longest wavelengths and the lowest frequency.
- X-rays and gamma rays have the shortest wavelength and the highest frequency.

Key Point

Visible light is just a small range of radiations. It is part of a much bigger range, called the electromagnetic spectrum.

The Electromagnetic Spectrum

Increasing frequency ←

| Gamma rays | X-rays | Ultraviolet | Visible light | Infared | Microwaves | Radio waves |

Increasing wavelength →

Different colours of visible light have different wavelengths.

- Our eyes detect only a small part of the electromagnetic spectrum.
- The following equation applies to all of the waves of the electromagnetic spectrum:

$$\text{wave speed (m/s)} = \text{frequency (Hz)} \times \text{wavelength (m)}$$

The speed of light is 3×10^8 m/s and the wavelength of visible light is about 5×10^{-7} m.

What is its frequency?

wave speed = frequency × wavelength ← Write out the equation.

$$\text{frequency} = \frac{\text{speed}}{\text{wavelength}}$$ ← Rearrange the equation to make frequency the subject.

$$= \frac{3 \times 10^8}{5 \times 10^{-7}}$$ ← Write out the matching values.

$$= 6 \times 10^{14} \text{Hz}$$

Using Different Kinds of Electromagnetic Radiation

- Radio and microwaves are used for communication – for sending signals between mobile phones, between radio stations and radio receivers (or 'radios'), and even to space probes far from Earth.
- Mobile phone networks use microwaves.
- Mobile phones emit and absorb (and so detect) microwaves.
- Microwaves with a frequency that water molecules are good at absorbing can be used to heat anything that contains water.
- Infrared radiation can cause heating.
- Infrared is emitted by all objects, and the higher their temperature the more energetic the radiation is.
- Infrared cameras can detect this, so they can detect objects that are warmer than their surroundings.
- Paint or ink that reflects UV radiation can be used to make marks on objects. The marks can only be seen using a UV light and UV detector.
- Bones absorb X-rays more strongly than the softer tissue, so shadow images of the human body can be produced, which clearly show bones and any other denser tissue.
- X-rays and gamma rays can be used to kill harmful organisms, such as bacteria.

Key Point

Radio waves are very useful for transmitting information. TV and radio broadcasting, mobile phones and Wi-Fi systems all use radio waves.

Ionising Radiation

- X-rays and gamma rays ionise atoms strongly. Some UV can also ionise.
- When materials absorb energy from these radiations, the atoms have enough energy for electrons to escape from them.
- This can cause chemical changes in complicated molecules within our bodies, such as DNA, and lead to cancer. To avoid this, we must limit exposure to these radiations.
- For routine X-ray health checks, the benefits of the very low exposure to radiation outweigh the hazards.

Key Words

electromagnetic wave
transverse wave
retina
electromagnetic
 spectrum
microwave
infrared
ultraviolet (UV)
X-ray
gamma ray
ionise

Quick Test

1. What do all electromagnetic waves have in common?
2. List the parts of the electromagnetic spectrum in order of decreasing wavelength.
3. What happens to the frequency of electromagnetic waves as wavelength decreases?

Nuclei of Atoms

You must be able to:

- Recall that nuclei have protons and neutrons, and that neutrons have no charge but protons have positive charge
- Use the form $^A_Z X$ to show different nuclear structures and isotopes
- Understand that most nuclei are stable, but some are unstable and can change by emission of particles and energy
- Distinguish between alpha, beta and gamma radiations.

Atoms, Nuclei and Ions

- The nuclei of atoms are very dense and positively charged.
- Electrons, with negative charge, orbit the nuclei in shells.
- The shells of electrons are different distances from nuclei.
- An electron in an atom can gain energy from electromagnetic radiation and move further away from the nucleus.
- When an electron moves closer to the nucleus, the atom emits electromagnetic radiation.
- If an atom loses one of its outer electrons it becomes an ion – it is no longer electrically neutral but has overall positive charge.
- Nuclei contain protons and neutrons.
- The protons have the positive charge.
- Neutrons do not have electric charge – they are neutral.

$^1_1 H$ $^4_2 He$

Absorption of Electromagnetic Radiation by an Atom

The electron gains energy and moves to a higher shell.

Emission of Electromagnetic Radiation by an Atom

The electron loses energy and falls to a lower shell.

Atoms of Different Sizes

- Hydrogen atoms are the smallest atoms and have just one proton and one electron. Some hydrogen atoms can have one or even two neutrons in the nucleus.
- Iron atoms have 26 protons and 26 electrons. They can have 28, 30, 31 or 32 neutrons.
- Forms of the same element, with the same number of protons but different numbers of neutrons, are isotopes.
- The number of neutrons affects the mass of an atom, but does not affect the charge.

Isotopes of Iron

$^{54}_{26} Fe$ $^{56}_{26} Fe$ $^{57}_{26} Fe$ $^{58}_{26} Fe$

Stable and Unstable Nuclei

- Most of the nuclei in the world around us change very rarely – they are stable.
- But some can change, by emitting particles or radiation – they are unstable.
- These changes are called radioactive emission or radioactive decay.
- It is impossible to predict when one nucleus will change in this way. The emission, or decay, is random.

Key Point

Most of the nuclei of the atoms in your body are stable. They will not change by radioactive decay. A very small proportion of your atoms have unstable nuclei. Your body is a little radioactive. That's normal and natural.

- Materials with very unstable nuclei have a very short **half-life** – it takes a short time for half of the nuclei in a sample to decay (see pages 186–187).

Alpha Emission

- In one kind of emission, two protons and two neutrons leave the nucleus.
- They come out together, and we call the group of four an alpha particle. A continuous flow of alpha particles is **alpha radiation**.
- The alpha particles have enough energy to knock electrons out of atoms as they travel. This is ionisation.

Beta Emission

- In another kind of emission, a neutron inside the nucleus changes into a proton. An electron is emitted.
- The electron usually has high speed. It is called a beta particle.
- **Beta radiation** is ionising radiation. It is hazardous.

Gamma Emission

- There is a third kind of emission, in which very high energy electromagnetic radiation carries energy away from the nucleus. This is **gamma radiation**.
- Gamma rays also ionise.

Ionisation

- Alpha particles quickly lose energy as they travel through material.
- They don't travel very far, or penetrate, through materials before they slow down and become part of the material.
- Alpha particles pass energy to the material, by ionising its atoms.
- Beta particles and gamma rays also ionise.
- They can travel further than alpha particles through material. They are more penetrating.

Alpha is absorbed by a few centimetres of air or a thin sheet of paper.

Beta passes through air and paper but is absorbed by a few millimetres of aluminium.

Gamma is very penetrating and needs many centimetres of lead or many metres of concrete to absorb most of it.

Quick Test

1. a) State which **three** of these are the same element?

   $^1_1Xx \quad ^2_1Xx \quad ^3_1Xx \quad ^3_2Xx \quad ^3_3Xx$

   b) Explain how you can deduce that they are the same element. Mention protons and neutrons.
2. Describe how radioactive emissions cause ionisation of matter.

Half-Life

You must be able to:

- Distinguish between irradiation and contamination
- Explain the concept of half-life
- Write balanced equations for nuclear decay and the emission of alpha, beta and gamma radiation.

Irradiation and Contamination

- Everyday material can be deliberately bombarded with ionising radiations. This is called irradiation.
- Irradiation can be used to kill microorganisms, such as bacteria, and it can be used to kill cancerous cells.
- The material that is exposed to the radiation does not become radioactive.
- If radioactive material becomes mixed up with other substances, the substances are contaminated. The mixture is radioactive.

Random Change and Half-Life

- A sample of radioactive material contains a very large number of atoms, so it contains a very large number of nuclei.
- The change or decay of a particular nucleus is unpredictable. It can be described as random.
- However, in very unstable materials the nuclei will change more quickly than the nuclei in more stable materials.
- In a sample of material, the number of nuclei that have not yet decayed decreases as, one by one, the nuclei decay.
- This follows a particular pattern – a decay curve.
- For a radioactive material, the time taken for the number of undecayed nuclei to reduce by half is always the same, no matter how many nuclei there are to start with.
- This time is called the half-life of the material.
- In a material with very unstable nuclei, the half-life is short.

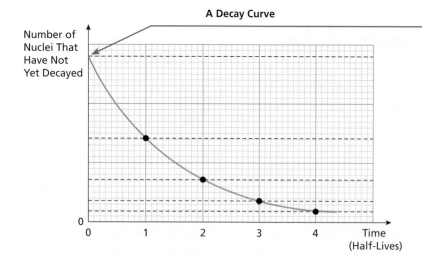

A Decay Curve

Number at the start

Number of Nuclei That Have Not Yet Decayed

Time (Half-Lives)

Nuclear Equations

Nuclear equations are used to represent radioactive decay:
- An alpha particle is represented by the symbol $^4_2$He.
- A beta particle is represented by the symbol $^0_{-1}$e.

When an alpha particle is emitted:
- the mass number of the element is reduced by 4
- the atomic number is reduced by 2.

This is because 2 protons and 2 neutrons are emitted from the nucleus, e.g.

$$^{219}_{86}\text{Rn} \rightarrow {}^{215}_{84}\text{Po} \quad {}^4_2\text{He}$$

Radon   Polonium   Alpha Particle

219 = 215 + 4 and 86 = 84 + 2

With beta decay:
- the mass number does not change
- the atomic number is increased by 1.

This is because a neutron turns into a proton and an electron, and the electron is emitted as the beta particle, e.g.

$$^{14}_{6}\text{C} \rightarrow {}^{14}_{7}\text{N} + {}^0_{-1}\text{e}$$

Carbon-14   Nitrogen   Beta Particle

14 = 14 + 0 and 6 = 7 – 1

The emission of a gamma ray does not cause a change in the mass or the charge of the nucleus.

You need to be able to be able to write balanced decay equations for alpha and beta decay, as shown by the examples above:
- The mass numbers on the right-hand side must add up to the same number as those on the left.
- The atomic numbers on the right-hand side must have the same total as those on the left.

Quick Test

1. In a sample of radioactive material, such as carbon-14, $^{14}_{6}$C, what happens to:
   a) the number of nuclei of the radioactive material?
   b) the total number of nuclei?
2. Fill in the spaces in this nuclear equation:

$$^{238}_{92}\text{U} \longrightarrow {}^{\square}_{90}\text{Th} + {}^4_{\square}\text{He}$$

Key Words

irradiation
contaminated
random
unstable
stable
decay curve
half-life

Systems and Transfers

You must be able to:

- Understand that the total energy of a system stays the same unless energy enters or leaves it
- Recall that energy can be stored by systems and can transfer from one system to another
- Calculate the energy stored as thermal energy, as kinetic energy, as elastic potential energy or as gravitational potential energy.

Conservation of Energy

- In a car engine, fuel burns and so the temperature of the gas inside a cylinder rises.
- Pressure also rises and the gas can push a piston.
- If there is no other energy entering or leaving the engine, then the total energy available from the fuel is equal to the energy transferred to the piston.
- In reality, some energy is lost to the surroundings as heat.
- Even so, the energy available from burning fuel can never be destroyed – it just dissipates (spreads out).
- This is an example of conservation of energy.

Sources and Transfers of Energy

- Energy is released from a fuel when it is burned (reacting with oxygen in the air). Effectively, the fuel stores energy.
- There are other kinds of energy store.
- Water high up in a dam stores energy as gravitational potential energy.
- Flowing water is a store of energy until the energy passes from the water, e.g. to a turbine in a hydroelectric system:
  - The flowing water stores energy as kinetic energy.
  - The transfer of energy to a turbine is a mechanical process. Work is done.
- A stretched spring also stores energy, as does a bow.
- A bow can transfer energy to an arrow, so the arrow gains kinetic energy.
- The stored energy of a stressed object is called elastic potential energy.
- Energy flows from a hotter object to cooler ones around it. The hotter object acts as an energy store. The energy transfer processes, such as emission of radiation, are thermal processes.
- A battery or electric cell acts as a store of energy.
- Components in a circuit can transfer energy to their surroundings by heating (thermal processes) or by doing work (mechanical processes.)

Energy for Overcoming Resistive Force

- Energy is required to provide force over a distance to produce acceleration of a car.
- Energy is also required to overcome resistive forces – friction and air resistance.

Key Point

The energy of any system stays the same whatever happens inside the system, provided no energy enters or leaves. We say that it is conserved.

Fuel and air

An explosion of the fuel pushes the piston

Piston

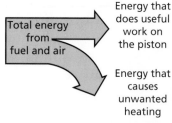

Total energy from fuel and air

Energy that does useful work on the piston

Energy that causes unwanted heating

Key Point

Resistive forces slow down a car and cause transfer of energy to the surroundings. The car will keep slowing until it stops, unless the energy is replaced.

Energy from fuel and air

For a car moving at steady speed on a flat road, energy from fuel is used to overcome resistive force. This causes heating.

Energy Calculation Summary

Energy is dissipated–it is spread into the surroundings.

Stretching a spring transfers energy to it, which is stored as elastic potential energy:

LEARN

> **energy transferred in stretching (J) =**
> **0.5 × spring constant (N/m) × (extension (m))²**

The energy stored in a spring is equal to the work done in stretching it.

Energy stored by a body raised above the ground is gravitational potential energy:

LEARN

> **In a gravity field: potential energy (J) =**
> **mass (kg) × height (m) × gravitational field strength, _g_ (N/kg)**

The gravitational field strength is about 10N/kg.
Energy stored by a moving body is kinetic energy:

LEARN

> **kinetic energy (J) = 0.5 × mass (kg) × (speed (m/s))²**

If one object is hotter than another, the hotter object acts as an energy store.
Energy can flow from a hotter to a cooler object:

> **energy available (to pass from hotter to cooler object) =**
> **mass × specific heat capacity × temperature fall**

Use the mass, specific heat capacity and temperature fall of the hotter object.

Energy transferred by an electrical component:

LEARN

> **energy transferred (J) =**
> **charge (C) × potential difference (V)**

This equation applies to energy transfer devices, such as a heater or motor. Remember, charge (C) = current (A) × time (s)

Quick Test

1. Energy cannot be destroyed, so describe what happens to the energy of a moving car when it stops.
2. Name **three** different kinds of energy store.
3. Calculate how much energy is effectively stored by:
   a) a kettle containing 0.5kg of water if the water is 70°C hotter than its surroundings
   b) a spring that is stretched by 0.05m by a final force of 15N
   c) 1000kg of water that is 50m above a hydroelectric power station
   d) a 0.03kg bullet moving at 400m/s.
      The specific heat capacity of water = 4200J/kg/°C.

Key Words

conservation
energy store
gravitational potential energy
kinetic energy
mechanical process
elastic potential energy
thermal process

Energy, Power and Efficiency

You must be able to:

- Calculate the power of a device from data on energy and time
- Calculate the power of electrical energy transfer from data on current and voltage
- Calculate the efficiency of energy transfer processes.

Power

- Power is the rate of transferring energy:

$$\text{power (W)} = \frac{\text{energy transferred (J)}}{\text{time (s)}}$$

Electrical Energy and Power

- The power of an electrical device is the rate at which it transfers energy. This is related to potential difference and current:

$$\text{power (W)} = \text{potential difference (V)} \times \text{current (A)}$$

- The unit of power is the watt (W).
- As a watt is quite small, the kilowatt (kW) is often used to measure the power of an electrical component or device.
- Rearranging the power equation gives:

$$\text{energy transferred (J)} = \text{power (W)} \times \text{time (s)}$$

- A higher power device transfers more energy per hour.

Efficiency

| total energy supplied = |
| useful output energy transfer + wasted or dissipated energy |

- A ratio can be used to compare the useful energy output to the total energy supplied.
- Multiply the ratio by 100, to create a percentage figure, which represents the efficiency.

$$\text{efficiency} = \frac{\text{useful output energy transfer (J)}}{\text{input energy transfer (J)}} \times 100\%$$

- A similar calculation involving power gives the same answer:

$$\text{efficiency} = \frac{\text{useful power output (W)}}{\text{total power input (W)}} \times 100\%$$

> **Key Point**
>
> For calculations with answers in joules (J) for energy, the SI system of units, including amp, volt, watt and second, are used. For calculations with answers in kilowatt-hours (kWh) for energy, the kilowatt (kW) is used for power and the hour for time.

A motor takes 20J of energy from its electrical supply. It supplies 8J to a load to lift it up. ←

Calculate the efficiency of the motor.

$$\text{efficiency} = \frac{\text{useful output energy transfer}}{\text{input energy transfer}} \times 100\%$$

$$= \frac{8}{20} \times 100\%$$

$$= 40\%$$

This is the useful energy output transfer.

Increasing Efficiency, Reducing Dissipation

- We normally want efficiency to be as high as possible. That means that the wasted or dissipated energy must be small.
- Lubrication with oil reduces heating and dissipation in mechanical energy transfers.
- Old **filament lamps** are very inefficient. They produce a lot of unwanted heat.
- Compact fluorescent and **light-emitting diode (LED)** lights produce less heat energy and are more efficient.
- We like our houses to be warm, but thermal energy transfers out from them, heating the world outside. The world outside gets only a very little bit warmer, because it is big. However, the energy lost from inside our homes is important.
- We **insulate** homes as much as possible to reduce energy loss, using materials such as foam boards. These have low **thermal conductivity**.

> **Key Point**
>
> All processes 'waste' some energy. The useful energy output is less than the energy supplied. The 'wasted' energy is spread thinly in the surroundings, often causing its temperature to rise by a small amount. The wasted energy is dissipated.

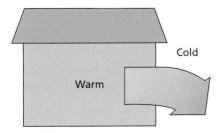

Poor insulation – high rate of energy transfer to the surroundings

Good insulation – low rate of energy transfer to the surroundings

> **Quick Test**
>
> 1. An electrical room heater has a current of 5A and a voltage of 230V.
>   a) Calculate its power in kilowatts (kW).
>   b) Calculate how much energy the room heater supplies to the room in i) 1 hour and ii) 6 hours.
> 2. Calculate the efficiency of a motor that provides a useful energy output of 1kJ when supplied with 1.25kJ of energy.

> **Key Words**
>
> power
> efficiency
> filament lamp
> light-emitting diode (LED)
> insulate
> thermal conductivity

Physics on the Road

You must be able to:

- Estimate the sizes of some everyday speeds and accelerations
- Describe how to measure human reaction time
- Understand that when a driver makes an emergency stop, the total distance needed to stop is the sum of the thinking distance and the braking distance
- Describe the danger of large deceleration.

Example Speeds

- If you walk quickly you can have a speed of about 1.5 metres per second (m/s). That's about 3.5 miles per hour (mph).
- A steady running speed for a fairly fit person is between 2.0 and 2.5m/s.
- An Olympic sprinter can run at about 10m/s.
- Acceleration at the start of a race is very important. A sprinter who goes from 0 to 1m/s in one second has an acceleration of 10m/s^2. If it takes two seconds, then the acceleration is only 5m/s^2.
- A fast but steady cycling speed is similar, although top cyclists can maintain an average of 14m/s for an hour.
- In a severe hurricane the wind speed can be 35m/s or more, but even a wind speed of 10m/s feels pretty strong.
- A commercial jet travels at about 140m/s, which is 500 kilometres per hour (km/h).

Human Reaction Times

- You can measure your reaction time by working with another person:
  1. They hold a ruler with its zero mark level with your open fingers.
  2. They let go at a random time and you close your fingers as quickly as you can.
  3. The distance the ruler falls depends on your reaction time.

$$\text{reaction time} = \sqrt{\frac{(2 \times \text{distance ruler falls})}{g}}$$

- Air resistance doesn't have much effect because the ruler does not reach high speed.
- You can improve the accuracy of your result by repeating the measurement several times and working out a mean (average) value.

> **Key Point**
>
> When we sense something happening, we do not react at that exact instant. There is a short delay – our reaction time.

g is the acceleration of the ruler, which is the acceleration due to gravity and is equal to 10m/s^2.

Stopping Distances of Cars

- When a driver has to stop a car, first he or she must react.
- The distance the car travels during the reaction time is sometimes called thinking distance.
- Only after the reaction time does the driver actually apply the brakes. Then the car slows down.
- The distance travelled during braking is called braking distance.

The total (or overall) **stopping distance** is the thinking distance plus the braking distance.

Key:

Thinking distance
Braking distance

Acceleration in a Car

- A car with high **acceleration** can reach more than 30m/s after just 10 seconds.
- The speed increases by an average of 3m/s every second. That's an acceleration of 3m/s².
- The acceleration needs a force.

Deceleration During Accidents

- In a car accident, rapid **deceleration** takes place.
- Deceleration requires force, just as acceleration does, but the force is now in the opposite direction to the motion.
- The decelerating force can hurt and kill.
- Seatbelts and airbags decrease the decelerating force on passengers in an accident.
- A seatbelt is designed to stretch, while ordinary surfaces such as windscreens and steering wheels do not stretch in the same way.
- When a seatbelt stretches, it increases the time during which the deceleration acts, so decreases the deceleration and, therefore, the force.
- Airbags and crumple zones have a similar effect.

> **Key Point**
>
> When a car accelerates, you accelerate too. The car seat exerts a force on you. Remember: force = mass × acceleration

> **Key Point**
>
> Safety features such as seatbelts and airbags are designed to reduce the force that decelerates you in a car accident.

> **Quick Test**
>
> 1. Calculate which is faster: a bullet that travels 100m in 0.4s or a plane that travels 1km in 3.3s.
> 2. Name the **two** distances that add up to make the total stopping distance of a car.

> **Key Words**
>
> reaction time
> thinking distance
> braking distance
> stopping distance
> acceleration
> deceleration

Energy for the World

You must be able to:

- Describe the main energy resources that are available
- Sort energy resources into renewable and non-renewable
- Explain why renewable energy resources are better for the future
- Recall that use of renewable resources has increased in the past decade.

Non-Renewable Energy Resources

- Electricity provides a convenient way of supplying energy to our homes, workplaces and leisure places.
- Electricity can be generated by burning **fossil fuels** – oil, coal and gas. Most of the world's electricity is generated in this way.
- However, once we take these fuels from the ground and use them, we can never replace them. They are **non-renewable**.
- **Nuclear fuel** also comes from the ground, from rocks, and is non-renewable.
- Nuclear fuel has the extra problem that it makes radioactive waste, which is very difficult to dispose of safely.
- Fossil fuels release carbon dioxide when they burn.
- Carbon dioxide is a greenhouse gas that can cause global climate change.
- Nuclear power stations don't directly produce carbon dioxide in the same way, but they produce radioactive waste products.

Key Point

Fossil fuels are the remains of organisms from the distant past. The fuels were created by energy storage by the living things, which took millions of years. Humans have used a large proportion of the world's fossil fuels in a much shorter time.

Renewable Energy Resources

- Wood is a **bio-fuel**. It will not run out, provided that we plant new trees to replace the ones we use – it is **renewable**.
- Other bio-fuels are produced from plant crops, such as oil seed rape and oil palm.
- Plants can store energy from sunlight by **photosynthesis**.
- We can use the energy that they store, but so far humans have not been able to create artificial photosynthesis.
- **Wind power** is also renewable.
- Winds in the atmosphere are caused by heating by the Sun, and by more heating in some places than others. As long as there is air and sunshine, there will be wind.

A Wind Turbine

Propeller blades

Wind

Generator

- **Hydroelectric power** stations generate electricity from moving water:
  - The water starts at a high point.
  - It travels down pipes to a lower point where it can turn turbines.
  - The water gets to the higher place by rain and, as long as there is water and sunshine, there will always be rain.
  - This energy source is renewable.

Hydroelectric Dam

- Tides also produce natural movement of water, which can turn turbines.
- Energy can be taken directly from sunlight using **solar panels** that heat water or **solar cells** that generate d.c. electricity.
- Renewable resources are less of a problem to the global environment than fossil fuels and nuclear energy.
- Because of this, most governments around the world are encouraging the use of renewable resources.

Quick Test

1. Group the following into **renewable** and **non-renewable energy** resources:
   A wind
   B tide
   C nuclear fuel (uranium)
   D coal
   E bio-fuel oil
   F gas (methane)
   G hydroelectricity.

> **Key Words**
>
> fossil fuel
> non-renewable
> nuclear fuel
> bio-fuel
> renewable
> photosynthesis
> wind power
> hydroelectric power
> solar panel
> solar cell

Energy at Home

You must be able to:

- Explain that the transmission of energy from power stations uses transformers to reduce heating of the cables that wastes energy
- Explain the roles of live, neutral and earth wires in wiring in homes
- Recall that UK homes use electricity with a.c. frequency of 50Hz and a voltage of about 230V.

Transmission of Energy from Power Stations to Users

- Power stations can be a long way from the places where people live, work and play.
- The energy must be transmitted to where it is needed using cables. The network of cables is called the National Grid.
- If there is a large current in the cables, a large amount of energy will transfer from them by heat, which isn't useful.
- The rate of transmitting the energy, or the power, in a circuit is related to current, voltage and resistance:

> **power (W) = potential difference (V) × current (A)**
> **= (current (A))² × resistance (Ω)**

- Fortunately, transmission can happen at high power using high voltage but low current. Then there is less heating of the cables and less energy loss.
- At power stations, voltage from the generators is made bigger using **step-up transformers**.
- High voltage in our homes would be dangerous. Near our homes, voltage is made smaller using **step-down transformers**.
- Transformers only work with a.c. (alternating current), so mains electricity is a.c. The current is always changing direction.
- Batteries and solar cells provide d.c. (direct current). This current is always in the same direction.
- In our homes, the voltage is about 230 volts (V). It is still a.c., and one cycle of alternation lasts $\frac{1}{50}$ of a second. The frequency is 50 hertz (Hz).

Key Point

The resistance of the transmission cables is fixed (by their length and other properties), so the power transferred from them is dependent on the square of the current in them.

Key Point

Transformers work using the changing magnetic field due to changing current in their coils. The current changes continuously – it is alternating current (a.c.).

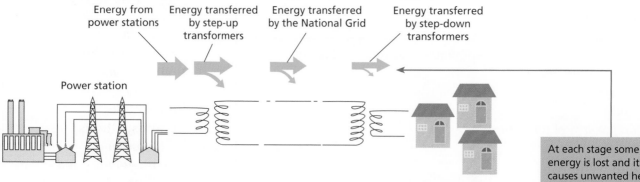

Energy from power stations → Energy transferred by step-up transformers → Energy transferred by the National Grid → Energy transferred by step-down transformers

Power station

Electricity users

At each stage some energy is lost and it causes unwanted heating of the surroundings – it dissipates.

Electrical Wiring at Home

- There is a potential difference or voltage between a live wire and a neutral wire.
- When a resistor is connected between live and neutral wires it carries a current and it becomes hot – it's a heater.
- When a motor is connected between live and neutral wires the current and the resulting magnetic forces make it spin.
- If you touch a live wire, there is a potential difference between you and anything else that you are touching, such as the ground and there will be a dangerous current through you.
- If a live wire is badly connected inside the metal casing of an appliance then the casing becomes 'live'. Touching it can have the same effect as touching the live wire directly.
- The casing is earthed. It has an extra wire – the earth wire.
- There is a potential difference between the live wire and the earth wire. Normally they are not connected together, so no current flows.
- However, if the live wire touches the metal casing, a current can flow between it and the earth wire.
- As there is very little resistance between the live and earth wires, the current will be large.
- The large current can melt a deliberate weak point in the live wire connection – a fuse. This cuts off the live wire from the power supply, and makes the appliance safe.
- A fuse in the plug and the wall switch, next to the wall socket, can cut off the appliance from the live wire in the house circuit.
- However, the live wire in the house circuit still provides a potential difference and touching it is dangerous.

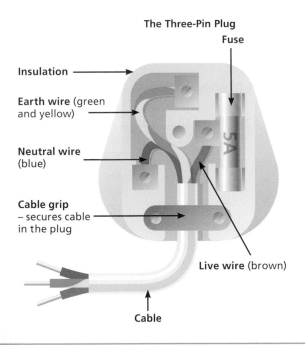

The Three-Pin Plug

Fuse

Insulation

Earth wire (green and yellow)

Neutral wire (blue)

Cable grip – secures cable in the plug

Live wire (brown)

Cable

Quick Test

1. Explain why electrical energy is transmitted using high voltage and low current.
2. Explain why electrical energy is transmitted using a.c. and not d.c.

Key Words

step-up transformer
step-down transformer
live wire
neutral wire
earth wire
fuse

Review Questions

Matter, Models and Density

1 What is the unit of density?

   A kgm   **C** kg/m^2

   B kg/m   **D** kg/m^3 **[1]**

2 Which of these models of an atom is **not** normally used now?

   A ● Dot

   B Ball

                                                                [1]

3 Which of the following best describes the nuclear model of the atom?

   A the radius of the nucleus is much smaller than the radius of the atom

   B the radius of the nucleus is the same as the radius of the atom

   C the radius of the nucleus is much bigger than the radius of the atom   **[1]**

4 What is the density of material in the space between the Earth and the Moon?

   A very much less than in our surroundings on Earth

   B a little less than in our surroundings on Earth

   C about the same as in our surroundings on Earth

   D more than in our surroundings on Earth   **[1]**

5 **a)** Calculate the density of a material if 1.0kg has a volume of $0.002m^3$.   **[3]**

    b) Explain, in terms of particles, why gases are much less dense than solids or liquids.   **[1]**

6 Explain the differences between:

a) an atom and a nucleus [2]

b) an atom and an ion [2]

c) an electron and a proton [2]

d) a proton and a neutron. [2]

Total Marks .... / 16

Temperature and State

1 In a gas, what does molecular bombardment cause?

A melting

B freezing

C energy

D pressure [1]

2 Which of the following describes a change in state?

A reversible

B irreversible

C chemical [1]

3 Which has most internal energy?

A an ice cube of mass 0.01kg and a temperature of −1°C

B a pan of water with mass 0.5kg and a temperature of 80°C

C a lake of water with mass 1×10^7kg and a temperature of 8°C

D a cloud of steam with mass 5kg and a temperature of 100°C [1]

4 How does a gas exert pressure on surfaces? [2]

Total Marks .... / 5

Review Questions

Journeys

1 What is 100 miles in kilometres?

$$\frac{1 \text{ mile}}{1 \text{ kilometre}} = \frac{8}{5}$$

A 160km

B 62.5km

C 60km

D 21.6km   [1]

2 How far can you walk in 2.5 hours at an average speed of 1m/s?

A 1440m

B 9000m

C 10800m

D 12600m   [1]

3 Which graph shows constant velocity?

A Displacement

C Velocity

B Displacement

D Velocity

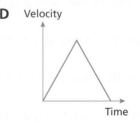   [1]

4 A car is travelling at 5m/s and then speeds up to 15m/s. It takes 10s to do this.

What is the car's acceleration?

A 0.5m/s²

B 1m/s²

C 2m/s²

D 10m/s² [1]

5 The diagram shows the velocity vectors of a car at two times, T_1 and T_2, one minute apart.

T_1 T_2

a) What has happened to the speed of the car? [1]

b) What has happened to the velocity of the car? [1]

6 a) A sports car can accelerate from standstill (velocity = 0) to 30m/s in 10s.

What is its acceleration? [3]

b) If the mass of the car is 1000kg, what is its kinetic energy:

i) when it is standing still? [1]

ii) when it is moving at 30m/s? [3]

c) What average force is needed to accelerate the car? [3]

d) Use the following equation

(final velocity (m/s))² – (initial velocity (m/s))² = 2 × acceleration (m/s²) × distance (m)

to work out the distance the car travels during this acceleration. [2]

e) Calculate the amount of work that is needed for the car's acceleration. [3]

f) What is the power at which the car gains energy? [2]

Total Marks _____ / 23

Review Questions

Forces

1 What type of force acts on the Earth to keep it in orbit?

    A electric or electrostatic force

    B gravitational force

    C magnetic force

    D resistive force
    [1]

2 Which of these always causes acceleration?

    A unbalanced or net force

    B balanced forces

    C constant velocity

    D constant pressure
    [1]

3 How much force is needed to accelerate a mass of 20kg by 4m/s²?

    A 5N

    B 16N

    C 24N

    D 80N
    [1]

4 **a)** When a person steps off a boat, what does their foot do to the boat? [1]

    b) What happens to the boat:

        i) if it is much more massive than the person? [1]

        ii) if it is not much more massive than the person? [1]

    c) Sketch the forces acting on the person and on the boat. [3]

5 Humans cannot jump very high. Why not? [1]

Total Marks _____ / 10

Force, Energy and Power

1 What is power the same as?

   A rate of change of velocity

   B kinetic energy

   C rate of energy transfer

   D strength   [1]

2 A person has to do work to push a cupboard across a room.

   a) If they push it for 2.5m with an average force of 180N, how much work do they do?   [3]

   b) If the cupboard is floating in space, and it experiences a force of 180N over a distance of 2.5m, how much kinetic energy does it gain?   [1]

   c) Why doesn't the cupboard in the room gain kinetic energy?   [1]

   d) On Earth, imagine that the cupboard experiences an **upwards** force equal to its weight, 300N, and rises steadily to a height of 2.5m.

      What can you say about the cupboard's energy?   [3]

Total Marks _____ / 9

Changes of Shape

1 Which of the following best describes the relationship between force and extension for an elastic spring?

   A constant

   B linear

   C non-linear

   D varying   [1]

2 What is the weight on Earth, in newtons (N), of a ball with mass of 1.2kg?   [3]

Total Marks _____ / 4

Review Questions

Electric Charge

1 Between which of these pairs of atomic particles will there be a force of attraction?

A (+)   (+)   **C** Neutral ⬤   (−)

B Neutral ⬤   (+)   **D** (+)   (−)   [1]

2 Inside atoms, which particles have electric charge?

A neutrons   **C** neutrons, protons and electrons

B neutrons and protons   **D** protons and electrons   [1]

3 What does the movement of many electrons in the same direction produce?

A an electric charge

B an electric current

C an electric resistance   [1]

4 What is the unit of charge?

A ampere   **C** joule

B coulomb   **D** volt   [1]

5 Which of these is a correct equation?

A current = charge × time   **C** charge = $\frac{\text{current}}{\text{time}}$

B current = $\frac{\text{charge}}{\text{time}}$ **D** time = current × charge   [1]

Total Marks _____ / 5

Circuits

1 What component is this the symbol for?

[1]

2   Explain:

   a) the difference between a volt, V, and kilovolt, kV. [1]

   b) the difference between a cell and a battery. [1]

   c) the difference between series and parallel connections. [1]

   d) the difference between an ammeter and a voltmeter. [2]

3   **a)** Draw a circuit diagram for a circuit you would use to investigate the relationship
      between current and voltage for a filament lamp. [5]

   b) A filament lamp contains a wire that gets hot.

      Sketch a current–voltage graph for a filament lamp. [4]

   c) Explain why the graph in part **b)** is not perfectly straight. [2]

> **Total Marks** .... / 17

Resistors and Energy Transfers

1   Which of these pairs are both units of energy?

   A volt and joule   **C** watt and kilowatt

   B watt and joule   **D** joule and kilowatt-hour [1]

2   What happens to:

   a) the resistance of a thermistor when its temperature increases? [1]

   b) the resistance of an LDR when light level decreases? [1]

3   A kettle is rated at 2.0kW.
   During 1 week, the kettle is used for a total of 2.5 hours.

   How much energy does it transfer in the week? [3]

> **Total Marks** .... / 6

Magnetic Fields

1. Which of these is a correct diagram of a magnetic field pattern?

A

C

B

D

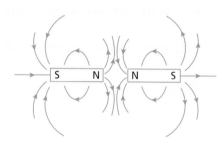

[1]

2. A compass is lying close to a coil of wire that is part of a circuit.

   When does the compass needle move?

   A   when the current in the coil is constant

   B   only when the current in the coil is turned on

   C   only when the current in the coil is turned off

   D   when the current in the coil is turned on or off

[1]

3. A north pole of a magnet:

   A   attracts another north pole

   B   repels another north pole

   C   repels a south pole

   D   attracts a north pole or a south pole.

[1]

4. How do we know that the Earth is magnetic?

[1]

Total Marks _____ / 4

Wave Behaviour

1 What term is given to the number of vibrations per second?

   A amplitude   **C** speed

   B frequency   **D** wavelength   [1]

2 If ripples on water have a wavelength of 0.1m and a frequency of 5Hz, what is their speed?

   A 0.5m/s   **C** 1.5m/s

   B 1.0m/s   **D** 50m/s   [1]

3 Which of these statements is **true**?

   A Only transverse waves carry energy.

   B Only longitudinal waves carry energy.

   C Transverse and longitudinal waves carry energy.

   D Neither transverse nor longitudinal waves carry energy.   [1]

4 What does a source of waves do?

   A absorbs waves   **C** reflects waves

   B emits waves   **D** transmits waves   [1]

5 Eyes and ears are detectors of waves.

   When a wave travels from a source to a detector, which of these does **not** travel?

   A energy

   B information

   C substance such as air or water

   D vibration   [1]

6 Ripples on water act as **models** of **transverse** waves.
   Sound waves are **longitudinal**.

   Explain the meaning of the three terms in **bold**.   [6]

Total Marks _____ / 11

Practice Questions

Electromagnetic Radiation

1 Which of these have the longest wavelength?

   A radio waves   **C** visible light waves

   B ultraviolet waves   **D** X-rays   **[1]**

2 Reflection of some frequencies of light but not others by different surfaces gives the surfaces:

   A brightness   **C** texture

   B colour   **D** gloss   **[1]**

3 Complete the sentence.

The colour that surfaces appear is due to different interactions with different:

   A amplitudes of light.

   B brightnesses of light.

   C speeds of light.

   D wavelengths of light.   **[1]**

4 The frequency of visible light travelling through glass is 4×10^{14} Hz and its wavelength is 5×10^{-7} m.

What is its speed?   **[3]**

5 When waves pass from one medium into another their speed usually changes.

What happens to frequency and wavelength?   **[2]**

Total Marks _____ / 8

Nuclei of Atoms

1. How many neutrons are there in a nucleus with this symbol $^{15}_{7}N$?

   A 22   **C** 8

   B 15   **D** 7   [1]

2. What happens to the charge of a nucleus that emits an alpha particle?

   A it decreases by two   **C** it stays the same

   B it decreases to zero   **D** it increases by two   [1]

3. Which of these cannot normally change an atom into an ion?

   A absorption of energy from electromagnetic radiation

   B high-energy collisions

   C gravity on Earth   [1]

4. Complete the sentence.

   Alpha particles, beta particles and gamma rays are all kinds of:

   A electromagnetic radiation.

   B light radiation.

   C ionising radiation.   [1]

5. Sketch an atom and show how:

   a) it can gain energy without becoming an ion   [2]

   b) it can gain energy and become an ion.   [1]

6. **a)** Describe what happens inside an atom when it absorbs energy from electromagnetic radiation, such as visible light or UV.   [3]

   b) Describe what happens inside an atom when it emits energy in the form of light or UV.   [3]

Total Marks _____ / 13

Half-Life

1 Different radioactive substances have different half-lives.

What is a half-life? [3]

2 Which graph shows the longest half-life?

A

C

B

D

[1]

3 What is contamination?

A exposing a material to ionising radiation

B adding radioactive substances to a material

C increasing the radioactivity of a material

D absorbing energy from a material [1]

4 Which of these represents a beta particle?

A $^{0}_{1}e$ **B** $^{0}_{-1}e$ **C** $^{1}_{0}e$ **D** $^{-1}_{0}e$ [1]

5 A small sample of material contains 1 000 000 nuclei of sodium-24.
After 15 hours there are only 500 000.
This is the nuclear equation:

$$^{24}_{11}Na \rightarrow {}^{24}_{12}Mg + {}^{0}_{-1}e + gamma\,rays$$

a) What is the half-life of sodium-24? [1]

b) What has happened to the 'missing' nuclei of sodium-24? [2]

c) Describe how the reaction might affect surrounding material. [2]

Total Marks .... / 11

Systems and Transfers

1 Which of the following is **not** a store of energy?

    A a wind-up toy   **C** a moving bullet

    B water high in a reservoir   **D** burned ash on the ground   [1]

2 How much energy is stored by a mass of 0.5kg if it is held on a stretched spring by a force of 20N?

    A 5J   **C** 20J

    B 10J   **D** 40J   [1]

3 Which of these transfers energy?

    A a battery in a circuit that is turned off   **C** a fuel in a car with the engine turned off

    B a resistor in a working circuit   **D** water resting in a high reservoir   [1]

4 Water has a higher specific heat capacity than ethanol.

What does this mean about amounts of energy?

    A It takes more energy to heat a kilogram of water by 20°C than a kilogram of ethanol.

    B It takes less energy to heat a kilogram of water by 20°C than a kilogram of ethanol.

    C It takes more energy to boil a kilogram of water than a kilogram of ethanol.

    D It takes less energy to boil a kilogram of water than a kilogram of ethanol.   [1]

Total Marks _____ / 4

Energy, Power and Efficiency

1 **a)** Calculate the efficiency of a motor that does 20J of useful work for each 50J of energy that is supplied to it.   [2]

    b) Explain what happens to the 'missing' energy.   [1]

2 **a)** These diagrams show energy transfers to the same scale. Which has the highest efficiency? [1

b) Explain your answer to part **a)**. [1]

Total Marks _____ / 5

Physics on the Road

1 Which of these is closest to normal walking speed?

A 0.2m/s   C 2m/s

B 1.2m/s   D 24m/s   [1]

2 A train is moving at 10m/s and accelerates to 35m/s in 5s.

Which of these is the train's acceleration?

A $0m/s^2$ C $5m/s^2$

B $1m/s^2$ D $10m/s^2$ [1]

3 A car of mass 900kg is travelling at 20m/s.

a) How much kinetic energy does it have? [3]

b) What happens to the energy if the car stops on a flat road? [3]

c) Why is the stopping distance longer when going downhill? [1]

Total Marks _____ / 9

Energy for the World

1 Which of these is a renewable energy resource?

    A coal   **B** gas   **C** oil   **D** wind   **[1]**

2 Which graph shows change in the use of wind energy resources in the UK over the last 20 years?

   [1]

> **Total Marks** .... **/ 2**

Energy at Home

1 What is the voltage in UK homes?

    A about 12V   **B** about 24V   **C** about 230V   **D** about 1kV   **[1]**

2 Complete the sentence.

A mains electric appliance and its on/off switch are connected between:

    A the live and neutral wires.   **C** the earth and neutral wires.

    B the live and earth wires.   **D** the positive and negative wires.   **[1]**

3 Which graph shows alternating current (a.c.)?

   [1]

4 Why is it a good idea to send electrical energy over long distances using low current?   **[4]**

> **Total Marks** .... **/ 7**

Review Questions

Magnetic Fields

1) Describe how you can show that a coil of wire carrying an electric current has a magnetic field around it. [2

2) A solenoid is a useful electromagnet.

How can you increase the magnetic effect in the space around the coil? [3

Total Marks _____ / 5

Wave Behaviour

1) Which of the following best describes a longitudinal wave?

A   direction of travel of the wave and line of vibration of the medium are the same

B   direction of travel of the wave and line of vibration of the medium are opposite

C   direction of travel of the wave and line of vibration of the medium are at right–angles

D   direction of travel of the wave and line of vibration of the medium are perpendicular [1

2) Which of these statements is **true**?

A   Ripples on water provide a good model of transverse waves.

B   Ripples on water provide a good model of longitudinal waves.

C   Sound waves in air are transverse.

D   Light waves are longitudinal. [1

3) Complete the sentence.

The period of one vibration is:

A   the same as amplitude.   C   how long it lasts.

B   the same as frequency.   D   the length of a wave. [1

Total Marks _____ / 3

Electromagnetic Radiation

1 Which of these statements is true?

A Light waves always have the same speed.

B Sound waves always have the same speed.

C Sound waves can travel through space.

D Light waves can travel through space. [1]

2 Which of these is not part of the electromagnetic spectrum?

A radio waves   **C** visible light waves

B sound waves   **D** X-rays [1]

3 Which of these are particularly hazardous?

A infrared waves   **C** visible light waves

B radio waves   **D** X-rays [1]

4 Which of the following is the same for all electromagnetic waves?

A amplitude in space   **C** speed in space

B frequency in space   **D** wavelength in space [1]

5 **a)** Make a large sketch of the electromagnetic spectrum showing the main parts. [7]

b) Add notes to your sketch to show what different parts of the spectrum can be used for. [7]

c) Show which end of the spectrum has the longest wavelength and lowest frequency. [1]

d) Add notes to your sketch to show some hazards of some of the parts. [2]

Total Marks .... / 21

Review Questions

Nuclei of Atoms

1 Which of these pairs are isotopes of the same element?

A   C   proton

neutron

B   D

[1

2 Which of these are kinds of electromagnetic radiation?

A alpha particles   C gamma rays

B beta particles   D neutrons   [1

3 What happens to the charge of a nucleus that emits a gamma ray?

A it decreases   C it stays the same

B it decreases to zero   D it increases   [1

4 How does an atom become an ion?

A it loses or gains one or more electron

B it loses or gains one or more proton

C it loses or gains one or more neutron

D it loses or gains one or more gamma ray   [1

5 What does 'random' mean?

A in bursts   C very fast

B without a pattern   D very slowly   [1

6 Which type of radiation can travel furthest through a material?

A alpha particles

B beta particles

C gamma rays   [1

7 What is irradiation?

    A increasing the radioactivity of a material

    B absorbing energy from a material

    C adding radioactive substances to a material

    D exposing a material to ionising radiation   [1]

Total Marks .... / 7

Half-Life

1 Which of the following describes the nuclei in radioactive material?

    A stable   **B** unstable   **C** big   **D** small   [1]

2 Replace x and y with the correct numbers in the following equations showing radioactive decay.

    a) $_{6}^{x}C \rightarrow {}_{y}^{14}N + {}_{-1}^{0}e$ [2]

    b) $_{x}^{238}U \rightarrow {}_{90}^{y}Th + {}_{2}^{4}He$ [2]

3 Draw a line from each symbol to the correct diagram.

$_{1}^{2}H$

$_{1}^{3}H$

$_{2}^{4}He$

$_{2}^{3}He$

proton

neutron

[3]

Total Marks .... / 8

Review Questions

Systems and Transfers

1 Which of these statements agrees with the principle of conservation of energy?

    A Energy can be created and destroyed.

    B Energy can be created but never destroyed.

    C Energy cannot be created but it can be destroyed.

    D Energy cannot be created or destroyed. [1]

2 Which of the following does **not** supply energy to a system?

    A absorption of light   **C** using fuel to accelerate

    B emission of light   **D** heating [1]

4 Which of these is the kinetic energy of a car of mass 800kg travelling at 20m/s?

    A 400J   **C** 1600J

    B 820J   **D** 160 000J [1]

> **Total Marks** _____ / 3

Energy, Power and Efficiency

1 A battery-powered motor uses 100J of energy to lift a load. The energy supplied to the load is 60J.

    What happens to the other 40J of the supplied energy?

    A it does work on the load   **C** it is stored by the motor

    B it causes heating and dissipates   **D** it is returned to the battery [1]

2 Which of these does **not** reduce the rate of unwanted energy transfer?

    A lubrication   **C** dissipation

    B thermal insulation   **D** streamlining [1]

3 The table contains two examples of energy storage devices and systems and one example of an energy transfer device and system.

Give **two** more examples of each.

Energy Storage Devices and Systems	Energy Transfer Devices and Systems
battery	resistor
arrow held in a bow	

[4]

4 An electric current carries energy from a supply, such as a battery or the a.c. mains, to energy transfer devices in the circuit.

What are the main types of energy transfer in the following devices?

a) a heater [1]

b) a motor [1]

c) a hair drier [1]

d) a lamp [1]

5 Which of the following transfers the most energy?

A a 2.0kW kettle used for 5 minutes

B a 0.8kW washing machine used for 30 minutes

C a 400W television used for 2.5 hours [1]

6 a) i) What is lubrication? [2]

  ii) How does lubrication reduce rate of energy transfer? [2]

b) i) What is thermal insulation? [2]

  ii) How does thermal insulation reduce rate of energy transfer? [2]

Total Marks _____ / 19

Review Questions

Physics on the Road

1 Which of the following measurements is closest to 100km/h?

A 100mph

C 30mph

B 60mph

D 10mph

[1]

2 What is reaction time?

A the time between an event happening and a person responding

B the time between a person seeing an event and responding

C the total time taken to stop a car after an event happens

D the braking time of a car after an event happens

[1]

3 Which graph shows how thinking distance changes as speed increases?

A Thinking distance / Speed

C Thinking distance / Speed

B Thinking distance / Speed

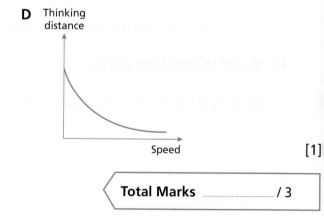

D Thinking distance / Speed

[1]

Total Marks _____ / 3

Energy for the World

1 **a)** Copy and complete this table adding at least **one** advantage and **one** disadvantage for each of the five different energy resources.

Energy Resource	Advantages	Disadvantages
coal		
oil		
wind		
solar		
nuclear		

[6]

b) Name **one** other energy resource and list its advantages and disadvantages. [3]

Total Marks _____ / 9

Energy at Home

1 What is the network of cables for transmitting energy over large distances called?

A National Grid

B step-up transformer

C step-down transformer

D power station [1]

2 What immediately happens in an electrical appliance if the live wire becomes connected to the earth wire?

A the voltage becomes very large

B no current can flow at all

C a very large current can flow

[1]

3 Which of these is an electrical insulator?

A copper

B iron

C PVC

D steel [1]

Total Marks _____ / 3

Mixed Exam-Style Biology Questions

1 The diagram below shows a heart.

What is the name of blood vessel **X**?

A aorta

C pulmonary vein

B pulmonary artery

D vena cava [1

2 Which of the bacteria below convert nitrates in the soil to nitrogen in the air?

A putrefying

C nitrifying

B denitrifying

D nitrogen-fixing [1

3 The movement of substances from an area of high concentration to an area of low concentration describes which one of the following processes?

A active transport

C transpiration

B diffusion

D osmosis [1

4 The following factors affect the distribution of organisms.

Which one is a **biotic** factor?

A light intensity

C number of predators

B pH of soil

D amount of rainfall [1

5   Some students wanted to investigate the effect of temperature on respiration of yeast.

They made a simple manometer as shown below.

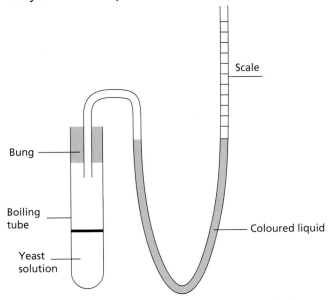

The students placed 0.5g of dried yeast, 0.05g of glucose and 10cm³ of water in the boiling tube. A thin layer of oil was poured onto the top of the water. The boiling tube was then put into a water bath at 20°C.

They left the apparatus for 30 minutes and then recorded how far the coloured liquid had moved on the scale.

They repeated the experiment at 40°C and 60°C.

a)   What type of microorganism is yeast?   [1]

b)   The yeast is respiring anaerobically in this experiment.

     What will the products be?   [2]

c)   Why does the coloured liquid move up the scale?   [1]

d)   Suggest **two** variables the students needed to keep the same for each experiment?   [2]

e)   What was the dependent variable in this investigation?   [1]

f)   The students recorded their results in a table.

A	20	40	60
Number of Divisions on Scale that Coloured Liquid Moved	12	4	0

    i)   Suggest a suitable title for row **A**.   [2]

    ii)   What can the students conclude from these results?   [1]

    iii) Why was there no movement of the coloured water at 60°C? [2

    iv) How could the students improve the accuracy of their results? [1

g) If the boiling tube at 20°C is left for several weeks, the yeast will eventually die.

Give **two** reasons why the yeast will die. [2]

6 The diagram below shows part of a phylogenetic tree.

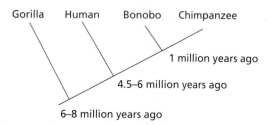

What can be deduced from the tree?

A The gorilla is more closely related to the bonobo than the human.

B The human and chimpanzee share a common ancestor from 1 million years ago.

C The gorilla and human share a common ancestor from 6–8 million years ago.

D Humans are most closely related to the chimpanzee. [1]

7 The diagram below shows the mechanism that plants use to allow gases to enter and exit the leaves and also to control transpiration.

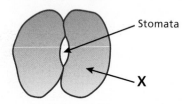

a) What is transpiration? [1]

b) What is the name of cell **X**, which opens and closes the stomata? [1]

c) Which gas will enter through the stomata when the plant is photosynthesising? [1]

8 Some students wanted to investigate if the number of stomata on the upper and lower side of leaves were similar or different.

They collected a leaf from the elephant ear plant, *Saxifrage bergenia*.

They painted the upper and lower surface of the leaf with clear nail varnish and left it to dry.

They then peeled the nail varnish from the leaf and were able to count the number of stomata in several fields of view using a microscope.

a) What is the genus of the plant the students used? [1]

b) The diagram below shows what the students could see in one field of view using a light microscope.

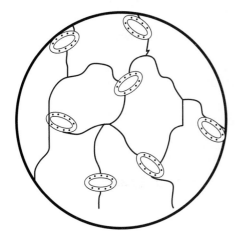

Stomata measure about 30–40µm.

What is likely to be the magnification the students used?

A ×4

B ×100

C ×10 000 [1]

c) The students recorded their results in a table.

Field of View	1	2	3	4	5
Number of stomata – upper side of leaf	2	3	2	2	1
Number of stomata – lower side of leaf	6	5	7	9	3

i) Calculate the mean number of stomata per field of view for the upper and lower surface of the leaf.

Show your working. [4]

ii) Explain why there are more stomata on the lower surface of leaves compared with the upper surface. [5]

9 Tall corn plants is the dominant trait to short corn plants.
A cross between two plants yielded 72 plants that were tall and 28 that were short.

What are the likely genotypes of the parent plants?

A TT and TT

C Tt and Tt

B TT and Tt

D tt and tt

[1,

10 Which one of the following is a communicable disease?

A cancer

C AIDS

B liver disease

D obesity

[1]

11 The diagram below shows the components of blood.

W

X

Y

Z

What is the function of component **W**?

A produce antibodies

C transport carbon dioxide and glucose

B trap microorganisms

D help the blood to clot

[1]

12 Colour blindness is an example of an X-linked recessive disease.

It is caused by an alteration in one gene which is on the X chromosome.

The altered gene will be expressed unless a 'normal' allele is present on a second X chromosome to 'cancel it out'.

a) Explain why males are much more likely to suffer from colour blindness than females.   [2]

b) A female can be a carrier of colour blindness.

What is the chance of a female carrier and a normal male having a son who is colour blind?

A   25%   C   75%

B   50%   D   100%   [1]

c) The diagram below shows the incidence of colour blindness in a family.

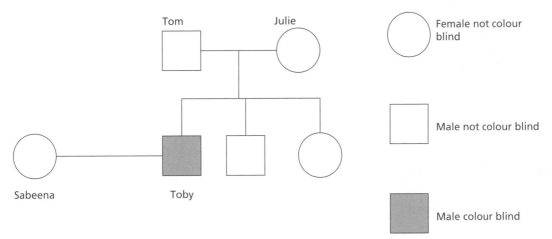

Has Toby inherited his colour blindness from his mother or father?   [1]

d) Toby marries Sabeena. Sabeena is not a carrier for colour blindness.

Which of the statements below is **true**?

A   there is a 50% chance any daughters they have will be carriers

B   none of their sons will be colour blind

C   there is a 50% chance any daughters will be colour blind   [1]

Mixed Exam-Style Biology Questions

13 Antibiotics are important medicines, which have been used to treat bacterial infections for over 70 years.

However, over recent years, many have become less effective as new antibiotic-resistant superbugs have evolved.

a) Explain how antibiotic-resistant bacteria develop. [3

b) Some serious illnesses such as tuberculosis are often treated with two different antibiotics simultaneously.

Explain how this regime is likely to reduce the emergence of a resistant strain. [2

c) Why are antibiotics **not** prescribed for viral infections? [1

d) The human body has several defence mechanisms to stop bacteria from entering our body.

Give **three** defence mechanisms and explain how each works. [6

14 Seed banks are an important store of biodiversity.

Which statement is **not** true when considering the use of seed banks to maintain biodiversity compared with storing whole plants?

A only uses a small amount of space

B suitable for storing all types of seeds

C relatively low labour costs

D seeds remain viable for long periods [1

15 The diagram on the right shows the parts of the nervous system.

Which letter represents the peripheral nervous system?

A W

B X

C Y

D Z [1

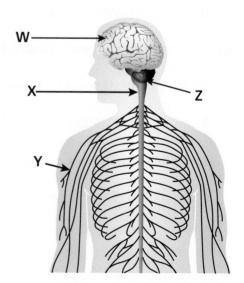

16 Scientists are worried about increased levels of carbon dioxide in the atmosphere.

Until 1950, the level of carbon dioxide in the atmosphere had never exceeded 300 parts per million.

The graph below shows levels of carbon dioxide over the last 10 years.

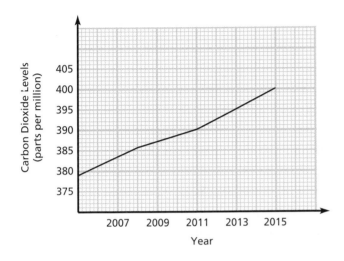

a) What was the level of carbon dioxide in 2008? [1]

b) Use the graph to predict carbon dioxide levels in 2017 if they continue to rise at their current rate. [1]

c) Explain why carbon dioxide levels have increased so much in the last 100 years. [2]

17 A transgenic organism is an organism that contains genes from another organism.

By incorporating a gene for human protein production into bananas, potatoes and tomatoes, researchers have been able to successfully create edible vaccines for hepatitis B, cholera and rotavirus.

a) Which type of human cells are likely to be used as a source of the gene.

   A red blood cells

   B white blood cells

   C brain cells

   D platelets [1]

b) Give **two** reasons why people might be reluctant to eat these transgenic plants. [2]

Total Marks _____ / 63

Mixed Exam-Style Chemistry Questions

1 Sturrock is investigating the reaction between calcium carbonate and dilute nitric acid.
He measures the reaction time for four different concentrations of nitric acid.
The only factor that was changed was concentration.
The results are shown in the table below.

Concentration	Reaction Time (s)
A	32
B	63
C	97
D	144

Explain, in terms of particles, why **A**, **B**, **C** and **D** had different reaction times. [4

2 Eliot is carrying out chromatography on inks from different pens.
He is trying to find out which ink was used to write a note.
He draws a start line in pencil and then puts a dot of each ink onto the line.
He then dips the filter paper into ethanol in a beaker.

a) What is the role of the **paper** in this experiment?

   A   mobile phase   C   solid phase

   B   gas phase   D   stationary phase   [1

b) Why did Eliot draw the start line in pencil?   [1

c) The results of Eliot's experiment are shown below.

   Which ink matches sample **X**, which was used on the note?   [1

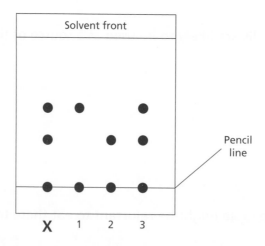

d) Calculate the R_f value for the ink in **sample 2**.
   Use a ruler to help you.   [1

3 During the electrolysis of molten lithium chloride, what is made at the anode?

   A chlorine

   B hydrogen

   C lithium

   D lithium hydroxide [1]

4 The diagrams below show the structures of two forms of carbon:

   a) Diamond is very hard material.
   Graphite is not very hard.

   Use ideas about bonding and structure to explain this observation. [4]

   b) What is the technical term given to the different forms carbon can take? [1]

   c) Describe **one** way of demonstrating that graphite and diamond are different
   physical forms of carbon. [2]

5 Ethane has the formula C_2H_6.
   Look at the three different representations of ethane.

                               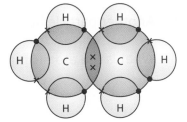

   Ball and stick model   Displayed formula   Dot and cross diagram

   a) What type of bonding is present in ethane?
   You must explain how the diagrams show this. [2]

   b) Describe the limitations of using displayed formulae to represent molecules. [2]

6 Lithium is extracted from its ore by electrolysis.
Iron is extracted from its ore by heating it with carbon.

a) Explain why different methods are used to extract lithium and iron. [2]

b) Molten lithium oxide contains ions.
The electrolysis of molten lithium oxide produces lithium and oxygen.

   i) Write the symbols for **atoms** of lithium and oxygen. [2]

   ii) Write the symbols for the **ions** of lithium and oxygen. [2]

   iii) Explain why solid lithium oxide cannot be electrolysed. [1]

7 The table contains information about some atoms and ions.

Particle	Atomic Number	Atomic Mass	Number of Protons	Number of Neutrons	Number of Electrons	Electronic Structure
A	7	14	7		7	2.5
B		40	20	20	18	2.8.8
C	8		8	8	8	
D	9	19		10	9	2.7

a) Complete the table. [5]

b) Explain why particle **D** is an atom and particle **B** is an ion. [2]

c) Particle A has the electronic structure 2.5.

   What does this tell you about the position of particle **A** in the periodic table?
   Explain your answer. [4]

d) Another particle has an atomic mass of 40 and contains 21 neutrons.

   What is the atomic number of particle **B**? [1]

8 Two isotopes of carbon are:

$^{12}_{6}C$ $^{14}_{6}C$

Explain the difference between isotopes of the same element in terms of subatomic particles? [4]

9 Ras Al-Khair in Saudi Arabia produces around one million cubic litres of drinking water a day from sea water.

Which of the following describes the process of extracting fresh water from sea water?

A chlorination

B filtration

C desalination

D sedimentation [1]

10 Magnesium sulfate is a salt.
It can be made by reacting magnesium oxide, MgO, with sulfuric acid, H_2SO_4.

a) Construct the **balanced symbol** equation for this reaction. [1]

b) Naomi suggests another method for preparing magnesium sulfate:

1. Measure 50cm³ of dilute sulfuric acid into a beaker.
2. Add one spatula of magnesium oxide.
3. Heat the mixture until only crystals of magnesium sulfate are left.

Give **one** safety precaution that Naomi should take when following this method. [1]

c) Naomi's method will **not** make a pure, dry sample of magnesium sulfate.

How can Naomi make sure that:

i) The reaction is complete? [1]

ii) The filtrate contains only magnesium sulfate solution? [1]

11 Look at the diagram of four different atoms:

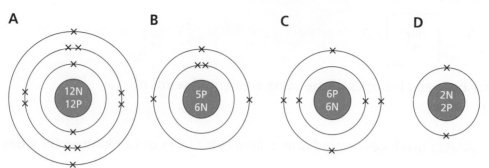

A   B   C   D

a) What is the centre of the atom called? [1

b) What subatomic particles make up the centre of the atom? [1

c) Which two elements shown are in the same **period** in the periodic table? [1

d) What are the names of elements **B** and **C**? [2

12 Look at the diagrams of compounds below.

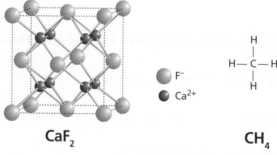

CaF₂   CH₄

a) Explain why the structure of calcium fluoride, CaF$_2$, means it has a high melting point. [3]

b) Explain why methane, CH$_4$, has a low melting point and boiling point. [3]

c) Draw dot and cross diagrams to show the ionic bonding in lithium oxide.
You should include the charges on the ions.
The electronic structure of lithium is 2.1.
The electronic structure of oxygen is 2.6. [2]

13 **a)** What is meant by the term **pure substance** in chemistry? [1]

b) Explain how this is different to the way in which pure is used to describe substances, e.g. orange juice, in everyday life. [1]

14 Look at the elements from the periodic table and answer the questions that follow.

| $_4^9Be$ | $_{12}^{24}Mg$ | $_{13}^{27}Al$ | $_9^{19}F$ | $_{15}^{31}P$ |

a) Which element has a relative atomic mass of 9? [1]

b) Which element has an atomic number of 9? [1]

c) An isotope of P has two fewer neutrons.

What is the relative atomic mass of the isotope? [1]

15 Magnesium and dilute sulfuric acid react to make hydrogen gas:

$Mg(s) + H_2SO_4(aq) \rightarrow MgSO_4(aq) + H_2(g)$

George measures the rate of this reaction by measuring the **loss in mass** of the reaction mixture. He finds that the change in mass is very small and difficult to measure.

a) Draw a labelled diagram to show a better way of measuring the rate of this reaction. [1]

b) The reaction between the magnesium and sulfuric acid takes longer than George would like.

What type of substance can George add to increase the rate of reaction? [1]

c) Suggest what safety precautions George needs to take when carrying out the experiment. [1]

16 Iodine is a non-metal.

Which statement is true about iodine **because** it is a non-metal?

A It is a solid at room temperature and pressure.

B It does not conduct electricity.

C It is a halogen.

D It is in Period 5 of the periodic table. [1]

17 Sea water contains many useful chemicals.
A company in the Middle East, specialising in desalination of sea water, decides that they can also extract particular chemicals and sell them onto the chemical industry.

a) What is desalination? [1]

b) Sodium chloride and sodium sulfate can both be extracted from sea water.

What is the chemical formula for sodium sulfate? [1]

c) It is important that people in all parts of the world have access to potable water. Explain why. [2]

18 What is the general formula for the reaction between a metal and an acid? [1]

19 Complete the word equations to show the products of each reaction:

a) magnesium + nitric acid [1]

b) zinc + sulfuric acid [1]

c) iron + hydrochloric acid [1]

20 What is the general formula for the reaction between metal carbonates and acid? [1]

21 Complete the word equations to show the products of each reaction:

a) magnesium carbonate + nitric acid [1]

b) copper carbonate + sulfuric acid [1]

c) sodium carbonate + hydrochloric acid [1]

22 Astra is carrying out experiments to identify gases.

Draw **one** line from each gas to the correct chemical test.

Name of Gas	Chemical Test
carbon dioxide	turns moist, red litmus blue
chlorine	turns moist, blue litmus red
hydrogen	turns lime water milky white
oxygen	burns with a squeaky pop
	relights a glowing splint

[4]

23 The majority of the world's scientists agree that the main causes of recent climate change are due to human actions. [1]

Which of the following is **not** a man-made cause of carbon dioxide emissions?

A flying aeroplanes

B driving cars

C planting trees

D burning plastics [1]

24 The table below shows the gases present in the air.

Gas	Percentage in Clean Air
nitrogen	78
oxygen	
carbon dioxide	0.04
other gases	1

a) Work out the percentage of oxygen in the air. [1]

b) What were the **two** main gases present in the Earth's early atmosphere? [2]

25 The table below shows some fractions of crude oil and the range of their boiling points. [1]

Fraction	Boiling Point Range (°C)
petrol	80–110
diesel	150–300
fuel oil	300–380
bitumen	400+

A hydrocarbon called hexadecane has a boiling point of 289°C.

In which fraction would you expect to find hexadecane? [1]

Total Marks .... / 93

Mixed Exam-Style Physics Questions

1 Which one of these statements is **false**?

   A Visible light is electromagnetic radiation.

   B Visible light is ionising radiation.

   C Visible light carries energy.

   D Visible light travels as a transverse wave. [1]

2 Dissipation of energy is reduced by which of the following?

   A having better insulation of houses

   B reducing the efficiency of an electric motor

   C using hot filament lamps instead of LED lamps

   D using step-up transformers to increase the voltage for long-distance transmission of electrical energy [1]

3 Which one of these statements is **false**?

   A Electrons can orbit the nuclei in atoms.

   B Electrons can flow in wires to make electric current.

   C Electrons are the same as beta particles.

   D Electrons all have positive electric charge. [1]

4 Which of the following has constant speed but changing velocity?

   A a car moving steadily along the road

   B the Earth in orbit around the Sun

   C a sprinter at the start of a race

   D a ball when you drop it to the floor [1]

5 a) Put the particles below in order of size, starting with the largest:

atom   electron   molecule   nucleus   [2]

b) During the change of state from liquid to gas, what happens to:

i)   atoms?   [2]

ii) nuclei?   [1]

c) Describe what happens to the molecules of a gas when it is heated.   [2]

d) The diagram shows a molecule of gas and its velocity before and after colliding with a wall.

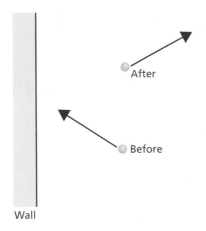

i)   What has happened to the speed of the molecule?   [1]

ii) What has happened to the velocity of the molecule?   [1]

iii) What does the wall do to the molecule?   [1]

iv) What does the molecule do to the wall?   [1]

e) i)   A molecule of gas has a mass of 4×10^{-26}kg and moves at 100m/s.

   Calculate the kinetic energy of the molecule.   [4]

ii) What is the total kinetic energy of a kilogram of the gas if all of the molecules move at 100m/s?   [1]

6 This bus has a constant forwards velocity.

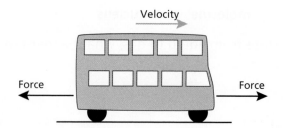

a) i)   What is the net force acting on the bus? [1

ii) What provides the forwards force? [1

iii) What provides the backwards force? [1

iv) What is its acceleration? [1

b) A girl standing on the bus holds an umbrella so that it is free to swing.

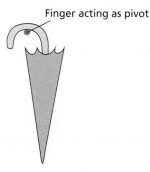

Finger acting as pivot

i)   The girl notices that when the bus accelerates, the umbrella seems to swing backwards.

Explain why that happens. [1

ii) What will happen to the umbrella when the bus decelerates to stop at a bus stop?
You must explain your answer. [2

c) i)   A child runs in front of the bus and the driver brakes hard to make the bus decelerate.
The girl falls forwards.

Explain why that happens. [1

ii) What is the difference between the reaction time of the driver and the braking time
of the bus? [2

iii) How do we use reaction time and braking time to work out the stopping time of the bus? [1

d) The moving bus has kinetic energy.

What happens to that energy when the bus brakes and stops? [3

7 This diagram represents an electric heater.
The supply voltage is 230V.

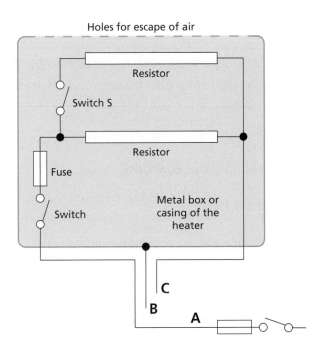

Holes for escape of air

Resistor

Switch S

Resistor

Fuse

Metal box or casing of the heater

Switch

C

B

A

a) What do the resistors do? [2]

b) Are the resistors connected in series or in parallel? [1]

c) What is the purpose of Switch S? [2]

d) What are the names of the three wires: **A**, **B** and **C**? [3]

e) When all the switches are closed, a current of 4.6A passes through each resistor.

   i) What is the value of each resistor? [3]

   ii) The total current through the fuse is 9.2A.

      Is their combined resistance bigger or smaller than your answer to part **i)**?
      Explain your answer. [2]

f) What is the maximum power of the heater? [3]

g) How much energy does the heater provide to a room in 3 hours? [3]

8 **a)** Sound waves in water have a frequency of 3000 Hz and a wavelength of 0.5 m.
Work out the speed of sound waves in water. [4

b) A student has written the following text but it contains same mistakes.

Longitudinal waves and transverse waves both transfer energy. But longitudinal waves need a medium to travel through and so they also transfer substances, such as air. Sound and light waves are examples of transverse waves, which means that their direction of travel is parallel to the direction of vibration.

Identify the mistakes and explain what is wrong. [3

c) Where are gamma rays emitted from? [1

d) Radio waves and gamma rays are electromagnetic radiation.

   i) State **two** things that are the same about radio waves and gamma rays. [2

   ii) State **two** things that are different about radio waves and gamma rays. [2

e) Visible light is part of the electromagnetic spectrum.

What is the electromagnetic spectrum? [3

f) How does your body respond to:

   i) visible light? [1

   ii) infrared radiation? [1

   iii) ultraviolet radiation? [1

   iv) X-rays? [1

   v) radio waves? [1

9 The diagram shows two houses. The temperature is the same inside them both.
The arrows show rate of energy transfer out from the houses.

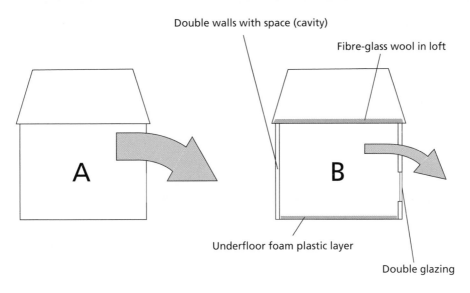

Double walls with space (cavity)

Fibre-glass wool in loft

A

B

Underfloor foam plastic layer

Double glazing

a) Explain why the arrows on the two diagrams are not the same. [2]

b) Why does the person who lives in House **A** pay much more money for heating? [1]

c) What happens to the energy that transfers out from the houses? [2]

d) What is another name for rate of transfer of energy? [1]

e) i) Name **three** energy sources that the people who live in the houses can use for heating. [3]

   ii) State whether the energy sources are based on renewable fuel, non-renewable fuel
       or a mixture of those. [3]

f) What are the advantages and disadvantages of using wind farms as sources of energy? [4]

g) What are the advantages and disadvantages of using oil as a source of energy? [4]

h) What changes in the use of different energy resources do you expect to happen in the next
   10 years?
   Explain your answer. [2]

10 **a)** Explain how atoms can emit different kinds of electromagnetic radiation. [4

This diagram shows pathways of three kinds of ionising radiation, travelling through air from three different radioactive sources.

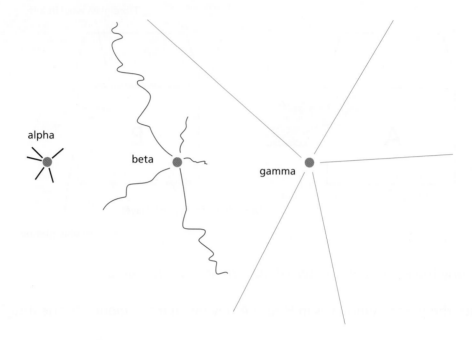

alpha

beta

gamma

b) What does 'radioactive' mean? [3

c) What does 'ionising' mean? [2

d) Which kind of radiation travels furthest through air? [1

e) i) Which kind of radiation runs out of energy soonest? [1

ii) How can you tell this from the diagram? [1

iii) Why does it run out of energy? [3

11 **a)** Describe how you could demonstrate that there is a magnetic field around a wire that carries a current. [2]

b) Describe how you can use a wire to provide a strong magnetic field. [2]

c) A magnetic effect produced when there is a current in a wire.

   i) What other effect is there? [1]

   ii) How does your answer to part **i)** affect transfer of energy from a circuit? [1]

   iii) Explain how this transfer of energy from a circuit can be useful. [1]

d) **i)** The graph of current against potential difference for a wire is like line **A** in the diagram below.

   Explain why it is like line **A** and not line **B**. [1]

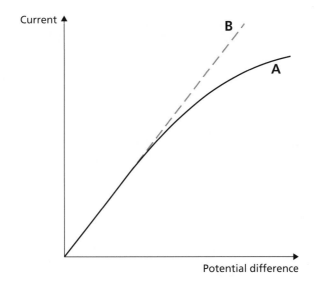

   ii) In what way is the graph for a thermistor different to the graph above? [2]

e) Nowadays, LEDs are usually used for lighting rather than wires in light bulbs. LEDs are much more efficient.

What does 'efficient' mean in this case? [1]

Total Marks .... / 121

ANSWERS

Pages 10–11 KS3 Biology Review Questions

1. **Any three from:** nucleus [1]; cell membrane [1]; cytoplasm [1]; mitochondria [1]; ribosomes [1]
2. For rigidity / support [1]
3. They are the site of photosynthesis [1]
4. A biological catalyst [1]
5. **Any one from:** amylase [1]; carbohydrase [1]
6. They are denatured / lose their shape [1]
7. Genes [1]
8. A [1]; B [1]; D [1]
9. In the nucleus [1]
10. Double helix [1]
11. To release energy [1]
12. oxygen + glucose → [1]; carbon dioxide (+ energy) [1]
13. water + carbon dioxide $\xrightarrow[\text{chlorophyll}]{\text{light}}$ [1]; oxygen + glucose [1]
14. Starch [1]
15. Cellulose [1]; proteins [1] (Accept any other named molecule, e.g. lignin)
16. The net movement of molecules from an area of high concentration to an area of low concentration [1]

> **Net** is a really important word. Molecules will be moving in both directions, so it is the overall (the **net**) direction that is important.

17. Between the alveoli [1]; and the blood [1]
18. **Any three from:** large surface area [1]; moist [1]; cells have very thin walls [1]; good supply of blood to carry oxygen away once it has diffused into blood [1]
19. cell, tissue, organ, organ system [2] (1 mark for two words in the correct position)

> The arrow means 'eaten by' and shows the flow of energy through the chain. Do **not** get it round the wrong way.

20. leaf → caterpillar → bird → fox [2] (1 mark if organisms are in the correct order; 1 mark if arrows are pointing in the correct direction)
21. Direction of flow of energy [1] (Accept 'eaten by')
22. Oxygen [1]
23. Carbon dioxide [1]
24. Carbon dioxide [1]
25. No longer exists [1]
26. A diet that contains foods from each food group [1]; in the correct proportions for that individual [1]; includes carbohydrates, fats, proteins, vitamins, minerals, fibre and water [1]

> Stating 'in the correct proportion' is important. For instance, the balance of foods in a bodybuilder's diet would be different from an elderly lady's. You need to show that you understand this.

27. Proteins [1]; fats [1]; carbohydrates [1]; minerals [1]; vitamins [1]
28. **Any three recreational drugs, such as:** alcohol [1]; nicotine [1]; cannabis [1]; heroin [1]
29. Liver [1]
30. Haemoglobin [1]
31. a) C [1]
    b) A [1]
    c) B [1]
    d) Alveoli / air sacs [1]
    e) Diffusion [1]
    f) To trap microorganisms [1]

Pages 12–13 KS3 Chemistry Review Questions

1. Distilled water = compound [1]; Gold = element [1]; Glucose = compound [1]; Salt water = mixture [1]
2. a) B [1]; C [1]
   b) magnesium + oxygen → magnesium oxide [2] (1 mark for correct reactants; 1 mark for correct product)
3. A correctly drawn diagram of the particles in a solid [1]; liquid [1]; and gas [1]

Solid   Liquid   Gas

4. D [1]
5. a) An alkali / base [1]
   b) B [1]
6. a) The elements are very unreactive [1]; and will not react with oxygen or other elements [1]
   b) **Any four from:** Aluminium is very reactive [1]; aluminium is higher than carbon in the reactivity series [1]; aluminium can only be extracted using electricity / electrolysis [1]; electrictiy was not readily available until the beginning of the 19th century [1]; gold and platinum would be found in elemental / unreacted form [1]
7. a) Red [1]
   b) Yellow [1]
   c) Green [1]
   d) Blue [1]
8. a) D [1]
   b) C [1]
   c) B [1]
9. Solid water / ice is less dense than liquid water [1]; this means that under the ice there is liquid water [1]

Pages 14–15 KS3 Physics Review Questions

1. A [1]
2. C [1]
3. B [1]
4. C [1]
5. B [1]
6. D [1]
7. B [1]
8. B [1]
9. D [1]

10. a) i) 1000kg [1]
       ii) 2400kg [1]
    b) mass = density × volume [1]; = 1000 × 0.01 [1]; = 10kg [1]
    c) 10kg [1]
    d) The Moon has weaker gravity / lower gravitational field strength [1]; because it is smaller / less massive (than Earth) [1]
    e) i) reduces it [1]
       ii) reduces it [1]
       iii) no change [1]
11. a) The particles in gases have large spaces between them [1]; and move around rapidly [1]; so the two different particles easily mix [1]
    b) The particles in solids are held together by strong forces [1]; and cannot move far away from their positions [1]

Pages 16–31 Revise Questions

Page 17 Quick Test
1. ×40
2. a) Mitochondria
   b) Chloroplasts
   c) Cell membrane
   d) Cytoplasm
3. **Any two from:** cell wall; vacuole; chloroplasts

Page 19 Quick Test
1. They increase the rate of reaction
2. **Any three from:** temperature; pH; substrate concentration; enzyme concentration
3. Enzymes have an active site in which only a specific substrate can fit

Page 21 Quick Test
1. oxygen + glucose → carbon dioxide + water (+ energy)

> When writing equations, always make sure the reactants are to the left of the arrow and the products are to the right.

2. Mitochondria
3. (Energy), alcohol and carbon dioxide
4. a) Protease
   b) Lipase
   c) Carbohydrase

Page 23 Quick Test
1. a) Water and carbon dioxide
   b) Oxygen and glucose
2. Chloroplasts
3. Enzymes are denatured

Page 25 Quick Test
1. In diffusion, substances move from a high to a low concentration (with a concentration gradient). In active transport, substances move from a

low concentration to a high concentration against the concentration gradient. Active transport requires energy.

2. Glucose; oxygen (accept amino acids and carbon dioxide)

3. To replace dead and damaged cells to allow growth and repair

4. a) From human embryos
   b) From adult bone marrow

Page 27 Quick Test

1. Large surface area to volume ratio; thin membranes; a good supply of transport medium

2. They are more complex and have a smaller surface area to volume ratio

3. It achieves a higher blood pressure and greater flow of blood to the tissues

Page 29 Quick Test

1. They have a small lumen and their walls are thick and muscular with elastic fibres

2. Substances are exchanged between blood and the tissues

3. Biconcave, which increases the surface area for absorbing oxygen; contains haemoglobin, which binds to oxygen; it does not have a nucleus – therefore, more space for oxygen

Page 31 Quick Test

1. Nitrates; phosphates; potassium

2. a) Water (and minerals)
   b) Glucose

3. Wind velocity; temperature; humidity

Pages 32–37 Practice Questions

Page 32 Cell Structures

1. Plant: all boxes ticked [1]; Animal: crosses against cell wall and chloroplasts, all other boxes ticked [1]; Bacteria: crosses against nuclear membrane and chloroplasts, all other boxes ticked [1]

2. a) i) Black / blue [1]
      ii) Pink [1]
   b) 10 × 40 = 400 [1]

3. Cell B [1]

Page 33 What Happens in Cells

1. a) Double helix [1]
   b) In the nucleus [1]

2. a)

   Substrate [1]
   Enzyme [1]
   Active site [1]

   b) Denatured / lose its shape [1]; will not work [1]
   c) **Any one from:** pH [1]; substrate concentration [1]; enzyme concentration [1]

Page 33 Respiration

1.

	Aerobic	Anaerobic
Where it Occurs	mitochondria [1]	cytoplasm [1]
Energy Release	high [1]	low [1]
Breakdown of Glucose	complete [1]	incomplete [1]

2. glucose [1] + oxygen [1] → water [1] + carbon dioxide [1] (+ energy)

Page 34 Photosynthesis

1. carbon dioxide [1] + water [1] $\xrightarrow{\text{light energy}}$ glucose [1] + oxygen [1]

2. a) Palisade cell [1]
   b) Chloroplasts [1]
   c) Chlorophyll [1]

Page 34 Supplying the Cell

1. a) **Any two from:** glucose [1]; oxygen [1]; water [1]
   b) Diffusion [1]
   c) Unicellular [1]

2. net [1]; high [1]; low [1]; against [1]; energy [1]

3. C [1]

4. Growth [1]; repair [1]

5. Bone marrow [1]

6. Embryos are 'killed' / embryos are disposed of (Accept any other sensible answer) [1]

Page 36 The Challenges of Size

1. a) The lungs [1]
   b) Red blood cell [1]
   c) Alveolus [1]
   d) Carbon dioxide [1]
   e) Oxygen [1]

Page 36 The Heart and Blood Cells

1. a) A = pulmonary artery [1]; B = aorta [1]; C = atrium [1]; D = ventricle [1]
   b) Atrioventricular valve [1]
   c) To stop blood flowing backwards from ventricle to atria [1]
   d) The lungs [1]

2. Capillary – smallest blood vessels [1]; and thin permeable walls [1]
   Artery – thick muscular walls [1]; and small lumen [1]
   Vein – large lumen [1]; and has valves [1]

3. **Any three from:** carbon dioxide [1]; glucose [1]; nutrients [1]; hormones [1]; antibodies [1]; water [1]; minerals [1]; vitamins [1]

Page 37 Plants, Water and Minerals

1. a) active transport [1]
   b) osmosis [1]
   c) diffusion [1]
   d) active transport [1]

2. To open / close stomata [1]; to control water loss in plants [1]

3. a) Increase [1]
   b) Increase [1]
   c) Decrease [1]

Pages 38–49 Revise Questions

Page 39 Quick Test

1. Central and peripheral

2. a) Carries impulses from sense organs to the CNS
   b) Carries impulses from the CNS to an effector
   c) Carries impulses from the sensory neurone to the motor neurone

   Always talk about nerve **impulses**, not messages.

3. a) Light
   b) Sound

4. Impulse arrives and triggers the release of neurotransmitters into the gap. Neurotransmitters cross the gap and bind to receptors on the next neurone, which triggers a new electrical impulse. The message goes from electrical to chemical and back to electrical.

   Remember, at the synapse the impulse changes from electrical to chemical then **back** to electrical.

Page 41 Quick Test

1. a) Testosterone
   b) Thyroxine

2. Hormonal messages give a slower response; they target a more general area; their effects are longer lasting

3. FSH encourages ovaries to produce oestrogen

Page 43 Quick Test

1. Oestrogen; progesterone

2. They are very effective; they can reduce the risk of getting some types of cancer

3. They do not protect against sexually transmitted diseases; they can have side effects

4. Social: involves people
   Economic: involves cost
   Ethical: involves morals

Page 45 Quick Test

1. Enzymes have an optimum temperature and their action slows / stops if the temperature is above or below the optimum temperature

   Enzymes are not denatured by low temperatures, they just have a slower rate of action.

2. Type 2

3. a) Pancreas
   b) It causes glucose to be converted to glycogen for storage and increases the permeability of cell membranes to glucose

Answers

Make sure you understand the difference between the terms glucose and glycogen. Do not get them mixed up.

Page 47 Quick Test
1. Water is needed to stay alive; the recycling of water influences climate and maintains habitats; recycling water brings fresh supplies of nutrients to habitats
2. Nitrogen-fixing; nitrifying; denitrifying; putrefying
3. Photosynthesis; dissolved in seas

Page 49 Quick Test
1. A community is all the organisms (plants and animals) within an ecosystem; a population is all the individuals of the same species within a community
2. **Any two biotic factors:** food; predators; pollinators; disease; human activity, e.g. deforestation
   Any two abiotic factors: temperature; light; moisture or pH of soil; salinity of water
3. **Any three from:** food; space; water; mates
4. Parasitism is when one organism lives in / on another organism and benefits; mutualism is when two organisms depend on each other and both benefit

Pages 50–53 Review Questions

Page 50 Cell Structures
1. Four correctly drawn lines **[3]** (2 marks for two lines; 1 mark for one)
   chloroplast – contains chlorophyll
   cell wall – gives support
   cell membrane – controls movement of substances in and out of the cell
   mitochondria – contains the enzymes for respiration

Page 50 What Happens in Cells
1. It becomes denatured / loses its shape **[1]**; and stops working **[1]**
2. protein **[1]**; amino acid **[1]**; speed up **[1]**; denatured **[1]**; optimum **[1]**

Page 50 Respiration
1. a) Lactic acid **[1]**
   b) His muscles are demanding more energy so respiration must go faster **[1]**; so his breathing rate increases to provide more oxygen for respiration **[1]**; if the demand is great he may go into anaerobic respiration **[1]**; in which case the heavy breathing will be to pay back the oxygen debt **[1]**
   c) i) Aerobic **[1]**
      ii) oxygen + glucose **[1]**; → carbon dioxide + water (+ energy) **[1]**
      iii) Mitochondria **[1]**

Page 51 Photosynthesis
1. a) Plants will photosynthesise more in warmer conditions **[1]**; therefore, grow faster **[1]**
   b) A paraffin heater will release carbon dioxide **[1]**; photosynthesis increases with increased levels of carbon dioxide **[1]**
   c) **Any one from:** increase light levels **[1]**; increase carbon dioxide levels **[1]**; use fertilisers **[1]**
   d) carbon dioxide + water **[1]**; → glucose + oxygen **[1]**
2. chlorophyll **[1]**; absorbs **[1]**; water **[1]**; carbon dioxide **[1]**

Page 52 Supplying the Cell
1. They have a large surface area **[1]**
2. a) Glucose **[1]**
   b) Red blood cell **[1]**
   c) C **[1]**

Page 52 The Challenges of Size
1. a) Diffusion **[1]**
   b) A specialised transport system is needed to transport materials over long distances in the monkey **[1]**; *Paramecium* has larger surface area / volume ratio **[1]**; so can rely on diffusion **[1]**

When asked about transport of materials in large and small organisms, always refer to surface area to volume ratio.

Page 53 The Heart and Blood Cells
1. a) A **[1]**
   b) A **[1]**
   c) B **[1]**
   d) B **[1]**
   e) A correctly drawn arrow labelled L **[1]**

   L ⟶ ◉

Page 53 Plants, Water and Minerals
1. Transpiration **[1]**
2. a) Xylem **[1]**
   b) Water / minerals **[1]**
   c) Made of dead cells with end walls removed **[1]**
3. Active transport **[1]**

Pages 54–57 Practice Questions

Page 54 Coordination and Control
1. a) Light **[1]**
   b) Ears **[1]**
   c) Smell **[1]**
   d) Tongue **[1]**
   e) and f) **Any two from:** touch **[1]**; pressure **[1]**; pain **[1]**; temperature change **[1]**

The skin cannot sense temperature, it can only sense a **temperature change**.

2. electrical **[1]**; synapse **[1]**; neurotransmitters **[1]**; receptors **[1]**
3. A **[1]**; C **[1]**
4. a) Motor neurone **[1**
   b) Sensory neurone **[1**
   c) Relay neurone **[1**

Page 55 The Endocrine System
1. In the blood stream **[1**
2. Three correctly drawn lines **[2** (1 mark for one)
   oestrogen – causes the lining of the uterus to thicken, progesterone – maintains the lining of the uterus, FSH – stimulates the release of an egg

Page 55 Hormones and Their Uses
1. a) Less effective than the combined pill **[1**
   b) Causes a thick sticky mucus which stops sperm reaching egg **[1**
   c) The ovaries **[1**
   d) Do not protect against STDs / can have side effects **[1**

Page 56 Maintaining Internal Environments
1. a) Diffusion **[1**
   b) Respiration **[1**
2. Graph B, **plus any two of:** because the blood glucose levels are higher to start with **[1]**; the rise in glucose is higher **[1]**; it takes a longer time for the glucose level to go down **[1]**

Page 57 Recycling
1. Four correctly drawn lines **[3]** (2 marks for two correct lines; 1 mark for one) nitrogen gas turned into nitrates by bacteria in plant roots – nitrogen-fixing,
   animal and plant material and waste products turned into ammonium compounds – putrefying, ammonium compounds turned into nitrates – nitrifying, nitrates turned into nitrogen gas – denitrifying
2. a) i) E **[1**
      ii) D **[1**
      iii) G **[1**
      iv) A **[1**
      v) F **[1**
   b) Death / excretion **[1**
   c) **Any one from:** combustion / burning **[1]**; evaporation of seas **[1]**

Page 57 Interdependence
1. Biotic: animals **[1]**; bacteria **[1]**; trees **[1]**; detritivores **[1]**
   Abiotic: rivers **[1]**; soil **[1]**; sea **[1]**
2. **Any three from:** amount of light / shade **[1]**; minerals in soil **[1]**; water content of soil **[1]**; temperature of soil **[1]**
3. a) Both organisms benefit **[1]**; the cleaner fish get food **[1]**; and the larger fish is clean / parasite free **[1]**
   b) Parasitism **[1**

Answers

Page 59 Quick Test
1. An organism's complete set of DNA, including all of its genes
2. A capital letter shows a dominant allele; a lower case letter shows a recessive allele
3. **Any two from:** height; weight; skin colour; intelligence (Accept any other sensible answer)
4. a) **Any one from:** height; weight (Accept any other sensible answer)
   b) **Any one from:** blood group; right or left handed; shoe size (Accept any other sensible answer)

Page 61 Quick Test
1. Haploid cells have half the number of chromosomes found in a diploid cell, as they have just one copy of each chromosome, e.g. sperm or egg cell; diploid cells have two copies of each chromosome, e.g. normal body cell.
2. Meiosis produces gametes with half the number of chromosomes as body cells; during fertilisation, two gametes from different individuals fuse together; this produces a new combination of genes creating variation
3. Female
4. Eggs will always carry an X chromosome; sperm cells may carry an X or a Y chromosome; there is a 50% chance that an egg will fuse with a sperm carrying an X chromosome = XX (female); and there is a 50% chance that an egg will fuse with a sperm carrying a Y chromosome = XY (male)

Page 63 Quick Test
1. There is natural variation within any population; organisms with characteristics best suited to the environment are likely to survive, breed and pass on their successful genes to the next generation; animals with poor characteristics less well suited to the environment are less likely to survive and breed

> Don't forget 'breed and pass on genes'. It is an easy way to get two marks.

2. A bacterium mutates to become resistant to the antibiotic that is being used; the antibiotic kills all the sensitive bacteria; the resistant bacteria multiply creating a population of antibiotic-resistant bacteria
3. Organisms that are found to have very similar DNA will share common ancestors

Page 65 Quick Test
1. Sweep net
2. $\dfrac{20 \times 10}{4} = 50$

Page 67 Quick Test
1. Measurements should be repeated
2. A result that does not fit the pattern of the rest of the results

3. Errors that are made every time that may be due to faulty equipment
4. It checks the design of the experiment and the validity of the data

Page 69 Quick Test
1. The genes may get into wild flowers or crops; they may harm the consumers; we don't know the long-term effects
2. Selecting organisms with desirable traits and breeding them
3. a) **Any two from:** hunting; overfishing; deforestation; farming single crops
   b) **Any two from:** creating nature reserves; reforestation; sustainable fishing

Page 71 Quick Test
1. **Any four from:** bacteria; viruses; fungi; protoctista; parasites
2. **Any three from:** air; water; food; contact; animals
3. **Any three from:** the skin; platelets; mucous membranes; stomach acid; eyelashes / tears
4. AIDS is the name of the disease; HIV is the name of the virus that causes the disease

Page 73 Quick Test
1. White blood cells recognise the antigens on the dead or weakened pathogen that is in the vaccination. They make antibodies but also form memory cells. In a subsequent infection, memory cells produce antibodies quickly and in large numbers.

> Antibodies are produced **rapidly** and in **large numbers** in subsequent infections. These two words may gain you two marks.

2. Antibiotics act on bacteria; antivirals act on viruses; antiseptics are used on skin and surfaces to kill microorganisms
3. Measles, mumps and rubella
4. To check they are safe (toxicity); to ensure they work (efficacy); to find out the correct dosage

Page 75 Quick Test
1. Too much carbohydrate / fat can lead to obesity, which leads to high blood pressure and cardiovascular disease; a high fat diet can lead to increased levels of cholesterol, which coats the smooth lining of the arteries, causing them to narrow, restricting blood flow and leading to heart attacks or strokes and high blood pressure; a diet high in salt can lead to high blood pressure.

> Remember, cholesterol coats **arteries** not veins.

2. Cancer is when cells grow and divide uncontrollably

3. Change in lifestyle; medication; surgery
4. Stem cells may develop into tumours / may be rejected by the patient

Page 76 Coordination and Control
1. a) Eyes [1]
   b) Voluntary response [1]
   c) Muscles in feet / legs [1]
2. a) Motor neurone [1]
   b) Arrow drawn pointing from left to right, i.e. ⟶ [1]

Page 76 The Endocrine System
1. Oestrogen levels will increase from day 2 to day 14 [1]

Page 77 Hormones and Their Uses
1. progesterone [1]; oestrogen [1]; more [1]; side effects [1]

Page 77 Maintaining Internal Environments
1. a) Active transport [1]
   b) Glucose enters cells [1]; Glucose is converted to glycogen [1]

Page 78 Recycling
1. a) Nitrogen-fixing [1]
   b) They turn nitrogen in the air into nitrates [1]; which plants need for growth [1]
2. a) Photosynthesis [1]
   b) Eaten by / consumption [1]

Page 78 Interdependence
1. **Any two from:** amount of space available [1]; amount of food / prey [1]; amount of water [1]; numbers of predators [1]
2. a) **Any three from:** space [1]; shelter [1]; water [1]; food [1]
   b) Grey squirrels have a more varied diet so they are less likely to be affected by shortages of food [1]; grey squirrels have two litters per year, therefore, they are outcompeting the red squirrels. [1]
3. natural [1]; community [1]; population [1]
4. **Abiotic:** A [1]; B [1]; E [1]
   Biotic: C [1]; D [1]

Page 80 Genes
1. cell, nucleus, chromosome, gene [1] (1 mark for three in the correct place)
2. a) Dominant [1]
   b) Heterozygous [1]
   c) ee [1]

Page 80 Genetics and Reproduction
1. 23 + [1]; 23 [1]; = 46 [1]
2. 4 [1]
3. a) 1 = FF [1]; 2 = Ff [1]; 3 = Ff [1]; 4 = ff [1]

Answers

b) 2 [1]; 3 [1]

c) 4 [1]

Page 81 Natural Selection and Evolution

1. A bacterium mutates to become resistant [1]; sensitive bacteria are killed by the antibiotic [1]; resistant bacteria multiply rapidly to form large population [1]

2. a) C and D [1]
   b) E and F [1]
   c) C and G [1]

Page 82 Monitoring and Maintaining the Environment

1. Four correctly drawn lines [3] (2 marks for two correct lines; 1 mark for one)
   The variety of water invertebrates in the canal – Pond net
   The variety of plants growing by the side of the canal – Quadrat
   The variety of flying insects in the long grass by the side of the canal – Sweep net
   The variety of invertebrates found under the hedges along the side of the canal – Pitfall trap

2. $\frac{12 \times 10}{4}$ [1]; = 30 [1]

Page 82 Investigations

1. Answer must have:
   Suitable number / range of temperatures (minimum of 3 temperatures at between 20 and 50°C) [1]
   Suitable number of peas used at each temperature (minimum 5) [1]
   Suitable time period to leave peas (2–3 days) [1]
   Simple method (must include adding water) [1]
   At least **two** other controlled variables (amount of water / size of peas / type of peas / amount of light / same growth medium, e.g. soil or cotton wool) [1]

Page 83 Resources and the Environment

1. B, E, A, C, D [1]

Page 83 Monitoring and Maintaining Health

1. Four correctly drawn lines [3] (2 marks for two correct lines; 1 mark for one)
   Malaria – Animal vector
   Cholera – By water
   Tuberculosis – By air
   Athlete's foot – Contact

2. lungs [1]; HIV [1]; immune [1]

3. A [1]; C [1]

> Do not confuse AIDS and HIV. HIV is the name of the virus. AIDS is the disease it causes.

4. a) A = microorganism, B = antibody, C = antigen [2] (1 mark for one correct)
   b) lymphocyte [1]

Page 84 Prevention and Treatment of Disease

1. a) Bacteria [1]
   b) Because there will still be microorganisms present even when he is feeling better [1]; without antibiotics these could start to multiply again, or even mutate into resistant strains [1]
   c) The sore throat may be due to a viral infection [1]; and antibiotics only kill bacteria [1]

2. D, A, B, C [3] (2 marks for two in correct places; 1 mark for one)

3. To test for efficacy / efficiency [1]; toxicity / safety [1]; dosage [1]

4. a) Bacteria / microorganisms [1]
   b) i) Antiseptic [1]
   ii) **Any one from:** gloves [1]; masks [1]; gowns [1]; all equipment sterilised [1]

Page 85 Non-Communicable Diseases

1. a) Statins [1]
   b) A stent [1]

2. High fat diet can lead to high cholesterol [1]; which narrows arteries [1]; causing high blood pressure, which puts a strain on heart [1] **OR** high salt intake [1]; causes high blood pressure [1]; which puts a strain on heart [1] **OR** eating more kJ energy / calories than used [1] leads to obesity [1]; which causes cardiovascular disease [1]

3. **Any four from:** drink less alcohol [1]; eat less [1]; lower salt intake [1]; switch to low fat products [1]; exercise more [1]

4. **Any two from:** Type 2 diabetes [1]; joint problems [1]; heart disease [1]; high blood pressure [1]; high cholesterol [1]

5. C [1]

Pages 86–95 Revise Questions

Page 87 Quick Test

1. Different forms of an element with the same number of protons but a different number of neutrons

2. 8 (14 – 6 = 8)

3. New experimental evidence has led to changes

Page 89 Quick Test

1. 58.3 g

2. Mixtures of substances in solution

3. CH_3

Page 91 Quick Test

1. By atomic number; by number of electrons in the outermost shell

2. Magnesium, 2.8.2

3. 2.8.7

Page 93 Quick Test

1. The electrons in the outermost shells of the metal atoms are free to move, so there are a large number of electrons moving between the metal ions.

2. **Any two from:** Distances between electrons and the nucleus are not realistic; bonds appear to be physical structures; bond lengths are not in proportion to the size of the atom; they do not give a good idea of the 3D shape of the atoms.

3. A 3D arrangement of a large number of repeating units (molecules / atoms) joined together by covalent bonds.

Page 95 Quick Test

1. A compound that contains carbon

2. It is a giant covalent molecule in which every carbon atom forms bonds with four other carbon atoms (the maximum number of bonds possible).

3. Allotropes are different physical forms of the same element, for example, graphite, graphene and diamond are all allotropes of carbon (they only contain carbon atoms but have different structures and, therefore, different properties)

Pages 96–101 Review Questions

Page 96 Genes

1. a) Combination [1]
   b) Genetics [1]
   c) Environment [1]
   d) Combination [1]
   e) Environment [1]

2. a) i) No sickle cell anaemia [1]
   ii) No sickle cell anaemia but a carrier [1]
   iii) Sickle cell anaemia sufferer [1]
   b) Aa [1]

3. a) Continuous: height [1]; weight [1]
   Discontinuous: eye colour [1]; shoe size [1]; freckles [1]
   b) i) Bar correctly plotted to show 7 people [1]
   ii) **Accept:** 0, 1 or 2 [1]

Page 97 Genetics and Reproduction

1. Meiosis [1]

2. a) Correct gametes [1]; correct offspring [1]

	Brown eyes	Brown eyes
Parents	Bb	Bb
Gametes	B b	B b
Offspring	BB Bb	Bb bb

   b) Heterozygous [1]

c) Three brown : one blue / 3 : 1 **[1]**

> Ratios can be expressed in a number of ways: 3 : 1, 75% : 25%, 0.75 : 0.25

d) 100% **[1]**

Page 97 Natural Selection and Evolution
1. a) Genus **[1]**
   b) New DNA evidence shows it to be very closely related to grey wolf **[1]**
   c) New fossils discovered **[1]**
   d) A group of similar animals that can breed to produce fertile offspring **[1]**

Page 98 Monitoring and Maintaining the Environment
1. a) A **[1]**
   b) $100 \times 50 = 5000 m^2$ **[1]**
   c) $1.7 \times 5000 = 8500$ **[1]**

Page 98 Investigations
1. a) Use the tape measure to mark a transect line from the river outwards across the field **[1]**; at suitable intervals, place a quadrat **[1]**; count the number of meadow buttercups in the quadrat **[1]**; measure the moisture content of the soil using the moisture meter **[1]**; repeat the transect in different areas / repeat and calculate and average **[1]**
   b) i) Mean = $39 \div 10 = 3.9$ **[1]**; mode = 4 **[1]**; median = 4 **[1]**
      ii) 1 **[1]**
      iii) **Any two from:** chance **[1]**; error made in counting **[1]**; net swept at different level **[1]**; net swept in different direction / angle **[1]**

Page 99 Resources and the Environment
1. A **[1]**
   Three correctly drawn lines **[2]** (1 mark for one correct line)
   wheat – large grain size,
   potato plant – large tubers,
   tomato plant – sweet tasting **[1]**

Page 100 Monitoring and Maintaining Health
1. a) Athlete's foot **[1]**
   b) Flu **[1]**
   c) Tuberculosis **[1]**
2. a) Phagocytosis **[1]**

> Remember, the word **phagocytosis** means to devour the cell.

   b) A phagocyte **[1]**
3. a) Form a clot **[1]**; which seals the wound **[1]**
   b) Trap microorganisms and dirt **[1]**
4. The antibodies produced against the tuberculosis (TB) bacterium are designed to recognise and lock onto the antigens on its surface (or accept:

specific to TB bacteria) **[1]**; the antigens on the cholera virus are different **[1]**; and the TB antibodies will not recognise them or fit onto them **[1]**

Page 101 Prevention and Treatment of Disease
1. a) Dead / weakened measles virus **[1]**
   b) Tanya already had antibodies against the measles virus **[1]**; she also has memory cells **[1]**; which can quickly produce large numbers of antibodies **[1]**
   c) In the air / moisture droplets **[1]**
   d) Measles is caused by a virus **[1]**; antibiotics cannot be used for viral infections / can only be used for bacterial infections **[1]**
2. **Any two from:** tested on cells **[1]**; animals **[1]**; computer models **[1]**; healthy volunteers **[1]**
3. To compare the results of people taking the drug to those who have not taken the drug **[1]**

Page 101 Non-Communicable Diseases
1. a) Correctly labelled axes **[1]**; correctly plotted points **[1]**; joined by a smooth curve **[1]**

   b) 37% **[1]**
   c) **Any two from:** heart disease **[1]**; type 2 diabetes **[1]**; high blood pressure **[1]**; liver disease **[1]**

Pages 102–105 Practice Questions

Page 102 Particle Model and Atomic Structure
1. a) D **[1]**
   b) The temperature is increasing **[1]**; so the particles in the solid ice start vibrating more quickly **[1]**
2. B **[1]**
3. a) Ne **[1]**
   b) Ca **[1]**
   c) $28 + 2 = 30$ **[1]**

> It is usual for mass numbers to be rounded to the nearest whole number.

4. a) A heating curve drawn showing a straight line at 100°C **[1]**; and a straight line at 0°C **[1]**; sloping down

in direction left to right **[1]**; with correctly labelled axes **[1]**

   b) The water molecules slow down **[1]**; as they lose kinetic energy **[1]**

5. a) charge = – / negative **[1]**; relative mass = 0.0005 / zero / negligible **[1]**
   b) charge = + / positive **[1]**; relative mass = 1 **[1]**
   c) charge = 0 / neutral **[1]**; relative mass = 1 **[1]**

Page 103 Purity and Separating Mixtures
1. a) Containing one type of atom or molecule only **[1]**
   b) Every substance has a specific boiling point at room temperature and pressure **[1]**; if the substance boils at a different temperature, it indicates that there are impurities **[1]**
2. a) Distance moved by the solvent = 28 **[1]**; $R_f = \dfrac{\text{distance moved by the compound}}{\text{distance moved by the solvent}}$,

   $R_f \text{ (pink)} = \dfrac{7.5}{28} = 0.27$ **[1]**;

   $R_f \text{ (purple)} = \dfrac{17.5}{28} = 0.63$ **[1]**
   b) D **[1]**
3. C_4H_4S **[1]**
4. $C = \dfrac{84}{12} = 7$ **[1]**; $H = \dfrac{16}{1} = 16$, $O = \dfrac{64}{16} = 4$ **[1]**;

   $C_7H_{16}O_4$ **[1]**

> Look for common factors to see whether an empirical formula can be simplified further.

5. A **[1]**

Page 103 Bonding
1. a) H = 1, Na = 11, Mg = 12, C = 6, O = 8, K = 19, Ca = 20, Al = 13 **[2]** (1 mark for 6–7 correct; 0 marks for 5 or less correct)
   b) $(2 \times 39.1) + 16 = 94.1$ **[1]** (Accept 94)
   c) $16 \times 2 = 32$ **[1]**
2. a) They all have the same number of electrons in their outer shell **[1]**
   b) They all have the same number of shells / they all have two shells **[1]**
3. a) C **[1]**
   b) B = 2.8.1 **[1]**; E = 2.8.7 **[1]**
   c) Electrons **[1]**

Answers

Page 104 Models of Bonding
1. a) An atom or molecule that has
      gained or lost electrons **[1]**
   b) A correctly drawn sodium ion (2.8) **[1]**;
      and chloride ion (2.8.8) **[1]**

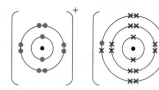

Sodium ion,   Chloride ion,
Na$^+$ Cl$^-$

2. a) A bond formed by the sharing **[1]**; of
      two outer electrons **[1]**
   b) Two correctly drawn chlorine atoms
      (each with 7 electrons) **[1]**; overlapping
      and sharing two electrons **[1]**

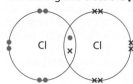

3. a) A large structure that is made up of
      repeating units (atoms / molecules) **[1]**;
      that are covalently bonded together **[1]**
   b) The atoms in the water / H_2O
      molecules are covalently bonded
      [1]; but each water molecule is
      separate – there is no covalent bond
      between the water molecules **[1]**

Page 105 Properties of Materials
1. a) **Any three from:** Carbon has four
      electrons in its outer shell **[1]**; it can
      form covalent bonds **[1]**; with up to
      four other atoms **[1]**; and can form
      chains **[1]**
   b) An allotrope is a different form of an
      element **[1]**
   c) **Any three from:** graphite **[1]**;
      diamond **[1]**; fullerene /
      buckminsterfullerene **[1]**; graphene
      [1]; lonsdaleite **[1]**; amorphous
      carbon **[1]**
2. a) It conducts electricity because it has
      free electrons **[1]**; and it is stronger
      than steel **[1]**
   b) Diamond does not conduct electricity **[1]**
   c) A diagram showing each carbon
      joined to four other carbon atoms **[1]**;
      with a minimum of five atoms shown
      in tetrahedral arrangement **[1]**

Diamond

Covalent bond
between two
carbon atoms

---

3. a) The ions must be either molten **[1]**;
      or dissolved in aqueous solution **[1]**
   b) In crystalline form, the distance
      between the ions is at its smallest /
      the ions are close together **[1]**; so the
      electrostatic forces are very high and
      have to be overcome for the crystal
      to melt **[1]**
4. C **[1]**

Page 107 Quick Test
1. $Ca(OH)_2$
2. $2Na(s) + Cl_2(g) \rightarrow 2NaCl(s)$
3. 2Mg, 2S, 8O ($2 \times O_4$)

Page 109 Quick Test
1. BaO, CuF_2, $AlCl_3$
2. Al_2O_3
3. The minimum amount of energy
   needed to start a reaction
4.

Reaction Profile for an
Endothermic Reaction

Energy ▲

Energy is
absorbed
from
surroundings

Products

Reactants

Progress of Reaction →

Page 111 Quick Test
1. Carbon dioxide
2. Zinc nitrate
3. copper oxide + sulfuric acid →
                      copper sulfate + water

Page 113 Quick Test
1. In solution (aq) / molten
2. The anode
3. Set up an electrolytic cell using a silver
   anode. Place the key at the cathode.
   Add a solution containing silver ions as
   the electrolyte.

Page 115 Quick Test
1. Iodine
2. The outermost electron in caesium is
   much further away from the nucleus
   than in lithium, so the force of
   attraction is weaker (it can lose this
   electron more easily)
3. Lithium

Page 116 Particle Model and Atomic Structure
1. a) It has evaporated **[1]**
   b) Increase the temperature of the
      room / switch on a fan **[1]**
   c) i) A diagram showing more
         than five particles, with at
         least 50% of the particles
         touching **[1]**

---

   ii) A diagram showing more than
       five particles, with none of the
       particles touching **[1]**

In cup   In air

2. D **[1]**
3.

Subatomic Particle	Relative Mass	Relative Charge
Proton **[1]** ●	1	+1 (positive) **[1]**
Neutron ●	1 **[1]**	0 (neutral)
Electron ✲	Negligible **[1]**	–1 (negative) **[1]**

4. a) Protons **[1]**
   b) The positively charged protons are at
      the centre of the atom **[1]**; so, only
      alpha particles travelling close to the
      centre of the atom will be repelled /
      deflected by them **[1]**

   Alpha particles are positively charged.
   Like charges repel each other.

5. He: 2 (4 – 2) **[1]**; Na: 12 (23 – 11) **[1]**;
   V: 28 (51 – 23) **[1]**

Page 117 Purity and Separating Mixtures
1. a) Measure its boiling point **[1]**;
      compare the boiling point with data
      from a data book / known values **[1]**
   b) The water is not pure **[1]**; it contains
      other substances **[1]**
2. a) CH_2O **[1]**

   In $C_6H_{12}O_6$ the common factor of all
   the numbers is 6, so divide by six to
   simplify the formula.

   b) CH_2O **[1]**

   Collect all the atoms of the same
   element together first, and then
   simplify: $CH_3COOH \rightarrow C_2H_4O_2 \rightarrow CH_2O$

   c) C_2H_4O **[1]**
3. a) $(6 \times 12) + (12 \times 1) + (6 \times 16) = 180$ **[1]**
   b) $(2 \times 12) + (4 \times 1) + (2 \times 16) = 60$ **[1]**
   c) $(1 \times 12) + (2 \times 16) = 44$ **[1]**
   d) $(2 \times 1) + (32.1) + (4 \times 16) = 98.1$ **[1]**
      (Accept 98)
4. Alloy **[1]**
5. C **[1]**

Page 118 Bonding
1. Mendeleev **[1]**
2. a) A **[1]**; E **[1]**
   b) A **[1]**; B **[1]**
   c) B **[1]**
   d) A = 3 **[1]**; B = 11 **[1]**; C = 13 **[1]**;
      D = 18 **[1]**; E = 4 **[1]**

a) **Any three from:** malleable **[1]**; sonorous **[1]**; ductile **[1]**; form a positive cation **[1]**; shiny **[1]**

b) Metal oxide **[1]**

c) An ionic compound **[1]**

Page 118 Models of Bonding

. C **[1]**

. One carbon atom drawn **[1]**; with covalent bonds with four hydrogen atoms **[1]**

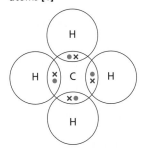

. Ball and stick models give a better picture of the 3D shape of the molecule **[1]**; and the bond angles / directions **[1]**

. A correctly drawn magnesium atom, 2.8.2 **[1]**; and magnesium ion (2.8)$^{2+}$ **[1]**

Magnesium atom, Mg

Magnesium ion, Mg^{2+}

Page 119 Properties of Materials

a) A different physical structure to other forms of the element **[1]**

b) Graphite is made of layers of atoms **[1]**; these are held together by weak forces **[1]**; so the layers can separate / slide over each other easily **[1]**; preventing the surfaces from rubbing together **[1]**

c) In diamond all possible covalent bonds have been used / each carbon atom is bonded to four other carbon atoms **[1]**; so it is extremely hard **[1]**; and has a high melting point **[1]**

> You need to mention high melting point to get the third mark. Drill bits get hot due to frictional forces, so it is an important property.

d) **Any one from:** electrical components **[1]**; solar panels **[1]**

2. C **[1]**

Page 120 Introducing Chemical Reactions

1. In a chemical reaction, the mass of the reactants will always equal the mass of the products **[1]** (Accept: No atoms are made or destroyed)

2. a) The number of atoms of that element present (the element before the number) **[1]**

b) i) C = 6, H = 12, O = 6 **[1]**
   ii) C = 3, H = 6, O = 2 **[1]**
   iii) H = 2, O = 2 **[1]**
   iv) Ca = 1, N = 2, O = 6 **[1]**

3. solid = (s), liquid = (l), gas = (g), aqueous = (aq) **[1]**

4. a) $2Mg(s) + O_2(g) \rightarrow 2MgO(s)$ **[2]**
   (1 mark for correct balancing; 1 mark for correct state symbols)

b) $4Li(s) + O_2(g) \rightarrow 2Li_2O(s)$ **[2]**
   (1 mark for correct balancing; 1 mark for correct state symbols)

c) $CaCO_3(s) + 2HCl(aq) \rightarrow CaCl_2(aq) + CO_2(g) + H_2O(l)$ **[2]** (1 mark for correct balancing; 1 mark for correct state symbols)

d) $4Al(s) + 3O_2(g) \rightarrow 2Al_2O_3(s)$ **[2]** (1 mark for correct balancing; 1 mark for correct state symbols)

Page 120 Chemical Equations and Energetics

1. a) 2+ **[1]**
   b) 2– **[1]**
   c) 3+ **[1]**
   d) 2– **[1]**

2. a) Exothermic **[1]**
   b) Endothermic **[1]**

3. **Any two from:** heating (water / central heating) **[1]**; produce electricity **[1]**; make sound **[1]**; make light **[1]**

4. The minimum energy required to start a reaction **[1]**

5. A correctly drawn reaction profile for an exothermic reaction **[1]**

Reactants

Energy is transferred to surroundings

Energy

Products

Progress of Reaction

6. A correctly drawn reaction profile for an endothermic reaction **[1]**

Energy is absorbed from surroundings

Products

Energy

Reactants

Progress of Reaction

Page 121 Types of Chemical Reactions

1. A **[1]**; C **[1]**

> Remember, oxidisation is the addition of oxygen.

2. a) $2Na(s) + Cl_2(g) \rightarrow 2NaCl(s)$ **[2]** (1 mark for correct balancing; 1 mark for correct state symbols); sodium is oxidised and chlorine is reduced **[1]**

b) $2Mg(s) + O_2(g) \rightarrow 2MgO(s)$ **[2]** (1 mark for correct balancing; 1 mark for correct state symbols); magnesium is oxidised and oxygen is reduced **[1]**

c) $2Li(s) + Br_2(g) \rightarrow 2LiBr(s)$ **[2]** (1 mark for correct balancing; 1 mark for

correct state symbols); lithium is oxidised and bromine is reduced **[1]**

d) $CuO(s) + H_2(g) \rightarrow Cu(s) + H_2O(l)$ **[2]** (1 mark for correct balancing; 1 mark for correct state symbols); copper is reduced and hydrogen is oxidised **[1]**

3. a) $H^+(aq)$ **[1]**
   b) $OH^-(aq)$ **[1]**

4. acid + base → salt + water **[1]**

5. a) $H_2SO_4(aq) + 2NaOH(aq) \rightarrow Na_2SO_4(aq) + 2H_2O(l)$ **[2]** (1 mark for correct reactants; 1 mark for correct products)

b) Na^+ **[1]**; SO_4^{2-} **[1]**

6. a) Samples of the mixture are taken and dabbed onto the paper **[1]**; the change of colour is compared to a pH chart (that shows the pH for each of the possible colours) **[1]**

b) B **[1]**

7. a) $NaOH(aq) + HNO_3(aq) \rightarrow NaNO_3(aq) + H_2O(l)$ **[2]** (1 mark for the correct reactants; 1 mark for the correct products)

b) H^+ / hydrogen **[1]**; Na^+ / sodium **[1]**

c) NO_3^{2-} / nitrate **[1]**; OH^- / hydroxide **[1]**

Page 122 Electrolysis

1. a) Cations **[1]**
   b) Anions **[1]**

2. The process of breaking down ionic compounds into simpler substances using an electric current **[1]**

3. Table salt is a solid at room temperature and pressure and electrolysis only works if the ion is in solution or molten **[1]**

4. a) Because they do not react with the products of electrolysis or the electrolyte **[1]**

b) Platinum electrodes are very expensive / the same results can be achieved using cheaper electrodes **[1]**

3. X = $Cu^{2+}(aq)$ **[1]**; Y = SO_4^{2-} (and OH^-) **[1]**

Page 123 Predicting Chemical Reactions

1. C **[1]**

2. 1 **[1]**

3. fluorine, chlorine, bromine, iodine **[1]**

4. a) A correctly drawn sodium atom (2.8.1) **[1]**; and potassium atom (2.8.8.1) **[1]**

Na

K

b) Potassium moves around more violently **[1]**; and burns with a lilac flame **[1]**

c) D **[1]**

5. Beryllium, Be **[1]**

> Group 2 elements are more reactive going down the group.

6. $Zn^{2+}(aq)$, $H^+(aq)$, $SO_4^{2-}(aq)$ **[1]**

7. Collect the gas in a test tube and bring a lit splint to the edge of the tube **[1]**; if

Answers

it burns with a squeaky pop, hydrogen is present [1]

Page 125 Quick Test
1. Rate of reaction increases
2. Increase the pressure
3. A large block of calcium carbonate has a low surface area to volume ratio compared to powder, which consists of lots of small particles with a high surface area to volume ratio.

Page 127 Quick Test
1. The steeper the line / the greater the gradient, the faster the rate of reaction
2. Catalysts reduce the activation energy (making a reaction more likely)
3. Enzymes

Page 129 Quick Test
1. Heat (in a blast furnace) with carbon
2. The oxygen that forms at the anode reacts with the carbon producing $CO_2(g)$, which then escapes, so the anode gradually wears away.

Page 131 Quick Test
1. Recycling is when the materials in an object are used for a new purpose – the refilled bottles are being reused, not recycled.
2. With some plastics, the materials may be contaminated, so it would be impractical / too expensive to recycle them.
3. To determine the environmental impact of a product throughout its life cycle, from sourcing materials through manufacture, use and disposal

Page 133 Quick Test
1. The breaking down of long-chain hydrocarbons into smaller molecules
2. The longer the chain, the greater the total amount of intermolecular forces that have to be overcome
3. **Any three from**: refinery gases / LPG – bottled gas; petrol – fuel for cars; naphtha – making other chemicals; kerosene / paraffin – aircraft fuel; diesel – fuel for cars / lorries / buses; fuel oil – fuel for power stations / ships; bitumen – tar for road surfaces / roofs (Accept any other sensible use for each fraction)

Page 135 Quick Test
1. Volcanic activity
2. Photosynthesis
3. Methane

Page 137 Quick Test
1. The burning / incomplete combustion of fossil fuels
2. Chlorine kills any bacteria in the water
3. Water that is safe to drink

Page 138 Introducing Chemical Reactions
1. a) H = 2, S = 1, O = 4 [1]
   b) Cu = 1, N = 2, O = 6 [1]
   c) C = 3, H = 6, O = 2 [1]
   d) C = 2, H = 6 [1]
2. a) $CuO(s) + H_2SO_4(aq) \rightarrow$ $CuSO_4(aq) + H_2O(l)$ [2] (1 mark for correct reactants; 1 mark for correct products)
   b) $2Mg(s) + O_2(g) \rightarrow 2MgO(s)$ [2] (1 mark for correct reactants; 1 mark for correct products)
   c) $Mg(OH)_2(aq) + 2HCl(aq) \rightarrow$ $MgCl_2(aq) + 2H_2O(l)$ [2] (1 mark for correct reactants; 1 mark for correct products)
   d) $CH_4(g) + 2O_2(g) \rightarrow CO_2(g) + 2H_2O(l)$ [2] (1 mark for correct reactants; 1 mark for correct products)
3. A [1]

Page 138 Chemical Equations and Energetics
1. a) Energy is taken in from the environment / surroundings [1]
   b) The energy comes from Atu's leg (heat energy) [1]
2. **From top to bottom:** CO_3^{2-} [1]; Li^+ [1]; iron(III) [1]; oxide [1]; SO_4^{2-} [1]

Page 139 Types of Chemical Reactions
1. A [1]; D [1]
2. a) Iron(III) oxide [1]
   b) Carbon monoxide [1]
   c) $Fe_2O_3(s) + 3CO(g) \rightarrow 2Fe(s) + 3CO_2(g)$ [2] (1 mark for the correct symbols; 1 mark for correct balancing)
3. a) $2HCl(aq)$ [1]
   b) $H_2SO_4(aq)$ [1]
   c) $2CH_3COOH(aq)$ [1]
   d) $2HF(aq)$ [1]
4. a) calcium + sulfuric acid → calcium sulfate + hydrogen [1]
   b) Above calcium [1]

Page 140 Electrolysis
1. Molten or in solution [1]
2. a) C [1]
   b) anion = oxygen [1]; cation = hydrogen [1]
   c) Metals such as aluminium have to be extracted by electrolysis [1]; which requires electricity [1]

Page 141 Predicting Chemical Reactions
1. C [1]
2. B [1]
3. caesium, rubidium, potassium, sodium, lithium [1]
4. a) i) 2.1 [1]
      ii) 2.8.2 [1]
      iii) 2.8.3 [1]
      iv) 2.6 [1]
   b) More bubbles should be drawn than in the Mg tube (at least 5 more) to show a more vigorous reaction [1]
   c) Hydrogen [1]

5. Collect the gas in a test tube and place a glowing splint into the tube [1]; if th splint relights, the gas is oxygen [1]

Page 142 Controlling Chemical Reactions
1. a) C [
   b) The higher the temperature, the faster the rate of reaction [
2. B [1]; C [1]

Page 143 Catalysts, Activation Energy and Equilibria
1. Catalysts lower the activation energy for a reaction [1]; this means that the reaction will happen more quickly whe the catalyst is present [1]
2. a) Catalase is the catalyst, so it is written over the arrow and not as a reactant [

> Remember, a catalyst is not used up in a reaction – it is not a reactant.

   b) Catalase is made of amino acids / is a protein / is an organic molecule [1]; manganese(IV) oxide is an inorganic molecule / catalyst [1]
3. a) i) A correct diagram showing particles at a low temperature [
      ii) A correct diagram showing particles at a high temperature [

Low Temperature

High Temperature

   b) The faster reactant particles move, the greater the chance of successful collisions with other reactant particles [1]; successful collisions lea to product particles being formed [1]; also, there will be more reactant particles with energy greater than the activation energy [1]
4. Nothing can enter or leave a closed system [1]; and the temperature and pressure remain the same [1]
5. B [1

Page 144 Improving Processes and Products

. B [1]
. a) copper(II) oxide + carbon →
   copper + carbon dioxide [1]
   b) For safety reasons / to prevent the
   hot contents from being ejected
   from the tube [1]
. D [1]
. B [1]

Page 145 Life Cycle Assessments and Recycling

. A, C, E and F [1]
. a) Recycled means to put the materials
   to another use / purpose [1]
   b) Extracting new materials uses a
   lot of energy, costs money and
   contributes to environmental
   pollution [1]; throwing away
   products means the materials /
   resources are no longer available [1];
   recycling means that the materials
   that would have been lost are now
   used in a different way [1]; this often
   involves less energy, lower costs
   and less waste than obtaining new
   materials [1]
   c) The cost (in money and pollution)
   is greater than the benefit gained
   from recycling the parts [1]
. A [1]; E [1]

Page 146 Crude Oil

. a) W = paraffin, X = diesel, Y = crude oil,
   Z = bitumen [3] (2 marks for two
   correct; 1 mark for one correct)
   b) At the top of the column [1]
. D [1]
. a) To break down into smaller
   molecules [1]
   b) There is not enough petrol in crude oil
   to meet demand [1]; and other more
   useful molecules can be made [1]
   c) **Any two from:** use a catalyst [1]; high
   temperatures [1]; high pressure [1]

Page 147 Interpreting and Interacting with Earth's Systems

1. a) As carbon dioxide levels increase, so
   does air temperature [1]
   b) Carbon dioxide is a greenhouse
   gas [1]; it traps heat energy in the
   atmosphere, leading to an increase
   in air temperature [1]

Page 147 Air Pollution and Potable Water

1. C [1]
2. a) Very small, solid particles [1]
   b) The lungs / respiratory system [1]

Pages 148–165 Revise Questions

Page 149 Quick Test

1. **Any three from:** Electrons are very
   small; have negative charge; in atoms
   they orbit the nucleus; they give an
   atom its negative charge to balance
   the positive charge of the nucleus;
   in metals some electrons are free to

move between atoms but in electrical
insulators there are no free electrons
2. Alpha particles were fired at atoms
   and some bounced back. That is only
   possible if atoms contain something
   very dense / positively charged.
3. Positive
4. Electric force, between atoms
5. The electric forces between gases are
   almost zero, but the forces are strong in
   solids so it's very hard to push particles
   of a solid apart.

Page 151 Quick Test

1. Quantity that changes: internal energy
   (also, volume and density may change)
   Quantity that does not change:
   (any one from) mass; temperature;
   chemical composition; atomic
   structure

   Remember that in changes of state,
   atoms or molecules do not change. The
   forces between them and their internal
   energy change.

2. No. Changes in state involve changes of
   internal energy without the need for
   temperature change.
3. thermal energy for a change in state
   = mass × specific latent heat
   = 267 000 × 1000
   = 2.67×10^8J
   (Accept 267 000 000J or 267 000kJ)
4. change in thermal energy
   = mass × specific heat capacity × change
   in temperature
   = 100 × 1006 × 10
   = 1.01×10^6J to 3 significant figures
   (Accept 1 006 000J or 1006kJ)
5. Increasing the temperature of a gas
   increases its internal energy / increases
   the kinetic energy of each molecule.
   The particles move faster, hit
   (bombard) surfaces harder and more
   often.

   Remember that 'normal' means at
   right angles (90°).

6. Increasing the volume increases the space
   in between molecules / they are more
   spread out so each area of the surfaces
   holding the gas experiences a smaller rate
   of collisions.

Page 153 Quick Test

1. kinetic energy = 0.5 × mass and speed²
   = 0.5 × 0.5 × 16²
   = 64J

   Do calculations like these step-by-
   step. Always start by writing the
   equation. Then put in the numbers.
   Do the arithmetic and don't forget
   to write the final unit. If you try to
   do everything all at once you'll
   often get confused and make
   mistakes.

2. time $= \dfrac{\text{distance}}{\text{speed}}$

   $= \dfrac{100}{40}$

   = 2.5 hours
3. acceleration $= \dfrac{\text{change in velocity}}{\text{time}}$

   $= \dfrac{(24-0)}{10}$

   = 2.4m/s²

Page 155 Quick Test

1. Gravity, or gravitational force (i.e. weight)
2. Electric or electrical force
3. Unbalanced (or net or resultant) force

   Remember that unbalanced force
   always causes acceleration of a body.

Page 157 Quick Test

1. The ice skater experiences low resistive
   force (friction) so loses little energy, and
   needs to do little work to replace lost
   energy.
2. A person leaning on a wall exerts a
   force on it, but the wall doesn't move
   and there is no distance involved. Work
   = force × distance = force × 0 = 0.
3. Power is rate of transferring energy
   / power measures how quickly energy is
   transferred.

Page 159 Quick Test

1. They can change its shape / cause
   extension or compression.

   If the forces acting on a body are
   balanced then there can be no
   acceleration, but shape can change and
   this can be extension or compression.

2. a) elastic
   b) plastic
   c) elastic
   d) plastic
3. Physics concerns the whole universe,
   and weight for an equivalent mass is
   very different in different places. On the
   Earth's surface, the weight of a particular
   mass is much the same everywhere so the
   distinction is not relevant.

Page 161 Quick Test

1. Electric force can be attractive or repulsive.
2. a) Electrons are transferred to or from
   the surface by friction.
   b) Electrons can flow within the metal,
   and even our skin can conduct some
   electricity. So when we hold the
   spoon, charge can flow to or from it
   and it doesn't stay charged.
3. Current is rate of flow of charge.
4. Current through resistance causes
   heating, so the surroundings are
   heated.

Answers

Page 163 Quick Test
1. **a)** An increase in voltage, or a decrease in resistance
   b) A decrease in voltage, or an increase in resistance
2. resistance = $\dfrac{\text{voltage}}{\text{current}}$. A metal wire's resistance increases when it is hot, so the ratio of voltage to current increases.
3. It decreases.

Page 165 Quick Test
1. They transfer energy by doing work (= force × distance) on objects outside the circuit, such as by lifting loads. (They may also become warm, and transfer some energy to the surroundings by heating.)
2. **a)** energy transfer =
   current × voltage × time
   = 1.5 × 12 × 60
   = 1080J
   b) power = current × voltage
   = 1.5 × 12
   = 18W
   OR
   power = $\dfrac{\text{energy}}{\text{time}}$
   = $\dfrac{1080}{60}$
   = 18W

Pages 166–171 Review Questions

Page 176 Controlling Chemical Reactions
1. **a)** B **[1]**; C **[1]**
   b) A graph drawn with a line steeper than the 25°C line **[1]**

Volume of CO_2 Produced

0   Time Taken for Cross to Disappear

Page 167 Catalysts, Activation Energy and Equilibria
1. **a)** A chemical that reduces the activation energy, making it more likely that the reaction will take place **[1]**
   b) Gases burned in a car engine are harmful for the environment **[1]**; the catalytic converter enables the reactions to take place leading to non-harmful gases and acceptable levels of gases **[1]**
   c) One graph line drawn showing the reaction without a catalyst **[1]**; a second

correctly drawn graph line showing the reaction with a catalyst **[1]**

[1];

2. C **[1]**
3. forward **[1]**; HI **[1]**; reverse **[1]**; reverse **[1]**

Page 168 Improving Processes and Products
1. A **[1]**
2. The carbon / graphite anode **[1]**

Page 168 Life Cycle Assessments and Recycling
1. **a)** B, D, C, A **[1]**
   b) Less waste **[1]**; less fresh water used in its manufacture **[1]**
   c) **Any two from:** more energy is required to melt the ore (bauxite / aluminium oxide) **[1]**; anode reacts with oxygen to form carbon dioxide **[1]**; more fossil fuel used in production **[1]**
   d) Cork **[1]**
   e) Aluminium is easily recycled **[1]**

Page 169 Crude Oil
1. petrol **[1]**

Page 170 Interpreting and Interacting with Earth's Systems
1. **a)** Carbon dioxide is a greenhouse gas **[1]**; increased carbon dioxide levels leads to greater levels of heat energy being trapped in the atmosphere **[1]**; this results in increased air temperature and climate change **[1]**
   b) Levels of CO_2 have risen faster than was expected **[1]**; so reducing the levels will require more wells **[1]**
   c) 60.4% increase **[1]**
   d) Carbon dioxide is released through the burning of fossil fuels in factories and cars **[1]**; large-scale deforestation has removed trees that would normally take in carbon dioxide for photosynthesis **[1]**
2. A **[1]**

Page 171 Air Pollution and Potable Water
1. Carbon monoxide is similar in shape to O_2 **[1]**; it binds with haemoglobin **[1]**; preventing O_2 from being transported to the cells **[1]**
2. B **[1]**
3. Desalination **[1]**; reverse osmosis **[1]**
4. **a)** A partially permeable membrane / semi-permeable membrane **[1]**

   b) In places that have a large population **[1]**; but a low rainfall / poor water supply **[1]**

Pages 172–177 Practice Questions

Page 172 Matter, Models and Density
1. D **[1]**
2. C **[1]**
3. A **[1]**
4. density = $\dfrac{\text{mass}}{\text{volume}}$ **[1]**;
   = $\dfrac{0.24}{0.0001}$
   = 2400kg/m³ **[1]**

Page 172 Temperature and State
1. B **[1]**
2. C **[1]**
3. They can escape from each other / evaporate / boil **[1]**; they gain energy / they gain kinetic energy **[1]**; they move faster **[1]**
4. They gain energy / they gain kinetic energy **[1]**; they move faster **[1]**

Page 173 Journeys
1. D **[1]**
2. D **[1]**
3. A **[1]**
4. B **[1]**
5. **a)** distance = speed × time **[1]**;
   = 24 **[1]**; kilometres **[1]**
   b) distance = speed × time
   = 40 **[1]**; miles **[1]**
   c) distance = speed × time
   = 4 **[1]**; × 3600 **[1]**;
   = 14400m **[1]**

   There are 60 × 60 = 3600 seconds in an hour.

6. **a)** A scalar has size, a vector has size and direction **[1]**
   b) **Any one from:** displacement **[1]**; force **[1]**; velocity **[1]**; acceleration **[1]**; momentum **[1]**
   c) **Any one from:** energy **[1]**; distance **[1]**; area **[1]**; speed **[1]**
7. **a)** speed = $\dfrac{\text{distance}}{\text{time}}$ **[1]**;
   = $\dfrac{6000}{12}$ **[1]**;
   = 500km/h **[1]**
   b) 500 × $\dfrac{1000}{3600}$ **[1]**; = 139 m/s **[1]**

Page 174 Forces
1. B **[1]**
2. C **[1]**
3. Friction / resistive force **[1]**
4. A body can't accelerate without force / the acceleration of a body is proportional to the resultant force acting on it / force = mass × acceleration **[1]**
5. Any body that exerts a force on another itself experiences an equal force in the opposite direction **[1]**

age 175 Force, Energy and Power

. A   [1]

age 175 Changes of Shape

. B   [1]
. C   [1]

age 176 Electric Charge

. C   [1]
. B   [1]
. C   [1]
. C   [1]

age 176 Circuits

. D   [1]
. C   [1]
. A   [1]
. A   [1]
. D   [1]
. **a)** To supply energy / create a potential difference or voltage [1]
  b) To measure current [1]
  c) To measure voltage / potential difference [1]
  d) To oppose current / to control current (or voltage) / or to provide heating [1]
  e) To allow current in only one direction [1]
  f) To change current (or voltage) [1]; depending on temperature [1]
  g) To change current (or voltage) [1]; depending on light brightness [1]

age 177 Resistors and Energy Transfers

. B   [1]

Pages 178–197 Revise Questions

age 179 Quick Test

. Sketch should show **looped** lines (magnetic field lines) that are closest together near the poles of the magnet. Arrows on the lines should point **away** from the north pole of the magnet and towards the south pole.

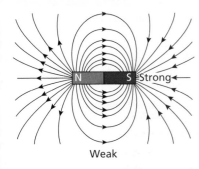

Weak

. The shape of the magnetic field lines around a solenoid is similar to the shape around a permanent bar magnet but the field around the solenoid can be turned on and off by turning the current on and off.

age 181 – Quick Test

. Wavelength = m; frequency = Hz; wave speed = m/s

. $\dfrac{320}{2}$ = 160Hz

---

3. In longitudinal waves the oscillations are parallel to the direction of energy transfer; in transverse waves the oscillations are at right-angles to the direction of energy transfer

Page 183 – Quick Test

1. All electromagnetic waves have the same speed in a vacuum.
2. radio waves, microwaves, infrared, visible (red to violet), ultraviolet, X-rays, gamma rays
3. Frequency increases as wavelength decreases

Page 185 Quick Test

1. **a)** ^1_1Xx, ^2_1Xx, ^3_1Xx
   b) Isotopes of the same element have the same number of protons, shown by the lower number, even if they have different total numbers of protons and neutrons, shown by the upper number.
2. Radiations carry a high concentration of energy, and when this energy is absorbed by atoms one or more of their orbital electrons can escape, leaving the atom as a positive ion.

Page 187 Quick Test

1. **a)** Decrease
   b) Stays the same / no change
2. 234; 2

Page 189 Quick Test

1. The energy is transferred to the environment, such as in moving air, and eventually spreads thinly causing heating of the environment (air, road). The energy dissipates / is dissipated.
2. **Any three from:** gravitational potential energy of a raised mass; kinetic energy of a moving mass; elastic potential energy of a stretched or compressed object; thermal energy of a hot object; electric potential energy of a battery
3. **a)** energy available to transfer to surroundings = mass × specific heat capacity × temperature difference
      = 0.5 × 4200 × 70
      = 147000J **OR**
      = 147kJ
   b) energy stored =
      (average) force × distance (extension)
      = $\left(\dfrac{15}{2}\right) \times 0.5$
      = 0.375J
   c) potential energy = mass × height × g
      = 1000 × 50 × 10
      = 500000J **OR**
      = 500kJ
   d) kinetic energy =
      0.5 × mass × speed²
      = 0.5 × 0.03 × 400²
      = 2400J **OR**
      = 2.4kJ

Page 191 Quick Test

1. **a)** power =
      current × potential difference
      = 5 × 230
      = 1150W = 1.15kW
   b) i) energy = power × time
      = 1150 × 3600
      = 4140000J **OR**
      = 4.14 × 10⁶J
   ii) 4140000 × 6 = 24840000J **OR**
      2.48(4) × 10⁷J
2. efficiency = $\dfrac{\text{useful output energy transfer}}{\text{input energy transfer}} \times 100\%$
   = $\dfrac{1}{1.25} \times 100\%$
   = 80%

Page 193 Quick Test

1. speed = $\dfrac{\text{distance}}{\text{time}}$
   For the bullet: speed = $\dfrac{100}{0.4}$
   = 250m/s
   For the plane: speed = $\dfrac{1000}{3.3}$
   = 303m/s
   The plane is faster.
2. Thinking distance and braking distance

> During thinking time speed is constant, but during braking time speed is decreasing.

Page 195 Quick Test

1. Renewable: A, B, E and G
   Non-renewable: C, D and F

Page 197 Quick Test

1. High current in cables causes heating. That means that the system loses a lot of energy. By transmitting at low current this energy loss is reduced. The power output from the power station is voltage × current, so if the current is to be low then the voltage needs to be high.
2. Transformers can transfer energy from one circuit to another. They allow energy to be transmitted at high voltage (stepped up) and then received by users at lower voltage (stepped down). But they don't work if the current in the transformers themselves is steady – it has to change. a.c. is continuously changing.

Pages 198–199 Review Questions

Page 198 Matter, Models and Density

1. D   [1]
2. C   [1]
3. A   [1]
4. C   [1]

Answers

5. a) density = $\dfrac{\text{mass}}{\text{volume}}$ **[1]**;

$= \dfrac{1.0}{0.002}$ **[1]**;

$= 500\text{kg/m}^3$ **[1]**

b) The particles are much further apart **[1]**

6. a) Any two from: an atom has electrons / a nucleus does not **[1]**; an atom is neutral / a nucleus has positive charge **[1]**; an atom has low density / a nucleus has high density **[1]**; a nucleus has a very much smaller radius than an atom **[1]**

b) An atom is neutral / an ion is charged or has charge **[1]**; an atom has equal numbers of protons and electrons, but an ion has different numbers **[1]**

Remember that in a neutral atom the numbers of protons and electrons are equal, but in an ion they are not.

c) Any two from: an electron is much smaller / a proton is much bigger **[1]**; an electron has negative charge / a proton has positive charge **[1]**; electrons orbit the nucleus / protons are in the nucleus **[1]**

d) Protons have positive charge **[1]**; neutrons are neutral **[1]**

Page 199 Temperature and State

1. D **[1]**
2. A **[1]**
3. C **[1]**
4. Particles / molecules moving very fast **[1]**; bombard / hit surfaces **[1]**

Page 200 Journeys

1. A **[1]**
2. B **[1]**
3. A **[1]**
4. B **[1]**
5. **a)** It has decreased **[1]**
   b) It has decreased and changed direction **[1]**

6. **a)** acceleration = $\dfrac{\text{change in speed}}{\text{time}}$ **[1]**;

$= \dfrac{30}{10}$ **[1]**;

$= 3\text{m/s}^2$ **[1]**

b) i) 0 **[1]**
ii) kinetic energy =
$0.5 \times \text{mass} \times \text{speed}^2$ **[1]**;
$= 0.5 \times 1000 \times 30^2$ **[1]**;
$= 450\,000\text{J}$ or 450kJ **[1]**

c) force = mass × acceleration **[1]**;
$= 1000 \times 3$ **[1]**;
$= 3000\text{N}$ **[1]**

d) distance = $\dfrac{(30^2 - 0)}{(2 \times 3)}$ **[1]**;

$= 150\text{m}$ **[1]**

e) work done = force × distance **[1]**;
$= (3000 \times 150)$ **[1]**;
$= 450\,000\text{J}$ or 450kJ **[1]**

f) power = $\dfrac{\text{energy or work}}{\text{time}}$ **[1]**;

$= 45\,000\text{W}$ or 45kW **[1]**

Page 202 Forces

1. B **[1]**
2. A **[1]**
3. D **[1]**
4. **a)** Pushes / exerts a force **[1]**
   b) i) little effect **[1]**
   ii) it accelerates / moves **[1]**
   c) Diagram to show: forces of the same size **[1]**; opposite directions **[1]**; acting on person and boat **[1]**

5. Gravity is too strong / weight is too big **[1]**

Page 203 Force, Energy and Power

1. C **[1]**
2. **a)** work = force × distance **[1]**;
   $= 180 \times 2.5$ **[1]**;
   $= 450\text{J}$ **[1]**
   b) 450J **[1]**
   c) Because of resistive forces / friction **[1]**
   d) It gains gravitational potential energy **[1]**; of 300×2.5 **[1]** $= 750\text{J}$ **[1]**

Page 203 Changes of Shape

1. B **[1]**
2. weight = mass × g **[1]**;
   $= 1.2 \times 10$ **[1]**;
   $= 12\text{N}$ **[1]**

Page 204 Electric Charge

1. D **[1]**
2. D **[1]**
3. B **[1]**
4. B **[1]**
5. B **[1]**

Page 204 Circuits

1. A diode **[1]**
2. **a)** A kilovolt is 1000 volts. **[1]**
   b) A battery has more than one cell. **[1]**
   c) In series circuits the current passes through one component after another, but in a parallel circuit it passes through one or the other / the current divides. **[1]**
   d) An ammeter measures current; a voltmeter measures voltage or potential difference **[1]**; the ammeter is connected in series with the component and the voltmeter is connected across it, in parallel with it **[1]**
3. **a)** Circuit drawn with: cell or battery and switch **[1]**; ammeter **[1]**; filament lamp **[1]**; the components all in a

series **[1]**; voltmeter in parallel with the lamp **[1]**

b) Graph drawn with: current labelled on y-axis **[1]**; voltage labelled on x-axis **[1]**; line is straight at low current **[1]**; line becomes curved, towards the voltage axis **[1]**

c) Resistance is higher when the wire is hot **[1]**; due to increased difficulty of electron flow **[1]**

Page 205 Resistors and Energy Transfers

1. D **[1**
2. **a)** It decreases **[1**
   b) It increases **[1**
3. energy = power × time **[1]**;
   $= 2 \times 2.5$ **[1]**;
   $= 5\text{kWh}$ **[1]** (Accept the correct answer in SI units, i.e. 18 000 000J)

Page 206 Magnetic Fields

1. A **[1**
2. D **[1**
3. B **[1**
4. It affects magnetic needles / compasses **[1**

Page 207 Wave Behaviour

1. B **[1**
2. A **[1**
3. C **[1**
4. B **[1**
5. B **[1**
6. **Model:** something that acts like something else / simulates reality **[1]**; used to help explain what is happening and make predictions **[1]**; **transverse:** a wave in which the vibration of the medium **[1]**; is at right-angles to the direction of travel of the wave **[1]**; **longitudinal:** a wave in which vibration of the medium **[1]**; is parallel to the direction of travel of the wave **[1]**

Page 208 Electromagnetic Radiation
1. A [1]
2. B [1]
3. D [1]
4. speed = frequency × wavelength [1];
    = $(4 \times 10^{14}) \times (5 \times 10^{-7})$ [1];
    = 2×10^8 m/s [1] (Accept 200 000 000 m/s)

> Using powers of ten for very large and very small numbers is easier than writing numbers in full and counting the zeros.

5. Frequency: stays the same [1]; wavelength: changes [1]

Page 209 Nuclei of Atoms
1. C [1]
2. A [1]
3. C [1]
4. C [1]
5. a) Atom with electron orbits [1]; representation of movement of electron to higher orbit [1]
   b) Representation of removal of electron from atom [1]
6. a) Electron(s) [1]; gain energy [1]; and move further from the nucleus (move to a higher energy level) [1]
   b) Electron(s) [1]; lose energy [1]; and move closer to the nucleus (or move to a lower energy level) [1]

Page 210 Half-Life
1. The time taken [1]; for half [1]; of the radioactive nuclei to decay [1]
2. D [1]
3. B [1]
4. B [1]
5. a) 15 hours [1]
   b) They have become nuclei of another element [1]; magnesium-24 [1]
   c) The beta radiation / electrons and gamma radiation emitted [1]; can cause ionisation in surrounding material [1]

Page 211 Systems and Transfers
1. D [1]
2. A [1]
3. B [1]
4. A [1]

Page 211 Energy, Power and Efficiency
1. a)
$$\text{efficiency} = \frac{\text{useful output energy transfer}}{\text{input energy transfer}} \times 100$$
   $= \frac{20}{50} \times 100$ [1];
   = 40% [1]
   b) It causes heating / temperature rise / it dissipates [1]

2. a) A [1]
   b) The 'lost energy' is a smaller proportion [1]

Page 212 Physics on the Road
1. B [1]
2. C [1]
3. a) kinetic energy = 0.5 × mass × speed² [1];
    = $0.5 \times 900 \times 20^2$ [1];
    = 180 000 J or 180 kJ [1]
   b) It transfers to the surroundings / dissipates [1]; (mostly) through the brakes [1]; (mostly) causing heating [1]
   c) The car has gravitational potential energy to dissipate as well as its kinetic energy. [1]

Page 213 Energy for the World
1. D [1]
2. B [1]

Page 213 Energy at Home
1. C [1]
2. A [1]
3. C [1]
4. Wires get hot and the bigger the current the hotter they get [1]; the heating transfers energy to the surroundings [1]; that energy is wasted [1]; so using low current reduces energy loss to the surroundings. [1]

Pages 214–221 Review Pages

Page 214 Magnetic Fields
1. Bring a compass close to the coil [1]; the compass will point along the magnetic field lines of the coil [1]
2. More turns in the coil [1]; more current in the coil [1]; have an iron core inside the coil [1]

Page 214 Wave Behaviour
1. A [1]
2. A [1]
3. C [1]

Page 215 Electromagnetic Radiation
1. A [1]
2. B [1]
3. D [1]

> Spectrum means 'range'. Electromagnetic waves have a range of wavelengths and range of frequencies, but they all have the same speed in space.

4. C [1]
5. a) The sketch should show: radio [1]; microwaves [1]; infrared [1]; visible [1]; ultraviolet [1]; X-rays [1]; gamma

rays [1] **(this order required, or its reverse)**

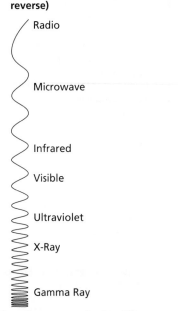
Radio
Microwave
Infrared
Visible
Ultraviolet
X-Ray
Gamma Ray

   b) Radio – communications [1]; microwaves – communications / cooking [1]; infrared – heating [1]; visible – seeing [1]; ultraviolet – security marking [1]; X-rays – medical imaging [1]; gamma rays – killing bacteria / treating tumours / medical imaging [1]
   c) The radio end of the spectrum [1]
   d) **Any two from:** ultraviolet – skin damage / cancer [1]; X-rays – tissue damage / cancer [1]; gamma rays – tissue damage / cancer [1]

Page 216 Nuclei of Atoms
1. A [1]
2. C [1]
3. C [1]
4. A [1]
5. B [1]
6. C [1]
7. D [1]

Page 217 Half-Life
1. B [1]
2. a) $x = 14$ [1]; $y = 7$ [1]
   b) $x = 92$ [1]; $y = 234$ [1]
3. Four correctly drawn lines [3] (2 marks for two correct lines; 1 mark for one)

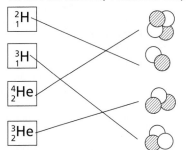
$^2_1$H
$^3_1$H
$^4_2$He
$^3_2$He

Page 218 Systems and Transfers
1. D [1]
2. B [1]
3. D [1]

Answers

Page 218 Energy, Power and Efficiency
1. B [1]
2. C [1]
3. Energy storage devices and systems – **any two from:** water in a reservoir [1]; fuel [1]; a hot kettle [1]; any moving object [1]; Energy transfer devices and systems – **any two from:** motor [1]; lamp [1]; engine [1]; any electrical appliance [1]

> A resistor with a steady current receives energy just as quickly as it passes energy to the surroundings by heating. It doesn't store energy.

4. a) heating [1]
   b) working / kinetic energy [1]
   c) heating and working / kinetic energy [1]
   d) emitting light [1]
5. C [1]
6. a) i) Separation of surfaces [1]; using oil (or similar) [1]
      ii) Reduces friction [1]; reduces heating / dissipation [1]
   b) i) A layer of material [1]; that is a poor thermal conductor [1]
      ii) Reduces thermal energy transfer [1]; from warmer to cooler place / system or vice versa [1]

Page 220 Physics on the Road
1. B [1]
2. A [1]
3. C [1]

Page 221 Energy for the World
1. a) 1 mark for each advantage / disadvantage (maximum of 6 points; for full marks there must be a balance of advantages and disadvantages)

Energy resource	Advantages	Disadvantages
coal	• cheap • still a lot in the ground	• causes pollution • releases carbon dioxide
oil	• cheap • convenient, widely usable • still a lot available	• causes pollution • releases carbon dioxide
wind	• renewable • clean	• requires large wind farms
solar	• renewable • good for local supply	• only suitable for mass use if large solar farms are built • expensive
nuclear	• uses little fuel • no polluting emissions	• produces radioactive waste material • expensive

b) **Any one resource, plus one advantage and one disadvantage, from:** gas [1]; advantage – widely available [1]; disadvantage – burning releases carbon dioxide [1]; bio-fuel [1]; advantage – renewable [1]; disadvantage – large land use needed [1]; hydroelectric [1]; advantage – renewable [1]; disadvantage – needs high dammed reservoirs [1]; tides [1]; advantage – renewable / always available [1]; disadvantage – barrage needed across estuary [1]

Page 221 Energy at Home
1. A [1]
2. C [1]
3. C [1]

Pages 222–229 Mixed Exam-Style Biology Questions

1. A [1]
2. B [1]
3. B [1]
4. C [1]
5. a) A fungus [1]
   b) Ethanol [1]; carbon dioxide [1]
   c) Pressure caused by carbon dioxide gas [1]
   d) **Any two from:** amount of yeast [1]; amount of glucose [1]; volume of water [1]; incubation time [1]
   e) Units that liquid moved up the scale [1]
   f) i) Temperature [1]; $\wp C$ [1]
      ii) The yeast respires at a faster rate at a temperature of 20 $\wp C$ [1]
      iii) The enzymes [1]; in the yeast had been denatured / were destroyed by the high temperature [1]
      iv) Use a smaller range of temperatures / smaller divisions on the scale [1]
   g) The yeast will run out of glucose [1]; the yeast is killed by increasing concentrations of ethanol [1]
6. C [1]
7. a) Movement of water through a plant and its evaporation from the leaves [1]
   b) Guard cell [1]
   c) Carbon dioxide [1]
8. a) *Saxifrage* [1]
   b) B [1]
   c) i) Upper: $\frac{10}{5}$ [1]; = 2 [1]; lower: $\frac{30}{5}$ [1]; = 6 [1]
      ii) On a hot day plants will open their stomata [1]; to allow exchange of gases [1]; for photosynthesis [1]; plants will lose less water through evaporation [1]; if the stomata are not in direct sunlight / are shaded [1]
9. C [1]
10. C [1]
11. D [1]

12. a) Males only have one X chromosome [1]; so if the allele for colour blindness is present, there is no chance of a second allele to cancel it out [1]
    b) B [
    c) Mother [
    d) B [
13. a) A mutation occurs that makes the bacterium resistant [1]; the sensitive bacteria are killed by the antibiotic [1] the resistant bacteria survive and multiply to form a resistant population [1]
    b) If a bacterium mutates to develop resistance to one antibiotic [1]; it is still likely to be killed by the second antibiotic [1]
    c) Antibiotics are not effective against viruses / only kill bacteria [
    d) **Any three defences, plus a correct explanation for a total of 6 marks:** skin [1]; physical barrier [1] OR platelets [1]; form clot to seal wounds [1] OR mucous membranes [1]; trap microorganisms [1] OR acid in stomach [1]; kills microorganisms [1] OR tears / sweat [1]; contain antimicrobial substances [1]
14. B [1
15. C [1
16. a) **Accept:** 385.5 OR 386ppm [1
    b) **Accept any value between:** 404–406ppm [1
    c) Increase in the burning of fossil fuels [1]; deforestation [1]
17. a) B [1
    b) Worried about safety for consumption / long-term effects not known [1]; dislike the idea of eating something that contains human genes [1]

> If asked for concerns about genetically engineered foods, your answer must include concerns about safety when **eaten / consumed**.

Pages 230–237 Mixed Exam-Style Chemistry Questions

1. The time taken to react increases from A to D [1]; this means that the more concentrated the acid, the faster the reaction [1]; in terms of particles, there are more ions available per unit volume in A than in D [1]; so there are more likely to be successful collisions [1]
2. a) D [1
   b) The line should not move – if it had been drawn in pen, the ink would have moved with the solvent front. [1
   c) Ink 3 [1
   d) 13/40 = 0.33 (Accept answers between 0.30 and 0.35) [1
3. A [1
4. a) Graphite has a giant covalent structure in which each carbon atom is bonded to three other carbon atoms [1]; the graphite structure

is in layers, held together by weak forces, so the layers separate easily **[1]**; diamond has a giant covalent structure in which each carbon atom is covalently bonded to four other carbon atoms / the maximum number of carbon atoms **[1]**; this makes it very strong **[1]**

b) Allotrope **[1]**

c) Burn / react diamond and graphite with oxygen **[1]**; to show that they produce the same product: carbon dioxide **[1]**

. a) Covalent bonds **[1]**; the dot and cross diagram shows that the electrons are shared / the ball and stick model and the displayed formula use a single lines or sticks to represent a covalent bond **[1]**

b) The bond angles are incorrect **[1]**; the model does not show the 3D shape of a molecule **[1]**

. a) Lithium is higher in the reactivity series than carbon, so it cannot be displaced by it – it can only be extracted by electrolysis **[1]**; iron is lower than carbon in the reactivity series, so it can be displaced by it **[1]**

b) i) Li **[1]**; O **[1]**

ii) Li⁺ **[1]**; O²⁻ **[1]**

iii) For electrolysis to work the ions have to be mobile (in solution / molten) / in a solid, the ions are not free to move **[1]**

. a) Particle A: 7 neutrons **[1]**; Particle B: atomic number of 20 **[1]**; Particle C: atomic mass of 16 **[1]**; and electronic structure 2.6 **[1]**; Particle D: 9 protons **[1]**

b) D is an atom because the number of electrons equals the number of protons (the overall charge is neutral) **[1]**; B is an ion because it has two electrons less than the number of protons (so it has an overall charge) **[1]**

c) It is in Group 5 **[1]**; and Period 2 **[1]**; the electronic configuration shows the numbers of electrons in each shell / energy level – the number of shells (two) gives the period number **[1]**; the number of electrons in the outermost shell / energy level (five) gives the group number **[1]**

d) 20 **[1]**

. The number of neutrons varies **[1]**; as neutrons have mass this means that the atomic mass changes **[1]**; whilst the number of electrons stays the same **[1]**; as the number of protons is the same in each isotope **[1]**

. C **[1]**

0. a) $MgO(s) + H_2SO_4(aq) \rightarrow$
$MgSO_4(aq) + H_2O(l)$ **[1]**

b) **Any one from:** wear eye protection / safety goggles **[1]**; beware of spitting acid when heating the mixture **[1]**; do not boil the mixture **[1]**

c) i) Keep adding magnesium oxide until no more dissolves (all acid has reacted) **[1]**

ii) Pass the mixture through a filter funnel to remove unreacted magnesium oxide **[1]**

11. a) The nucleus **[1]**

b) Protons and neutrons **[1]**

c) B and C **[1]**

d) B = boron **[1]**; C = carbon **[1]**

12. a) The compound is ionic **[1]**; the ions of calcium and fluoride are arranged in a giant lattice structure in the solid form of the ion **[1]**; this means that it is extremely difficult to break the strong electrostatic forces between ions to melt it **[1]**

b) Methane has a simple molecular structure **[1]**; it only has very weak intermolecular forces between molecules, so is easy to separate from other methane molecules **[1]**; so the melting point and boiling points are low **[1]**

c) Correctly drawn lithium ion **[1]**; and oxide ion **[1]**

Li⁺   O²⁻

13. a) A substance that contains only one type of atom or molecule **[1]**

b) In everyday life, pure means a substance comes from one source with no other contaminants **[1]**

14. a) Be **[1]**

b) F **[1]**

c) 29 **[1]**

15. a) Correctly drawn diagram **[1]**

Gas syringe system

b) Add a catalyst **[1]**

c) Wear eye protection **[1]**

16. B **[1]**

17. a) The removal of salt from seawater to produce pure water **[1]**

b) Na_2SO_4 **[1]**

c) Fresh water is needed for people to survive **[1]**; if the water is contaminated with disease-causing organisms or high in salts then the person drinking it is likely to become ill and die **[1]**

18. metal + acid → salt + hydrogen **[1]**

19. a) magnesium nitrate + hydrogen **[1]**

b) zinc sulfate + hydrogen **[1]**

c) iron(II) chloride + hydrogen **[1]**

20. metal carbonate + acid → salt + carbon dioxide + water **[1]**

21. a) magnesium nitrate + carbon dioxide + water **[1]**

b) copper sulfate + carbon dioxide + water **[1]**

c) sodium chloride + carbon dioxide + water **[1]**

22. carbon dioxide – turns limewater milky white **[1]**; chlorine – turns moist, red litmus blue **[1]**; hydrogen – burns with a squeaky pop **[1]**; oxygen – relights a glowing splint **[1]**

23. C **[1]**

24. a) (100 – 78 – 0.04 – 1 =) 20.96% **[1]**

b) Ammonia **[1]**; carbon dioxide **[1]**

25. Diesel **[1]**

Pages 238–245 Mixed Exam-Style Physics Questions

1. B **[1]**

2. A **[1]**

3. D **[1]**

4. B **[1]**

5. a) molecule, atom, nucleus, electron **[2]** (1 mark for one error)

b) i) The forces between them become weaker **[1]**; they move further apart **[1]**

ii) There is no change **[1]**

c) They gain energy **[1]**; and move faster **[1]**

d) i) No change **[1]**

ii) It changes (because direction changes) **[1]**

iii) Exerts / applies a force **[1]**

iv) Exerts / applies a force **[1]**

e) i) energy = 0.5 × mass × (speed)² **[1]**
= 0.5 × (4 × 10⁻²⁶) × 100² **[1]**; = 2 × 10⁻²² **[1]**; J **[1]**

ii) 5000J **[1]**

6. a) i) Zero **[1]**

ii) Driving force / engine **[1]**

iii) Resistance (air, friction) **[1]**

iv) Zero **[1]**

b) i) Inertia / resistance to acceleration / need for a force for acceleration **[1]**

ii) Swing forward **[1]**; inertia / resistance to deceleration / need for a force for deceleration **[1]**

c) i) Inertia / resistance to deceleration / need for a force for deceleration **[1]**

ii) Reaction time – time between event and driver acting **[1]**; braking time – time between driver acting and vehicle stopping **[1]**

iii) Add them together **[1]**

d) Heating **[1]**; in brakes (and / or road, air) **[1]**; dissipation / spread thinly in surroundings **[1]**

Answers

7. a) Oppose current [1]; and produce heating (electrical energy is transferred to heat) [1]
    b) In parallel [1]
    c) To switch the supply to second resistor on and off [1]; control heating / turn heater up [1]
    d) A = live [1]; B = earth [1]; C = neutral [1]
    e) i) resistance = $\dfrac{\text{potential difference}}{\text{current}}$ [1]
       $= \dfrac{230}{4.6}$ [1];
       $= 50\Omega$ [1]
       ii) Smaller [1]; the current can take more than one route [1]
    f) power =
       potential difference × current [1];
       = 9.2 × 230 [1];
       = 2116W [1]
    g) energy transferred = power × time [1];
       = 2.116 × 3 [1];
       = 6.35kWh [1]

8. a) wave speed = frequency × wavelength [1]; = 3000 × 0.5 [1]; = 1500 [1]; m/s [1]
    b) Longitudinal waves do not transfer material [1]; sound waves are not transverse [1]; in transverse waves, the directions of travel and vibration are perpendicular (at right-angles) [1]
    c) Nuclei (of atoms) [1]
    d) i) Speed in space / vacuum [1]; can travel through space / vacuum / do not need a medium [1]
       ii) Any two from: wavelength [1]; frequency [1]; ionising ability [1]; penetrating ability [1]
    e) The range / set [1]; of different wavelengths / frequencies [1]; of the family of electromagnetic waves that travel with the same speed through space [1]

Radio waves are not harmful to us because our bodies absorb them extremely weakly. They transfer very little energy to our bodies, either for heating or for ionisation.

    f) i) The eyes detect / respond to visible light [1]
       ii) There is a warming effect [1]
       iii) Possible sunburn [1]
       iv) Ionisation effects / no noticeable sensation [1]
       v) There is no (measurable) response [1]

9. a) There is more / faster energy loss from A than B [1]; A has poorer insulation [1]
    b) They must replace the lost energy [1]
    c) It heats the surroundings [1]; spreads thinly / dissipates [1]
    d) Power [1]
    e) i) and ii) Any three sources, plus correct identification of type of resource, from:
       gas – non-renewable [2];
       oil – non-renewable [2];
       coal – non-renewable [2]; electricity – a mixture [2]; wood or other biofuel – renewable [2]; solar cells – renewable [2]; solar panels – renewable [2] (1 mark for source; 1 mark for correct type)
    f) Advantages: renewable [1]; low pollution / low CO_2 emission [1]; Disadvantages: use large areas of land / not always beautiful [1]; power output not high [1]

25 years ago there were very few wind farms in the world. Now there are many. You need to be able to explain this change.

    g) Advantages: widely available [1]; easy to transport [1]; Disadvantages: non-renewable [1]; polluting / high CO_2 emission [1]
    h) More renewables [1]; primarily due to concern over climate change [1]

10. a) Vibrating / oscillating charged particles [1]; emit (electromagnetic radiation) electrons [1]; that can fall towards nucleus / lose energy [1]; within atoms, nuclei can emit gamma rays [1]
    b) The emission [1]; of ionising radiation [1]; from substances with unstable nuclei [1]
    c) The removal (or sometimes addition) of electrons from atoms when energy is absorbed [1]; which results in atoms becoming charged [1]
    d) Gamma rays [
    e) i) Alpha [
       ii) Shortest tracks [
       iii) It causes ionisation [1]; and passes energy to atoms [1]; of the surrounding substance [1]

11. a) Use a plotting compass [1]; turn current on and off and watch movement of the needle [1]
    b) Make a coil [1]; have many turns on coil / add an iron core [1]
    c) i) Heating [
       ii) The surroundings are heated / energy transfers thermally to the surroundings [
       iii) We can use it for heating rooms for heating spaces / appliances [
    d) i) The wire gets hot, resistance increases [
       ii) Gradient [1]; slopes down / is negative [1]
    e) Less / slower rate of waste of energy [

Notes

Notes

Periodic Table

Key

atomic number
symbol
name
relative atomic mass

(1)	(2)		3	4	5	6	7	8	9	10	11	12	(3) 13	(4) 14	(5) 15	(6) 16	(7) 17	(0) 18
1 **H** hydrogen 1.0																		2 **He** helium 4.0
3 **Li** lithium 6.9	4 **Be** beryllium 9.0												5 **B** boron 10.8	6 **C** carbon 12.0	7 **N** nitrogen 14.0	8 **O** oxygen 16.0	9 **F** fluorine 19.0	10 **Ne** neon 20.2
11 **Na** sodium 23.0	12 **Mg** magnesium 24.3												13 **Al** aluminium 27.0	14 **Si** silicon 28.1	15 **P** phosphorus 31.0	16 **S** sulfur 32.1	17 **Cl** chlorine 35.5	18 **Ar** argon 39.9
19 **K** potassium 39.1	20 **Ca** calcium 40.1	21 **Sc** scandium 45.0	22 **Ti** titanium 47.9	23 **V** vanadium 50.9	24 **Cr** chromium 52.0	25 **Mn** manganese 54.9	26 **Fe** iron 55.8	27 **Co** cobalt 58.9	28 **Ni** nickel 58.7	29 **Cu** copper 63.5	30 **Zn** zinc 65.4		31 **Ga** gallium 69.7	32 **Ge** germanium 72.6	33 **As** arsenic 74.9	34 **Se** selenium 79.0	35 **Br** bromine 79.9	36 **Kr** krypton 83.8
37 **Rb** rubidium 85.5	38 **Sr** strontium 87.6	39 **Y** yttrium 88.9	40 **Zr** zirconium 91.2	41 **Nb** niobium 92.9	42 **Mo** molybdenum 95.9	43 **Tc** technetium	44 **Ru** ruthenium 101.1	45 **Rh** rhodium 102.9	46 **Pd** palladium 106.4	47 **Ag** silver 107.9	48 **Cd** cadmium 112.4		49 **In** indium 114.8	50 **Sn** tin 118.7	51 **Sb** antimony 121.8	52 **Te** tellurium 127.6	53 **I** iodine 126.9	54 **Xe** xenon 131.3
55 **Cs** caesium 132.9	56 **Ba** barium 137.3	57-71 lanthanides	72 **Hf** hafnium 178.5	73 **Ta** tantalum 180.9	74 **W** tungsten 183.8	75 **Re** rhenium 186.2	76 **Os** osmium 190.2	77 **Ir** iridium 192.2	78 **Pt** platinum 195.1	79 **Au** gold 197.0	80 **Hg** mercury 200.5		81 **Tl** thallium 204.4	82 **Pb** lead 207.2	83 **Bi** bismuth 209.0	84 **Po** polonium	85 **At** astatine	86 **Rn** radon
87 **Fr** francium	88 **Ra** radium	89-103 actinides	104 **Rf** rutherfordium	105 **Db** dubnium	106 **Sg** seaborgium	107 **Bh** bohrium	108 **Hs** hassium	109 **Mt** meitnerium	110 **Ds** darmstadtium	111 **Rg** roentgenium	112 **Cn** copernicium		114 **Fl** flerovium			116 **Lv** livermorium		

Physics Equations

You must be able to recall and apply the following equations using the appropriate SI units:

Word Equation
density (kg/m³) = $\dfrac{\text{mass (kg)}}{\text{volume (m}^3\text{)}}$
distance travelled (m) = speed (m/s) × time (s)
acceleration (m/s²) = $\dfrac{\text{change in velocity (m/s)}}{\text{time (s)}}$
kinetic energy (J) = 0.5 × mass (kg) × (speed (m/s))²
force (N) = mass (kg) × acceleration (m/s²)
work done (J) = force (N) × distance (m) (along the line of action of the force)
power (W) = $\dfrac{\text{work done (J)}}{\text{time (s)}}$
force exerted by a spring (N) = extension (m) × spring constant (N/m)
gravity force (N) = mass (kg) × gravitational field strength, g (N/kg)
(in a gravity field) potential energy (J) = mass (kg) × height (m) × gravitational field strength, g (N/kg)
charge flow (C) = current (A) × time (s)
potential difference (V) = current (A) × resistance (Ω)
energy transferred (J) = charge (C) × potential difference (V)
power (W) = potential difference (V) × current (A) = (current (A))² × resistance (Ω)
energy transferred (J, kWh) = power (W, kW) × time (s, h)
wave speed (m/s) = frequency (Hz) × wavelength (m)
efficiency = $\dfrac{\text{useful output energy transfer (J)}}{\text{input energy transfer (J)}}$ × 100%

You must be able to select and apply the following equations using the appropriate SI units:

Word Equation
change in thermal energy (J) = mass (kg) × specific heat capacity (J/kg°C) × change in temperature (°C)
thermal energy for a change in state (J) = mass (kg) × specific latent heat (J/kg)
(final velocity (m/s))^2 – (initial velocity (m/s))^2 = 2 × acceleration (m/s^2) × distance (m)
energy transferred in stretching (J) = 0.5 × spring constant (N/m) × (extension (m))^2
potential difference across primary coil (V) × current in primary coil (A) = potential difference across secondary coil (V) × current in secondary coil (A)

Glossary and Index

Notes

Notes

Notes

Notes

Notes

Notes

Collins

OCR GCSE Revision

Combined Science

Foundation

OCR
Gateway
GCSE

Workbook

Fran Walsh, Eliot Attridge
and Trevor Baker

Revision Tips

Rethink Revision

Have you ever taken part in a quiz and thought *'I know this!'* but, despite frantically racking your brain, you just couldn't come up with the answer?

It's very frustrating when this happens but, in a fun situation, it doesn't really matter. However, in your GCSE exams, it will be essential that you can recall the relevant information quickly when you need to.

Most students think that revision is about making sure you **know** stuff. Of course, this is important, but it is also about becoming confident that you can **retain** that *stuff* over time and **recall** it quickly when needed.

Revision That Really Works

Experts have discovered that there are two techniques that help with all of these things and consistently produce better results in exams compared to other revision techniques.

Applying these techniques to your GCSE revision will ensure you get better results in your exams and will have all the relevant knowledge at your fingertips when you start studying for further qualifications, like AS and A Levels, or begin work.

It really isn't rocket science either – you simply need to:

- **test yourself** on each topic as many times as possible
- **leave a gap** between the test sessions.

Three Essential Revision Tips

1. **Use Your Time Wisely**

   - Allow yourself plenty of time.
   - Try to start revising at least six months before your exams – it's more effective and less stressful.
   - Your revision time is precious so use it wisely – using the techniques described on this page will ensure you revise effectively and efficiently and get the best results.
   - Don't waste time re-reading the same information over and over again – it's time-consuming and not effective!

2. **Make a Plan**

   - Identify all the topics you need to revise (this All-in-One Revision & Practice book will help you).
   - Plan at least five sessions for each topic.
   - One hour should be ample time to test yourself on the key ideas for a topic.
   - Spread out the practice sessions for each topic – the optimum time to leave between each session is about one month but, if this isn't possible, just make the gaps as big as realistically possible.

3. **Test Yourself**

   - Methods for testing yourself include: quizzes, practice questions, flashcards, past papers, explaining a topic to someone else, etc.
   - This All-in-One Revision & Practice book provides seven practice opportunities per topic.
   - Don't worry if you get an answer wrong – provided you check what the correct answer is, you are more likely to get the same or similar questions right in future!

Visit our website to download your free flashcards, for more information about the benefits of these techniques, and for further guidance on how to plan ahead and make them work for you.

www.collins.co.uk/collinsGCSErevision

Contents

Contents

Contents

Cell Structures

1 **a)** Draw a line from each cellular structure to its function.

Structure	Function
Nucleus	Contains chlorophyll
Cell membrane	Contains receptor molecules
Chloroplast	Contains enzymes for respiration
Mitochondria	Contains genetic material

[3]

b) Which of the structures above is only found in plant cells?

....

[1]

2 Which of the following are features of an electron microscope? Tick (✓) **two** boxes.

Higher resolution than light microscope	
Does not require specimens to be stained	
Uses more powerful lenses than a light microscope	
Uses magnets to focus an electron beam	

[2]

3 Jade wants to look at some blood using a light microscope.
She pricks her finger and places a drop of blood on a glass slide.

a) Once the blood has dried, what can Jade do to make the cells easier to see under the microscope?

....

[1]

b) The diagram shows what Jade can see under the microscope.

i) What type of cell is cell **X**?

....

[1]

ii) What type of cell is cell **Y**?

....

[1]

c) Jade is using a microscope with a ×4 magnification eyepiece and a ×100 magnification objective lens.

What is the total magnification she is using?

....

[1]

Total Marks .... / 10

What Happens in Cells

1 Underline the correct word from each pair in bold to complete the passage about DNA.

DNA is found in the **nucleus / cytoplasm** of cells. It is a **monomer / polymer** and is made of strands of nucleic acids that are coiled to form a **double helix / triple helix**. [3]

2 **a)** Protease enzyme digests proteins. What does carbohydrase enzyme digest?

_____ [1]

b) An enzyme reaction can be summarised as: enzyme + substrate ⟶ products (+ enzyme)

Complete the equation to show the reaction for lipase enzyme.

lipase + _____ ⟶ _____ + _____ (+ lipase) [3]

c) Enzymes are denatured by high temperatures.

Suggest **one** other factor that may denature enzymes.

_____ [1]

3 Pepsin and trypsin are both enzymes that digest proteins. Pepsin is found in the stomach and trypsin is found in the intestines.
The graph shows how pH affects the rate of action of both enzymes.

a) What is the substrate for both enzymes?

_____ [1]

b) What is the optimum pH for trypsin?

_____ [1]

c) When the contents of the stomach pass to the intestine, pepsin stops digesting any remaining proteins.

Suggest why.

_____

_____ [2]

Total Marks _____ / 12

Respiration

1 The table below shows the percentage of a person's blood that is delivered to different areas of the body during exercise and at rest.

Body Parts	Percentage of Blood Delivered to Each Part	
	At Rest	**During Exercise**
Muscles	15	65
Brain	17	5
Liver	30	8
Other	38	22

a) Plot these results on the graph paper. [4

b) Suggest why there is more blood flowing to the muscles during exercise than at rest.

....

....

.... [3

2 The diagram shows a yeast cell.

a) To what group of microorganisms does yeast belong?

.... [1

b) Which **two** structures are present in both yeast and plant cells, but not animal cells?

.... [2

c) Yeast can respire in the absence of oxygen. Write the word equation for this reaction.

.... [3

3 Most living things use oxygen when they respire. This is known as aerobic respiration.

a) Write the word equation for aerobic respiration.

.... [2

b) How are the reactants in this equation delivered to body cells?

.... [1

Total Marks .... / 16

Photosynthesis

1 The following questions are about plants and food:

a) What is the name of the process plants use to make food?

.... [1]

b) What is the name of the food molecule made by plants?

.... [1]

c) What is this food molecule used for?

....

.... [2]

d) Explain why the concentration of carbon dioxide in a greenhouse may be higher
at night than during the day.

....

....

.... [2]

2 a) Complete the word equation for photosynthesis.

carbon dioxide + ... $\xrightarrow[\text{chlorophyll}]{\text{light energy}}$ glucose + ...   [2]

b) The chlorophyll needed for photosynthesis is found inside which subcellular structures?

.... [1]

c) Photosynthesis is an endothermic reaction.

What does this mean?

....

.... [1]

Total Marks .... / 10

Supplying the Cell

1 The diagram below shows the stages in the cell cycle.

A   B   C   D   E

a) Put the stages in the correct order. The first one has been done for you.

B _____ _____ _____ _____   [1]

b) What is the name of the type of cell division shown in the diagram?

_____   [1]

c) Apart from growth, state **one** other reason for this type of cell division.

_____   [1]

2 The boxes below represent the concentrations of salts inside and outside a cell.

| Low salt concentration | | High salt concentration |

Draw **three** arrows on the diagram and label them to show the direction of movement for:

a) diffusion   [1]

b) active transport   [1]

c) movement of water by osmosis.   [1]

3 A stem cell is a cell that can differentiate into many different types of cell.

a) Name **two** places from where human stem cells can be obtained.

_____   [2]

b) By which process does glucose move from the small intestine into the blood stream?

_____   [1]

c) By which process does oxygen move from the alveoli into the blood stream?

_____   [1]

Total Marks _____ / 10

The Challenges of Size

1   The diagram shows two cells from different parts of a plant.

a) What is the name of cell **Y**?

    _____   [1]

b) In which part of a plant would you find cell **Z**?

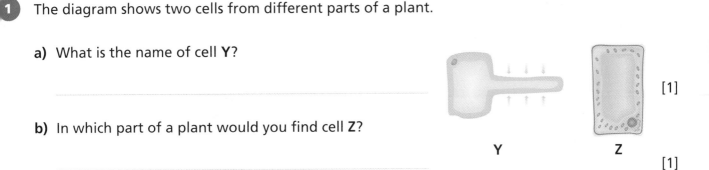

    _____   [1]

    Y   Z

2   a) Match the image to the name of the blood vessel and its function by joining them with a line.

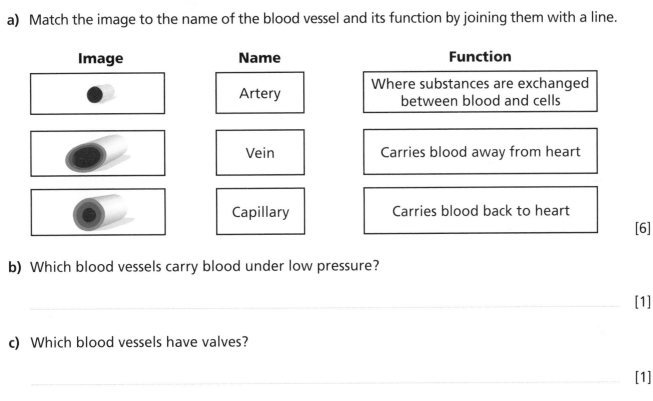

Image	Name	Function
	Artery	Where substances are exchanged between blood and cells
	Vein	Carries blood away from heart
	Capillary	Carries blood back to heart

    [6]

b) Which blood vessels carry blood under low pressure?

    _____   [1]

c) Which blood vessels have valves?

    _____   [1]

d) The diagram shows a network of capillaries in a muscle.

    Tick (✓) the boxes next to the two substances that are most likely to be found in the blood flowing through an artery.

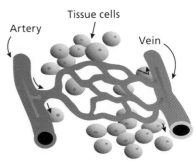

Tissue cells
Artery
Vein

Carbon dioxide	
Glucose	
Urea	
Starch	
Oxygen	

    [2]

    Total Marks _____ / 12

The Heart and Blood Cells

1 The diagram shows a human heart.

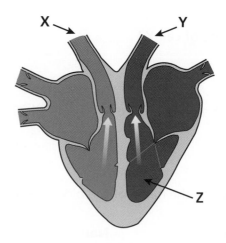

The bottom chambers are contracting, forcing blood through the blood vessels labelled **X** and **Y**.

a) What name is given to the bottom chambers of the heart?

.... [1

b) Are blood vessels **X** and **Y** arteries or veins?

Explain your answer.

....

.... [2

c) Where is blood flowing to when it flows through blood vessel **X**?

.... [1

d) How is the chamber labelled **Z** adapted to its function?

....

....

.... [3

2 Name **three** substances carried by plasma.

.... [3

Total Marks .... / 10

Plants, Water and Minerals

1 The diagram below shows two similar plants in different conditions.

Plant X

Plant cells short of water so the plant wilts

Not enough water in soil

Plant Y

H_2O H_2O H_2O H_2O H_2O H_2O

Plant cells full of water so the plant stays erect

Plenty of water in soil

Plants lose water through pores in the leaves called stomata.

a) In which plant will the stomata be closed?

_____ [1]

b) Explain why plant **X** will not be photosynthesising.

_____ [2]

c) Which terms describes the cells of plant **Y**?

Tick (✓) the correct answer.

Turgid	
Flaccid	
Wilting	

[1]

d) Water moves from the roots to the leaves before being lost from the leaves.

What is this process called?

_____ [1]

e) How do the following factors affect water loss from a plant's leaves?

i) Wind speed _____ [1]

ii) Temperature _____ [1]

f) The diagram shows a stoma.

What is the role of the cell labelled **A**?

A

_____ [1]

g) Explain why it is usual to find more stomata on the lower surface of a leaf compared with the upper surface.

_____

_____ [2]

Total Marks _____ / 10

Coordination and Control

1 Match the part of the nervous system to its function by drawing a line between them.

Nervous System Part   **Function**

Sensory neurone		Carries impulses from relay neurone to effector

Receptor		Carries impulses from receptor to relay neurone

Brain		Detects a stimulus

Motor neurone		Responsible for coordinating a response

[3

2 The diagram below shows a neurone.

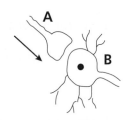

Impulse travels towards cell body and then away from cell body

What type of neurone is it?

....

[1

3 The diagram shows the junction between two nerve cells, **A** and **B**.
The arrow shows the direction of the nerve impulse.

Complete the passage below about transmission of nerve impulses by
filling in the gaps.

A receptor receives a .... and generates an .... impulse in

the .... neurone. The impulse travels along the neurone until it reaches a

.... The sensory neurone releases a chemical called a ....

This crosses the gap and binds to .... on the next neurone. This generates

another electrical impulse.

[6

4 Which statement is true for a nervous response? Tick (✓) one box only.

A very quick response	
A generalised response	
Carried by chemical impulses	
Long-lasting effect	

[1]

Total Marks .... / 11

The Endocrine System

1 The diagram shows the major glands in the body that produce hormones.

a) What is the name of gland **C**?

_____ [1]

b) Name the hormone produced by gland **A**.

_____ [1]

c) The glands labelled **E** are found on top of which organs?

_____ [1]

d) The organs labelled **F** produce the male sex hormone. What are the organs called?

_____ [1]

e) How do hormones travel to their site of action?

_____ [1]

C [1]

D [1]

A

E [1]

B

F [1]

2 Which of the following statements are true about hormones? Tick (✓) two boxes.

They are fast acting	
They are chemicals	
They are proteins	
Their response is long lasting	

[2]

3 The flow diagram is about control of blood glucose levels.

a) Process **A** happens in which organ?

_____ [1]

b) Process **B** happens in which organ?

_____ [1]

Blood glucose levels rise

↓

A Insulin produced

↓

B Glucose converted to glycogen

↓

C Increased permeability of membrane to glucose

c) People with type 1 diabetes often need to inject themselves with insulin before a meal.

Explain why.

_____

_____ [2]

Total Marks _____ / 11

Hormones and Their Uses

1 A woman's fertility can be controlled by drugs made from female sex hormones.

a) What hormone can be combined with oestrogen in the female contraceptive pill?

.... [1]

b) Give **two** disadvantages of taking the contraceptive pill.

....

.... [2]

c) What hormone stimulates the release of the egg?

.... [1]

2 The table below gives information about three methods of birth control used by women of different ages.

	% of Women per Age Range						
Age Range	16–19	19–24	25–29	30–34	35–39	40–44	45–49
Contraceptive Pill	48	64	55	48	28	17	11
Contraceptive Injection	1	11	8	6	6	5	4
Condoms	63	39	37	28	26	20	16

a) What method of contraception is most popular in women of 16–19 years of age?

.... [1]

b) In which age range is use of the contraceptive pill most popular?

.... [1]

c) Suggest **one** advantage of using contraceptive injections compared to the contraceptive pill.

.... [1]

d) Give **one** advantage of condoms compared to contraceptive pills or injections.

.... [1]

Total Marks .... / 8

Maintaining Internal Environments

1 The internal temperature of the body needs to be kept constant.

  a) What is the normal body temperature of humans?

  _____ [1]

  b) Enzymes have an optimum temperature at which they work.

  Explain what happens to the enzymes if the temperature of the body:

  i) increases _____ [1]

  ii) decreases _____ [1]

2 Describe the similarities and differences between type 1 and 2 diabetes.

  _____

  _____

  _____

  _____

  _____ [3]

3 Homeostasis is the maintenance of a constant internal environment.

  Name **three** factors that need to be controlled to maintain a constant internal environment.

  _____ [3]

4 Underline the word in bold that best completes each sentence.

  Insulin is a **neurotransmitter / enzyme / hormone**.

  Insulin is released from the **liver / pancreas / stomach**.

  Insulin is released when blood glucose levels are **low / high**.

  Insulin is most likely to be released **before a meal / during a meal / after a meal**. [4]

> **Total Marks** _____ / 13

Recycling

1 **a)** In the carbon cycle, carbon is returned to the atmosphere by the respiration of **three** groups of organisms.

What are the **three** groups?

....

....

....

[3

b) Which molecule do plants convert atmospheric carbon dioxide into during photosynthesis?

....

[1

2 **a)** Some plants have nitrogen fixing bacteria in their root nodules.
These bacteria can turn nitrogen into nitrates.

What natural process also fixes nitrogen?

....

[1

b) Plants need nitrogen to make certain kinds of molecules.

What are these molecules?

....

[1

3 The flow diagram below shows part of the nitrogen cycle.

Nitrogen in plants → **A** → Nitrogen in animals → **B** → Ammonium compounds

a) What process is shown by the letter **A**?
Underline the correct answer from the list below.

lightning   **decomposition**   **feeding**   **nitrogen fixation**   [1]

b) What process is shown by letter **B**?
Underline the correct answer from the list below.

lightning   **decomposition**   **feeding**   **nitrogen fixation**   [1]

Total Marks .... / 8

Interdependence

1 The diagram shows a farmland food web.

a) Name **two** animals that are in competition with each other for food.

.... [1]

Hawk   Fox

Stoat

Rabbit   Bird   Mouse

Grass   Barley

b) Name **one** primary consumer from the web.

.... [1]

c) Name **one** producer from the web.

.... [1]

2 The graph shows the population of foxes in a woodland over time.

a) Suggest **three** reasons for the decrease in fox numbers at point **A**.

....

....

.... [3]

Number of Foxes

A

Time

b) Give **three** resources for which foxes will compete.

.... [3]

c) The trees in the woodland will also be in competition with each other. Give **three** resources for which trees will compete.

.... [3]

3 The image shows a buffalo and some oxpecker birds. The birds feed on tiny parasites on the buffalo's skin.

a) What sort of relationship is this?

....

.... [1]

b) Marcus says that the oxpecker bird is a parasite.

Why is Marcus wrong?

....

.... [1]

Total Marks .... / 14

Genes

1 Complete the following sentences by filling in the missing words.

An inherited characteristic is controlled by _____, which are found on structures

called chromosomes. Chromosomes are made of _____, which is coiled to form a

_____ _____. Body cells have pairs of chromosomes and are said to be

diploid, while gametes have single chromosomes and are said to be _____.　　　[4

2 Draw **one** line from each word to the correct definition.

Word	Definition
gamete	to have one recessive and one dominant allele
phenotype	the appearance of an individual
gene	a sperm or egg cell
heterozygous	a section of DNA

[3

3 Chelsea is describing herself on a dating website.

*I am 27 years old, 150cm tall and quite thin. I have blonde hair and blue eyes. I have my ears
and eyebrows pierced. I work in a sports shop and am a very good swimmer.*

a) Which **two** characteristics are inherited?

_____　[2

b) Name **one** characteristic that is most likely due to a combination of inherited and
environmental factors.

_____　[1]

4 Match the pairs of alleles to the correct description by drawing a line between them.

tt	Heterozygous
Tt	Homozygous dominant
TT	Homozygous recessive

[2]

Total Marks _____ / 12

Genetics and Reproduction

1 A scientist carried out many investigations into breeding pea plants.

He concluded that the height of the pea plants was controlled by 'determiners' (which we now know are genes) and that plants are always tall or short.

The scientist crossed two pure bred pea plants – one tall and one short, and found that all the offspring were tall.

a) Which is the dominant trait?

_____ [1]

b) The scientist then crossed two of the offspring and found that in the next generation the ratio of tall to small plants was 3 : 1.

Draw a genetic cross to show why this happened.

[2]

2 A camel body cell has 70 chromosomes.

a) Following mitosis, how many chromosomes will each resulting cell have? _____ [1]

b) Following meiosis, how many chromosomes will each resulting cell have? _____ [1]

c) What is the **haploid** number of chromosomes in a camel? _____ [1]

d) A goat sperm cell has 30 chromosomes.

What is the **diploid** number of chromosomes in a goat? _____ [1]

3 The 23rd pair of chromosomes in humans is responsible for determining sex.

Draw a genetic diagram to show how sex is determined.

[3]

Total Marks _____ / 10

Natural Selection and Evolution

1 The phylogenic tree shows the classification of some of the big cats together with their Latin names.

a) Jordan says the snow leopard will be more closely related to the clouded leopard than the tiger, because the tiger is not a leopard.

Explain why Jordan is **not** correct.

....

....

....

....

Lion *Panthera leo*	
Jaguar *Panthera onca*	
Leopard *Panthera pardus*	
Tiger *Panthera tigris*	
Snow leopard *Panthera uncia*	
Clouded leopard *Neofelis nebulosa*	

[2

b) Scientists use fossil evidence to help classify organisms.

What other technique can they use that helps to show the evolutionary relationships between animals?

....

[1

2 Write the letters for the stages below in the correct order to show how evolution occurs.

A Genes for successful adaptations will be passed onto the next generation.

B Individuals best adapted to the environment are more likely to survive.

C There is always variation within a population.

D The best adapted individuals will reproduce.

....

[1

3 Which statement best describes a **species**?

A A group of similar individuals, which produce offspring with the same genes.

B A group of similar individuals, which share the same features and genes.

C A group of similar individuals, which can breed to produce fertile offspring.

Your answer [ ] [1

Total Marks .... / 5

Monitoring and Maintaining the Environment

1 Recent estimates suggest that if deforestation continues at its present rate, the world's rainforests will have vanished by the year 2150.

Explain why this is a problem.

....

....

....

[4]

2 The chart below lists some endangered animals and gives an estimate of how many survive in the wild at present.

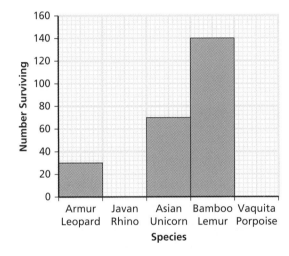

a) There are an estimated 50 Javan rhino and 90 vaquita porpoise surviving in the wild.

Add these to the bar chart. [2]

b) Suggest **two** reasons why animals become endangered.

....

....

[2]

c) What is meant by 'conservation'?
Give an example in your answer.

....

....

....

[2]

Total Marks .... / 10

Investigations

1 A local wildlife group wanted to find out about the number of hedgehogs in an area.
They spent a night in the area and counted and marked each hedgehog they found.
A week later, they returned to the area and repeated the exercise.
This time they counted the hedgehogs and noted if they were marked or not.
On the first night, 12 hedgehogs were counted and marked.
On the second night, 10 hedgehogs were counted, 6 of which were marked.

a) What is the name of the technique used by the wildlife group?

_____ [1

b) Calculate the number of hedgehogs in the area. Show your working.

Answer: _____ [2

2 Some students investigated the effect of different concentrations of acid rain on the growth of broad bean plants.
They germinated 50 bean plants and selected five plants that had roots and shoots of the same length
The students planted the five plants in different pots and watered each pot weekly with a different concentration of acid rain.
After six weeks they measured the height of the bean plants.
Their results are shown in the table.

pH of Rainwater	7.0	6.5	6.0	5.5	5.0	4.5
Height of Bean Plant (cm)	47	48	47	42	20	8

a) Suggest **two** variables that needed to be controlled when planting the bean plants in pots.

_____ [2

b) Which of these conclusions could the students draw from the results?

A The plants with the highest pH grew best.

B Increasing the pH resulted in taller plants.

C When the pH gets too acid, plants stop growing.

D Bean plants are not affected until the pH drops to 5.5.

Your answer ☐ [1]

c) Describe **one** way by which the students could improve the reliability of their results.

_____

_____ [2]

Total Marks _____ / 8

Resources and the Environment

1 Scientists have developed a genetically modified variety of wheat that produces bigger grains than the traditional variety.

Scientists are hoping the wheat will grow in nutrient-poor soil in developing countries where drought is often a problem.

Traditional wheat   GM wheat

a) Why is this GM variety of wheat more desirable than the traditional variety?

_____ [1]

b) Suggest **two** other useful characteristics that scientists could introduce into the wheat to make it more beneficial to developing countries.

_____

_____ [2]

c) Some people are concerned about the use of GM crops.
Suggest **two** concerns that people might have.

_____

_____ [2]

2 The table below gives some information about different varieties of tomato plants.

Plant Variety	Characteristics Present (+) or Absent (−)				
	High Yield of Fruit	Large Fruit	Drought Resistant	Resistant to Pests	Fast Growing
A	+	−	−	+	−
B	+	−	+	−	+
C	−	+	+	−	−
D	−	+	−	−	+

A farmer wants to grow tomato plants that give a high yield of large fruit and are fast growing.

a) What **two** plants should the select as parent plants to give the best chance of achieving the desired characteristics?

_____ [1]

b) The seeds produced from the cross grow into new tomato plants.
Not all the new plants have the desired characteristics.

How can the farmer use selective breeding to increase the likelihood of getting plants with the desired characteristics?

_____

_____ [2]

Total Marks _____ / 8

1 Which of the following diseases are communicable diseases?
Tick (✓) **three** correct boxes.

AIDS		Haemophilia	
Measles		Cholera	
Diabetes		Liver disease	
Cancer		Goitre	

[1

2 Match each microorganism to its size and the disease that it causes by drawing lines between the boxes.

Type of Microorganism	Size	Disease
Virus	10µm	Thrush
Bacteria	1µm	Malaria
Protozoa	100µm	Tuberculosis
Yeast	0.1µm	Chickenpox

[4

3 The graph is about the number of people infected with HIV from 2000 to 2014.

a) Describe what the graph shows about how the number of people infected with HIV changed between 2000 and 2014.

_____

_____

_____

_____

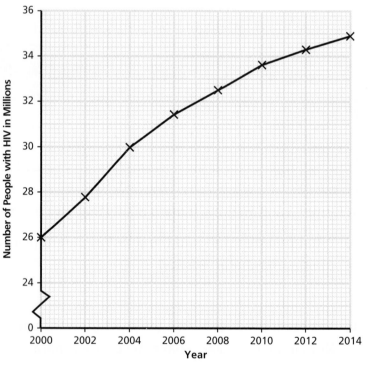

[2

b) What disease is caused by HIV?

_____

[

c) Explain why people with HIV infection are more susceptible to tuberculosis than people without HIV.

_____

_____

[

Total Marks _____ / 11

Prevention and Treatment of Disease

1 The human body has a number of mechanisms to prevent pathogens from entering.

   a) Describe the role of platelets in defence to disease.

   [2]

   b) The respiratory system produces mucus.

   What is the role of mucus in defence to disease?

   [1]

2 **a)** Name **two** tests that may be carried out on new drugs before clinical trials.

   [2]

   b) In clinical trials, some patients are given the drug, and others are given a sugar pill that contains no drugs.

   Explain why.

   [2]

3 Vaccinations are available for many diseases.

   a) Explain how vaccination prevents people from catching diseases.

   [6]

   b) Name **two** common childhood illnesses that there are vaccines for.

   [2]

Total Marks _____ / 15

Non-Communicable Diseases

1 By studying the human genome, scientists are able to predict the likelihood of an individual having a particular disease.

Potentially, this could be used to predict the chances of someone getting cancer.

Suggest **one** advantage and **one** disadvantage of being able to use the human genome in this way.

Advantage: _____

Disadvantage: _____ [2

2 Body mass index (BMI) is a simple measurement that is commonly used to classify a person as underweight, normal weight, overweight, or obese.

It is calculated using the following equation:

$$BMI = \frac{weight\,(kg)}{height^2\,(m)}$$

A BMI greater than or equal to 25 is overweight.
A BMI greater than or equal to 30 is obese.

Karanjit is 1.62 metres tall and weighs 74kg

a) Calculate Karanjit's BMI to one decimal place.

Answer: _____ [2

b) Name **two** health risks associated with obesity.

_____ [2

3 Evidence suggests that certain lifestyle choices are linked to an increased chance of developing certain illnesses.

Give an example of an illness / disease that is associated with:

a) excessive alcohol consumption.

_____ [1

b) a high fat diet.

_____ [1

Total Marks _____ / 8

Particle Model and Atomic Structure

1 The smallest particle that retains the properties of the element is the:

A neutron   B proton   C atom   D Higgs boson

Your answer [ ] [1]

2 Which of the following correctly explains why an atom has no charge?

A The number of neutrons equals the number of protons.

B The number of protons equals the number of electrons.

C The number of neutrons equals the number of electrons.

D The total number of protons and neutrons equals the number of electrons.

Your answer [ ] [1]

3 This table about the three main isotopes of carbon, is missing some key information.

Isotope	Symbol	Mass Number	Atomic Number	Protons	Neutrons	Electrons
Carbon-12	$^{12}_{6}C$	12	6	B	6	D
A	$^{13}_{6}C$	13	6	6	7	6
Carbon-14	$^{14}_{6}C$	14	6	6	C	6

a) Fill in the missing sections of the table.   [4]

b) What is the name of the particle whose number defines an element?   [1]

....

c) Palladium has an atomic mass of 106 and atomic number of 46.

   How many **neutrons** are in the nucleus?   [ ] [1]

4 A gas is condensing into liquid.

a) What happens to the speed of the water molecules?

.... [1]

b) What type of energy is lost from the molecules?

.... [1]

Total Marks .... / 10

Topic-Based Questions   309

Purity and Separating Mixtures

1 Glucose, $C_6H_{12}O_6$, can be bought at the following price points:

- Supermarket: £3/kg
- Industrial chemical supplier: £6/kg; £18/kg; £114/kg

Suggest why the chemical supplier can charge £114/kg for glucose.

....

.... [2

2 Which of the following is the empirical formula of glucose, $C_6H_{12}O_6$?

A $C_6H_{12}O_6$ **B** $C_2H_3O_2$ **C** CHO   **D** CH_2O

Your answer ☐ [1

3 Calculate the relative formula mass of $Mg(OH)_2$. Show your working.

relative formula mass = ... [2

4 What is the empirical formula of a chemical containing 60g of carbon, 12g of hydrogen and 16g of oxygen? Show your working.

empirical formula = ... [2]

5 Sandy wants to extract the pigment in ink so that she can transport it easily on a camping expedition.

Explain how she can separate the pigment from the ink.

....

....

.... [3]

Total Marks .... / 10

Bonding

1. Tungsten is a metal. Which of the following is **not** a reason why it is a metal.

   A It conducts electricity easily.

   B It is malleable.

   C It is a good conductor of heat.

   D It has the symbol W.

   Your answer ☐ [1]

2. Which of the following shows the **electronic structure** for magnesium?

   A 2.8.2   **B** 2.8.1   **C** 2.8.8.2   **D** 2.8.8.1

   Your answer ☐ [1]

3. Explain the differences between a **covalent bond** and an **ionic bond**.

   ....

   ....

   ....

   .... [4]

4. Sodium, Na, is a metal. It has the atomic number 11.

   Which of the following can you **not** deduce using the atomic number?

   A The electronic structure.   **B** The period sodium is in.

   C The number of isotopes.   **D** The group sodium is in.

   Your answer ☐ [1]

5. Draw the electronic structure for the element chlorine, Cl.

   [1]

Total Marks .... / 8

Models of Bonding

1 Methane has the formula CH_4.

   a) Draw a dot and cross diagram and the displayed formula for methane in the spaces below.

     Dot and Cross Diagram   **Displayed Formula**   [2

   b) Give **one** advantage that ball and stick models have over displayed formulae.

    ....   [1

2 Aluminium forms an ion.

   Draw a dot and cross diagram to show an aluminium cation.

                                                                                                    [1

3 Hydrogen sulfide, H_2S, is a covalent compound.

   a) Draw a dot and cross diagram to show a molecule of H_2S.

                                                                                                    [1

   b) How many electrons are there in a **single** covalent bond?

    ....   [1

Total Marks .... / 6

Properties of Materials

1 Which of the following best describes an **allotrope**?

   A An element with the same number of protons and neutrons.

   B An element with the same number of protons but a different number of neutrons.

   C An element that can form different physical forms.

   D An element that can form long-chained molecules.

   Your answer ☐ [1]

2 Many of the metals used to make products are alloys.
One of the most commonly used alloys is steel.
Steel is a mixture of the elements carbon and iron.

Explain, with the aid of a diagram, how the addition of carbon to iron makes the steel alloy much stronger and less likely to fracture.

[6]

3 Which of the following is **not** an allotrope of carbon?

   A glucose   **B** diamond   **C** fullerenes   **D** graphene

   Your answer ☐ [1]

4 Why is diamond such a hard material?

[2]

Total Marks .... / 10

Introducing Chemical Reactions

1 Write the number of atoms of each element for each formula below:

a) H_2O

.... [1

b) H_2SO_4

.... [1

c) $Ba(PO_3)_2$

.... [1

d) CH_3COOH

.... [1]

2 Copper oxide reacts with sulfuric acid.

Which of the following is the correct **word** equation for this reaction?

A   copper oxide + sulfuric acid → copper sulfate

B   copper oxide + sulfuric acid → copper sulfate + water

C   copper oxide + sulfuric acid → copper + hydrogen sulfate

D   copper oxide + sulfuric acid → copper sulfate + carbon dioxide + water

Your answer [ ] [1]

3 Magnesium carbonate reacts with nitric acid.

magnesium carbonate + nitric acid → magnesium nitrate + carbon dioxide + water

Write the **balanced symbol** equation for this reaction.

.... [2]

Total Marks .... / 7

Chemical Equations and Energetics

1 This question is about the four ions: **iron(II)**, **magnesium**, **sulfate** and **hydrogen carbonate**.

Which of the following correctly shows the charges on each ion?

	Iron(II)	Magnesium	Sulfate	Hydrogen Carbonate
A	3+	2+	2+	2−
B	2+	3+	2−	1−
C	2+	2+	2−	1−
D	2+	2+	2−	1+

Your answer ☐ [1]

2 Give the definition of the following terms:

a) cation .... [1]

b) anion .... [1]

3 Here is a word equation for a chemical reaction:

copper(II) oxide + sulfuric acid → copper(II) sulfate + water

What does the (II) indicate?

.... [1]

4 Which of the following shows a reaction profile for an **endothermic** reaction?

A

B

C

D

Your answer ☐ [1]

5 A series of reactions was carried out and the overall bond energies are recorded below.

For each example, state whether the reaction is **exothermic** or **endothermic**.

a) Striking a match .... [1]

b) Adding vinegar to calcium carbonate .... [1]

c) Cold packs used for sports injuries .... [1]

d) Chemical hand warmers .... [1]

Total Marks .... / 9

Types of Chemical Reactions

1   Draw a (circle) around the substance that is being **reduced** in each reaction.

a) beryllium + oxygen → beryllium oxide   [1

b) lead oxide + hydrogen → lead + water   [1

2   Look at the following reaction:

lead oxide + carbon → lead + carbon dioxide

a) Which species is being **reduced**?

.... [1

b) Which species is being **oxidised**?

.... [1

c) Write the **balanced symbol** equation for the reaction.

.... [2

3   Underline the **acid** in each of the following reactions.

a) $MgCO_3(aq) + 2HCl(aq) → MgCl_2(aq) + CO_2(g) + H_2O(l)$ [1

b) $HNO_3(aq) + NaOH(aq) → NaNO_3(aq) + H_2O(l)$ [1,

c) $2CH_3CH_2COOH(aq) + 2K(s) → H_2(g) + 2CH_3CH_2COOK(aq)$ [1

d) $2HBr(aq) + Mg(s) → MgBr_2(aq) + H_2(g)$ [1

4   Trevor is measuring the pH of a local river.
He uses universal indicator.

Explain why using universal indicator is **less** accurate than using a data logger with a pH probe.

....

....

....

.... [3]

Total Marks .... / 13

Electrolysis

1 When a metal is reacted with an acid it forms a metal salt, plus hydrogen gas.
A reactivity series is shown on the right.

Look at the following reactions:

W sodium + sulfuric acid → sodium sulfate + hydrogen

X calcium + sulfuric acid → calcium sulfate + hydrogen

Y potassium + sulfuric acid → potassium sulfate + hydrogen

Z magnesium + sulfuric acid → magnesium sulfate + hydrogen

Potassium
Sodium
Calcium
Magnesium
Aluminium
Carbon
Zinc
Iron
Tin
Lead
Hydrogen
Copper
Silver
Gold
Platinum

a) Which of the following shows the **correct order** of reactivity for these reactions, least to most reactive?

    A WXYZ

    B ZWXY

    C ZXWY

    D YWXZ

                        Your answer   ☐   [1]

b) Element **V** can displace zinc from zinc oxide. It cannot be displaced by carbon.

    Suggest where element **V** would appear in the reactivity series.

    .... [1]

2 Explain why some metals have to be extracted from their ores by electrolysis.

....

....

....

....

.... [3]

> **Total Marks** .... / 5

Predicting Chemical Reactions

1. Which of the following correctly explains the reactivity of **Group 1** metals?

   A As the outermost electron is closest to the nucleus it is easier to remove that electron.

   B As the outermost electron is furthest from the nucleus it is easier to remove that electron.

   C The outermost electrons are closest to the nucleus and are easier to remove.

   D The outermost electrons are closer to the nucleus and are harder to remove.

   Your answer [ ]   [1

2. Argon is a noble gas. It has the atomic number 18.

   Which of the following correctly shows the electronic structure of argon?

   A   B   C   D

   Your answer [ ]   [1

3. Describe how you would test if the gas produced in a reaction is oxygen.

   ....

   ....   [2

4. Fluorine and oxygen are next to each other in the periodic table in Period 2.

   Describe the similarities and differences between the reactivity of fluorine and oxygen.

   ....

   ....

   ....

   ....

   ....   [3

   Total Marks .... / 7

Controlling Chemical Reactions

1 Which of the following shows the correct units for measuring the rate of reaction?

A g/s **B** g/m **C** m/s **D** cm^2/s

Your answer ☐ [1]

2 Which of the following correctly shows the reason why a chemical reaction stops?

A The maximum quantity of reactant has been made.

B The minimum quantity of reactant has been made.

C A reactant is used up.

D A product is used up.

Your answer ☐ [1]

3 Give **two** ways in which the rate of a reaction can be changed.

....

.... [2]

4 Look at the following diagrams.

A   B   C   D

The diagrams all show the same mass of calcium carbonate.
Calcium carbonate reacts with nitric acid.

a) Which diagram shows the calcium carbonate that would react the **slowest** with nitric acid?

Your answer ☐ [1]

b) Describe how surface area affects the rate of reaction.

....

.... [2]

Total Marks .... / 7

Catalysts, Activation Energy and Equilibria

1 Explain how a catalyst affects the rate of reaction.

....

....

....

.... [4]

2 What is meant by the term **irreversible** reaction?

....

.... [1]

3 Which of the following reactions are classed as being **reversible**? Write down the correct letters.

A $CH_4(g) + 2O_2(g) \rightarrow CO_2(g) + 2H_2O(l)$ **C** $H_2(g) + I_2(g) \rightleftharpoons 2HI(g)$

B $2Li(s) + 2HCl(aq) \rightarrow 2LiCl(aq) + H_2(g)$ **D** $NH_4Cl(s) \rightleftharpoons NH_3(g) + HCl(g)$

.... [1]

4 The graph on the right shows a dynamic equilibrium.

Which of the following shows the correct labels for the graph?

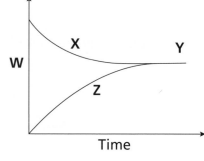

A W = forward reaction   X = reaction rate   Y = equilibrium   Z = backward reaction

B Y = forward reaction   Z = reaction rate   W = equilibrium   X = backward reaction

C X = forward reaction   W = reaction rate   Y = equilibrium   Z = backward reaction

D X = forward reaction   Y = reaction rate   W = equilibrium   Z = backward reaction

Your answer ☐ [1]

5 Explain what is meant by the term 'dynamic equilibrium'.

....

....

.... [2]

Total Marks .... / 9

Improving Processes and Products

1 What is the name given to a rock containing minerals of metal compounds?

.... [1]

2 Which of the following is the element that most metals on the planet are bonded to?

A sulfur   **B** silica   **C** oxygen   **D** carbon

Your answer ☐ [1]

3 Andy is carrying out the experiment shown in the diagram below.

Loose plug of mineral wool to stop mixture shooting out

Mixture of copper oxide and carbon

Heat

a) The loose plug of mineral wool in the top of the test tube is a safety precaution.

Give **two** other safety precautions that should be carried out when doing the experiment.

....

.... [2]

b) Andy reacts copper(II) oxide with carbon.

Write a **word** equation for the reaction that takes place.

.... [2]

c) Cuprite, an ore of copper, has the formula Cu_2O.

Write a **balanced symbol** equation for the reaction between cuprite and carbon.

.... [2]

Total Marks .... / 8

Life Cycle Assessments and Recycling

1   Lochmara Lodge Cafe prides itself on being environmentally friendly.
Inside the cafe the lights have lampshades made out of used computer circuit boards.

The lampshades are an example of recycling.

Give **three** reasons why recycling is beneficial.

....

....

....
[3

2   Radka manufactures garden gnomes.

Before the garden gnomes were produced, Radka had to carry out a life cycle assessment.

Give the **four** stages of the life cycle.

....

....
[4

Total Marks .... / 7

Crude Oil

1   The diagram shows a fractional distillation column.

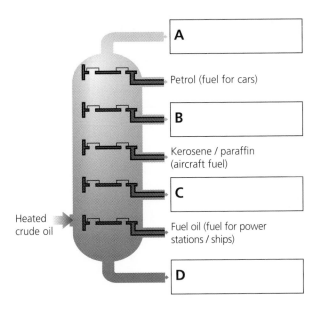

A

Petrol (fuel for cars)

B

Kerosene / paraffin
(aircraft fuel)

C

Heated
crude oil

Fuel oil (fuel for power
stations / ships)

D

The diagram is missing the following labels:

Bitumen   Diesel   Naphtha   Refinery gases

Write each label in the correct place on the diagram.   [4]

2   Explain why short chain hydrocarbons have a low boiling point and long chain hydrocarbons
have a high boiling point.

....

.... [2]

3   Not all of the products from fractional distillation are useful.
To make them useful, they have to be cracked.

What is meant by the term 'cracking'?

.... [1]

4   Crude oil is used for a number of purposes.
It is a finite resource.

Explain why crude oil is a finite resource.

....

.... [2]

Total Marks .... / 9

Interpreting and Interacting with Earth's Systems

1 The atmosphere of our Earth currently is made up of the following gases.

Gas	Proportion of the Atmosphere (%)
Nitrogen	78
Oxygen	21
Carbon dioxide	0.04
Other gases	1

a) The numbers in the table do not add up to 100%.

Suggest why this is the case.

.... [1

b) Scientists have created models of the atmosphere of early Earth.
One of the models is shown below. It is in the **incorrect** order.

Put these statements into the correct order.

A These newly formed oceans removed some carbon dioxide by dissolving the gas.

B Primitive plants that could photosynthesise removed carbon dioxide from the atmosphere, and added oxygen.

C Levels of nitrogen in the atmosphere increased as nitrifying bacteria released nitrogen.

D A hot volcanic Earth released ammonia, carbon dioxide and water vapour.

E The Earth cooled and water vapour condensed into liquid water.

The **correct** order is:

[2

2 What part of the electromagnetic spectrum is affected by greenhouse gases?

A gamma   **B** ultraviolet   **C** infrared   **D** heat

Your answer [ ] [1

Total Marks .... / 4

Air Pollution and Potable Water

1 Draw a line from each air pollutant to the effect it produces.

Carbon monoxide		coats surfaces with soot
Sulfur dioxide		kills plants and aquatic life
Nitrogen oxides		forms photochemical smogs
Particulates		air poisoning

[3]

2 Clean drinking water is essential for everyday life.

Look at the flowchart.

It shows the treatment of sewage water leading to fresh drinking water.

a) What is **removed** from the water treatment system at **A** and **B**?

A ....

B .... [2]

b) What is **added** to the water treatment system at **C** and **D**?

C ....

D .... [2]

3 Draw a diagram to show how **thermal desalination** takes place.

[2]

Matter, Models and Density

1 Describe the forces between the molecules in a gas.

....

[1

2 State the evidence that led to Rutherford claiming that the atomic nucleus was positively charged.

....

....

[2

3 Explain why solid aluminium has a higher density than molten aluminium.

....

....

[2

4 A 2m³ cube of copper has a mass of 1.792×10^4kg.

Calculate the density of copper.

density = ... [2

5 Name the particle that J. J. Thomson discovered.   Answer: .... [1

6 State how the Bohr model of the atom differed from Rutherford's model.

....

....

[2

7 1kg of steam condenses to water at 100°C.

In the boxes below sketch how the molecules might appear in the two states.

Steam (gas)	Water (liquid)

[2

Total Marks .... / 12

Temperature and State

Refer to the Data Sheet on page 444 when answering these questions.

1 A small block of aluminium is given just sufficient energy to melt.

Identify **one** factor that remains unchanged when it melts.

_____ [1]

2 What type of change is a change of state?

_____ [2]

3 State **two** factors that are linked to the internal energy of a solid or liquid.

_____

_____ [2]

4 a) The latent heat of vaporisation of water is 2.26×10^6 J/kg.

Calculate how much energy is released if 0.1kg of steam condenses to water at 100°C.

energy released = _____ [2]

b) The specific heat capacity of water is 4200J/kg/°C.

Calculate how much energy is released when 0.1kg of water at 100°C cools by 65°C.

energy released = _____ [2]

5 Carla is eating jam sponge pudding.
Although the jam and sponge are the same temperature, the jam burns her mouth but the sponge does not.

Explain why.

_____

_____ [2]

Total Marks _____ / 11

Journeys

Refer to the Data Sheet on page 444 when answering these questions.

1 Describe the difference between speed and velocity.

....

.... [2]

2 A car travels at an average speed of 30m/s.

Calculate how far it travels in 40 seconds.

distance = ... [2]

3 A car travelling at 30m/s increased its speed to 70m/s in 8 seconds.

Calculate the acceleration.

acceleration = ... [2]

4 A person travels five miles north and then three miles east.
They stop for a break before travelling four miles south.
Finally they travel three miles west.

What is their **final** displacement?

Answer: .... [1]

5 A 50kg athlete is running at 8m/s.

Calculate how much kinetic energy they have.

kinetic energy = ... [3]

Total Marks .... / 10

Forces

1 What is the difference between a gravitational force and an electric force?

....

.... [1]

2 State Newton's first law of motion.

....

.... [2]

3 The Earth makes a complete orbit of the Sun each year.

Describe the forces acting on the two bodies while this is happening and compare their magnitude.

....

....

....

.... [3]

4 A 30N force is applied to a stationary truck of mass 15kg.

Calculate the acceleration of the truck.

acceleration = ... [2]

5 A student says:

When standing, there is a force called weight acting through my feet on the floor.

What piece of information from Newton's third law has been left out of this statement by the student?

....

.... [2]

6 State the name of the force that always opposes motion.

.... [1]

Total Marks .... / 11

Force, Energy and Power

1 Vinay needs to get a barrel into the back of his van.

Suggest why he might prefer to push the barrel up a ramp rather than lift it straight in.

_____

_____

_____
[3]

2 A 60kg person climbs to the top of a 12m high flight of stairs.

Calculate how much potential energy the person gains.
(g = 10m/s^2)

potential energy = _____ [2]

3 A machine can lift a 150kg load 12m vertically in 90 seconds.

Calculate the power of the machine.
(g = 10m/s^2)

power = _____ [2]

4 A car is released from rest. It accelerates down a hill until the brakes are applied and comes to a stop at the bottom of the hill.

Describe the main energy changes that take place.

_____

_____

_____
[3]

5 Explain why a person might find that pushing a piano is difficult, despite it having wheels.

_____

_____
[2]

Total Marks _____ / 12

Changes of Shape

Refer to the Data Sheet on page 444 when answering these questions.

1 What is meant by a 'plastic material'?

_____

_____ [1]

2 Explain why the value for gravitational field strength is larger on Jupiter than it is on Mars.

_____ [1]

3 A spring extends 2cm when a force of 1N is applied.

Calculate the value of the spring constant.

spring constant = _____ [2]

4 A student added weights to a spring, recording the extension for each weight.
A graph was plotted of the results, as shown below.

Explain the shape of the graph.

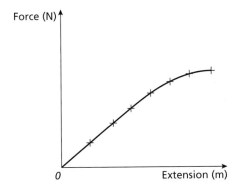

_____

_____

_____

_____ [3]

5 A spring with spring constant 80N/m is stretched 30cm.

Calculate how much energy is transferred.

energy transferred = _____ [2]

> **Total Marks** _____ / 9

Electric Charge

1 What name is given to the space around a charged object in which another charged object would experience a force?

Answer: _____ [1

2 A flow of charge will produce a reading on an ammeter.

Give the **two** other detectable effects that a flow of charge can produce.

_____

_____ [2

3 Explain why a plastic comb is an insulator, despite containing electrons.

_____ [2

4 A battery produces a current of 5A for 10 seconds.

Calculate how much charge flows.

charge = _____ [2]

5 A teacher rubs a plastic rod with a woollen cloth. Both the rod and cloth are insulators.

a) Explain why the plastic rod becomes positively charged and the woollen cloth becomes negatively charged.

_____

_____

_____ [3]

b) A student holds the positive rod over a discharged electroscope.

Explain why the gold leaf inside the electroscope rises.

_____

_____ [3]

Total Marks _____ / 13

Circuits

1 On a current–potential difference (I–V) graph for a component, what does the gradient represent?

Answer: .... [1]

2 A student varied the potential difference across a component in a circuit and measured the current.
They used their results to plot the graph below.

a) Suggest what the component was most likely to be.

Answer: .... [1]

b) Explain why the graph in part **a)** has that shape for the component.

....

....

....

.... [4]

The student repeated the experiment with a different component and produced the graph below.

c) Name the component.

Answer: .... [1]

d) State what the graph indicates about the current direction.

.... [1]

Total Marks .... / 8

Resistors and Energy Transfers

1 Calculate the value of the potential difference across **V** in the circuit below.

Current

12Ω

36V

4Ω

V

potential difference = _____ [3]

2 Calculate the combined resistance of the two parallel resistors below.

24V

4A

4A

24Ω

8Ω

resistance = _____ [3]

3 A 2kW kettle is plugged into a 250V supply and switched on.

Calculate the current that flows.

current = _____ [2]

4 A 2Ω, a 3Ω and a 5Ω resistor are connected in series with a 20V battery.

Calculate the current that flows through them.

current = _____ [2]

Total Marks _____ / 10

Magnetic Fields

Refer to the Data Sheet on page 444 when answering these questions.

1 A wire carrying a current passes through a piece of card.
Three plotting compasses are placed on the card.
The direction of the pointer for one of the plotting
compasses is shown on the diagram below.

Complete the diagram by drawing in the pointers on
plotting compasses **X** and **Y**.

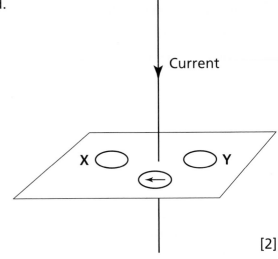

[2]

2 A coil of wire is connected to a 12V battery via a closed switch.
A compass is placed close to the coil of wire.
After 15 seconds, the switch is opened.
The compass needle moves and points in a different direction.

Suggest a reason for this.

_____

_____

_____

[2]

3 A student investigates the magnetic field due to a coil placed on a piece of paper and
connected to a 6V battery.
They sprinkle iron filings around the coil.

Suggest how they would identify the strongest region of the magnetic field.

_____

_____

[1]

4 Explain what is meant by 'induced magnetism'.

_____

_____

[2]

Total Marks _____ / 7

Wave Behaviour

1 What type of wave is a sound wave?   Answer: _____ [1

2 A student uses a 0.9m long ripple tank to measure the velocity of a water wave.
The wave travels the length of the tank in 3 seconds.
The distance between waves is 0.01m.

a) Calculate the velocity of the wave.

velocity = _____ [2

b) What is the frequency of the wave?

frequency = _____ [2

3 Below is a picture of water in a ripple tank, taken 2 seconds after the dibber started
to oscillate up and down.

What is the speed of the waves?

0.5m

Dibber

wave speed = _____ [2

4 The diagram below shows the refraction of water waves as they pass into shallow water.

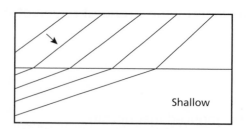

Shallow

What **two** wave measurements have changed during refraction?

_____ [2]

Total Marks _____ / 9

Electromagnetic Radiation

1 A pebble is dropped into a ripple tank, producing a water wave.
This can model an electromagnetic wave.

State what property of the wave cannot now be changed.

Answer: _____ [1]

2 A dentist will leave the room when a patient is having an X-ray.

Suggest the reason for this.

_____ [2]

3 A microwave oven uses microwaves to heat food.
A jacket potato on a plate is placed inside the oven, which is then switched on for a few minutes.
When removed, the potato is hot but the plate is cool.

Explain why this is.

_____

_____

_____ [3]

4 A radio station broadcasts by using radio waves of wavelength 1500m.
The speed of electromagnetic radiation is 3×10^8 m/s.

Calculate the frequency of the station.

frequency = _____ [3]

5 X-rays and gamma rays are forms of ionising radiation.

Describe how they can affect the body.

_____

_____ [2]

Total Marks _____ / 11

Nuclei of Atoms

1 Name the particles that are found in an atomic nucleus.

_____ [2

2 Uranium atoms (atomic number 92) can be found with different numbers of neutrons.

What word describes these different forms of the same element?

Answer: _____ [1

3 Gamma rays are known as ionising radiation.

Describe how they can affect atoms.

_____

_____ [2

4 A teacher puts different absorbers between a radioactive source and a Geiger counter.
When paper is used, the count rate on the Geiger counter doesn't change.
However, the count rate drops when aluminium is used and drops further when lead is used.

Name the types of radiation that the source emitted.

_____ [2

5 State the values for **X** and **Y** in the equation for radioactive decay below.

$$^{235}_{92}U \rightarrow\ ^{Y}_{X}Th +\ ^{4}_{2}He$$

_____ [2

6 Two nuclei of carbon have different numbers of neutrons.

$$^{12}_{6}C \qquad ^{14}_{6}C$$

a) Describe the structure of each nucleus.

_____

_____ [2

b) State the charge on each nucleus.

_____ [1

Total Marks _____ / 12

Half-Life

1 Explain what is meant by the term 'half-life'.

[2]

2 Explain what is meant by the term 'irradiation'.

[1]

3 Americium-241 is used in smoke detectors. It emits alpha particles.
The equation for the radioactive decay is shown below.

$$^{241}_{95}\text{Am} \rightarrow {}^{237}_{x}\text{Np} + {}^{y}_{2}\text{He}$$

a) What are the values of x and y?

$x =$ [1]

$y =$ [1]

b) Americium-241 has a half life of 432 years, so will not need to be replaced in the smoke detector.

Suggest why this is an advantage.

[2]

4 Suggest **two** ways in which atoms can be affected when they are bombarded by radiation from a radioactive source.

[2]

Total Marks _____ / 9

Systems and Transfers

Refer to the Data Sheet on page 444 when answering these questions.

1 A hot saucepan is dropped into a sink full of cold water.

   a) Explain why the saucepan cools down.

   _____

   _____ [2

   b) Describe what happens to the cold water as a result.

   _____ [1

2 Calculate the amount of heat required from an electric kettle to raise the temperature of 1.2kg of water from 20°C to boiling point at 100°C.
(Take the specific heat capacity of water to be 4200J/kg/°C.)

heat energy = _____ [2

3 A farm has a hydroelectric system to produce electrical power from a generator. 20kg of water falls 15m down a vertical hillside every second.

   a) State the main energy changes that take place in the system.

   _____

   _____ [3

   b) Calculate the amount of energy that will be changed from one form to another every second as the water falls down the hillside.
   ($g = 10m/s^2$)

energy = _____ [2

   c) In reality, energy will be lost from the system. State what form that energy is likely to take.

Answer: _____ [1

Total Marks _____ / 11

Energy, Power and Efficiency

1. When charging a mobile phone from the mains, not all the electrical energy is transferred through the transformer (charger).

   Describe how energy is 'lost'.

   .... [1]

2. State **two** ways in which the heating of a house can be improved by reducing heat loss.

   ....

   .... [2]

3. A 250V mains fan draws a current of 2A from the power supply.

   a) Calculate the power of the fan.

   power = ... [2]

   b) Calculate how much energy the fan will draw from the mains power supply if it is on for 10 minutes.

   energy = ... [2]

4. A mains kettle is used to raise the temperature of 2kg of water by 70°C in order for it to boil. (Specific heat capacity of water = 4200J/kg/°C)

   a) Calculate how much energy the water would receive from the kettle.

   energy = ... [2]

   b) If the kettle provided 8×10^5J of electrical energy to the water, calculate the efficiency of the kettle.

   efficiency = ... [3]

   Total Marks .... / 12

Physics on the Road

1 State **two** distances that determine the total stopping distance of a car when the driver needs to brake suddenly.

.... [2

2 **a)** A car travelling at a velocity of 25m/s is brought to rest in 10 seconds.

Calculate the deceleration.

deceleration = ... [2

b) Calculate the force that would act on a person of mass 70kg sitting inside the car and wearing a secure seat belt.

force = ... [2

3 Two students carry out an experiment to measure their reaction time.
They use a metre ruler and a stopwatch.
They found the following equation useful:

$$\text{reaction time} = \frac{\sqrt{2 \times \text{distance (m)}}}{g}$$

a) Describe how they could carry out the experiment.

....

....

....

....

....

.... [6

b) Suggest what would be a sensible result for their reaction time.

.... [1

Total Marks .... / 13

Energy for the World

1 Explain what is meant by a 'non-renewable' energy source.

....

.... [2]

2 A steam engine uses coal as a fuel.

a) Describe the energy changes that take place in the engine as it moves along the track.

....

....

.... [4]

b) Alcohol is a renewable bio-fuel that can be produced from crops on farms.
It could be used to run steam engines by burning it in a boiler.

Suggest **two** reasons why this would not be a good idea.

....

....

.... [2]

3 Nuclear power stations use uranium-235 as a fuel.
Uranium-235 has a long half-life of 7×10^8 years.

a) Suggest why uranium is considered to be a non-renewable fuel.

....

.... [1]

b) State **one** advantage and **one** disadvantage of using nuclear power.

....

....

.... [2]

Total Marks .... / 11

Energy at Home

Refer to the Data Sheet on page 444 when answering these questions.

1 What is the difference between an a.c. supply and a d.c. supply?

....

.... [2

2 State the **potential difference** and **frequency** of the mains electricity supply.

.... [2

3 What is the function of the earth wire in an appliance?

....

.... [2

4 A teacher sets up a model electricity transmission system.
A diagram of the apparatus is shown below.

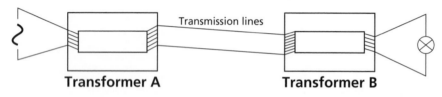

Transformer A   Transmission lines   **Transformer B**

a) State what type of transformer is represented by **Transformer B**.

.... [1]

b) Explain why transformers are used in the transmission of power in the National Grid.

....

....

....

.... [3]

Total Marks .... / 10

Collins

GCSE (9–1)
Combined Science (Biology)

F

Paper 1 (Foundation Tier)

You may use:

- a scientific calculator
- a ruler.

Time allowed: 1 hour 10 minutes

Instructions

- Use black ink. You may use a HB pencil for graphs and diagrams.
  Answer **all** the questions.
- Write your answer to each question in the space provided.
  Additional paper may be used if required.

Information

- The total mark for this paper is **60**.
  The marks for each question are shown in brackets [ ].
- Quality of extended responses will be assessed in questions marked with an asterisk (*).

SECTION A

Answer **all** the questions.

You should spend a maximum of 20 minutes on this section.

1   The diagram shows a light microscope.

What is **X**?

A   lens

B   stage

C   spine

D   mirror   Your answer ☐ [1]

2   Which cell does **not** have a nucleus?

A   red blood cell

B   white blood cell

C   neurone

D   root hair cell   Your answer ☐ [1]

3   How many strands of nucleic acid form the helical structure of DNA?

A   1

B   2

C   3

D   4   Your answer ☐   **[1]**

4   The following statements are about enzymes.

Which statement is **not** true?

A   The optimum temperature for all enzymes is 37°C.

B   All enzymes are biological catalysts.

C   All enzymes have an active site.

D   All enzymes are denatured by high temperatures.   Your answer ☐   **[1]**

5   The diagram shows a plant cell.

What is the name of this cell?

A   root hair cell

B   epithelial cell

C   mesophyll cell

D   palisade cell   Your answer ☐   **[1]**

Turn over

6   Where is meristematic tissue found?

   A   central nervous system

   B   peripheral nervous system

   C   bone marrow

   D   plant roots and shoot tips   Your answer ☐ [1

7   Villi are found in the small intestine.
   They are important in the absorption of the products of digestion.

   Which of the following statements is **true** about villi?

   A   Villi are destroyed by the nicotine in cigarette smoke.

   B   Villi have thick walls to aid absorption.

   C   Villi provide a large surface area for absorption of molecules.

   D   Villi absorb only glucose from the intestines.   Your answer ☐ [1]

8   The diagram shows a working muscle cell.

   What letter is most likely to represent plasma?   Your answer ☐ [1]

9   Terri looks at a piece of skin under a microscope using a high powered lens.
     She can see cells, but is unable to see clearly the structures within the cells.

     What is the most likely reason for this?

     A The specimen is too thick.

     B The resolution of the microscope is not high enough.

     C The microscope is not focused correctly.

     D There is insufficient light.   Your answer ☐ **[1]**

10   Some students investigated the rate of reaction of amylase enzyme in turning starch
     into glucose.
     They used temperatures between 0°C and 70°C.
     They plotted their results as a line graph.

     Which graph are they most likely to obtain?

  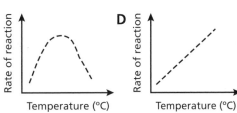

                                                              Your answer ☐ **[1]**

Turn over

SECTION B

Answer **all** the questions.

11   Catalase is an enzyme that breaks down hydrogen peroxide to release oxygen gas.
Catalase is present in liver.
Some students wanted to investigate the effect of pH on catalase activity.
They took five boiling tubes and placed a piece of liver in each.
They then added to each tube hydrogen peroxide that had been buffered to a different pH.

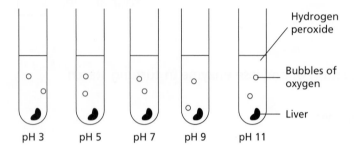

pH 3   pH 5   pH 7   pH 9   pH 11

The students counted the number of bubbles produced in five minutes.

(a) Why is counting bubbles **not** an accurate way of measuring the amount of
    oxygen produced?

    ....

    ....

    ....

                                                                                            [2]

(b) Another group of students carried out the same experiment but decided to collect the oxygen using a gas syringe.

(i) Explain why this will give a more accurate measure.

....

.... **[1]**

(ii) Name **two** variables the students should control in the experiment.

....

.... **[2]**

(c) On the axes below, sketch the graph you would expect to get from the results.

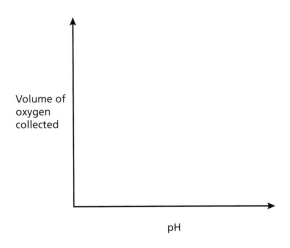

[1]

Turn over

12 Some students wanted to investigate the link between surface area to volume ratio (SA : V)
    and rate of diffusion.

    They found the following information in a textbook.

Side length of cube	Surface area	Volume	SA : V ratio
2 cm	$2 \times 2 \times 6 = 24$ cm^2	$2 \times 2 \times 2 = 8$ cm^3	24 to 8 = 3 : 1
4 cm			
6 cm	$6 \times 6 \times 6 = 216$ cm^2	$6 \times 6 \times 6 = 216$ cm^3	216 to 216 = 1 : 1
8 cm	$8 \times 8 \times 6 = 384$ cm^2	$8 \times 8 \times 8 = 512$ cm^3	384 to 512 = 0.75 : 1

(a) Complete the table for the cube with a side length of 4 cm.   [3

(b) In which cube will diffusion occur fastest?
    Explain your answer.

    _____

    _____   [2

3 Adam, Ben and Tommy want to find out who has the quickest reactions.

They use a computer program.

When they see the shape change from green to red, they have to press the mouse button as quickly as they can. The computer calculates their reaction times and puts them in a table.

User name	1st attempt	2nd attempt	3rd attempt	Mean average
Adam	0.52	0.49	0.46	0.49
Ben	0.66	0.62	0.61	
Tommy	0.45	0.42	0.42	0.43

(a) Calculate the mean for Ben's results.

mean = ... **[2]**

(b) In this experiment, the pupils are making a voluntary response.

Write down the stages of the pathway represented by **A**, **B** and **C**.

receptor $\longrightarrow$ **A** .... $\longrightarrow$ relay neurone $\longrightarrow$ **B** .... $\longrightarrow$ **C** .... $\longrightarrow$ response

A ....

B ....

C .... **[3]**

Turn over

(c) The Babinski reflex is a reflex action in infants.

Stroking the sole of the foot with a firm stimulus causes the big toe to bend upwards.

(i) How do you know this is a reflex action?

_____

_____ [1

(ii) What is the function of the reflex action?

_____

_____ [1

4   Some children are born with a hole in the heart.

When this happens, there is a hole at point **X** on the diagram, between the left and right side of the heart.

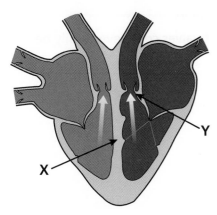

Dionne is 13 years old. She has had a hole in the heart since she was born.
She easily gets short of breath and finds physical exercise very tiring.

(a) Explain why she has these symptoms.

....

....

....

....

....   **[2]**

(b) Aortic valve stenosis is when the valve labelled **Y** is too narrow.

What will be the likely effect of this condition on the heart?

....

....

....   **[1]**

Turn over

(c) When heart valves become damaged they may need to be replaced with either mechanical (artificial) valves or tissue (animal donor) valves.

There is a higher risk of blood clots when mechanical valves are used and patients need to take blood thinning medication for the rest of their lives.

Valves from animal donors usually only last a maximum of 20 years.

Using stem cell technology, it is hoped that replacement heart valves could eventually be grown from a person's own cells.

(i) What is the function of heart valves?

_____

_____ [1

(ii) Suggest **two** reasons why someone might be reluctant to have a heart valve from an animal donor.

_____

_____

_____ [2

(iii) What are the advantages of using stem cells to produce heart valves?

_____

_____ [2

15   In 1921, two scientists called Banting and Best performed a number of experiments on dogs.

In their first experiment they removed the pancreas from a dog.
The dog's blood glucose levels rose and the dog developed diabetes.

In a second experiment, they removed a pancreas from a healthy dog, froze it, ground it and filtered it.
The filtrate they extracted was injected into the diabetic dog with high blood glucose levels.
The dog's blood glucose levels returned to normal and it became healthier.

(a) What substance had Banting and Best discovered?

.... [1]

(b) Glucose is needed for respiration.

Complete the word equation below for aerobic respiration.

glucose + ... → carbon dioxide + ... [2]

(c) Yeast respires anaerobically to produce alcohol.
Colin wanted to make some homemade pear wine.
He mashed some pears, added water, yeast and sugar and left the mixture for a week.

(i) Why did Colin add sugar?

.... [1]

(ii) After a week, Colin noticed a lot of bubbles in the mixture.

Explain why there were bubbles.

.... [1]

Turn over

(d) For each of the statements below, write down whether they are describing **aerobic** or **anaerobic** respiration.

   i)   Occurs in the mitochondria

   ii) Releases a lot of energy

   iii) Breakdown of glucose is incomplete

   iv) Requires oxygen

[4]

6   The photograph shows a water lettuce, which is a floating water plant.
    It is not anchored to the ground, but has hair-like roots.

(a) Explain how water moves into the water lettuce.

    ....

    ....

    ....

    .... [3]

(b) Water lettuce is a freshwater plant.

    What would happen to the net movement of water if the water lettuce was placed
    in sea water?
    Give a reason for your answer.

    ....

    ....

    ....

    .... [2]

(c)* Explain how glucose and minerals are transported through a plant.

[6

(d) In which organ of a plant is glucose produced?

[1

(e) In humans, the blood transports substances around the body.

Name **three** substances transported by plasma in the blood.

[3

END OF QUESTION PAPER

Collins

GCSE (9–1)
Combined Science (Biology)
Paper 2 (Foundation Tier)

F

Time allowed: 1 hour 10 minutes

You may use:
- a ruler
- a scientific calculator.

Instructions

- Use black ink. You may use a HB pencil for graphs and diagrams.
- Answer **all** the questions.
- Write your answer to each question in the space provided.
- Additional paper may be used if required.

Information

- The total mark for this paper is **60**.
- The marks for each question are shown in brackets [ ].
- Quality of extended responses will be assessed in questions marked with an asterisk (*).

Practice Exam Paper 2

SECTION A

Answer **all** the questions.

You should spend a maximum of 20 minutes on this section.

1   An egg cell from a human female usually contains

   A   one X chromosome

   B   two X chromosomes

   C   one X and one Y chromosome

   D   one Y chromosome   Your answer [ ]   [1

2   Carla uses a quadrat to count the number of dandelion plants growing in different areas of a field.

   Her results are shown below.

Quadrat number	Number of dandelions
1	7
2	9
3	8
4	8
5	6

   Each quadrat measures one square metre.

   The total area of the field is 60 square metres.

   What is the estimated number of dandelions in the field?

   A   98

   B   228

   C   380

   D   456   Your answer [ ]   [1

3   What type of organisms would you expect to catch using the apparatus below?

A   moths

B   beetles

C   voles

D   worms   Your answer [ ]   **[1]**

4   Which of the following is an example of sustainable development?

A   Introducing fishing quotas to limit the amount of fish that can be caught.

B   Clearing rainforests to grow food for the population.

C   Imposing large taxes on fossil fuel use.

D   Building museums to preserve the past.   Your answer [ ]   **[1]**

Turn over

5 An association between two individuals in which the association benefits both is called:

A mutualism

B competition

C commensalism

D parasitism   Your answer [ ] **[1]**

6 An example of a discrete variable is:

A height

B blood group

C weight

D width of hand span   Your answer [ ] **[1]**

7 The table below shows part of the classification of the long nosed common dolphin, D. capensis.

Phylum	Chordata
Class	Mammalia
Order	Cetacea
X	Delphinidae
Y	Delphinus
Species	D. capensis

Which of the following statements is **correct**?

A X is the genus.

B Y is the genus.

C X is the kingdom.

D Y is the kingdom.   Your answer [ ] **[1]**

8   A person who has been infected with human papilloma virus (HPV) has an increased risk of developing:

   A tuberculosis

   B influenza

   C autism

   D cervical cancer   Your answer ☐ **[1]**

9   Which of the following is an example of an **abiotic** factor in a pond?

   A the temperature of the water

   B the mass of pond weed

   C the number of frogs

   D microorganisms that feed on decaying plant material   Your answer ☐ **[1]**

10   Sometimes a mutation occurs in DNA.

   Which statement is **correct** about mutations?

   A Mutations will only affect phenotype.

   B Mutations will only affect genotype.

   C Mutations may affect both phenotype and genotype.

   D Mutations affect neither phenotype nor genotype.

                                                        Your answer ☐ **[1]**

Turn over

Practice Exam Paper 2

SECTION B

Answer **all** the questions.

11 Look at the article from a nature magazine about ospreys.

> Although the osprey population has increased over recent years in the UK, they remain the fourth rarest bird of prey in the UK. They are at risk because they feed on fish and, therefore, depend on high water quality of rivers and lakes. Their eggs are often stolen by collectors and migrating ospreys are at risk from being shot by hunters.
>
>
>
> The Lake District Osprey Project has been running for several years to encourage these birds to breed in the UK. In 2001, a pair of ospreys nested beside Bassenthwaite Lake. They were the first wild osprey to breed in the Lake District for over 150 years. The Forestry Commission built a nest to encourage the birds to stay, which they did. Once the eggs were laid, wardens kept a round the clock watch to prevent disturbance and deter egg thieves. Bassenthwaite Lake is a National Nature Reserve and provides valuable habitats for a variety of wildlife.

(a) Ospreys were once endangered in the UK.

What does endangered mean?

....

....

[1]

(b) Give **two** ways in which humans have caused the ospreys to become endangered.

....

....

....

[2]

(c) How has the osprey been protected and encouraged to breed
in the Lake District?

....

.... **[1]**

12   The graph below shows the smoking habits and incidence of lung cancer for people living in a European country.

Smoking habits and lung cancer incidence in a European country

KEY

✖✖✖ Male smoking data

●●● Female smoking data

——— Male incidence of lung cancer

- - - - Female incidence of lung cancer

(a) Describe the patterns in male and female smoking habits from 1948 to 2000.

....

....   [2]

(b) Calculate the percentage difference in female smokers between 1968 and 1988.
Show your working.

percentage difference = ...   [3]

(c) Does the data support the hypothesis that smoking causes lung cancer?
Give a reason for your answer.

....

....

....   [2]

(d)* A healthy heart is essential for good health.

Describe the effect of diet and exercise on the cardiovascular system.

[6]

13 Below is one of the stages in the carbon cycle.

carbon in dead animals and plants → carbon dioxide in the atmosphere

(a) What is the name of this process?

.... **[1]**

(b) Nitrogen is another element that is recycled.

Below is part of the nitrogen cycle.

nitrates in soil → nitrogen in the air

(i) Which type of bacteria is involved in this process?

.... **[1]**

(ii) Plants cannot use nitrogen gas.

What substance must nitrogen be converted into so that plants can make use of it?

.... **[1**

4 The table contains information about three mammals.

Animal	Binomial name	Diet
Horse	*Equus ferus*	Eats grasses and plant materials. Has only one simple stomach.
Deer	*Dama dama*	Eats shoots, fresh grass, twigs, fruit. Has a complex stomach and can bring food back up into its mouth to chew again.
Zebra	*Equus zebra*	Eats mainly grasses. Has one simple stomach.

(a) Which two animals are most closely related?

Give **two** reasons for your answer.

....

....

.... **[2]**

The table gives some information about donkeys and horses.

Donkeys	Horses
Stubborn but hard working	Hard workers
Sure footed	Delicate legs
Difficult to train	Easy to train
Slower runners	Fast runners
Average life span 30–50 years	Average life span 25–30 years
Ferments food in a hind gut so less prone to colic	Cannot vomit so prone to colic
Not very intelligent	Intelligent

A mule is a cross between a donkey and a horse.

Mules are often used to carry heavy loads on their backs in mountainous regions.

(b) List the qualities required from the donkey and the horse to make the mule suitable for this work.

(i) Qualities from the donkey.

....

....

.... **[2]**

Turn over

(ii) Qualities from the horse.

[2

(c) Mules cannot reproduce.
It is wrong to call a mule a 'species'.

Explain why.

[1

(d) Scientists believe the modern-day horse evolved from a horse with four toes.
The four toes were useful for spreading the load on a soft forest floor.
As the ground hardened, a large central toe, similar to the hoof of today's horses,
was better for running over open country.

Suggest how the modern day horse with a hoof could have evolved through
natural selection.

[4

5 The diagram shows sections of a pair of chromosomes from a cat, which contain genes for eye colour, ear shape and fur pattern.

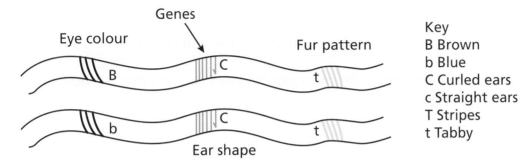

Key
B Brown
b Blue
C Curled ears
c Straight ears
T Stripes
t Tabby

(a) Describe the phenotype of the cat for these three characteristics.

....

....

.... [3]

(b) The cat above mates with a cat that is heterozygous for fur pattern.

(i) Complete the genetic cross diagram.

Parents

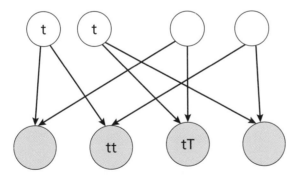

Gametes

Offspring   [2]

(ii) What is the ratio of striped cats to tabby cats in the offspring?

.... [1]

(c) Polycystic kidney disease (PKD) is an inherited disease that affects cats.
PKD is controlled by a single pair of genes.
The allele for PKD is dominant.

A cat breeder is concerned that some of his kittens may have inherited PKD.

(i) Draw a diagram to show the results of a cross between two cats that are both heterozygous for PKU.

[3]

(ii) In a litter of eight kittens, how many kittens would you expect to have PKU if both parents were heterozygous for the condition?

[1

6 A patient has developed a wound infection following surgery.

Some pus from the wound is examined and found to contain a bacteria called *P. aeruginosa*.

Doctors need to know which antibiotic will be best to treat the patient.

They spread the bacteria onto some agar in a Petri dish and add two filter paper discs that have been soaked in different antibiotics.

After incubation at 37°C they examine the Petri dish.

The diagram shows the actual size of the dish after incubation.

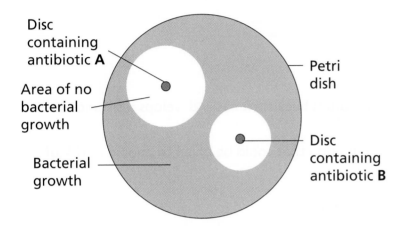

If the area of no bacterial growth around the disc (including the disc) is greater than 200 mm², the antibiotic can be used successfully to treat the infection.

(a) Work out if either or both of the antibiotics could be used to treat the infection.

Use area of a circle = 3.14 × r^2.

You must clearly state your answer.

_____

_____

_____

_____

[3]

Turn over

(b) Suggest **one** other factor that might determine which antibiotics should be used to treat an infection, other than whether the organism is sensitive or resistant to the antibiotic.

....

.... [1

(c) Explain the action of phagocytic white blood cells when *P. aeruginosa* first enters a wound.

....

....

....

.... [3

(d) *P. aeruginosa* can cause problems in hospitals because it easily develops resistance to a range of antibiotics.

Scientists would like to develop a vaccination that could be given to people at risk of post-surgical infections.

What would scientists use in the vaccination?

....

.... [1

(e) Antibiotics are not not suitable for treating all infectious diseases.

Give **one** example of an infectious disease that would **not** be treated with antibiotics.

.... [1

END OF QUESTION PAPER

Collins

GCSE (9–1)
Combined Science (Chemistry)

F

Paper 3 Foundation Tier

Time allowed: 1 hour 10 minutes

You must have:

- the Data Sheet (page 443)

You may use:

- a scientific calculator
- a ruler

Instructions

- Use black ink. You may use an HB pencil for graphs and diagrams.
- Answer **all** the questions.
- Write your answer to each question in the space provided.
- Additional paper may be used if required.

Information

- The total mark for this paper is **60**.
- The marks for each question are shown in brackets **[ ]**.
- Quality of extended responses will be assessed in questions marked with an asterisk (*).

SECTION A

Answer **all** the questions.

You should spend a maximum of 20 minutes on this section.

1   Athina wants to separate a mixture of amino acids.
    She carries out thin layer chromatography.
    The amino acid samples are placed onto silica gel and a solvent is added.

    After two hours the silica gel is sprayed with ninhydrin, which makes the amino acids become visible.

    What is the name given to the **silica gel** in this experiment?

    A   gas phase

    B   mobile phase

    C   solid phase

    D   stationary phase

    Your answer ☐ **[1]**

2   The diagram below shows the chromatogram before and after spraying with ninhydrin.

    What is the R_f value for sample **3**?
    Use a ruler to help you.

    A   0.16

    B   0.27

    C   0.81

    D   0.95

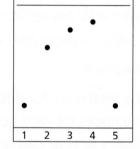

Before   After

    Your answer ☐ **[1]**

The diagrams show the electronic structure of four different atoms.

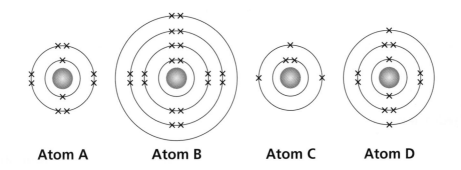

Atom A   **Atom B**   **Atom C**   **Atom D**

Which two atoms are in the same **group**?

A   atom A and atom B

B   atom B and atom D

C   atom C and atom D

D   atom A and atom C

Your answer [ ]   [1]

An element, **X**, has an atomic mass of 88 and the atomic number 38.

Which of the following is correct for element **X**?

A   No. of protons = 38   No. of neutrons = 50   No. of electrons = 50

B   No. of protons = 50   No. of neutrons = 38   No. of electrons = 38

C   No. of protons = 38   No. of neutrons = 38   No. of electrons = 50

D   No. of protons = 38   No. of neutrons = 50   No. of electrons = 38

Your answer [ ]   [1]

Turn over

5   During the electrolysis of aqueous copper sulfate, what is made at the cathode?

    A sulfate

    B hydrogen

    C copper

    D copper hydroxide

                                           Your answer   ☐   **[1**

6   Which of these shows the balanced symbol equation for the reaction between sodium and oxygen to make sodium oxide?

    A $Na + O_2 \rightarrow NaO_2$

    B $4Na + O_2 \rightarrow 2Na_2O$

    C $S + O_2 \rightarrow SO_2$

    D $4S + O_2 \rightarrow 2S_2O$

                                           Your answer   ☐   **[1**

7   What is the best description of the particles in a solid?

	Distance between particles	Movement of particles
A	Close together	In continuous random motion
B	Close together	Vibrating about a fixed point
C	Far apart	In continuous random motion
D	Far apart	Vibrating about a fixed point

                                           Your answer   ☐   **[1**

3 The molecular formula of octadecane is $C_{18}H_{38}$.

What is the empirical formula of octadecane?

A CH_2

B C_2H_4

C C_9H_{19}

D $C_{36}H_{76}$

Your answer ☐ [1]

9 Limestone is the common name for calcium carbonate.

Limestone reacts with hydrochloric acid.

Which of the following shows the correct balanced symbol equation for the reaction between limestone and hydrochloric acid?

A $CaCO_3 + HCl \rightarrow CaCl + H_2O$

B $CaCO_3 + HCl \rightarrow CaCl + H_2O + CO_2$

C $CaCO_3 + 2HCl \rightarrow CaCl_2 + H_2O + CO_2$

D $CaCO_3 + 2HCl \rightarrow CaCl_2 + H_2O + CO_3$

Your answer ☐ [1]

10 Which of the following shows the reaction profile for an exothermic reaction?

A B

C D

Your answer ☐ [1]

SECTION B

Answer **all** the questions.

11   Rosanne is reacting magnesium with sulfuric acid.

(a) Complete the general word equation for a reaction between a metal and an acid:

metal + acid → _____ + _____   [2]

(b) Rosanne noticed that the test tube containing the reaction mixture grew warm during the reaction.

She decided to measure 30 cm³ of acid into a glass beaker.
She measured the temperature of the acid.
She then added 0.1 g of magnesium metal to the acid and measured the temperature change.

Rosanne repeated the experiment four more times using different masses of magnesium metal.
Here is her table of results.

Mass of magnesium (g)	Temperature change (°C)			Mean temperature change (°C)
	Test 1	Test 2	Test 3	
0	0	0	0	
0.1	3	3	4	
0.2	6	6	5	
0.3	7	9	9	
0.4	12	13	12	
0.5	15	16	16	

(i) Calculate the mean temperature change for 0.4 g of magnesium.
Write your answer in the table.
Give your answer to one decimal place.   [2]

(ii) Plot the graph of the results for Test 1 below.

[2]

(iii) One of the points is anomalous.

Which one?
Explain how you can tell from the graph.

....

....

....

[2]

(c) Rosanne measured the temperature using a data-logger with a temperature probe.

Suggest why a data-logger with temperature probe enables more accurate readings.

.... [1]

(d) Give **one** safety precaution that Rosanne should have taken when carrying out
the experiment.

.... [1]

Turn over

12 Look at the graph of boiling points of elements against their atomic numbers for Period 2 of the periodic table.

(a) What does the graph tell you about the boiling point as you go across a **period**?

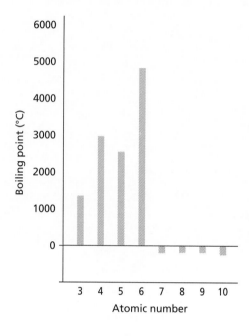

....

.... [2]

(b) Explain why the properties of elements change across a period.

....

....

....

.... [2]

(c) Particle **X** is a particle with the atomic number of 18 and the electronic structure 2.8.8.
Particle **Y** is a particle with the atomic number of 20 and the electronic structure 2.8.8.

Which particle is an atom and which is an ion?
Explain your answer.

....

....

.... **[2]**

(d) A diagram of a hydrogen atom is shown below.

(i) Explain what the **problems** are in representing the atom in this way.

....

....

....

.... **[3]**

(ii) Niels Bohr was the scientist who devised this particular model of the atom.

Explain how his model **improved** upon earlier models.

....

.... **[2]**

13 * Look at the table of data below.

Material	Strength (arbitrary units)	Resistance to corrosion	Density (g/cm3)	Electrical conductivity	Cost (UKP per tonne)
Aluminium	230	Excellent	2.8	Very good	800
Carbon-fibre	2500	Very good	1.5	Very good	11000
PVC plastic	70	Good	1.3	Poor	500
Steel	255	Poor	7.8	Good	60
Titanium alloy	855	Good	4.4	Good	8000

A modern sculptor is making a sculpture for display at the winter Olympics.

The sculptor needs to decide which material to use for her sculpture.

Some of the materials are metals and some are polymers.

Describe and compare the bonding of the materials in the table.

Suggest which of them would be best for making the sculpture, giving reasons for your answer.

[6

4 The diagram below shows an allotrope of carbon called graphene.

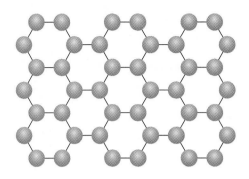

(a) Graphene is used in solar panels.

Explain what **properties** make graphene useful for solar panels.

....

.... **[2]**

(b) Another form of carbon is graphite.

As well as being a good conductor of electricity, it can be used as a dry lubricant.

Draw the structure of graphite in the space below.

[2]

(c) Diamond and graphite have been known for thousands of years.

Graphene was discovered in 2004 whilst another form of carbon, the fullerenes, were discovered in 1985.

Suggest why graphene and the fullerenes were only discovered relatively recently.

....

.... **[2]**

Turn over

15   Look at the diagram. It shows the electrolysis of copper sulfate solution.

Carbon electrodes

Copper sulfate solution

(a) Explain what happens to the copper ions during electrolysis.

_____

_____

_____   [3]

(b) Copper can also be extracted from copper oxide by heating with carbon.

Explain why aluminium **cannot** be extracted from its oxide using this method.

_____

_____   [2]

(c) Tom decides to use electrolysis to extract copper from copper bromide solution. Copper is made.

What is the name of the other product that is produced?

_____   [1]

16 Look at this information about an atom of an element:

Number of neutrons   10
Number of protons   8
Number of electrons   8

(a) What is the mass number of the atom?

.... **[1]**

(b) What is the atomic number of the element?

.... **[1]**

(c) What is the name of the element?
Use the periodic table on your data sheet (page 443) to help you.

.... **[1]**

(d) Glucose has the formula $C_6H_{12}O_6$.

Show that the relative formula mass, M_r, of glucose is 180.
The M_r of C is 12.0, of H is 1.0 and of O is 16.0.

....

....

....

.... **[2]**

Turn over

17 A teacher carries out a thermite reaction.
The thermite reaction is shown below.

aluminium + iron(III) oxide → iron + aluminium oxide

(a) Write a **balanced symbol** equation to show this reaction.

.... [2]

(b) Suggest **two** safety precautions a person carrying out this reaction should take.

....

....

.... [2]

(c) The thermite reaction is an example of an oxidation / reduction reaction.

(i) What is **oxidation**?

.... [1]

(ii) What is **reduction**?

.... [1]

END OF QUESTION PAPER

Collins

GCSE (9–1)
Combined Science (Chemistry)

F

Paper 4 Foundation Tier

You must have:

- the Data Sheet (page 443)

You may use:

- a scientific calculator
- a ruler.

Time allowed: 1 hour 10 minutes

Instructions

- Use black ink. You may use an HB pencil for graphs and diagrams.
- Answer **all** the questions.
- Write your answer to each question in the space provided.
- Additional paper may be used if required.

Information

- The total mark for this paper is **60**.
- The marks for each question are shown in brackets **[ ]**.
- Quality of extended responses will be assessed in questions marked with an asterisk (*****).

Practice Exam Paper 4

SECTION A

Answer **all** the questions.

You should spend a maximum of 20 minutes on this section.

1 Which of the following is a property of all Group 0 elements?

   A They have eight electrons in the outermost shell.

   B They are chemically unreactive.

   C They form positive ions.

   D They are less dense than air.

Your answer ☐ [1]

2 Look at the fractionating column.

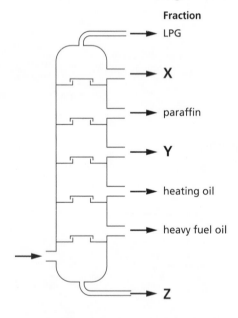

Fraction
LPG
X
paraffin
Y
heating oil
heavy fuel oil
Z

Which fraction is **X**?

   A petrol

   B aviation fuel

   C bitumen

   D alcohol

Your answer ☐ [1]

Look at the diagrams showing the electron structures of four elements.

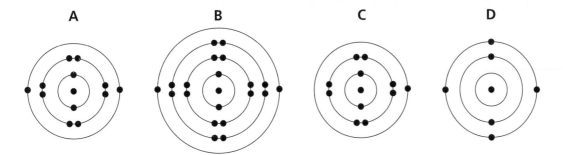

Which element is in **Period 4** of the periodic table?

Your answer ☐ **[1]**

A group of students wants to extract pure water from sea water.

Which technique should they use?

A crystallisation

B evaporation

C filtration

D distillation

Your answer ☐ **[1]**

Turn over

5 Wayne is investigating the reaction between hydrogen peroxide and a catalyst.
He collects the oxygen gas produced and plots the graph shown below.

What is the rate of oxygen production between 0 and 5 s?

A   23 cm³/s

B   7 cm³/s

C   1.4 cm³/s

D   0.7 cm³/s

Your answer ☐   [1

Miranda is investigating the breakdown of hydrogen peroxide into water and oxygen.

$$2H_2O_2 \rightarrow 2H_2O + O_2$$

The reaction is extremely slow.

Miranda takes four black powders which she adds to the hydrogen peroxide.

She records the amount of gas produced.

Look at the graph of her results.

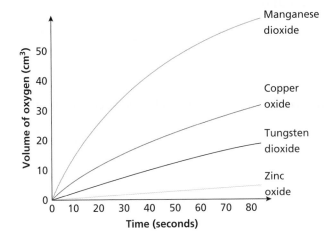

Which of the catalysts tested would be the best for catalysing this reaction?

A   copper oxide

B   manganese dioxide

C   tungsten dioxide

D   zinc oxide

Your answer ☐   **[1]**

7   Which statement is true for a **Group 0** element?

   A   It dissolves in water to form bleach.

   B   It is a metal.

   C   It is an inert gas.

   D   It reacts with an acid to form a salt and hydrogen gas.

Your answer [ ]   [1

8   Which of the following is the name given to the process by which fractions of crude oil are converted into smaller, more useful molecules?

   A   fractional distillation

   B   cracking

   C   chromatography

   D   filtration

Your answer [ ]   [1

Crude oil is a mixture of hydrocarbons in the alkane series.

Which of the following is **not** an alkane?

A CH_4

B C_2H_4

C C_3H_8

D C_4H_{10}

Your answer ☐ [1]

0 Which relative molecular mass, M_r, is **not** correct for the molecule given?

A water, H_2O $M_r = 18.0$

B sulfur dioxide, SO_2 $M_r = 64.1$

C carbon monoxide, CO $M_r = 28.0$

D chlorine, Cl_2 $M_r = 72.0$

Your answer ☐ [1]

SECTION B

Answer **all** the questions.

11 (a) Give the electronic structure of potassium.

.... [1

(b) Draw a diagram to show the metallic bonding in potassium.

[2

(c) A small piece of potassium is added to water.

Describe what observations you would make when a small piece of potassium is added to a trough of water.

....

....

.... [2

(d) Write the word equation to show the reaction between water and potassium.

.... [2]

(e) Describe how the reactivity of the **two** metals above potassium in the reactivity series will differ to potassium.

....

....

.... [2]

12 The table below shows the composition of the Earth's atmosphere at 3 billion and 2 billion years ago (bya).

Gas	3 bya (%)	2 bya (%)	Present (%)
Nitrogen	91	82	
Oxygen	0	10	
Carbon dioxide	9	8	

(a) Complete the table to show the present day proportion of gases.

[1

(b) Describe how the percentages of the gases in the atmosphere have changed between 3 bya and 2 bya.

Give reasons for the changes.

....

....

....

[3

(c) The graph shows how humans are likely to have caused the increase in greenhouse gases.

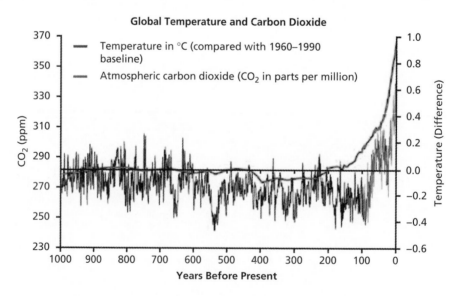

Global Temperature and Carbon Dioxide

Temperature in °C (compared with 1960–1990 baseline)

Atmospheric carbon dioxide (CO_2 in parts per million)

CO_2 (ppm)

Temperature (Difference)

Years Before Present

(i) Calculate the change in carbon dioxide concentration between 1000 and 100 years before present.

change = ... [2]

(ii) What is the current temperature difference?

.... [1]

(d)* Methane and carbon dioxide are greenhouse gases.
Methane is a far more powerful greenhouse gas than carbon dioxide.

Explain the greenhouse effect and discuss the consequences that increased levels of carbon dioxide and methane have on the greenhouse effect.

Suggest ways to reduce greenhouse gas emissions.

....

....

....

....

....

....

....

....

....

....

....

.... [6]

Turn over

13   Stephen and Nicci are investigating displacement reactions.
     They strongly heat copper oxide with carbon powder.

(a) What is a displacement reaction?

....

....   [

(b) Write the balanced symbol equation for the reaction between copper oxide and carbon.

....   [2

(c) Stephen says that he could extract aluminium from aluminium oxide powder.

Is he correct?
Explain your answer.

....

....   [2

(d) What is the symbol formula for aluminium oxide?

....   [1

4   Theo is carrying out an experiment cracking long-chain hydrocarbons.

He sets up the experiment shown below.

(a) What is meant by the term **cracking** long-chain hydrocarbons?

....

.... **[2]**

(b) What is a hydrocarbon?

.... **[1]**

(c) What is the function of the porcelain fragments?

.... **[1]**

Turn over

(d) The paraffin on the mineral wool has the formula $C_{14}H_{30}$.
The products of the cracking reaction are C_3H_8 and another hydrocarbon.

What is the formula for the other hydrocarbon produced?

.... [1

(e) Name **three** useful products obtained from crude oil.

....

.... [3

5   A teacher is carrying out an experiment to demonstrate the reactivity of different metals
     to her class.
     One of the metals is lithium.
     Lithium is stored under oil in a sealed bottle.

(a) Explain why the lithium is stored under oil.

     ....

     ....

     ....   [2]

(b) The teacher then places a small piece of lithium into a bowl of water.
     The lithium reacts with the water.
     It moves about on the surface of the water and the class can see bubbles of a gas.

     What gas is formed in this reaction?

     ....   [1]

(c) Write the word equation for the reaction between lithium and water.

     ....   [2]

(d) Potassium is in the same group of the periodic table as lithium.

     Describe how the reaction between potassium and water would compare to that of
     lithium and water.
     Give a reason for your prediction.

     ....

     ....

     ....   [3]

Turn over

16 Magnesium reacts very slowly with cold water to produce an alkaline solution and hydrogen gas.

(a) Describe the test for hydrogen gas.

....

....

....

[2

(b) Magnesium is in Group 2 of the periodic table.

Describe the **difference** in the reaction that would be seen with the element immediately before magnesium in the periodic table.

....

[1

(c) Magnesium cannot be extracted from its ore with carbon.

Explain why this is the case and suggest how magnesium can be extracted from its ore.

....

....

....

....

....

[3

END OF QUESTION PAPER

Collins

GCSE (9–1)
Combined Science (Physics)

Paper 5 (Foundation Tier)

F

Time allowed: 1 hour 10 minutes

You must have:

- the Data Sheet (page 444)

You may use:

- a scientific calculator
- a ruler

Instructions

- Use black ink. You may use a HB pencil for graphs and diagrams.
- Answer **all** the questions.
- Write your answer to each question in the space provided.
- Additional paper may be used if required.

Information

- The total mark for this paper is **60**.
- The marks for each question are shown in brackets [ ].
- Quality of extended responses will be assessed in questions marked with an asterisk (*).

SECTION A

Answer **all** the questions.

You should spend a maximum of 20 minutes on this section.

1 Which of these symbols is used in a circuit to show a **thermistor**?

A   B

C   D

Your answer [ ] [1

2 A train travels at 40 km/h.

How far does it travel in 2.5 hours?

A 100m

B 90km

C 100km

D 90m

Your answer [ ] [1]

Which of the following statements describing an atom is **incorrect**?

A The atom has a positively charged nucleus.

B Most of an atom's mass is in the nucleus.

C The nucleus has a similar radius to the atom.

D The nucleus is surrounded by negative electrons.   Your answer ☐ [1]

A 30-turn solenoid is connected to a battery, as shown below.

Coil 30 turns

Which of the following changes would **not** increase the strength of the magnetic field in the solenoid?

A increasing the number of turns on the solenoid to 50

B reversing the connections on the battery

C increasing the current in the solenoid

D placing a soft iron core inside the solenoid   Your answer ☐ [1]

Turn over

5   Which of the graphs below best shows the relationship between the current and potential difference across a diode?

A

B

C

D

Your answer ☐ [1]

6   A positively charged plastic rod is held near the top of the metal disc on a gold leaf electroscope, as shown below.

Which of the following statements is **true**?

A   The gold leaf becomes negatively charged and rises.

B   Electrons move up to the metal disc.

C   The metal stem has an opposite charge to the gold leaf.

D   Positive charges flow down into the gold leaf.   Your answer ☐ [1]

The graph below shows how the extension of a spring varies as the load on it increases.

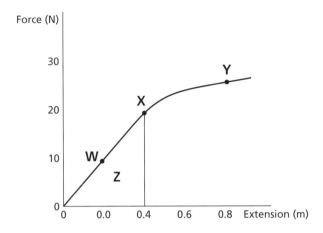

Which statement is **not** true about the graph?

A Region Z represents the work done stretching the spring 0.4m.

B The graph is non-linear between points X and Y.

C The gradient at W is the energy stored in the spring.

D Point X is the elastic limit.   Your answer ☐ **[1]**

2 kg of water is heated from 20°C to 90°C.
Specific heat capacity of water = 4200 J/kg/°C.

The quantity of heat required in joules is:

A 5.88×10^5 J

B 58800J

C 1.68×10^5 J

D 7.56×10^5 J   Your answer ☐ **[1]**

9   Which of the following diagrams correctly shows the magnetic field lines between two permanent magnets with identical but opposing north poles?

A

B

C

D

Your answer ☐   [1

10   A suspended spring, of spring constant 12 N/m, is stretched 40 cm when a load is added.

Calculate how much work is done.

Use the formula:
energy transferred in stretching = 0.5 × spring constant × (extension)^2

A   480J

B   2.4J

C   1.92J

D   0.96J   Your answer ☐   [1

SECTION B

Answer **all** the questions.

1   Evelyn is using several plotting compasses to investigate the magnetic field around a solenoid.
She sets up the apparatus as shown below.
The solenoid is placed in the middle of a large piece of paper on a bench.

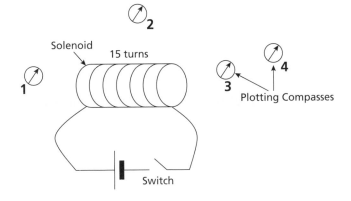

(a) Before Evelyn switches the circuit on, she looks at the needles on the plotting compasses.
They are all pointing in the same direction, away from the solenoid.

Give a reason for this.

_____

_____   **[1]**

(b) Evelyn closes the switch.
The compass needles move to a new position.
The needles of compasses **3** and **4** appear as shown below.

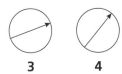

On the compasses below, draw in the new needle positions for compasses **1** and **2**.

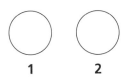

[2]

Turn over

(c) Evelyn wanted to increase the strength of the magnetic field in the solenoid.

Give **three** ways in which she could increase the magnetic field.

....

....

....

.... [3]

(d) Evelyn decided to test the strength of the electromagnet by seeing how many pieces of copper it could pick up.

What is wrong with that idea?

....

.... [1]

2   A student rubs a plastic comb with a woollen cloth.
The comb becomes positively charged.

(a) Explain how the comb becomes charged.

....

.... **[2]**

(b) Suggest a way to show that the comb is charged.

....

.... **[2]**

(c) For your suggestion in part **(b)**, what would you expect to see and why?

....

.... **[2]**

13 A person pushes a 100kg container, which has small wheels, up a ramp into the back of a van. The vertical height is 0.7m as shown in the diagram.

Use the acceleration of gravity, $g = 10m/s^2$.

(a) How much work does the person do putting the container in the van?

Show your working.

work done = _____ J   [4]

(b) The same quantity of work would have been done if the person lifted the container directly into the van, without using the ramp.

Explain why they chose to use the ramp.

_____

_____

_____ [2]

4   A student is investigating how the resistance of a wire
     varies with length.
     They set up the circuit shown.
     A metre rule was placed alongside the wire.

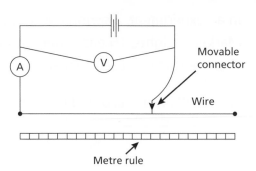

(a) Explain why the reading on the voltmeter remained
    constant throughout the experiment.

     ....

     ....   **[1]**

(b) The student used an 18V battery and obtained the following results:

Resistance (Ω)	Length of wire (cm)
25	100
22	90
18	75
15	60
12	50
10	40
9	30
8.5	20

(i)   What trend do the results in the table suggest?

      ....

      ....   **[1]**

(ii) What is the resistance of the wire when it is 50cm long?

                                        resistance = ... Ω   **[1]**

(iii) What current flowed when the wire was 50cm long?

                                        current = ... A   **[3]**

15 In an experiment, a spring was suspended vertically from a horizontal beam.
Marked weights, 1N each, were attached to the bottom of the spring, one at a time.
A metre rule was used to measure the extension when each weight was added.

The results were recorded in the table below.

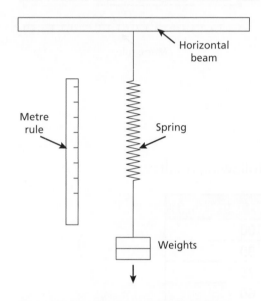

Force (N)	Extension (cm)
1	1.6
2	3.2
3	4.8
4	6.4
5	8.1
6	9.6
7	11.2
8	12.8
9	14.4
10	15.9

(a) Calculate the spring constant for the spring using the extension when 4N was the weight.

spring constant = ... N/m **[3**

(b) A graph was plotted of the results.

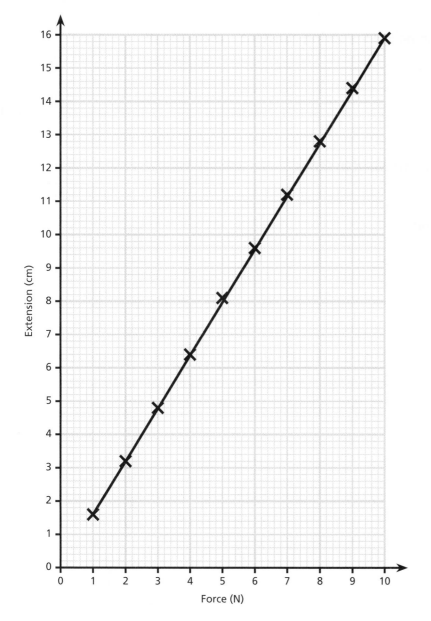

Suggest **one** reason why the line of best fit **cannot** be extended to predict the extension for a force of 12N.

_____ [2]

(c) Calculate how much work was done when the spring was stretched by the 4N weight.
Use the formula:

energy transferred in stretching = 0.5 × spring constant × (extension)²

work = ... J   [2]

(d) A second identical spring was attached in series, as shown.

The experiment was repeated.

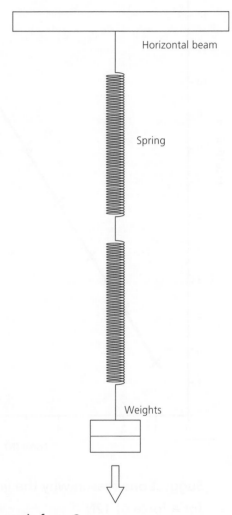

Horizontal beam

Spring

Weights

What would you expect to notice about the results for each force?

....

....   [1]

16   A student is investigating the behaviour of a thermistor.

They set up the circuit shown here.

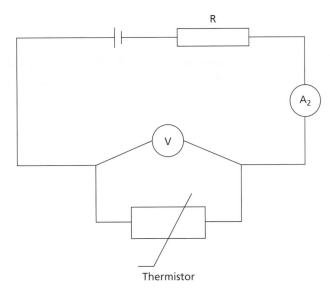

(a)* The student was given a kettle, two thermometers, two beakers and some crushed ice.

Explain how the student could use this apparatus to demonstrate the behaviour of a thermistor at different temperatures.

....

....

....

....

....

....

....

....   [6]

Practice Exam Paper 5

(b) The student replaced the voltmeter with a multimeter to directly record the resistance of the thermistor at different temperatures.

The results were recorded in the table below.

Temperature (°C)	Resistance (kΩ)			
	Reading 1	Reading 2	Reading 3	Mean
0	28.1	28.1	28.2	28.1
10	20.4	20.3	20.2	20.3
20	14.1	14.3	14.1	14.2
30	11.1	11.1	11.2	11.1
40	8.9	9.1	9.2	9.1
50	7.9	9.1	7.9	7.9
60	7.1	7.2	7.1	7.1
70	6.6	6.5	6.4	6.5
80	6.1	5.9	5.9	5.9
90	5.5	5.4	5.5	5.5

(i) There is an anomaly in the table of results.

Identify the anomaly and explain how the student should deal with it.

_____

_____

_____ [2]

(ii) Write down a conclusion you can you draw from the table of results.

_____

_____ [1]

7 A student sets up the apparatus below to measure the specific latent heat of ice.

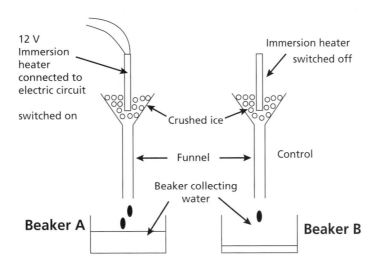

(a) Complete the circuit diagram below.

Include an ammeter and a voltmeter to show how the immersion heater should be connected to the 12V supply so that the power of the immersion heater can be calculated.

[2]

Turn over

(b) Suggest extra apparatus that might be needed and the measurements that should be taken to successfully calculate the specific latent heat of ice.

[4

(c) Explain why the student set up a control experiment.

[1

(d) The student repeats the experiment five times to have more confidence in the conclusion. One of the calculations gives too high a value for the specific latent heat of ice.

Suggest **one** error in measurement that might have caused this.

[1

END OF QUESTION PAPER

Collins

GCSE (9–1)
Combined Science (Physics)

Paper 6 (Foundation Tier)

F

Time allowed: 1 hour 10 minutes

You must have:

- the Data Sheet (page 444)

You may use:

- a scientific calculator
- a ruler

Instructions

- Use black ink. You may use a HB pencil for graphs and diagrams.
- Answer **all** the questions.
- Write your answer to each question in the space provided.
- Additional paper may be used if required.

Information

- The total mark for this paper is **60**.
- The marks for each question are shown in brackets [ ].
- Quality of extended responses will be assessed in questions marked with an asterisk (*).

SECTION A

Answer **all** the questions.

You should spend a maximum of 20 minutes on this section.

1   Which of the following statements is **false**?

   A   Infrared cameras are used to show up heat loss from houses.

   B   Gamma, X-rays and ultraviolet light are ionising radiations.

   C   Satellites use microwaves for communication.

   D   Ultraviolet light has a longer wavelength than red light.   Your answer [ ]   [1

2   The diagram below shows red light passing from air into glass at an angle to the surface.
     Refraction occurs.

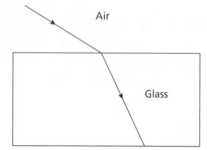

Red light

Air

Glass

Which of the following is **true** about the waves of red light being refracted in this example?

   A   the velocity increases

   B   the frequency remains the same

   C   the wavelength increases

   D   the frequency decreases as the wavelength increases   Your answer [ ]   [1]

Two isotopes of radium are shown below.

$^{228}_{88}$**Ra** $^{226}_{88}$**Ra**

Which statement is correct about the two isotopes?

A They have the same number of neutrons.

B They have identical masses.

C They have different numbers of protons.

D Radium-228 has two more neutrons than radium-226.   Your answer [ ]   **[1]**

Which of the following sources of energy is **not** renewable?

A nuclear

B wind

C solar

D hydroelectric   Your answer [ ]   **[1]**

Turn over

5   In an experiment a signal generator is connected to a loudspeaker.
     A microphone connected to an oscilloscope is placed in front of the loudspeaker,
     as shown below.

     Traces on the oscilloscope, obtained for two different settings on the signal generator,
     are shown below.

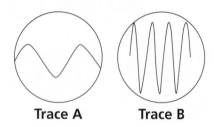

     Trace A   **Trace B**

     Identify which of the following have changed from **Trace A** to **Trace B**.

     A   Only the amplitude has increased.

     B   The amplitude and frequency have increased.

     C   Only the frequency has increased.

     D   The amplitude has increased but the frequency has decreased.   Your answer ☐ **[1**

A radioactive source emits two types of radiation.

The paths of the particles passing through an electric field were tracked and are shown below.

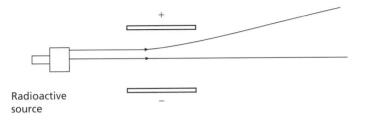

Radioactive
source

Identify the types of radiation shown in the diagram.

A   beta particles and gamma rays

B   alpha particles and beta particles

C   alpha particles and gamma rays

D   beta particles and protons   Your answer ☐ [1]

A person lifts an 800g book from the floor and places it on a shelf 1.6m above the ground.

How much potential energy does the book gain?
Use the acceleration due to gravity, g = 10m/s^2

A   128J

B   12.8J

C   1280J

D   12800J   Your answer ☐ [1]

Turn over

8   Which of the following could affect the thinking distance of a driver making an emergency stop

   A   a wet road

   B   bald tyres

   C   worn brakes

   D   tiredness   Your answer ☐ [1

9   Which of the following statements about transmission of electrical power from power stations ir
     the National Grid is **not** true?

   A   Large currents flow in the overhead cables.

   B   High voltages are used to reduce energy losses.

   C   The frequency of the mains supply is 50Hz.

   D   Transformers can only be used when the supply is a.c.   Your answer ☐ [1

10   For every 50 joules of energy put in, a car engine only produces 10 joules of useful energy.

     Which row of the table is **correct** about the car engine?

	Efficiency	Most energy is lost as:
A	40%	sound
B	5%	heat
C	20%	heat
D	2%	sound

                                                                 Your answer ☐ [1]

SECTION B

Answer **all** the questions.

1   A model wind turbine is being tested.

A fan is used to generate the wind.

As the blades rotate, they drive a dynamo and produce a potential difference.

The potential difference is measured for different distances between the turbine and the fan, using a voltmeter.

The results are in the table below.

Distance between fan and turbine (m)	Potential difference (V)
0.2	7.5
0.3	6.8
0.4	6.2
0.5	5.9
0.6	5.6
0.7	5.4
0.8	5.3
0.9	5.2
1.0	5.1

(a) Suggest why no reading was taken at 0.1m.

_____   **[1]**

Turn over

(b) The potential differences at lengths 1m and 0.9m have been plotted on the graph below.

(i) Plot the rest of the results onto the graph and join them with a smooth curve.

[2

(ii) At which distance was the measured potential difference 5.5V?

Use your graph to answer this question.

_____

[1

(c) Explain what could be done to make the results more reliable.

....

.... [2]

(d) Large wind turbines are used to generate electricity.
The aim is to use them to help cut down on the use of fossil fuels in power stations.

Suggest **one** advantage and **one** disadvantage of using wind turbines.

....

....

....

.... [2]

Turn over

12 A teacher was demonstrating waves by shaking a slinky.
The pattern is shown below.

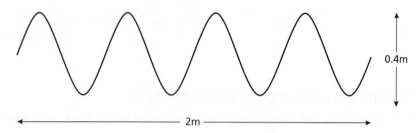

0.4m

2m

The frequency of the wave was 2Hz.

(a) What type of wave is the teacher demonstrating?

Answer: .... [1

(b) (i) State the amplitude of the wave.

amplitude = ... m [1

(ii) State how the amplitude relates to energy.

....

.... [2

(iii) Using the diagram above, work out the wavelength of this wave.

wavelength = ... m [2

ok

(iv) Calculate the velocity of the wave.

velocity = _____ m/s   **[2]**

(c)* The teacher then sets up a ripple tank with a cork floating on top of the water, as shown below.

A vibrator can generate waves by moving the dipper up and down.

Ripple tank

Explain how the apparatus shown could be used to demonstrate that it is only the wave that travels and not the water.

_____

_____

_____

_____

_____

[4]

13 A 60kg driver is travelling in a car at 12m/s.

A child runs out from the kerb and the driver has to do an emergency stop.

The graph below shows the changes in the car's velocity.

It covers the time from when the driver first saw the child (time = 0).

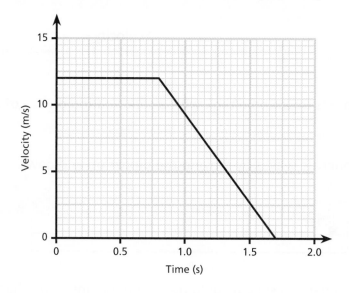

(a) What distance (thinking distance) did the driver cover before applying the brakes?

thinking distance = ... m [2

(b) Calculate the deceleration of the driver once the brakes were applied.

deceleration = ... m/s² [2

(c) Suggest **one** factor that might have increased the braking distance.

_____

_____ **[1]**

(d) The graph on the previous page showed the thinking and braking distances for an alert driver.

Sketch a graph below to show how it would have appeared had the driver been under the influence of alcohol or drugs.

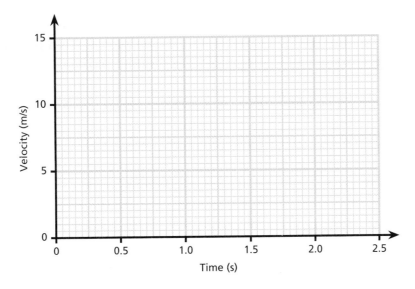

[2]

14 A teacher uses 100 dice to explain the idea of half-life.
Each dice is a cube and the faces are numbered 1 to 6.

The teacher rolls all 100 dice from a container at the same time.
When a dice lands with a 6 on top, it represents a decayed nucleus.

a) What is meant by the term 'half-life'?

....

.... [2]

b) Describe how the teacher could use the dice to show that there is a pattern to
radioactive decay.

....

....

....

.... [4]

15 (a) Coal is used in some power stations to generate electricity.
The electricity is sent to homes and businesses via power lines in the National Grid.

A model power line is shown below.

(i) Explain why coal is a **non-renewable** energy source.

....

.... [2]

(ii) What type of transformer is at **Y**?

.... [1]

(iii)Explain why electricity is sent at such high voltages in a power line.

....

....

.... [2]

(b) What are the potential difference and frequency of the mains supply in the home?

potential difference = ... V [1]

frequency = ... Hz [1]

Turn over

16 Below is a diagram of the electromagnetic spectrum.

Increasing wavelength ———→

Gamma rays	X-rays	**Y**	Visible spectrum Blue ———→ Red	Infrared	**Z**	Radio waves

(a) What type of waves in the electromagnetic spectrum are **Y** and **Z**?

Y = ... [1]

Z = ... [1]

(b) In a vacuum, which property is the same for all parts of the electromagnetic spectrum?

.... [1]

(c) Give **two** uses of X-rays.

....

....

.... [2]

(d) What type of wave in the electromagnetic spectrum is used by satellites for communication?

.... [1]

17 There are heat losses in a power station.

The diagram below shows these heat losses.
They are calculated for every 100 joules stored in the coal.

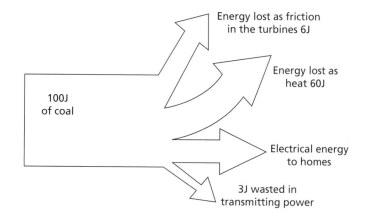

(a) Calculate how much electrical energy reaches the homes for every 100 joules of coal in this power station.

Answer: _____ J per 100J of coal   **[2]**

(b) Calculate the efficiency of this power station.

efficiency = _____ %   **[2]**

END OF QUESTIONS

There are no questions printed on this page

The Periodic Table of the Elements

(1) 1	(2) 2												(3) 13	(4) 14	(5) 15	(6) 16	(7) 17	(0) 18
1 **H** hydrogen 1.0																		2 **He** helium 4.0
3 **Li** lithium 6.9	4 **Be** beryllium 9.0												5 **B** boron 10.8	6 **C** carbon 12.0	7 **N** nitrogen 14.0	8 **O** oxygen 16.0	9 **F** fluorine 19.0	10 **Ne** neon 20.2
11 **Na** sodium 23.0	12 **Mg** magnesium 24.3	3	4	5	6	7	8	9	10	11	12		13 **Al** aluminium 27.0	14 **Si** silicon 28.1	15 **P** phosphorus 31.0	16 **S** sulfur 32.1	17 **Cl** chlorine 35.5	18 **Ar** argon 39.9
19 **K** potassium 39.1	20 **Ca** calcium 40.1	21 **Sc** scandium 45.0	22 **Ti** titanium 47.9	23 **V** vanadium 50.9	24 **Cr** chromium 52.0	25 **Mn** manganese 54.9	26 **Fe** iron 55.8	27 **Co** cobalt 58.9	28 **Ni** nickel 58.7	29 **Cu** copper 63.5	30 **Zn** zinc 65.4		31 **Ga** gallium 69.7	32 **Ge** germanium 72.6	33 **As** arsenic 74.9	34 **Se** selenium 79.0	35 **Br** bromine 79.9	36 **Kr** krypton 83.8
37 **Rb** rubidium 85.5	38 **Sr** strontium 87.6	39 **Y** yttrium 88.9	40 **Zr** zirconium 91.2	41 **Nb** niobium 92.9	42 **Mo** molybdenum 95.9	43 **Tc** technetium	44 **Ru** ruthenium 101.1	45 **Rh** rhodium 102.9	46 **Pd** palladium 106.4	47 **Ag** silver 107.9	48 **Cd** cadmium 112.4		49 **In** indium 114.8	50 **Sn** tin 118.7	51 **Sb** antimony 121.8	52 **Te** tellurium 127.6	53 **I** iodine 126.9	54 **Xe** xenon 131.3
55 **Cs** caesium 132.9	56 **Ba** barium 137.3	57-71 lanthanides	72 **Hf** hafnium 178.5	73 **Ta** tantalum 180.9	74 **W** tungsten 183.8	75 **Re** rhenium 186.2	76 **Os** osmium 190.2	77 **Ir** iridium 192.2	78 **Pt** platinum 195.1	79 **Au** gold 197.0	80 **Hg** mercury 200.5		81 **Tl** thallium 204.4	82 **Pb** lead 207.2	83 **Bi** bismuth 209.0	84 **Po** polonium	85 **At** astatine	86 **Rn** radon
87 **Fr** francium	88 **Ra** radium	89-103 actinides	104 **Rf** rutherfordium	105 **Db** dubnium	106 **Sg** seaborgium	107 **Bh** bohrium	108 **Hs** hassium	109 **Mt** meitnerium	110 **Ds** darmstadtium	111 **Rg** roentgenium	112 **Cn** copernicium			114 **Fl** flerovium		116 **Lv** livermorium		

Key

atomic number
symbol
name
relative atomic mass

Physics Data Sheet

change in thermal energy = mass × specific heat capacity × change in temperature

thermal energy for a change in state = mass × specific latent heat

$(\text{final velocity})^2 - (\text{initial velocity})^2 = 2 \times \text{acceleration} \times \text{distance}$

energy transferred in stretching = $0.5 \times \text{spring constant} \times (\text{extension})^2$

potential difference across primary coil × current in primary coil =
potential difference across secondary coil × current in secondary coil

Answers

Workbook Answers

You are encouraged to show all your working out, as you may be awarded marks for method even if your final answer is wrong.

Page 286 – Cell Structure

1. a) Four correctly drawn lines [3]
        (2 marks for two correct lines;
        1 mark for one)
        Nucleus – Contains genetic
        material
        Cell membrane – Contains receptor
        molecules
        Chloroplast – Contains chlorophyll
        Mitochondria – Contains enzymes
        for respiration
    b) Chloroplasts   [1]
2. Higher resolution than light
    microscope [1]; Uses magnets to focus
    an electron beam [1]
3. a) Stain them   [1]
    b) i) White blood cell / phagocyte   [1]
        ii) Red blood cell   [1]
    c) 4 × 100 = 400, ×400 magnification [1]

Page 287 – What Happens in Cells

1. nucleus [1]; polymer [1]; double
    helix [1]
2. a) Carbohydrates   [1]
    b) fats / lipids [1]; fatty acids [1];
        glycerol [1] (fatty acids and
        glycerol can be given in any order)
    c) A change in pH   [1]
3. a) Protein   [1]
    b) 9   [1]
    c) Pepsin is denatured when the pH
        rises above 5 / 6 [1]; the pH of the
        intestine is above this / is alkaline [1]

Page 288 – Respiration

1. a) Bar chart drawn with each axis
        labelled [1]; appropriate scale [1];
        two data sets clearly shown [1];
        accurately drawn bars [1]

    b) Muscles will require more glucose
        and oxygen [1]; to release more
        energy during exercise [1]; these are
        delivered to cells by the blood [1]

        > Energy is **released**. Do not state
        > that it is made or produced.
        > This will lose you the mark.

2. a) Fungi   [1]
    b) cell wall [1]; vacuole [1]

    c) glucose → ethanol + carbon
        dioxide [3] (1 mark for each
        correct chemical)
3. a) glucose + oxygen [1]; → carbon
        dioxide + water [1]

        > When writing equations,
        > make sure the reactants are to
        > the left of the arrow and the
        > products to the right.

    b) In the blood   [1]

Page 289 – Photosynthesis

1. a) Photosynthesis   [1]
    b) Glucose   [1]
    c) Respiration [1]; makes other
        molecules [1] (Accept named
        molecules, e.g. cellulose)
    d) At night, plants respire and
        produce carbon dioxide [1]; in
        the day, the plants respire but
        they will be also be
        photosynthesising, using up
        some carbon dioxide [1]

        > Remember, plants **respire** as
        > well as **photosynthesise**.

2. a) water [1]; oxygen [1]
    b) Chloroplasts   [1]
    c) Requires / takes in energy   [1]

Page 290 – Supplying the Cell

1. a) B, E, A, C, D   [1]
    b) Mitosis   [1]
    c) Repair of tissues   [1]
2. a) Diffusion: ←   [1]
    b) Active transport: →   [1]
    c) Osmosis: →   [1]
3. a) bone marrow [1]; embryos [1]
    b) Active transport   [1]
    c) Diffusion   [1]

Page 291 – The Challenges of Size

1. a) Root hair cell   [1]
    b) Leaf   [1]
2. a) Six correctly drawn lines [6]
        (1 mark for each correct line)

    b) Veins   [1]
    c) Veins   [1]
    d) Glucose [1]; Oxygen [1]

        > **Arteries** carry blood **away** from
        > the heart. Remembering that
        > both 'arteries' and 'away' start
        > with the letter **A** should help
        > you recall the right answer.

Page 292 – The Heart and Blood Cells

1. a) Ventricles   [1]
    b) Arteries [1]; carry blood away from
        heart [1] OR X = pulmonary artery
        [1]; and Y = aorta [1]
    c) Lungs   [1]
    d) Thick muscular walls [1]; for strong
        contractions [1]; to send blood
        under high pressure to body [1]
2. **Any three from:** carbon dioxide [1];
    urea [1]; amino acids [1]; glucose [1];
    antibodies [1]; hormones [1]

Page 293 – Plants, Water and Minerals

1. a) Plant X   [1]
    b) Plants take in carbon dioxide for
        photosynthesis through stomata
        [1]; but stomata are closed to
        prevent water loss [1]
    c) Turgid   [1]
    d) Transpiration   [1]
    e) i) Increased wind speed increases
            water loss   [1]
        ii) Increased temperature increases
            water loss   [1]
    f) Guard cells open and close stomata [1]
    g) Underneath of leaf shaded / not
        in direct sunlight [1]; therefore
        less water will be lost through
        evaporation [1]

Page 294 – Coordination and Control

1. Four correctly drawn lines [3] (2
    marks for two correct lines; 1 mark
    for one)
    Sensory neurone – Carries impulses
    from receptor to relay neurone
    Receptor – Detects a stimulus
    Brain – Responsible for coordinating
    response
    Motor neurone – Carries impulse from
    relay neurone to effector
2. Relay   [1]
3. stimulus [1]; electrical [1]; sensory [1];
    synapse [1]; neurotransmitter [1];
    receptors [1]
4. A very quick response   [1]

Page 295 – The Endocrine System

1. a) Pituitary   [1]
    b) Insulin   [1]
    c) Kidneys   [1]
    d) Testes   [1]
    e) In the blood   [1]
2. They are chemicals [1]; Their response
    is long lasting [1]
3. a) Pancreas   [1]
    b) Liver   [1]
    c) Blood glucose levels will rise
        after a meal [1]; and they cannot
        produce their own insulin to lower
        glucose levels [1]

Page 296 – Hormones and Their Uses

1. a) Progesterone **[1]**
   b) **Any two from:** easily forgotten **[1]**; doesn't provide protection against sexually transmitted infections **[1]**; possible side effects **[1]** (Accept any other sensible answer)
   c) Oestrogen **OR** FSH **[1]**
2. a) Condoms **[1]**
   b) 19–24 years of age **[1]**
   c) **Any one of:** injections are longer lasting **[1]**; can't be forgotten like the pill can **[1]**
   d) **Any one from:** they protect against sexually transmitted diseases **[1]**; easier to obtain / don't need to see a doctor **[1]**; no side effects **[1]**

Page 297 – Maintaining Internal Environments

1. a) 37°C **[1]**
   b) i) Denatured / destroyed **[1]**
      ii) Rate of reaction decreases / stops **[1]**
2. Type 1 has an earlier onset, whereas type 2 tends to develop later in life **[1]**; in type 1 the pancreas does not produce insulin, whereas in type 2 the insulin is produced but not effective **[1]**; type 1 requires insulin injections, whereas type 2 can usually be controlled by diet **[1]** (Accept any other sensible comparisons)
3. Temperature **[1]**; blood water levels / water potential / concentration of ions **[1]**; blood glucose **[1]**
4. hormone **[1]**; pancreas **[1]**; high **[1]**; during a meal **[1]**

Page 298 – Recycling

1. a) animals **[1]**; plants **[1]**; microorganisms / decomposers **[1]**
   b) Glucose **[1]**
2. a) Lightning **[1]**
   b) Proteins **[1]**
3. a) Feeding **[1]**
   b) Decomposition **[1]**

Page 299 – Interdependence

1. a) Bird and mouse / hawk and fox **[1]**
   b) **Any one from:** rabbit **[1]**; bird **[1]**; mouse **[1]**
   c) Grass / barley **[1]**
2. a) Disease **[1]**; lack of food / prey **[1]**; introduction of new predator / hunted **[1]**
   b) **Any three from:** mates **[1]**; space / territory **[1]**; food **[1]**; water **[1]**
   c) **Any three from:** light **[1]**; water **[1]**; space **[1]**; nutrients **[1]**
3. a) Mutualism **[1]**
   b) The oxpecker bird is not harming the buffalo **[1]**

Page 300 – Genes

1. genes **[1]**; DNA **[1]**; double helix **[1]**; haploid **[1]**

2. Four correctly drawn lines **[3]** (2 marks for two correct lines; 1 mark for one) gamete – a sperm or egg cell, phenotype – the appearance of an individual, gene – a section of DNA, heterozygous – to have one recessive and one dominant allele
3. a) Blonde hair **[1]**; blue eyes **[1]**
   b) A good swimmer / thin / height **[1]**
4. Three correctly drawn lines **[2]** (1 mark for one correct line) tt – Homozygous recessive Tt – Heterozygous TT – Homozygous dominant

Page 301 – Genetics and Reproduction

1. a) Tall **[1]**
   b) Correct genotypes for both parents **[1]**; correct outcomes of cross **[1]** (Accept either a Punnett square or cross diagram)

Parent 1

		T	t
Parent 2	T	TT	Tt
	t	Tt	tt

2. a) 70 **[1]**
   b) 35 **[1]**
   c) 35 **[1]**
   d) (30 × 2 =) 60 **[1]**
3. Correct genotypes for both parents **[1]**; correct outcomes of cross **[1]**; identifying XX as female and XY as male offspring **[1]** (Accept a Punnett square or a cross diagram)

Mother

		X	X
Father	X	XX FEMALE	XX FEMALE
	Y	XY MALE	XY MALE

Page 302 – Natural Selection and Evolution

1. a) The snow leopard and tiger have evolved from a common ancestor **[1]**; who lived less time ago compared with the common ancestor of snow leopard and clouded leopard **[1]**
   b) DNA analysis **[1]**
2. C, B, D, A **[1]**
3. C **[1]**

Page 303 – Monitoring and Maintaining the Environment

1. Loss of habitat **[1]**; loss of biodiversity **[1]**; loss of potential medicines and drugs **[1]**; rainforests important in cycling carbon / removing excess carbon dioxide from the atmosphere through photosynthesis **[1]**
2. a) A correctly drawn bar chart with a bar drawn at 50 for Javan

rhino **[1]**; and 90 for vaquita porpoise **[1]**

   b) **Any two of:** hunting **[1]**; habitat destruction **[1]**; pollution **[1]**; disease **[1]**
   c) Conservation is the act of preserving or protecting organisms **[1]**; **plus any one of:** national parks **[1]**; nature reserves **[1]**; anti-poaching laws **[1]**; fishing quotas **[1]**; captive breeding programmes **[1]** (Accept any other sensible example)

Page 304 – Investigations

1. a) Capture–mark–recapture method **[1]**
   b) $\frac{12 \times 10}{6}$ **[1]**; $= \frac{120}{6} = 20$ **[1]**
2. a) **Any two from:** size of pot **[1]**; amount / mass / type of compost **[1]**; amount / volume of acid rain used to water **[1]**; size of beans **[1]**; light **[1]**; temperature **[1]**; length of roots and shoots **[1]**
   b) B **[1]**
   c) Plant more beans at each pH **[1]**; and calculate mean result **[1]**

Page 305 – Resources and the Environment

1. a) it produces a higher yield for same area of wheat / number of plants **[1]**
   b) **Any two of:** disease resistance **[1]**; pest resistance **[1]**; drought resistance **[1]**; inclusion of additional nutrients / minerals / vitamins **[1]**
   c) The genes could get into wild plants **[1]**; possible harmful effects if eaten **[1]** (Accept any other sensible reason)
2. a) A and D **[1]** (Both are needed for the mark)
   b) Choose plants with the best characteristics and cross them again **[1]**; repeat this many times **[1]**

Page 306 – Monitoring and Maintaining Health

1. AIDS **[1]**; Measles **[1]**; Cholera **[1]**
2. All microorganisms correctly matched **[4]** (2 marks if two are correctly matched; 1 mark if one is correctly matched)

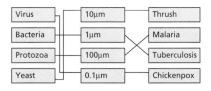

3. a) There has been an increase in numbers [1]; the rate of increase seems to be slowing down [1]
   b) AIDS [1]
   c) Their immune system is already weakened [1]

Page 307 – Prevention and Treatment of Disease

1. a) Help blood to clot [1]; forms a scab, which prevents entry of microorganisms [1]
   b) Microorganisms and small particles of dirt are trapped by mucus [1]
2. a) **Any two from:** computer simulations [1]; tests on cells grown in laboratory [1]; tests on animals [1]; tests on healthy people [1]
   b) The sugar pill (placebo) is a control [1]; to compare the effect of using the drug and using no drug (with no psychological influences) [1]
3. a) A vaccine contains a dead / weakened version of the pathogen / microorganism [1]; white blood cells [1]; recognise the pathogen / antigens and produce antibodies [1]; and memory cells [1]; in subsequent infections, the memory cells produce antibodies rapidly (and in large numbers) [1]; the antibodies immobilise the pathogens / cause them to clump together [1]
   b) **Any two of:** measles [1]; mumps [1]; chickenpox [1]; rubella [1]; diphtheria [1] (Accept any other sensible answer)

Page 308 – Non-Communicable Diseases

1. Advantage: potential for people to change lifestyle / get early treatment / regular screening [1];
   Disadvantage: could lead to depression / people unable to get jobs / insurance (Accept any other sensible answer) [1]
2. a) $BMI = \dfrac{74}{1.62 \times 1.62}$ [1] = 28.2 [1]
   b) **Any two from:** heart disease [1]; stroke [1]; diabetes [1]; cancer [1]; joint / muscular problems / arthritis [1]
3. a) **Any one of:** liver disease [1]; cancer (breast, mouth, bowel or unspecified) [1] (No mark for lung cancer)
   b) **Any one of:** heart attack [1]; heart disease [1]; obesity [1]; high blood pressure [1]

Page 309 – Particle Model and Atomic Structure

1. C [1]
2. B [1]
3. a) A = carbon-13 [1]; B = 6 [1]; C = 8 [1]; D = 6 [1]
   b) proton [1]
   c) 60 [1]
4. a) They slow down [1]
   b) Kinetic energy [1]

Page 310 – Purity and Separating Mixtures

1. Each price is for a different purity [1]; the most expensive is the purest grade of glucose / no contaminants [1]
2. D [1]
3. A_r: Mg = 24, O = 16, H = 1, 24 + (2 × 1) + (2 × 16) [1]; = 58 [1]
4. A_r: C = 12, H = 1, O = 16, $\dfrac{60}{12}$ = 5, $\dfrac{12}{1}$ = 12, $\dfrac{16}{16}$ = 1 [1]; $C_5H_{12}O$ [1]
5. Sandy should carry out evaporation / crystallisation [1]; pour the ink into a conical flask / suitable glass container and then gently heat [1]; the liquid component of the ink will evaporate leaving the dried ink pigments [1]

Page 311 – Bonding

1. D [1]
2. A [1]
3. Covalent bonds occur where one electron in the outer shell of each atom [1]; is shared by each of the atoms (two shared electrons = one covalent bond) [1]; ionic bonds occur where the metal element donates an electron or electrons and the non-metal receives the electron(s) [1]; both atoms end up with a full outer shell [1]
4. C [1]
5. A correctly drawn diagram (2.8.7) [1]

Page 312 – Models of Bonding

1. a) A correctly drawn dot and cross diagram [1]; and displayed formula [1]

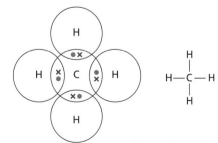

Dot and Cross   Displayed Formula

b) Ball and stick models can give an indication of bond angles / the 3D shape of the molecule. [1]
2. A correctly drawn diagram [1]

Al^{3+}

3. a) A correctly drawn diagram [1]

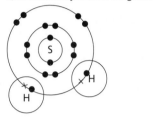

b) 2 [1]

Page 313 – Properties of Materials

1. C [1]
2. A diagram showing two different sizes of atoms in a regular arrangement [1]; correctly labelled / with a correct key [1]

Key
● C
○ Fe

The carbon atoms fit into the gaps between the iron atoms [1]; this means that the iron atoms cannot slide over one another [1] two hydrogens and an oxygen [1]; the water molecules are all joined together by weak forces, making them easy to separate from each other [1]

3. A [1]
4. The carbon atoms are each covalently joined to four other carbon atoms [1]; this makes the carbon atoms extremely difficult to separate from each other [1]

Page 314 – Introducing Chemical Reactions

1. a) H = 2, O = 1 [1]
   b) H = 2, S = 1, O = 4 [1]
   c) Ba = 1, P = 2, O = 6 [1]
   d) C = 2, H = 4, O = 2 [1]
2. B [1]
3. $MgCO_3 + 2HNO_3 \rightarrow Mg(NO_3)_2 + CO_2 + H_2O$ [2]
   (1 mark for the correct chemical symbols; 1 mark for correct balancing numbers)

Page 315 – Chemical Equations and Energetics

1. C [1]
2. a) A positively charged ion [1]
   b) A negatively charged ion [1]

3. The copper ion has a charge
   of 2+ [1]
4. A [1]
5. a) exothermic [1]
   b) endothermic [1]
   c) exothermic [1]
   d) endothermic [1]

Page 316 – Types of Chemical Reactions

1. a) oxygen [1]
   b) lead oxide [1]
2. a) lead oxide [1]
   b) carbon [1]
   c) $2PbO(l) + C(s) \rightarrow$
      $2Pb(s) + CO_2(g)$ [2]
      (1 mark for correct reactants; 1 mark
      for correct products)
3. a) $HCl(aq)$ [1]
   b) $HNO_3(aq)$ [1]
   c) $CH_3CH_2COOH(aq)$ [1]
   d) $HBr(aq)$ [1]
4. Using universal indicator is a
   qualitative measurement [1]; it is
   possible for two people to arrive at
   two different pH levels [1]; a data
   logger gives a precise, quantitative
   measurement [1]

Page 317 – Electrolysis

1. a) C [1]
   b) Above zinc, but below carbon [1]
2. Metals below carbon can be
   removed from their ores by
   displacement by carbon [1]; more
   reactive metals will not be
   displaced [1]; electrolysis separates
   the molten ions [1]

Page 318 – Predicting Chemical Reactions

1. B [1]
2. C [1]
3. Hold a glowing splint at the end of
   a test tube containing the gas [1];
   if the gas is oxygen, the splint will
   reignite [1]
4. Both are in Period 2, which means
   their outer electrons are close to
   the nucleus / they have a strong
   attraction for electrons [1]; oxygen
   requires 2 more electrons to fill the
   outer shell, whilst fluorine requires
   just 1 extra electron [1]; it is easier to
   attract 1 electron than 2, so fluorine
   is more reactive [1]

Page 319 – Controlling Chemical Reactions

1. A [1]
2. C [1]
3. Any two from: use a catalyst [1];
   increase temperature [1]; increase
   pressure [1]; increase concentration [1]
4. a) B [1]
   b) The larger the surface area [1];
      the greater the opportunity
      for the reactants to come
      together and have a successful
      reaction [1]

Page 320 – Catalysts, Activation Energy and Equilibria

1. A catalyst speeds up the rate
   of reaction [1]; it does this by
   lowering the activation energy [1];
   so the reaction needs less energy
   to start [1]; it does this without
   being involved directly / it is not a
   reactant [1]
2. A reaction that only goes in one
   direction / cannot go back / cannot
   re-form reactants [1]
3. C and D [1]
4. C [1]
5. There is no change in the amount /
   concentration of reactants and
   products [1]; the rate of the forward
   reaction equals the rate of the reverse
   reaction [1]

Page 321 – Improving Processes and Products

1. ore [1]
2. C [1]
3. a) Wear eye protection / safety
      goggles [1]; tilt the tube away
      from your body [1]
   b) copper(II) oxide + carbon →
      carbon dioxide + copper [2]
      (1 mark for each correct product)
   c) $2Cu_2O(s) + C(s) \rightarrow$
      $CO_2(g) + 4Cu(s)$ [2]
      (1 mark for correct reactants; 1
      mark for correct products)

Page 322 – Life Cycle Assessments and Recycling

1. Recycling reduces the amount of
   waste going to landfill [1]; the
   materials that would be lost are still
   in circulation [1]; energy costs of
   dumping the product are reduced [1]
2. Obtaining raw materials [1];
   manufacture [1]; use [1]; disposal [1]
   (Accept in any order)

Page 323 – Crude Oil

1. A = refinery gases [1]
   B = naphtha [1]
   C = diesel [1]
   D = bitumen [1]
2. Short chain hydrocarbons only have a
   few intermolecular forces keeping
   them together [1]; long chain
   hydrocarbons have a lot of
   intermolecular forces keeping
   the chains together, making it much
   more difficult to separate them [1]
3. Cracking is taking long chain
   hydrocarbons and breaking them into
   smaller, more useful short-chained
   molecules [1]
4. It formed over millions of years [1]; it
   is being used up faster than it is being
   replaced [1]

Page 324 – Interpreting and Interacting with Earth's Systems

1. a) The numbers in the table will have
      been rounded (up and down) [1]

   b) D, E, A, B, C [2] (1 mark for A after
      D; 1 mark for C after B)
2. C [1]

Page 325 – Air Pollution and Potable Water

1. Four correctly drawn lines [3] (2 marks
   for two correct lines; 1 mark for one)
   Carbon monoxide – air poisoning,
   Sulfur dioxide – kills plants and aquatic
   life, Nitrogen oxides – photochemical
   smogs, Particulates – coat surfaces
   with soot
2. a) A = large solids [1];
      B = small particulates [1]
   b) C = bacteria [1]; D = chlorine [1]
3. Correctly drawn apparatus and
   process [1]; all correctly labelled [1]

Page 326 – Matter, Models and Density

1. The forces are weak [1]
2. The nucleus repelled [1]; positive
   alpha particles [1]
3. The aluminium atoms are more
   closely packed in the solid form (than
   when in the liquid state) [1]; so the
   density is higher [1]
4. $\text{density} = \dfrac{\text{mass}}{\text{volume}} = \dfrac{1.792 \times 10^4}{2}$ [1];
   $= 8.96 \times 10^3 \text{kg/m}^3$ [1]
5. The electron [1]
6. Bohr's model had the electrons in
   orbits [1]; around the nucleus [1]
7. A correct sketch of molecules in steam
   [1]; and water [1]

Steam (gas)   Water (liquid)

Page 327 – Temperature and State

1. Any one from: temperature [1]; mass
   [1]; the number of aluminium atoms [1];
   the structure of aluminium atoms [1]
2. A reversible [1]; physical change [1]
3. The forces between the solid / liquid's
   atoms or molecules [1]; the motion
   of the atoms or molecules [1]
4. a) Energy = $0.1 \times (2.26 \times 10^6 J)$ [1];
      $= 2.26 \times 10^5 J$ [1] (Accept 226 000J
      or 226kJ)
   b) Energy = $0.1 \times 4200 \times 65$ [1];
      $= 2.73 \times 10^4 J$ [1] (Accept 27 300J
      or 27.3kJ)
5. The jam has a higher specific heat
   capacity than the sponge [1]; as both
   cool, the jam gives more heat energy
   to the mouth than the sponge [1]

Page 328 – Journeys

1. Speed is a scalar quantity as it only has magnitude [1]; velocity is a vector as it has both magnitude and direction [1]
2. Distance = average speed × time [1]; distance = 30 × 40 = 1200m [1]
3. Acceleration = $\dfrac{\text{change in velocity}}{\text{time}}$

   $= \dfrac{(70-30)}{8}$ [1]; = 5m/s² [1]
4. 1 mile north (of origin) [1]
5. kinetic energy = 0.5 × mass × (speed)² [1]; = 0.5 × 50 × 8² [1]; = 1600J [1]

Page 329 – Forces

1. A gravitational force can only be attractive, an electrical force can be repulsive or attractive [1]
2. A body stays still or keeps moving at constant velocity [1]; unless an external force acts on it [1]
3. There is an attractive force from the Sun pulling on the Earth [1]; there is also an attractive force from the Earth pulling on the Sun [1]; these forces are equal in magnitude but opposite in direction [1]
4. force = mass × acceleration, 30 = 15 × a [1]; $a = \dfrac{30}{15}$ = 2m/s² [1]
5. There is an equal and opposite force [1]; of the floor pushing against the feet of the student [1]
6. Friction [1]

Page 330 – Force, Energy and Power

1. The work done is the same whether the ramp is used or the barrel is lifted up directly into the van (same load and same vertical height through which the load is moved) [1]; the ramp increases the distance over which the work is done [1]; so less effort (force) is required [1]
2. Potential energy = 60 × 10 × 12 [1]; = 7200J [1]
3. Power = $\dfrac{150 \times 10 \times 12}{90}$ [1]; = 200W [1]
4. Potential energy [1]; changes to kinetic energy as the car accelerates down the hill [1]; kinetic energy is then changed to heat energy in the brake pads at the bottom [1]
5. The work done by the person has to overcome friction [1]; as well as to move the piano [1]

Page 331 – Changes of Shape

1. A material that is deformed when a force is applied and does not return to its original shape when the force is removed [1]
2. Jupiter has greater mass than Mars [1]
3. spring constant = $\dfrac{\text{force}}{\text{extension}} = \dfrac{1}{2 \times 10^{-2}}$ [1]; = 50N/m [1]

> You must be able to recall the following equation and rearrange it to make the spring constant the subject:
> force = spring constant × extension

4. The straight line part of the graph shows the spring obeying Hooke's law and behaving elastically [1]; the point at which the graph just stops showing proportionality (begins to curve) is the elastic limit [1]; after that point, the graph curves, showing plastic behaviour [1]
5. Energy = 0.5 × spring constant × (extension)² = 0.5 × 80 × (0.3)² [1]; = 3.6J [1]

> The extension is given in cm, so it must be converted to m before making your calculation.

Page 332 – Electric Charge

1. An electric field [1]
2. A magnetic field [1]; and heat [1] (Accept produces light)
3. The electrons are not free to move [1]; so charge cannot flow [1]
4. charge = current × time = 5 × 10 [1]; = 50C [1]
5. a) Electrons are transferred from the rod to the cloth [1]; having lost electrons, the rod is now positively charged [1]; having gained electrons, the cloth is now negatively charged [1]
   b) Electrons are attracted up to the plate at the top [1]; leaving both the stem and gold leaf positively charged [1]; the leaf is repelled by the stem and rises [1]

Page 333 – Circuits

1. Resistance [1]
2. a) A (filament) light bulb / lamp [1]
   b) The graph is linear for low values of current and obeys Ohm's law [1]; then as the current increases, the graph becomes non-linear as the wire in the bulb (lamp) heats up [1]; this increases the resistance [1]; due to more collisions between the moving electrons and (increasingly) vibrating metal atoms [1]
   c) A diode [1]
   d) Current can only flow one way through it [1]

Page 334 – Resistors and Energy Transfers

1. current = $\dfrac{\text{potential difference}}{\text{resistance}}$

   $= \dfrac{36}{12}$ = 3A [1]; so potential difference across 4Ω resistor = 3 × 4 [1]; = 12V [1]
2. potential difference = current × resistance, 24 = 4 × R [1]; $R = \dfrac{24}{4}$ [1]; = 6Ω [1]
3. power = volts × current, 2000 = 250 × current [1]; current = $\dfrac{2000}{250}$ = 8A [1]
4. Total resistance = 2 + 3 + 5 [1]; potential difference = current × resistance, 20 = current × 10, current = 2A [1]

Page 335 – Magnetic Fields

1. Correct drawings showing the arrow pointing up for X [1]; and down for Y [1]

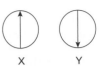

2. The compass needle is no longer affected by the magnetic field of the coil, as no current is flowing through the wires of the coil [1]; therefore, the needle moves to point towards the Earth's magnetic north pole [1]
3. There will be a greater density of iron filings (in the strongest region of the magnetic field) [1]
4. Induced magnetism is when some iron or steel objects become magnetic [1]; when placed in a magnetic field [1]

Page 336 – Wave Behaviour

1. A longitudinal wave [1]
2. a) velocity = $\dfrac{0.9}{3}$ [1]; = 0.3m/s [1]
   b) frequency = $\dfrac{\text{velocity}}{\text{wavelength}} = \dfrac{0.3}{0.01}$ [1]; = 30Hz [1]
3. frequency = $\dfrac{4}{2}$ (4 waves in 2 seconds) = 2Hz [1]; speed = 2 × 0.5 = 1m/s [1]
4. Velocity (speed) [1]; wavelength [1]

Page 337 – Electromagnetic Radiation

1. Frequency [1]
2. The dentist takes many X-rays in a day [1]; the risk to the health of the dentist is high [1]
3. The potato contains water, the plate does not [1]; water is a strong absorber of microwaves of a certain frequency [1]; the water molecules gain energy / increase their vibrations, producing heat [1]
4. speed = frequency × wavelength [1]; frequency = $\dfrac{3 \times 10^8}{1500}$ [1]; = 2 × 10⁵Hz [1] (Accept 200 000Hz)
5. If absorbed by cells of the body [1]; they ionise atoms and can cause chemical changes that can be harmful [1] (Accept they can cause cells to become cancerous)

Page 338 – Nuclei of Atoms

1. Protons [1]; and neutrons [1]
2. Isotopes [1]
3. Ionising radiation can cause atoms to lose electrons [1]; and become ions [1]
4. Beta particles [1]; and gamma rays [1]
5. X = 90 [1]; Y = 231 [1]
6. a) Both have six protons [1]; but the carbon-12 nucleus has six neutrons and the carbon-14 nucleus has eight neutrons [1]
   b) The charge on both nuclei is the same, +6 [1]

Page 339 – Half-Life

1. Half-life is the time taken for the number of radioactive nuclei [1]; in a sample to halve [1]
2. Irradiation is the exposure of an object to ionising radiation [1]
3. a) $x = 93$ [1]; $y = 4$ [1]
   b) It doesn't need to be handled or replaced [1]; so avoids exposure to alpha particles [1]
4. Electrons gain energy (are excited) and rise to a higher energy level [1]; atoms become ionised [1] (Accept 'electrons escape from the outer orbit around the nucleus' for 1 mark)

Page 340 – Systems and Transfers

1. a) Energy in the form of heat [1]; is transferred from the saucepan to the water [1]
   b) The water warms up as it gains energy [1]
2. Heat = 1.2 × 4200 × 80J [1]; = 4.032×10^5J [1] (Accept 403 200J)
3. a) Gravitational potential energy [1]; changes to kinetic energy [1]; which changes to electrical energy [1]
   b) energy transferred every second = 20 × 10 × 15 [1]; = 3000J [1]
   c) Heat / thermal [1]

Page 341 – Energy, Power and Efficiency

1. It is transferred in the form of thermal energy in the transformer [1]
2. **Any two from**: reduce air flow between the inside and outside of the house [1]; insulate the loft [1]; use double glazing [1]; use carpets [1] (Accept any other sensible suggestion)
3. a) power = 250 × 2 [1]; = 500W [1]
   b) energy = 500 × 10 × 60 [1]; = 3×10^5J [1] (Accept 300 000J)
4. a) energy = 2 × 4200 × 70 [1]; = 5.88×10^5J [1]
   b) efficiency = $\frac{\text{useful output energy transfer}}{\text{total input energy transfer}} \times$ 100% [1]; = $\frac{5.88 \times 10^5}{8 \times 10^5} \times$ 100% [1]; = 73.5% [1]

Page 342 – Physics on the Road

1. Thinking distance [1]; and braking distance [1]
2. a) acceleration (deceleration) = $\frac{\text{change in velocity}}{\text{time}} = \frac{25}{10}$ [1]; = 2.5m/s² [1]
   b) force = 70 × 2.5 [1]; = 175N [1]
3. a) One student holds the ruler vertically [1]; the other puts their open hand level with the 0cm mark, so that the ruler is between their fingers and thumb [1]; the student drops the ruler [1]; the other student catches it [1]; the length at which the ruler was caught is recorded [1]; the reaction time is calculated [1]

b) Any value between 0.15 and 0.3 seconds [1]

Page 343 – Energy for the World

1. A non-renewable energy source is one that once it is used cannot be replaced [1]; in a reasonable time scale [1] (Accept: A natural resource that cannot be grown or produced [1]; at the same time as it is consumed [1])
2. a) Stored chemical energy (in coal) [1]; changes to heat in the boiler [1]; which produces steam [1]; which gives the engine kinetic energy [1]
   b) **Any two from:** burning alcohol still emits carbon dioxide [1]; alcohol is highly flammable so it is a hazard to people near the engine [1]; if farms produce alcohol, it would reduce the number of fields for food production [1]; there would be difficulty in transporting it, either by road or on the train [1]; extra emissions would be a factor with transportation [1] (Accept any other sensible response)
3. a) The amount of uranium in rocks on Earth is decreasing because of its decay [1]
   b) **Any one advantage from:** it doesn't emit carbon dioxide or particulates into the atmosphere [1]; a small amount of fuel produces an enormous quantity of energy [1] (Accept any similar sensible response)
   Any one disadvantage from: waste products are radioactive and dangerous [1]; waste products need to be transported for reprocessing [1]; radioactive waste is problematic to dispose of [1]; radioactive waste has a long half-life so will remain dangerous for hundreds of years [1] (Accept any similar sensible response)

Page 344 – Energy at Home

1. An a.c. supply produces a current that keeps rapidly changing direction [1]; the current from a d.c. supply only goes one way [1]
2. 230V [1] (Accept 240V or 250V); 50Hz frequency [1]
3. The earth wire offers a safe route into the ground / to earth for an electric current [1]; if a fault occurs in the appliance [1]
4. a) A step-down transformer [1]
   b) The potential difference is stepped up at the power station to a high value in the power lines [1]; this reduces energy losses in the power lines (energy is lost as heat) [1]; the potential difference is then stepped down for use in the home [1] (or similar answer).

Page 345–360 – Practice Exam Paper 1

Section A
1. B [1]
2. A [1]
3. B [1]
4. A [1]
5. D [1]
6. D [1]
7. C [1]
8. C [1]
9. B [1]
10. B [1]

Section B
11. (a) Bubbles could be different sizes [1]; individual bubbles difficult to count if produced quickly [1]
    (b) (i) Can measure volume of gas produced [1]
       (ii) **Any two from:** amount / mass liver [1]; volume of hydrogen peroxide [1]; strength of hydrogen peroxide; time [1]; temperature [1]
    (c) A correct curve drawn [1]

12. (a) Surface area = 4 × 4 × 6 = 96cm² [1]; Volume = 4 × 4 × 4 = 64cm³ [1]; SA : V ratio = $\frac{96}{64}$ = 1.5 : 1 [1]
    (b) The 2cm / smallest cube [1]; because it has the largest surface area to volume ratio [1]
13. (a) 0.66 + 0.62 + 0.61 = 1.89 [1]; mean = $\frac{1.89}{3}$ = 0.63 [1]
    (b) A = sensory neurone [1]; B = motor neurone [1]; C = effector [1]
    (c) (i) Happens automatically / no conscious decision made [1]
       (ii) To protect the body from pain / harm [1]
14. (a) Some deoxygenated blood will pass through hole from right side to left side [1]; and be sent round body without going to the lungs [1] **OR** some oxygenated blood will pass from left side to right side [1]; so less oxygenated blood goes to the body [1]
    (b) The heart will have to work harder to force blood out, causing chest pain / feeling weak or dizzy when exercising [1]
    (c) (i) To stop blood flowing backwards [1]
       (ii) **Any two from:** only last 20 years [1]; dislike idea of using non-human tissue [1]; chance of being infected with animal viruses [1]
       (iii) Should last longer [1]; no need to take antirejection medication [1]
15. (a) Insulin [1]
    (b) oxygen [1]; water [1]
    (c) (i) Sugar / glucose is a substrate for respiration [1]
       (ii) Carbon dioxide gas was produced [1]

(d) (i) Aerobic **[1]**
(ii) Aerobic **[1]**
(iii) Anaerobic **[1]**
(iv) Aerobic **[1]**

16. (a) Water moves into root hair cells **[1]**; moving from area of high water concentration to area of low concentration **[1]**; by osmosis **[1]**
(b) Net water movement would be out of plant **[1]**; because concentration of water would be higher in plant cells than outside **[1]**
(c)* Glucose moves by diffusion **[1]**; from areas of high concentration to areas of low concentration **[1]**; via the phloem tissue **[1]**; minerals enter plant by active transport **[1]** and move through plant due to the transpiration stream **[1]**; from roots to leaves through the xylem tissue **[1]**

> In the exam, if you see an asterisk (*) next to a question, it means that the quality of your response will be assessed. This means you must give all your ideas in a clear and logical way to avoid losing marks.

(d) Leaf **[1]**
(e) Hormones **[1]**; nutrients (Accept names substances, e.g. glucose, amino acids, water) **[1]**; waste substances (Accept names substances, e.g. carbon dioxide, urea) **[1]**

Page 361–376 – Practice Exam Paper 2

Section A
1. A **[1]**
2. D **[1]**

> $$\frac{(7 + 9 + 8 + 8 + 6)}{5} = 7.6$$
> $$7.6 \times 60 = 456$$

3. B **[1]**
4. A **[1]**
5. A **[1]**
6. B **[1]**
7. B **[1]**
8. D **[1]**
9. A **[1]**
10. C **[1]**

Section B
11. (a) At risk of extinction **[1]**
(b) Hunting / taking eggs **[1]**; polluting lakes / rivers (which reduced food source) **[1]**
(c) **Any one from:** nest built for breeding pairs **[1]**; wardens protect nests from disturbance / egg thieves **[1]**
12. (a) The number of male and female smokers has decreased steadily **[1]**; since 1968 **[1]**
(b) $40 - 25 = 15$ **[1]**; $\frac{15}{40} \times 100$ **[1]**; $= 37.5\%$ **[1]**

(c) Yes – because as % of males who smoked decreased **[1]**; so did incidence of cancer in males **[1]** **OR** No – because as % females who smoked decreased **[1]**; the incidence of cancer increased **[1]**
(d)* **Marks are awarded for identifying links between aspects of diet and exercise and their effect on the cardiovascular system. To gain the full 6 marks, there must be at least one example for exercise and one example for diet, e.g.**
Diet: a high fat diet can lead to narrowing of arteries **[1]**; which increases blood pressure **[1]**; and puts strain on the heart / can lead to a heart attack **[1]** **OR** a high salt diet can lead to high blood pressure **[1]**; which puts a strain on the heart / can lead to a heart attack **[1]** OR taking in more calories / energy than is needed can lead to becoming overweight / obesity **[1]**; which puts a strain on the heart / can lead to heart attack **[1]**
Exercise: exercise strengthens heart muscle **[1]**; and makes the heart more efficient **[1]**; reducing the chance of cardiovascular disease **[1]**
13. (a) (Microbial) respiration **[1]** (Accept decomposition)
(b) (i) Denitrifying **[1]**
(ii) Nitrates **[1]**

> Sometimes students get confused and think that the decaying matter gives off carbon dioxide. It doesn't. **Respiration** of the **microorganisms / decomposers** which feed on the decaying matter is where the carbon dioxide comes from.

14. (a) Horse and zebra: share same genus / both *Equus* **[1]**; both have simple stomach, whereas deer has complex stomach **[1]**
(b) (i) Donkey: sure-footed, less prone to colic, long life span, hardworking **[2]** (1 mark for more than two qualities; 2 marks for all qualities)
(ii) Horse: intelligent **[1]**; easy to train **[1]**
(c) Because species can breed with each other to produce fertile offspring **[1]**
(d) A mutation produced a horse with a larger central toe **[1]**; this horse was better at running so more likely to survive **[1]**; and breed **[1]**; and pass on genes to offspring **[1]**

15. (a) A tabby pattern **[1]**; with brown eyes **[1]**; and curled ears **[1]**
(b) (i) Gametes: T and t **[1]**; offspring (in order): Tt and tt **[1]**
(ii) 1 : 1 **[1]**
(c) (i) Correct genotypes of parents **[1]**; correct genotypes of offspring **[1]**; correct phenotypes of offspring **[1]** (Accept any correct genetic diagram)

		Parent 1	
		P	p
Parent 2	P	P P PKU	P p PKU
	p	P p PKU	p p no PKU

(ii) 6 **[1]**

> ¾ have PKU, so in a litter of 8 that would be 6 kittens with PKU.

16. (a) Antibiotic A can be used, B cannot **[1]**; Disc A: radius in range of 8.5–9.5mm, so $8.5 \times 8.5 = 72.25 \times 3.14 = 226.9mm^2$ **[1]**; Disc B: radius in range 6.5–7.5mm, so $6.5 \times 6.5 = 42.25 \times 3.14 = 132.7mm^2$ **[1]**
(b) Cost / if patient allergic to antibiotic **[1]**
(c) White blood cell engulfs the bacterium **[1]**; destroyed within white blood cell **[1]**; mention of phagocytosis or lysozyme or egestion of debris **[1]**
(d) Dead / weakened form of bacterium **[1]**
(e) Fungal infection / viral infection / any named infectious disease caused by a fungus, virus or protozoan **[1]**

Page 377–390 – Practice Exam Paper 3

Section A
1. D **[1]**
2. C **[1]**
3. B **[1]**
4. D **[1]**
5. C **[1]**
6. B **[1]**
7. B **[1]**
8. C **[1]**
9. C **[1]**
10. D **[1]**

Section B
11. (a) Salt **[1]**; hydrogen **[1]** (In any order)
(b) (i) 12.3 **[2]** (1 mark for 12 or 12.33)

(ii) A graph with accurately plotted points [1]; connected by straight lines / line of best fit drawn [1]

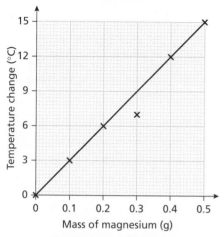

(iii) The point for 0.3g [1]; because it does not fit the pattern / the temperature change is too low [1]

(c) **Any one from:** It removes human error [1]; it does not rely on the eye sight / judgement of the observer [1]; it can record more precisely [1]

(d) Wear safety goggles (Accept any other reasonable safety precaution) [1]

12. (a) The boiling point tends to increase as you go across the period from Groups 1 to 4 [1]; with a drop in Groups 5, 6, 7 and 0 [1]

(b) **Any two from:** the period indicates the number of electron shells around the nucleus [1]; as you move across a period, the elements on the left-hand side are more likely to be metals, as they donate electrons [1]; those on the right are non-metals, as they receive electrons [1]; there is a change from metallic bonding to covalent bonding [1]; as you move right across the period in the metals section, the metals become less reactive relative to each other [1]; as you move left in the non-metals section, the non-metals become less reactive relative to each other [1]

(c) Particle X is an atom, Y is an ion [1]; the atomic number indicates the number of protons. If the number of electrons, which can be found from the electronic structure, matches the atomic number it must be neutral, i.e. an atom [1] (Or reverse argument)

(d) (i) The atom is not to scale [1]; the proton is drawn too large [1]; and the electron is too close to the nucleus [1]

(ii) One early model had the charges distributed evenly throughout the atom [1]; Bohr had electrons in discrete shells / energy levels [1]

13.* For the full 6 marks, your answer must describe the bonding in

polymers and metals and make comparisons between the two. It must clearly state your choice of materials for the sculpture and give justified reasons for your choice, e.g. The monomers / molecules in a polymer contain covalent bonds [1]; there are weak intermolecular forces between the monomers / molecules [1]; metals form giant structures / lattices [1]; in which the electrons in the outer shells of the atoms are free to move [1]; polymers are weaker because the intermolecular forces are weaker than in metals [1]; **plus any one of:** aluminium, because it is strong, resistant to corrosion and has a low density (so easy to create a sculpture from it) [1]; steel because it is strong and cheap and could be painted to protect it from corrosion [1]; PVC, because it is resistant to corrosion, easy to shape and low density, which means the cost of the sculpture would be low [1] (No marks to be awarded for carbon-fibre or titanium as the cost of these materials is too high)

14. (a) Graphene is a single lattice of atoms, making it very thin [1]; it also allows electrons to travel through the connected atoms / it conducts electricity [1]

(b) Drawing showing at least two layers of carbon atoms (arranged with three bonds per carbon atom) [1]; labelled intermolecular / weak forces between layers [1]

Weak forces
between layers

(c) We did not have the instrumental analysis / ability to detect the new forms [1]; there is far more diamond and graphite available today [1]

15. (a) The copper ions have a 2+ charge, they will move to the negative electrode / cathode [1]; where they will pick up 2 electrons [1]; this means that the outer shell will have 2 electrons in it / it is the same as the elemental form of copper [1]

(b) Metals below carbon in the reactivity series can be extracted by heating with carbon [1]; aluminium is higher in the reactivity series, so cannot be extracted in this way [1]

(c) Bromine gas [1]

16. (a) 18 [1]

(b) 8 [1]

(c) Oxygen [1]

(d) $6 \times 12.0 = 72$, $12 \times 1.0 = 12$, $6 \times 16.0 = 96$ [1]; $72 + 12 + 96 = 180$ [1]

17. (a) $2Al(s) + Fe_2O_3(s)$ [1]; $\rightarrow 2Fe(s) + Al_2O_3(s)$ [1]

(b) **Any two from:** eye protection [1]; carry out behind a safety screen [1]; use a fuse to start the reaction [1]; do not do the reaction inside [1]

(c) (i) Oxidation is the addition of oxygen [1]

(ii) Reduction is the loss of oxygen [1]

Page 391–406 – Practice Exam Paper 4

Section A

1. B [1]
2. A [1]
3. B [1]
4. D [1]
5. C [1]
6. B [1]
7. C [1]
8. B [1]
9. B [1]
10. D [1]

Section B

11. (a) 2.8.8.1 [1]

(b) Diagram that shows positive ions arranged in solid-like formation [1]; indication of sea of delocalised electrons [1]

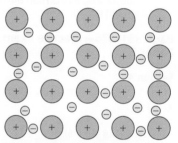

(c) The potassium moves around rapidly on the surface of the water [1]; and a gas ignites with a lilac flame [1]

(d) potassium + water → potassium hydroxide + hydrogen [2] (1 mark for each correct product)

(e) The higher up the group [1]; the less reactive they will be [1]

12. (a) $N_2 = 78$, $O_2 = 21$, $CO_2 = 0.04$ (accept 0.03) [1]

(b) The amount of nitrogen has dropped by 9%, because of the increase in oxygen levels [1]; there was no oxygen 3bya but 2bya 10% of the atmosphere was oxygen, due to the appearance of photosynthesising plants [1]; the amount of carbon dioxide remained relatively constant, this was due to volcanic activity [1]

(c) (i) 275ppm +/– 5 at 1000 years ago and 295 +/– 5 at 100 years ago [1]; change = 295 – 275 = 10ppm [1] (Accept 0.001%)

(ii) 1.0°C +/– 0.2 [1]

(d)*Answer must explain the effect of CO_2 and CH_4 on the greenhouse effect (trapping increased heat energy which is unable to escape the Earth) and make at least two suggestions on how to reduce emissions, e.g. The greenhouse effect is the term used for the ability of the atmosphere to trap some of the infrared radiation [1]; this causes the temperature of the Earth to increase to a higher level [1]; methane and carbon dioxide are greenhouse gases and increased levels of these gases in the atmosphere increases the amount of infrared radiation trapped, so the temperature of the Earth increases [1]; to reduce the greenhouse effect we need to find alternative sources of energy that do not produce carbon dioxide or methane [1]; for example, if we were to use hydrogen fuel cells instead of fossil fuels such as petrol, then there would be zero emissions [1]; methane is a more powerful gas than carbon dioxide, so minimising organic waste in landfill or reducing the amount of livestock, such as cows, would help to reduce the greenhouse effect [1]

13. (a) A displacement reaction is where a more reactive metal 'pushes' out a less reactive metal from a compound [1] (Or reverse argument)
   (b) $2CuO(s) + C(s) \rightarrow 2Cu(l) + CO_2(g)$ [2] (1 mark for correct formulae on both sides; 1 mark for correct balancing)
   (c) No [1]; because aluminium is higher on the reactivity series than carbon [1]
   (d) Al_2O_3 [1]

14. (a) Breaking up long-chain molecules [1]; into smaller / more useful molecules [1]
   (b) A molecule made up of carbon and hydrogen only [1]
   (c) They act as a catalyst [1]
   (d) $(C_{14}H_{30} - C_3H_8 =) C_{11}H_{22}$ [1]
   (e) **Any three from:** petrol [1]; diesel [1]; LPG / bottled gas [1]; kerosene [1]; paraffin [1]; fuel oil [1]; bitumen [1]; naphtha [1]

15. (a) It reacts violently with water [1]; the oil provides a barrier to water [1]
   (b) Hydrogen / H_2 [1]
   (c) $2Li + 2H_2O \rightarrow 2LiOH + H_2$ [2] (1 mark for correct formulae on both sides; 1 mark for correct balancing)
   (d) The potassium would react more violently [1]; and catch fire / spit [1]; as it is higher in the reactivity series than lithium [1]

16. (a) Hold a lighted splint at the end of the test tube [1]; if it makes a squeaky pop, hydrogen is present [1]
   (b) The reaction would be faster / more vigorous [1]
   (c) Magnesium is higher than carbon in the reactivity series [1]; electrolysis [1]; of the molten ore is required [1]

Pages 407–424 – Exam Practice Paper 5

Section A

1. D   [1]
2. C   [1]
3. C   [1]
4. B   [1]
5. A   [1]
6. B   [1]
7. C   [1]
8. A   [1]
9. D   [1]
10. D   [1]

Section B

11. (a) The compass needles are all pointing to magnetic north (as there is no magnetic field around the solenoid) [1]
   (b) Arrows drawn pointing left to right in compass 1 [1]; and right to left in compass 2 [1]

1   2

   (c) Increase the number of turns on the solenoid [1]; increase the current in the solenoid (accept increase potential difference / use more batteries) [1]; place a piece of soft iron inside the solenoid to act as a core [1]
   (d) Copper is not a magnetic metal (so will not be attracted to an electromagnet) [1]

12. (a) Electrons are transferred from the comb to the woollen cloth when it is rubbed [1]; removal of electrons results in the comb becoming positively charged [1]
   (b) Comb held near a running tap [1]; will attract the water [1] OR comb brought near an uncharged electroscope [1]; will cause the leaf to rise [1] OR comb will pick up small pieces of paper or attract hair [1]; if held over it [1] (Accept any other similar suggestion)
   (c) Mention of opposite charges attracting, like charges repelling [1]; the explanation must include a mention of electrostatic induction [1]

13. (a) work done = force × distance [1]; force = 100 × 10 =1000N [1]; work done = 1000 × 0.7 [1]; = 700J [1]
   (b) When using a ramp, the vertical distance the load lifted is the same, but the horizontal distance moved by the load (and, therefore, time for lifting) is much longer [1]; this reduces the force needed by the person to lift the load into the van [1]. (Accept a similar argument)

14. (a) The voltmeter measured the potential difference of the battery [1]
   (b) (i) As the length of the wire increases, so does the resistance [1]

(ii) 12Ω [1]
(iii) voltage = current × resistance [1]; 18 = current × 12, current = $\frac{18}{12}$ [1]; = 1.5A [1]

15. (a) force = spring constant × extension [1]; 4 = spring constant × 0.064 [1]; spring constant = 62.5N/m [1]
   (b) The elastic limit is not known [1]; so the force may not be proportional to the extension after 10N [1] (Accept a similar argument)
   (c) Energy transferred = 0.5 × 62.5 × (0.064)² [1]; = 0.128J (Accept 0.13J) [1]
   (d) The extension for each force would be greater   [1]

16. (a)*For the full 6 marks your answer must include a clear and complete explanation of how to carry out the experiment, including which measurements are to be recorded and reference to calculating the resistance, e.g. Pour hot water in one beaker and put crushed ice in another, place a thermometer in each beaker [1]; lower the thermistor into each beaker in turn, measure and record the temperature [1]; and the corresponding readings on the voltmeter and ammeter [1]; keep the thermometer and the thermistor in the beaker of hot water and repeat the measurements as the water cools [1]; the resistance at each temperature can now be calculated [1]; and a conclusion drawn [1]
   (b) (i) The 'reading 2' at 50°C is too high at 9.1Ω [1]; ignore the anomaly and just use the other two readings to calculate the average resistance at 50°C OR repeat the faulty measurement of resistance at 50°C [1]
      (ii) An inverse relationship: as the temperature of the thermistor rises, its resistance decreases [1]

17. (a) A circuit drawn with a battery, ammeter in series [1]; and a voltmeter connected in parallel to the heater/ battery, as shown [1] (or similar arrangement)

Immersion heater

(b) Apparatus: balance to measure the mass of the water collected (accept a measuring cylinder to calculate mass from the volume if known density of water is referred to, but not on its own) **[1]**; stopwatch to measure the time the heater was on **[1]**
Measurements: mass of water collected due to the immersion heater (by subtracting the mass in the control beaker B from the mass collected in beaker A) **[1]**; time the heater was on **[1]**

(c) To measure the mass of ice that melted due to the room temperature and not due to the heater **[1]**

(d) Too low a measurement of the mass of water collected or too high a reading of the time the heater was on **[1]**

Pages 425–442 Exam Practice Paper 6

Section A
1. D   **[1]**
2. B   **[1]**
3. D   **[1]**
4. A   **[1]**
5. B   **[1]**
6. A   **[1]**
7. B   **[1]**
8. D   **[1]**
9. A   **[1]**
10. C   **[1]**

Section B
11. (a) The wind speed would have been too high **[1]** (Accept the potential difference would have been too high)

(b) (i) All points plotted **[1]**; with a smooth curve drawn **[1]**

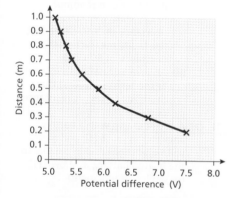

(ii) 0.64m (Accept any value between 0.63m and 0.65m) **[1]**

(c) For each distance, repeat each reading **[1]**; and calculate a mean value / an average of the results **[1]**

(d) Any one advantage from: don't emit greenhouse gases **[1]**; don't produce particulates **[1]**; wind energy is renewable **[1]**; no waste products to be disposed of **[1]**; have a long lifespan **[1]**; require little maintenance **[1]**; can be used in remote areas where there is no mains electricity **[1]** (Or any other sensible response)
Any one disadvantage from: expensive to build **[1]**; don't produce electricity on still days with no wind **[1]**; not very attractive to look at (visual pollution) **[1]**; noisy **[1]**; have a detrimental effect on wild life **[1]**

12. (a) Transverse waves **[1]**

(b) (i) $\frac{0.4}{2} = 0.2m$ **[1]**

(ii) The greater the amplitude, the greater the amount of energy **[1]**; the wave is carrying **[1]**

(iii) wavelength = $\frac{2m}{4\ waves}$ **[1]**; = 0.5m **[1]**

(iv) velocity = frequency × wavelength **[1]**; = 2 × 0.5 = 1m/s **[1]**

(c)* For the full 4 marks your answer must include a complete explanation of how to carry out the experiment, including which measurements are to be taken and how this leads to the conclusion that only waves travel (not the medium), e.g. The vibrating dipper produces transverse waves **[1]**; these travel along the surface of the water for the length of the tank **[1]**; the cork bobs up and down (as the waves pass) **[1]**; and does not move along with the transverse wave **[1]**

13. (a) From the graph: velocity = 12m/s, time = 0.8 seconds **[1]**; distance travelled = 12 × 0.8 = 9.6m **[1]**

(b) Change in velocity = 12m/s – 0, time for the change = 0.9 seconds **[1]**;
deceleration = $\frac{12}{0.9}$ = 13.3m/s² **[1]**

(c) Any one from: a wet road **[1]**; worn brakes **[1]**; worn tyres **[1]**; poor road surface **[1]**; increased load in the car due to passengers **[1]** (or any other suitable answer)

(d) A graph similar to below, having a longer thinking distance **[1]**; but the **same** braking distance **[1]**

14. (a) Half-life is the time taken for half the nuclei **[1]**; in a sample of a radioactive element to decay **[1]**

(b) Throw the dice and remove all those with a six showing **[1]**; keep repeating the process with the remaining dice, removing those with a six on the top face each time, until only a few dice remain **[1]**; record the number removed for each throw in a table **[1]**; plot a graph of the throw number against number of sixes to show a pattern **[1]**

15. (a) (i) A non-renewable source cannot be replaced **[1]**; in a reasonable time period / in a lifetime **[1]**

(ii) A step-down transformer **[1]**

(iii) A step-up transformer increases the voltage, which reduces the current to a small value in the power line **[1]**; this reduces the amount of energy lost in the power line as heat **[1]**

> Remember that when a step-up transformer steps up the potential difference by a certain ratio, it reduces the current by the same ratio. It is the heating effect of the current that leads to energy losses, so it must be kept as low as possible.

(b) potential difference = 240V (Accept 230V or 250V) **[1]**; frequency = 50Hz **[1]**

16. (a) Y = ultraviolet **[1]**; Z = microwaves **[1]**

(b) The velocity **[1]** (Accept speed)

(c) Any two from: for producing images of bone fractures **[1]**; by dentists to show tooth decay **[1]**; airport security **[1]**; to examine stress fractures in aircraft **[1]**; to identify corrosion inside parts of a bridge **[1]** (Accept any other sensible suggestion)

> 'For broken bones' or 'for fractured bones' are not acceptable answers. The answer must state that a picture or image is produced of the break / fracture.

(d) Microwaves **[1]**

17. (a) total energy lost = 6 + 60 + 3 = 69J **[1]**; electrical energy to the homes = 100 – 69J = 31J per 100J of coal **[1]**

(b) efficiency = $\frac{useful\ output\ energy}{useful\ input\ energy} \times 100\%$
= $\frac{31}{100} \times 100\%$ **[1]**; = 31% **[1]**
(Accept 0.31)

Notes

Notes

GCSE Combined Science Workbook

Notes

Notes

GCSE Combined Science Workbook

Notes

Notes